Chaucerian Problems
and Perspectives

Chaucerian Problems and Perspectives

ESSAYS PRESENTED TO
PAUL E. BEICHNER C.S.C.

EDITED BY
Edward Vasta
and
Zacharias P. Thundy

UNIVERSITY OF NOTRE DAME PRESS
NOTRE DAME   LONDON

Acknowledgment

The editors and the University of Notre Dame Press gratefully acknowledge the generous gift toward the publication of this volume secured by Reverend James T. Burtchaell, C.S.C., and the University of Notre Dame.

Library of Congress Cataloging in Publication Data

Main entry under title:

Chaucerian problems and perspectives.

    1. Chaucer, Geoffrey, d. 1400—Criticism and inter-
pretation—Addresses, essays, lectures. 2. Beichner,
Paul E.   I. Beichner, Paul E.   II. Vasta, Edward,
1928–   III. Thundy, Zacharias P., 1936–
PR1924.C47   821'.1   78-62971
ISBN 0-268-00728-4

Contents

CHAUCERIAN PROBLEMS: MAJOR WORKS

CHAUCERIAN PROBLEMS: MINOR WORKS

CHAUCERIAN PERSPECTIVES

Foreword

I appointed Father Paul Beichner Dean of the Graduate School at Notre Dame soon after becoming President in 1952. He was in office for about nineteen years—an all-time record as graduate deans go, at Notre Dame and elsewhere.

Under his aegis, the Graduate School grew from a very small to a quite large body. It progressed in quality as well as in size. In budgetary terms, graduate research grew from less than one to ten million dollars annually. From a graduation of a few Ph.D.'s the year when he began, almost 150 Ph.D.'s were graduating annually by the end of his deanship, and over six hundred Masters.

Having dealt with many academic deans, I can testify that Father Paul was an unusual dean. He was not given to the bureaucratic multiplication of papers. I would write him an inquiry on occasion and be sure that the answer would be back the next day—a curt, but adequate, response scribbled (yes, his handwriting was undistinguished, as is mine) on a scrap of paper generally used already for some other purpose. Sometimes he answered on the very note I sent him. He did not waste words or cultivate style when giving a quick answer to a pressing question. Style was for other purposes—not to embellish bureaucratic communications.

On certain matters, he could be counted on to be emphatic, sometimes passionate. He always had a good word for endeavors that had quality; he sensed immediately the excellence of good works and backed them faithfully. In a word, he was, for nineteen years of growth, a no-nonsense dean, a promoter only of things good and excellent.

All the time, despite the growing burden of administrative tasks, Father Paul continued to contribute to the understanding of his beloved Chaucer, by his teaching and his writings. As a monk, he understood nuances that laymen could miss. His insights into the various tales will illumine them for years to come. Never pedestrian, his commentaries always impressed me for their dry humor.

All of this is not yet the measure of the man. I well remember the long hours that went into the preparation of his *chef d'oeuvre,* the *Aurora* of Peter Riga. As he finally neared completion of this two-volume edition, a new manuscript would appear and he would begin again, true to his own personal demands for complete excellence in scholarship.

In 1954, Father Paul and I took a trip to Europe to visit the best universities and, we hoped, to induce some outstanding scholars to join us at Notre Dame. It was a long summer, with many university visits, many academic adventures, and not a few victories—some still in evidence at Notre Dame. Father Paul is and was a private person; this mission was not really his métier. Yet he was a good companion and partner-in-arms all summer long—from Oxford and Cambridge to Bonn and Munich and Fribourg. He had his own exciting moments in the British Museum and the Bibliotheque Nationale in Paris. He delighted to find Ruskin in error from a carving on a column in Venice (I think it had to do with Tubal or Jubal—the makers of music). He delighted to find the scratchings of Lord Byron on a temple at Sounion in Greece. All in all, it was quite an unusual summer for both of us. One thing certainly he will have forgotten. I drove long distances the days we traveled between university towns. The Breviary was a duty that in those days required about an hour a day in Latin. He could easily have acquitted himself of his prayers as we drove along, leaving me, the tired driver, with my hour's obligation after the long day's driving was done. But he never did. We arrived at our destination each night with an equal obligation and prayed the Breviary together. That is a kind of brotherhood that is rather rare. I appreciated it then and still remember it now.

Father Paul has always been an artist of sorts—carving totem poles from beaver-cut branches, making unusual prints for his own Christmas cards, and, lately, to illustrate his book of modern fables. Again, I must admit to a special pleasure when I opened that book and found it dedicated to me. I was especially impressed by the fact that, characteristically, he had never mentioned it to me. If I had not read the book, which I did with great pleasure, I might well have missed the dedication.

The last time I was with him (at Land O'Lakes, Wisconsin), he was cleaning out turtle shells and using them as planting places for a variety of miniature pines—yellow and white—as well as hemlocks and cedars. The results were not just biologically impressive, but aesthetic as well, and again like himself, unusual. A quiet, unpretentious man is Paul Beichner, with plenty to be vocal about, but he never will be. This makes me all the more happy that his colleagues have decided to produce a *Festschrift* in his honor. It will come as a great surprise to him. Even though he has richly deserved it, he will be modestly diffident about it, while secretly pleased with this sign of regard from his friends.

May his students follow in his large and unpretentious footsteps.

REV. THEODORE M. HESBURGH, C.S.C.
President, University of Notre Dame

PAUL E. BEICHNER, C.S.C.

Paul Edward Beichner, C.S.C., whose academic career reaches back four decades, is primarily a Chaucer scholar, but his teaching and writing have probed a wide field of medieval studies. During virtually his entire academic career, moreover, Father Beichner has served on the University of Notre Dame's administration. He belongs to a generation of Congregation of Holy Cross priests who, in the late thirties and early forties, dedicated themselves to raising the professional caliber of the University which their predecessors founded.

During the presidency of Reverend Theodore Hesburgh, Father Beichner saw the Graduate School through its most dramatic and exciting growth in size and quality. His administrative position at Notre Dame also carried him into regional and national bodies which, together with his writings, established his role as a national educator.

Underlying the opportunities and labors of his academic career is Paul Beichner's priesthood, which began and continues at Notre Dame. The oldest of four children, he left his Pennsylvania home at sixteen to complete his novitiate on the University campus and to take undergraduate study in philosophy. After an additional four years of theological studies at the Order's Holy Cross College in Washington, Father Beichner was ordained (1939). He returned to Notre Dame and two years later earned an M.A. in English, a field he chose both for its own sake and because it touched his other interests in art and philosophy. He taught Freshman English at the seminary and in 1941 became Assistant Prefect of Religion at the University.

Father Beichner's aptitude for scholarship led to the Order's decision that he should seek a Ph.D., whereupon he enrolled at Yale University. There he studied under Karl Young, Tucker Brooke, Robert J. Menner, and Clyde DeVane, the Dean of Yale College. While a graduate student he published his first scholarly article, which showed how canon law, imposing conditions upon the seal of confession, applies to Fra Celestino's affidavit regarding Pompilia in Browning's *The Ring and the Book.*[1] In bringing his special knowledge as a cleric to bear on a literary work, Beichner opened a vein of scholarship that he would continue to explore throughout his scholarly career. Similarly, in undertaking a dissertation on the *Aurora* of Peter Riga, Beichner again learned that his clerical background had application to literature through scholarship. The Yale dissertation initiated a project which he pursued on and off for twenty years and ultimately published in a two-volume critical edition. Beichner completed his doctorate in three years (1944), and for a fourth year at Yale he was awarded a Sterling Post-Doctoral Fellowship for medieval research.

Meanwhile, World War II changed the scene at Notre Dame. The entire University had been taken over by the U.S. Navy for the training of officers. Thus Beichner's conscious purpose at Yale was not only to acquire a Ph.D. and train himself as a scholar, but also to prepare himself for what he calls the University's "academic reconstruction." He returned to Notre Dame after the war and soon resumed his career as administrator as well as teacher and scholar. He rose from Assistant Head of the Department of English (1947–49) to Assistant Dean of the College of Arts and Letters (1949–50), then to Assistant Vice President for Academic Affairs (1950–52). In 1952 Father Hesburgh appointed him Dean of the Graduate School. He held that office for nineteen years.

From the beginning the scholar-teacher-administrator was identified with a (benign) group of radicals in the C.S.C. Order who supported the more scholarly members of the faculty and worked to increase their numbers and influence on a campus heavily committed to undergraduate education. Beichner remembers with amusement how Waldemar Gurian, Notre Dame's famed political scientist and founder of the *Review of Politics,* became abruptly warm and friendly once he discovered an article of Beichner's in *Speculum.* Beichner strove to attract seminarians to scholarship and to advanced degrees. He successfully urged the University administration to stimulate faculty and student interest in the national competitions for study grants, not only Rhodes and Marshall scholarships but also the newly created Fulbright, Wilson, and Danforth fellowships. He further persuaded the University to send its best M.A. faculty on to doctoral studies. He emphasized the need to admit only the most highly qualified students to the University, and as Dean of the

Graduate School he personally examined every admissions application. Toward the same end he created first-year and dissertation fellowships for doctoral students. Conscious of the graduate school's national standing, he was gratified to see a number of Notre Dame departments ranked in the 1965 Cartter Report. Higher rankings and a larger number of departments, including his own Department of English, were listed in the 1970 Roose-Andersen survey. He was also centrally involved in establishing a full-fledged university press, a goal he undertook in 1950 at the instance of then president Father John Cavanaugh and achieved in 1960 with the appointment of Emily Schossberger as the first Director. Beichner held the Chairmanship of the Press's Editorial Advisory Board for fourteen years (1960-74) and conducted a major re-evaluation of the Press before his retirement.

Meanwhile, he carried on his own teaching and writing without interruption. His publications include the articles which, as the contributions to the present volume imply, identify him primarily as a Chaucerian.[2] He is neither theorist nor philologist, he explains, but an eclectic scholar who deals "with what I can prove." His mastery of Latin and his knowledge of the Bible, the Office, Canon Law, the Sacraments, and the teachings and customs of the Church impressively inform his original contributions about religious and clerical characters in the *Canterbury Tales*. Characteristically his articles not only clarify Chaucer's intention and demonstrate the extent of Chaucer's knowledge and art, but they also refine one's appreciation for the subtlety of Chaucer's treatment.

Despite his renown as a Chaucer scholar, Father Beichner's *opus majus* is his two-volume edition of Peter Riga's versified Bible, the *Aurora*.[3] Enormously popular in the Middle Ages, with some two hundred and fifty manuscripts extant, the *Aurora* had not been printed until Beichner's edition. Indeed, except for a few small fragments, it had never been available to modern readers in any form. Beichner's edition has greatly facilitated the editing of Old French verse bibles by a group now working in Leiden under the direction of J. R. Smeets. Separate articles from Beichner's project, two of which lent inspiration to the Leiden editions, significantly expanded his contribution to the subject of versified bibles, their allegorical glosses, and their use by such writers as Gower and Chaucer.[4] The project also resulted in a monograph on the confusion of Jubal and Tubalcain as the medieval representative of music.[5]

As his publications brought national and international acknowledgment, so his services as Dean of the Graduate School carried him into office in national organizations. Keeping abreast of trends and opportunities and carrying that information to Notre Dame, he served through this country's most challenging era in graduate education. He was an early member of the Midwest Conference on Graduate Study and Research (now the Midwestern Association of Graduate Schools), an organization founded after World War II. He served on the Conference's Executive Committee for three years (1965–68) and in 1966–67 served as its Chairman. When the Council of Graduate Schools was formed in 1960, Notre Dame was one of the "Holy Hundred" invited to the organizational meeting. Father Beichner served on its Executive Committee for three years (1966–69). He further served for nine years (1958–67) on the National Selection Committee of the Woodrow Wilson Fellowship Program, and for three years (1969–72) on the Advisory Council on Graduate Education of the U.S. Office of Education.[6]

By 1968 he could foresee an end to graduate education's overheated growth. Although Notre Dame's undergraduate enterprise has always remained virtually unaffected by national trends, Beichner knew that the University's graduate programs would be sharply affected by the coming change. He expected the "fall" to arrive in 1975. To prepare the University for it, he resigned the deanship in 1971. "I knew I had gone through an era," he says, "I saw the change coming. As long as I was in office, our people would think no change was taking place and would expect the Graduate School to continue to expand." As it happened, the down-turn came sooner than he expected.

Father Beichner returned to full-time research and teaching in Notre Dame's Medieval Institute and its Department of English. He also indulged more liberally in his life-long hobbies of woodcarving, sculpture, and making block prints of rubber or wood. Self-taught in these arts, which developed from his boyhood habit of whittling, he had never abandoned them, even when the press of studies demanded his time. In fact, the hobbies which afforded pleasant distraction soon combined with his scholarly and literary abilities to produce a book of modern fables. One day while strolling on campus, he and Astrik Gabriel amused themselves by exchanging medieval anecdotes. Dr. Gabriel's remarking on the unfortunate obscurity of such material gave Father Beichner the idea of translating some of Odo of Cheriton's fables, which he happened to be reading. To bring them alive for a present-day audience he invented morals for the fables in modern-day terms. Eventually he left the medieval works behind and wrote his own fables after the medieval pattern. Independently of his fable writing, he was cutting block prints of outdoor scenes in a small size, the size of a page of type. The scenes eventually connected with the fables until the two merged arts resulted in the publication, in 1974, of *Once Upon a Parable: Fables for the Present,*[7] with fifty-two hand-cut illustrations.

Father Beichner's expanding interests have brought expanded teaching, including a course entitled "Fables, Allegories, and Utopias." Expanded also are his services to his religious community and to the Department of English. On the other hand, he still inhabits the same two small rooms in the Presbytery, adjacent to the campus church and the Main Building, whose golden dome is crowned by a statue of the Blessed Virgin. Amid a profusion of books and papers, scattered wood sculptures and block prints, a tank of swarming guppies, and *bonsai* plants on the windowsills, he studies and writes. Thirty additional illustrated fables, at last count, are collected toward perhaps another volume, although their eventual publication is to him a matter of some indifference. His hobbies are for his own pleasure; his continuing research and writing are for the University.[8] The prosperity of scholarship at Notre Dame is still his preoccupation, although he pauses now and then to look back over the history of the University with satisfaction. "This University," he has remarked, "has come farther than it has a right to expect with its limited resources and necessarily small investments. Conservatively managed, the University has somehow made relatively few mistakes."

Some people attribute Notre Dame's remarkable growth to particular individuals, including Father Beichner, or to historical conditions, or to lucky breaks; others attribute it to the Holy Spirit. Father Beichner defers the whole matter, as he puts it, to "the Lady on top of the Dome."

EDWARD VASTA

NOTES

1. "Fra Celestino's Affidavit and *The Ring and the Book,*" *Modern Language Notes,* 58 (1943), 335–40.
2. "Chaucer's Man of Law and *Disparitas Cultus,*" *Speculum,* 23 (1948),

70–75. "Absolon's Hair," *Mediaeval Studies,* 12 (1950), 222–33. "Chaucer's Hende Nicholas," *Mediaeval Studies,* 14 (1952), 151–53. "Non Alleluia Ructare," *Mediaeval Studies,* 18 (1956), 135–44. "Daun Piers, Monk and Business Administrator," *Speculum,* 34 (1959), 611–19; reprinted in *Chaucer Criticism: The Canterbury Tales,* ed. Richard Schoeck and Jerome Taylor (Notre Dame: University Press, 1960), pp. 52–62. "Characterization in the Miller's Tale," *Chaucer Criticism,* pp. 117–29. "The Grain of Paradise," *Speculum,* 36 (1961), 302–307. "Baiting the Summoner," *Modern Language Quarterly,* 22 (1961), 367–76. "Chaucer's Pardoner as Entertainer," *Mediaeval Studies,* 25 (1963), 160–72. "The Allegorical Interpretation of Medieval Literature," *PMLA,* 82 (1967), 33–38; reprinted in *Chaucer and His Contemporaries: Essays on Medieval Literature and Thought,* ed. Helaine Newstead (New York: Fawcett and World Library, 1968), pp. 112–23. "Confrontation, Contempt of Court, and Chaucer's Cecilia," *The Chaucer Review,* 8 (1974), 198–204.

3. *Aurora, Petri Rigae Biblia Versificata: A Verse Commentary on the Bible,* Publications in Mediaeval Studies, 19 (Notre Dame: University Press, 1965), 2 vols.

4. "The Old French Verse *Bible* of Macé de la Charité, A Translation of the *Aurora,*" *Speculum,* 22 (1947), 226–39. "The *Cursor Mundi* and Petrus Riga," *Speculum,* 24 (1949), 239–50. "La Bible versifiée de Jehan Malkaraume et l'*Aurora,*" *Le Moyen Age,* 61 (1955), 63–78. "Gower's Use of *Aurora* in *Vox Clamantis,*" *Speculum,* 30 (1955), 582–95. "Cantica Canticorum Beatae Mariae," *Marianum,* 21 (1959), 1–15. "The Champagne Letter Writer and Peter Riga," *Recherches de Théologie ancienne et médiévale,* 30 (1963), 336–40. "The *Floridus Aspectus* of Peter Riga and Some Relationships to the *Aurora,*" *Classica et Mediaevalia,* 30 (1969), 451–81. In *Dictionnaire des Lettres Françaises,* 4 (1964): "Chevalerie de Judas Macabé," 178; "Herman de Valenciennes," 375; "Hystore Job," 390; "Joseph," 438; "Macé de la Charité," 483; "Machabées," 483; "Jean Malkaraume," 422; "Psaumes," 607; "Pierre Riga," 598. In *Lexikon für Theologie und Kirche,* 8 (1963), "Petrus Riga," 378. In *New Catholic Encyclopedia,* 6 (1967), "Gower, John," 655.

5. *The Medieval Representative of Music, Jubal or Tubalcain?* Texts and Studies in the History of Mediaeval Education, 2 (Notre Dame: Medieval Institute, 1954).

6. His many influential papers in the field of higher education include "Preparation of College Teachers," *Bulletin of the National Catholic Educational Association,* 54 (1957), 142–44. "Faculty Recruitment," *College Newsletter of the N.C.E.A.,* 21 (1958), no. 2. "How to Keep Your Faculty," *College Newsletter of the N.C.E.A.,* 21 (1958), no. 3; reprinted in *President's Bulletin Board Reprint:* Division of Educational Institutions, Board of Education, The Methodist Church (Sept. 1958). "Selection of Undergraduates for Academic Careers in Colleges and Universities," *Bulletin of the National Catholic Educational Association,* 57 (1960), 189–

92. "The Identification of Graduate Students," *Council of Graduate Schools in the United States,* Proceedings of the Fifth Annual Meeting, Washington, D.C. (1965), pp. 32–37.

7. University of Notre Dame, 1974; Sheed and Ward (paperback), 1975.

8. Book reviews published by Father Beichner are: Margaret Aldum Gist, *Love and War in the Middle English Romances,* in *Speculum,* 23 (1948), 484–89; Beverly Boyd, *Chaucer and the Liturgy,* in *Speculum,* 44 (1969), 115–16; Phyllis B. Roberts, *Stephanus de Lingua-Tonante: Studies in the Sermons of Stephen Langton,* in *Speculum,* 45 (1970), 164–65; "An Adventure in International Education," review of Walter Johnson and Francis J. Colligan, *The Fulbright Program: A History,* in *Review of Politics,* 30 (1968), 86–88; Ernest G. Mardon, *The Narrative Unity of the Cursor Mundi,* in *Speculum,* 47 (1972), 539–40; Thomas W. Ross, *Chaucer's Bawdy,* in *Notre Dame English Journal,* 8 (1972), 52–54; Marcelle Thiébaux, *The Stag of Love: The Chase in Medieval Literature,* in *Medievalia et Humanistica,* N.S. 6 (1975), 218–19.

Other brief items include: "Preface to the American Edition," *A Mirror for Fools* by Nigel Longchamp, tr. J. H. Mozley (Notre Dame: University Press, 1963), pp. iii–vi; "Foreword to the American Edition," W. A. Pantin, *The English Church in the Fourteenth Century* (Notre Dame: University Press, 1962), pp. v–vi.

Chaucerian Problems: Major Works

E. TALBOT DONALDSON

Briseis, Briseida, Criseyde, Cresseid, Cressid: Progress of a Heroine

Legendary figures recurrent in literature may vary in their personalities from one appearance to another, but the particular attribute that made them legends in the first place is not subject to change. It is inconceivable that Doctor Faustus, when he asked of Helen,

> Was this the face that launched a thousand ships
> And burned the topless towers of Ilium?

could actually have meant,

> Was *this* the face that launched a thousand ships?
> Dear me, how disappointing.

Beauty may lie in the eye of the beholder, but no beholder of Helen's imagined beauty will ever find it deficient, no matter how idiosyncratic his own tastes may be: her legendary loveliness is the source of her persistent vitality, and because of it she exists virtually independently of the many literary imaginations of which she is the composite product. Similarly Briseida, Criseyde, or Cressida—no matter how you spell her—has existed ever since her appearance in Benoît de Sainte Maure only because of her infidelity to her lover; this fact, that her principal constant is inconstancy, has recently been persuasively demonstrated by Gretchen Mieszkowski in her study of Criseyde's reputation from Benoît to Henryson.[1] In this paper I shall discuss several other enduring attributes of the Criseyde character that are associated with her infidelity, complicating if not mitigating it.

Criseyde's infidelity, though it is the only reason for her appearance in any narrative, does not explain the charm she exerted on Boccaccio, Chaucer, Henryson, and, I think, Shakespeare, as well as on the imaginations of untold readers. For the Middle Ages and Renaissance she was a more interesting figure than her far better known contemporary, Helen of Troy; and I suspect that from the time of Benoît, and perhaps much earlier, she may have been a kind of surrogate for Helen. Helen seems always to have been so dominated by—and so domineering in—her beauty that poets have tended to shy away from her, to be hesitant to assign her much human personality: she may remind them of those Nicean barks of yore, but not of any one they know. It may be, too, that the fact that Helen's beauty had so early earned her a bad name was discouraging to the poetic imagination. In Homer, of course, everything about her but her beauty is ambiguous: sometimes she seems to regret her abduction, but at others seems perfectly content with her Trojan alliance. But she ends up, after all the slaughter, alive and well and living with Menelaus, as we learn in the *Odyssey*. The later legends eliminate Homer's ambiguity, and she becomes a woman who passes from man to man with remarkable adaptability. Plutarch says that when she was a young girl she was abducted by Theseus, and bore him Iphigenia; others, including Dictys,[2] relate that after Paris' death she married Deiphebus, whom she passively watched Menelaus butcher when the city was taken. The Ovidian epistle assigned to her makes her out as a tiresome girlish flirt, leading Paris on to abduct her by pushing him away. Post-classical poets similarly unable to try to construct a personality worthy of so gorgeous if immoral a creature had revenge on her by writing her down: Dares notes sardonically that she left Troy for home more sad than eager;[3] Spenser, of course, reduces her to Helen-Whore (Hellenore), while Chaucer and Shakespeare present her as an over-sophisticated society lady a bit past her prime, though still the rather wearily acknowledged preeminent beauty of Greece and Troy. She lives up in beauty to Faustus' expectations: but Marlowe allows her not a word, and she has no personality.

Criseyde, however, from the very start engaged sympathy as a woman unwillingly transferred from one man to another. In her earliest manifestation, she was partly Chryseis, the girl in the *Iliad* who was taken away from Agamemnon and sent back to her priestly father, and she was also partly Briseis, the widow who was taken away from Achilles and given to Agamemnon to make up for his loss of Chryseis. Briseis, unlike the later Criseyde, was eventually returned to her first lover, but only after a protracted separation during which Achilles sulked. Ovid sentimentalized Briseis by exploiting the pathos of her involuntary separation from Achilles—and this potential pathos, along with the sense of insecurity that Briseis suffers, has been an abiding element in the stories of Criseyde: in Ovid's epistle Briseis rather hysterically reproves Achilles for refusing to accept the large reward (including herself) that Agamemnon had offered him in order to get him to rejoin the war.[4]

Dares, whoever he was, does not seem to have known who Briseis was: this is suggested by his giving her name a double accusative, adding a Latin *m* to a Greek delta-alpha. Yet though she plays no part in his narrative, his description of her is longer and far more attractive than his description of Helen, who plays a large role. Briseida was beautiful, not of high stature, white-skinned, with soft yellow hair, joined eyebrows, lovely eyes, of *corpore aequali*—by which I guess Dares meant well-proportioned—seductive (*blanda*), affable, modest, full of pity, and of sincere mind (*animo simplici*): Helen is, in precisely the same Latin words, beautiful, seductive, of sincere mind, and, in addition, she has wonderful legs, a small mouth, and a mole between her eyebrows.[5] If Briseida had had any luck, the poet to lift her from Dares into a narrative of her own would have allowed her to display the admirable character Dares assigned her. It is unfortunate that Joseph of Exeter, who versified Dares, also gave her nothing to do, for he was evidently much impressed by her; in his description of her his normally turgid rhetoric overflows the banks to which his reader has learned to cling, but when the passage is deciphered, she sounds even nicer than she does in Dares.[6] As fate would have it, it was Benoît who gave her a story. Benoît, as Mrs. Mieszkowski rightly insists, distrusted all beautiful women (except his patroness, a twelfth-century Martha Blount), and did so noisily and long-windedly. I suppose he had only to note that Briseida, like that slut Helen, was said to be seductive and of honest mind and had, like her, a peculiarity about the eyebrows, to decide that Briseida was a bad one, too; so he invented for her a situation where he could prove she was. He began by adding to Dares' list of the most amiable and attractive characteristics the ambiguous phrase that she was much loved and loved much, along with the unambiguous remark that her heart was subject to change.[7]

It is interesting that Benoît, who certainly didn't know who Briseida had originally been, should have assigned her her original Homeric role of a woman who is shuttled involuntarily from one man to another. I suppose it was just chance, plus the obvious analogy to Helen, that led him to do so. In any case, his description of Briseida originated the paradox that Criseyde has been ever since: a woman with every quality a man might admire and love except an inconstant heart and joined eyebrows (which Benoît considered a minor blemish). And despite his antifeminism, he had enough sensitivity to realize that this was an interesting paradox, as has every poet since his time. Moreover, he was quite aware of, and even exploited, the pathos inherent in a woman's being involuntarily removed from the man she loves, and he realized fully the sense of insecurity that such a woman might have. Indeed, Benoît's Briseida is allowed more extenuating circumstances for her betrayal of her lover than were usually permitted her by later writers. She leaves Troy feeling unfairly rejected by her countrymen: when her exchange is suggested to Priam, he is happy to be rid of her; indeed, it is only his sense of economy—for he admits that she is noble, worthy, wise, and beautiful—that stops him from having her burned and torn to pieces because of her kinship with the hated Calchas. Her own reproach of her father for his treachery is admirable—although I suppose it is also ironical, for she is about to prove that a bad tree brings forth bad fruit. She does not complain that Troilus has done nothing to prevent her departure, though she seems aware of the failure. She recognizes that she is behaving badly in entertaining Diomede, and shows her utter lack of security when she says that she could have remained faithful if she had had help from Troy, but that she would have died in the Greek camp if it had not been for Diomede's loving her. In her final soliloquy she justifies her betrayal of Troilus solely by her need to survive, and realizes that henceforth no good of her "shal neither been ywriten nor ysonge"—a remark less unexpected than it is in Chaucer, since Briseida's Troilus has been shouting her infidelity all over the battlefield and all over Troy.[8]

Benoît's Briseida's interior monologues enlist a large measure of sympathy from a kindly reader. Yet it is true that while they do this, Benoît himself is constantly interrupting the narrative to prophesy her infidelity before it occurs, to put the worst possible construction on her holding off Diomede as long as she does, and generally to impugn any good motive she might conceivably have had. Indeed, Benoît anticipates Shakespeare's Thersites. This separation between the narrative itself and the narrator's reaction to it is, I am sure, something that Chaucer noticed in Benoît, for he adapts it to his own purposes in his poem, though there it is the narrator who is sympathetic and the facts of the narrative harsh. Yet as I have tried to show elsewhere,[9] the interruptions that Chaucer's narrator makes in the action of Book V in order to excuse Criseyde's behavior have an effect exactly opposite to the one presumably intended: the ineptness of the excuses are more damaging to her character than silence would have been, than Benoît's outright condemnation is. Both poets, however, manage—Benoît stumblingly, Chaucer brilliantly—to achieve two distinct points of view toward their heroine, and thus render her as pathetic as she is unstable. For some of this effect Chaucer had to reach around Boccaccio back to Benoît: Boccaccio's primary interest is Troilo, and he gives very little information about Criseida after her departure from Troy. Indeed, of all treatments of Criseyde Boccaccio's is the least substantial and the least sympathetic, and Chaucer was well advised to return to Benoît for hints about the wonderfully complex character he was to recreate.

Benoît's Briseida seems to have taken a new lover for reasons more psychological than physical—and this is perhaps true of Chaucer's Criseyde, but not incontrovertibly so, as I shall suggest. But the other later Criseydes are frankly passionate, and tend to evoke a strong sexual response from men, whether poets or persons in the narratives. For this development I suppose we have to credit—or blame—Guido de Columnis' Latin translation of Benoît. As Mrs. Mieszkowski observes,[10] love to Guido is lechery, as appears in his translation of the initial portrait of Briseida. While, as I have noted, Benoît's Briseida is said to have been much loved and to have loved much, Guido's translation removes any possible ambiguity: she attracted, he says, many lovers because of her seductive ways (a phrase rendered not by the relatively mild word *blanditiae,* but by the strong word *illecebrae*), and loved many men, inasmuch as she maintained no constancy of heart to her lovers.[11] I said earlier that Benoît had anticipated Thersites; but Guido is the real Thersites, whose snarling and gloating refrain is "Fry, lechery, fry."

It is characteristic of Criseyde's ill luck—though a very fortunate thing for English poetry—that Briseida's aptitude for loving and being loved should have made its way, by scribal error, into Joseph of Exeter's otherwise chaste translation of Dares' chaste portrait of her. Joseph, with characteristic ventosity, wrote that she "exposes her womanly features to sight"—that is, *in aspectum;* but at least one scribe rendered *aspectum* as *affectum,* which could mean that she exposed herself to love or desire, or to ignoble passion and base desire.[12] The appearance of this misreading in the St. John's manuscript of Chaucer's *Troilus* in the margin opposite the portrait of Criseyde in Book V suggests that this was the reading Chaucer knew. Joseph of Exeter also wrote that the "distinctive marks of her character (*morum*) strive with the riches of her beauty"; and, as the same manuscript testifies, at least one scribe mistook *morum* for *amorum,* an accident that was to produce those marvelously erotic Chaucerian lines,

> And with her riche beautee everemore
> Stroof love in hire ay which of hem was more.
> (V:818–19)

Of course, Chaucer's couplet is sufficiently ethereal so that it will not mean to every reader that Criseyde was a passionate woman; but it will mean so to many.

Every one remarks, of course, upon the fact that, unlike Chaucer's Criseyde, Boccaccio's is almost aggressively passionate. The chief reason that she initially fails to encourage Troilus, for instance, is that she is ashamed of how much she wants him for her lover (compare Shakespeare's Cressida), and in the consummation scene she needs none of the preliminaries of a jealous and fainting lover to prepare her emotions: she responds to the opportunity naturally and with enthusiasm. But I think the contrast between Boccaccio's and Chaucer's heroine is in this respect frequently overstated. Criseyde is not without strong passion, though Chaucer is subtle in his indication of it. There is, of course, the famous question, "Who yaf me drinke?" which she asks on seeing Troilus return from battle.[13] But the scene contains hints less ambiguous (and here I expand a brief footnote I wrote some years ago).[14] The very next line after her question provides an interesting gloss on it: "For of hir owene thought she weex al reed." I suppose it is not fair—though I shall do it anyhow—to point out that the nearest equivalent to this line in Chaucer, "And of his owene thought he weex al reed," occurs in the Shipman's Tale, and the blusher is the lecherous monk who has just been thinking how the merchant's wife has been belabored by her husband during the night (CT VII:111). The comparison is odious. Nevertheless, in the third stanza before Criseyde's blush there occurs a reinforcement for it. The narrator is describing Troilus as Criseyde sees him riding by:

> So lik a man of armes and a knight
> He was to seen, fulfilled of heigh prowesse;
> For bothe he hadde a body and a might
> To doon that thing, as wel as hardinesse;
> And eek to seen him in his gere him dresse,
> So fressh, so yong, so weeldy seemed he,
> It was an hevene upon him for to see.
>
> (II:631–37)

For the adjective *weeldy* Root reads *worthy*—a violation of the editorial principle of *durior lectio,* for *weeldy* is a relatively rare word, occurring only here in Chaucer's works, while *worthy* occupies a full page in the Chaucer *Concordance:* scribes do not ordinarily substitute rare words for common ones. The OED defines *wieldy* as "capable of 'wielding' one's body or limbs," placing "wielding" in quotation marks in order to refer the reader to the verb. Unfortunately, under the verb the OED does not list one of the fairly common Middle English usages: to wield a woman, that is, to possess, enjoy, or swive a mistress. The adjective should, I think, be redefined as "capable of wielding one's own body, or someone else's." And if my evidence seems so tenuous that of my own thought I ought to be waxing all red, let me point to a phrase earlier in the stanza:

> For bothe he hadde a body and a might
> To doon that thing.

What thing? This time the OED does not let us down, though it upholds us with a positively Chaucerian indirection: *thing,* 7 c: "Used indefinitely to denote something which the speaker is not able or does not choose to particularize." We recall the Wife of Bath's use of *thing* and its French cousin, *bele chose;* and the word is frequently used in Middle English to denote the sexual act. For all Criseyde's hesitancies, she is a sufficiently passionate woman, and when she considers taking a lover she notes all the potentialities of the venture. I suspect that at least some of her uncle's play-acting to get Troilus in bed with her was unnecessary—typical Pandarian overkill.

Henryson, who despite the vilification he has received for "spoiling" Chaucer's Criseyde, was as sensitive a reader of his master as any poet could wish, plays up the sexual potential of Cresseid, though not in his direct handling of her, but in his handling of the narrator. A hot spell in the Scottish spring has come to a sudden end with a hailstorm; when the weather clears it becomes very cold; Henryson's narrator, however, stands at his window gazing on the planet Venus, praying that his "faidit hart of lufe scho wald mak grene."[15] But his spring has passed too, and the cold of the weather and the cold of his heart—his "curage"—are one, and he is driven from the window and from Venus; after a passing reference to aphrodisiacs, he takes a drink and mends the fire, whose heat, he says, is best for an old man. He then takes down Chaucer's book of *Troilus:* no Shunammite woman for poor old poet Robert, but imagined Criseyde, flower of love in Troy. The pose is, of course, a variation on Chaucer's, rather coarser than anything Chaucer would have done, but nevertheless very effective in establishing the ironies of the narrator's love-sick attitude toward the heroine whom the second, non-Chaucerian book he consults punishes so cruelly.

I have not the time to discuss at length the most controversial of all Criseydes, Shakespeare's Cressida. I shall merely assert that Shakespeare emphasizes two aspects of her that, beside her infidelity, had come to distinguish her, her lack of security and her high sexuality. The former appears in her skittishness both in Troy and in the Greek camp; the latter in her night with Troilus and again in the Greek camp, especially in the scene (which Shakespeare got from the older Benoît-tradition, probably through Lydgate) in which she is greeted by the Greek officers. Ulysses' harsh comment (T&C IV: v, 55–57),

> There's language in her eye, her cheek, her lip,
> Nay, her foot speaks; her wanton spirits look out
> At every joint and motive of her body,

is a long way from her description in Benoît, and perhaps a longer way from her description in Chaucer, where it is said that the very way she moved ("the pure wise of hir mevinge") suggested to the masculine onlooker that she possessed "Honour, estaat, and wommanly noblesse" (Tr I: 285–87). But it is her sexuality that Ulysses observes, though his imputation of "wanton spirits" to her may be the revenge of an elderly intellectual who has just been—rather wittily—refused a kiss: surely another part of Ulysses' comment, that Cressida is one of those "That give a coasting welcome ere it comes" is false, since Cressida does not speak until halfway through the kissing-game that Ulysses himself has initiated. Still, his comment accurately anticipates the Cressida we see shortly thereafter flirting with Diomede; this great scene, in which the flirting couple is viewed by Troilus and Ulysses, and both couples by Thersites (T&C V: iii, 146), summarizes the paradox that Benoît first presented: that the lovely creature Troilus loved should become the fit subject for Thersites' scurrility. Many readers who remember earlier Criseydes will, as they watch this very attractive, very vulnerable girl proving unfaithful, join in Troilus' agonized cry: "This is, and is not Cressid."

But it is Criseyde, if only because she is being unfaithful.

Perhaps before closing it would be only fair to note that the origin and development of Criseyde has been exclusively the work of males, many of whom had a very low opinion of women and some of whom had no opinion at all of a woman's right to take the initiative in her own survival since they took it for granted that she had no such right. To such there was no essential difference between Homeric slave-girls (which is what Briseis and Chryseis as prisoners-of-war were) and a medieval lady who could be used as a slave-girl if it seemed militarily desirable. It was perfectly possible to deplore her behavior in using her sexuality to gain security in a bad situation by pretending that she had been got into the situation by fate rather than by men practicing politics. And the various Troiluses were never much help—even the nicest of them, Chaucer's, suggests to the lady that she will not remain faithful to him if she leaves Troy, and Shakespeare's romantic young idealist not only does that, but also fails even to consider raising a finger to prevent her departure: indeed, he positively bundles her into Diomede's arms, as if anxious to get on with the job of proving that he can be faithful to her without her physical presence. One might suppose that some narrators would have perceived that if you treat a woman as a pawn, limiting her moves as severely as a pawn's, you cannot expect her to show the virtue of a queen, who can go in any direction: if the move open to the pawn is one that previously brought her security she can scarcely be blamed for making it again. This is what Criseyde's story proves. I think both Chaucer and Shakespeare understood this—Shakespeare perhaps more fully than Chaucer, even though one's sympathies for Chaucer's Criseyde are greater than for Shakespeare's. But of course for either of them to have fully understood his heroine and to have made the reader understand would have been to destroy the lovely paradoxical artifice that Criseyde is.

NOTES

1. Gretchen Mieszkowski, "The Reputation of Criseyde 1155–1500," *Transactions of the Connecticut Academy of Arts and Sciences,* 43 (1971), 71–153.
2. The most convenient if not most authoritative editions of Dictys, Dares, and Joseph of Exeter are those in vol. 77 of the Delphin Classics (London, 1825). For Helen's marriage to Deiphebus, see pp. 254–55.
3. Delphin Classics 77, p. 338.
4. *Heroides,* ed. Grant Showerman, Loeb Classical Library (Boston, 1943), III: 25–42.
5. Dares says that "Briseidam formosam [non] alta statura, candidam, capillo flavo et molli superciliis iunctis, oculis venustis, corpore aequali, blandam, affabilem, verecundam, animo simplici, piam," while "Helenam similem illis, formosam, animi simplicis, blandam cruribus optimis, notam inter duo supercilia habentem, ore pusillo" (Delphin Classics 77, pp. 311, 308–309). Other manuscripts describe Briseida as "non alta statura," as apparently Joseph of Exeter's did, for he places her "in medium statum." The variation may account for Chaucer's mildly contradictory statements in I:

281, "She nas nat with the leeste of hir stature," and V: 806, "Criseide mene was of hir stature."

6. See Delphin Classics 78, p. 473. The portrait is printed by R. K. Root, ed., *Chaucer's Troilus and Criseyde* (Princeton: University Press, 1926), p. 543.

7. "Mout fu amee e mout amot, / Mais sis corages li chanjot" (*Le Roman de Troie par Benoit de Sainte-Maure*, ed. L. Constans, Société des anciens textes français, 12 [Paris: Firmin-Didot, 1904–12], I: 5285–86). My discussion of Benoît is greatly indebted to Mrs. Mieszkowski's, pp. 79–89.

8. The relevant passages have been translated by R. K. Gordon, *The Story of Troilus* (New York: Dutton, 1964), pp. 8, 12–13, 19–20. Gordon's volume also contains his translation of Boccaccio's *Filostrato*, which I have used in this study.

9. See "Criseide and Her Narrator" in *Speaking of Chaucer* (New York: Norton, 1970), pp. 65–83.

10. *The Reputation of Criseyde*, p. 92.

11. "Multos traxit propter suas illecebras amatores multosque dilexit, dum suis amatoribus animi constantiam non seruasset": Guido de Columnis, *Historia Destructionis Troiae*, ed. N. E. Griffin (Cambridge, Mass.: Mediaeval Academy of America, 1936), p. 85.

12. The scribal variations were first noted by Root in his edition of *Troilus*, p. 543, n. to lines 806–26. The Delphin Classics edition actually reads *affectum*.

13. Tr. II: 651. Readings are from my edition, *Chaucer's Poetry*, 2nd ed. (New York: Ronald, 1975).

14. *Speaking of Chaucer*, p. 66, n. 1.

15. *The Testament of Cresseid*, ed. Denton Fox (London: Nelson, 1968), line 24. I have adopted Professor Fox's fine interpretation of the meteorological conditions described at the beginning of the poem.

2

STEPHEN MANNING

Chaucer's Constance, Pale and Passive

Although poor Constance is by no means the most endearing of Chaucer's heroines, critics are still trying to cope with her and her tale. If the number of recent commentaries is any criterion, she seems to exert as forcible a presence on the modern reader as she does on the characters in her tale and on the Narrator himself, despite her much lamented passivity. But the aesthetic and ethical challenges of the Man of Law's tale remain. Some find the tale artistically satisfying, but only through the characterization of the Narrator as the Man of Law; most admit to disaffection, rising chiefly from too great an aesthetic distance. The reasons for this distance vary widely, but are generally found in either the narrative mode or the ethical values. Of those who object to various elements in the narrative mode, most object to the element itself rather than to Chaucer's handling of it. Thus the objection that Constance is not a realistic character, rather than that Chaucer presents an unrealistic character badly. Of those who object to the ethical values, most object to the passivity or detachment of Constance, rather than to Chaucer's failure to probe meaningfully into these qualities.[1] It is possible, however, to accept both the narrative mode and the ethical values and still find the tale unsatisfying. Most of the problems focus in the characterization of Constance, and neither the rhetoric in which Chaucer shrouds her nor a Narrator who hovers protectively is adequate solution. Chaucer was not unique in not knowing quite what to do with Constance: Trivet had his problems, and so did Gower, so perhaps the problems are built into the hagiographic romance and medieval aesthetic practice as well as in the male psyche.

Specifially, in the Man of Law's Tale Chaucer has difficulty harmonizing the elements of the cosmic and the human in Constance; as usual in the hagiographic romance, the scale of virtue is grand indeed, and the action bears clear implications of the cosmic struggle between God and Satan. Moreover, by her very name of Constance she drifts into waters allegorical as well as hagiographical. And finally, she has a theological/mythic/psychological content as the Feminine; Sheila Delany with considerable justice calls her Everywoman (p. 64). But despite these larger dimensions, Chaucer also seeks to make her more recognizably human; in fact his plot calls for a less cosmic and more human character in Part III when she is reconciled to her husband and father, and then must accept Alla's death. So while Chaucer strives for a typically hagiographic sense of wonder through the cosmic overtones, he also seeks pathos at times. Interestingly enough, he succeeds best when he combines the two. In the course of the poem, then, Constance descends from the more cosmic to the more human: Part I is more cosmic than human, Part II presents her as both, and Part III is more human than cosmic. But Chaucer explores neither the theological nor the psychological dimensions of Constance, and his treatment of his theme seems ultimately superficial. His interest may have well been more philosophical than religious; P. M. Kean finds its importance to Chaucer as a "further comment on the theme of Fortune and free will; it is not developed as a religious poem in its own right."[2] Even as further commentary, however, it lacks depth.

We see much of Constance, of course, through the eyes of the Narrator, who seldom remains indifferent to the events he narrates: he sympathizes, bristles, scolds, marvels, wearies, interprets, but he does not always understand. Unfortunately he does not emerge with much of a personality of his own (quite apart from his identification with the Man of Law) whose limitations could give depth to both Constance and the thematic content. He does seem to be conscious of her in his own way as an aspect of the Feminine, and in perhaps typical male fashion responds by protectiveness and bluster. Chaucer employs a similar technique when another of his narrators encounters the Feminine: in his response to Criseyde, the Narrator's bluster and protectiveness offer insight, but here they merely bounce off; there the technique is sophisticated and controlled, here it is at best half-formed. Further, the Narrator and his rhetoric are difficult to part, and together they create an aesthetic distance which, on the face of it, neither the Narrator nor the rhetoric intends. Part of our uneasiness stems from the fluctuation of the distance between closeups and long shots; the fluctuation at times calls attention to the distance between the two techniques, and when the closeup has been effective, we are that much less satisfied with the long shot.

Although Constance thus emerges as a somewhat pallid creature, she is not the passive ninny she has been accused of being. First of all, she possesses a presence, a *mana,* which demands and receives forcible response from those with whom she comes into contact directly or indirectly. Second, she moves in her world not only with detachment but with a self-sufficiency which her submission to Providence gives

her. This, I think, is one of the major stumbling blocks for our acceptance of her as a human being. Third, her virtue is on a scale and of a
complexity which modern spiritual writers advisedly call *heroic*. Finally, she realizes and feels the emotional implications of all her circumstances, and her ability to accept what God sends despite her
awareness gives her an imposing strength. This is the aspect of the
human that Chaucer handles best.

Constance's peculiar *mana* we see immediately: it is her impact on
the people of Rome, which they relate to the Syrian merchants, which
they in turn relate to the Sultan, who immediately falls in love with her
and determines to marry her despite the religious and legal complica-
tions. Notably, in the course of the poem, two men fall in love with her
and one is slain as a result; two want to rape her and both are appropriately slain for their efforts. Of the three significant women in the
tale, two hate her and attempt to dispose of her (although the means
they use is indirect: do they instinctively recognize an aspect of themselves in her and realize they cannot really destroy her and what she
represents?), and they are both slain; the remaining woman befriends
her only to be slain for her friendship. Yet Constance lives to sail
another sea. Since she creates such havoc, is it any wonder that the
Narrator does not seem to understand her? Not that much of this is
really her fault; the narrative mode of the entire poem is to create a
series of reactions, and while others react to Constance by greater
activity, she acts to a considerable extent only by exerting the *mana* she
possesses. Significantly, it is not she who cures the blind man, but
Hermengild, whom Constance encourages and gives something of her
own strength. Only here, and at times with Alla, does she interact with
another character. Generally, each character has his or her own space,
which allows for reaction but inhibits interaction.[3] Similarly, she responds to her circumstances as though they, too, were in a separate
space. For note how Chaucer isolates her in her moments of crisis: we
hear and see her address her parents and take leave of them and her
friends, but we are only dimly aware of the others' presence (274–87,
316–21). We see her look about, pale, for a champion, but we cannot
distinguish the surrounding press (645–51). We see her kneel on the
shore, pray to Christ and Mary, reassure her little son, and, turning her
head, bid farewell to a ruthless husband, but we are only dimly conscious of others on shore (825–68). Significantly, we see no reaction
from the constable when she offers her child to his care, but we see only
her acknowledgment of his unwillingness (858–61). And when she sets
sail the Narrator creates a sense of timelessness and spacelessness both

times by the vagueness of detail, and the first time by expanding the meaning of her journey in terms of a divine transcendence of space and time (470–504). The other characters react to Constance far more intensely than she to them; she thus remains almost independent of the results she creates.

Such isolation and emotive control are perhaps disturbing, but theologically it all has much to do with the nature of Constance. There is, first of all, her acceptance of what Divine Providence sends. If there is perfect trust in God, then there can be no concern for the worst that fortune can bring. She has thus learned the lesson of Lady Philosophy, of Innocent III, and of others. Her virtue is constancy, but it is also patience and fortitude. Emile Mâle mentions a representation of Fortitude on the doorways of Paris and Amiens cathedrals as a female warrior, "seated in an attitude full of repose and dignity," flanked by Patience and Perseverance. She waits "with clear mind and direct gaze, ready for any turn of fortune," and then Mâle comments: "No presentation of Fortitude has been conceived with truer nobility, none comes closer to the theological definition, 'a force of soul which ever acts in accordance with reason.'"[4] Thus Constance's force of soul: her constancy is such that she can remain detached from what befalls her. This is not mere passivity, but instead the *agere et pati* [activity and passivity] topos, which the representation of Fortitude suggests.[5] Indeed, Aquinas distinguishes among constancy, fortitude, patience, and perseverance, a foursome which also suggests more than passivity. He reminds us that, according to Luke, it is through patience that a man possesses his soul.[6]

Despite the detachment from the world which her submission to the will of God brings, Constance is always aware of what emotional stress such yielding to Providence costs. Even at the very beginning when Constance is to marry the Sultan, she feels her situation keenly (274–87). Although she fully expects to be drowned when set afloat by the Sultaness, she nonetheless commends herself to Christ and begs for amendment of her life (449–62). Immediately upon landing in Northumbria, however, the experience has been too much for her, and "In hir langage mercy she bisoghte, / The lyf out of hir body for to twynne" (516–17). But this is only momentary, for upon being led to shore by the constable, she kneels and thanks God (523). The climax of this acceptance of Providence occurs at the end of Part II in the long scene when she leaves Northumbria, openly accepting what Christ sends, while at the same time fully aware of the needs of her little son and of the hard-heartedness of her husband (826–63). Unfortunately, Chaucer drops this awareness in Part III.

All these various qualities which invest Constance with more than passivism are part of the basic set of cosmic and personal qualities that Chaucer has difficulty blending satisfactorily. Her cosmic qualities are multiple; to start with, as holy woman if not actually saint, Constance partakes in the cosmic battle between God and Satan characteristic of the saint's life. Her missionary activity in general suggests something of this scale, but more specifically it is Satan himself who enviously arouses the hatred of the Sultaness (365–71) and the passion of the young knight (582–86). In turn, the voice from heaven accuses the knight of slandering "The doghter of hooly chirche in heigh presence" (674–75). The miracle which accompanies the voice as well as the cure of the blind man and Constance's preservation while adrift, are the stuff of which saints' lives are made. The scale of her virtue also approaches the cosmic: her patience, chastity, constancy. It is this virtue which Satan sees in its perfection that causes him to inflame the knight (582–88).

Constance's allegorical dimension also suggests what I have been terming the cosmic. If not actual personification, she is an *exemplum.* Her travels aboard ship remind us of the sea of life or of the passions, and so forth.[7] Most important is her role as Everywoman, i.e., of *Anima,* man's soul as well as woman's. The theological connotations of *Anima* are, of course, multiple, and to this extent Constance may be said to partake of a dimension of the Feminine. The frequent medieval equation of *Anima* and *Ecclesia,* for example, reinforces Constance's role of giver of the spiritual life of faith to both the Syrians and the Northumbrians. Other implications of the Feminine from myth and psychology reinforce the theological overtones of the metaphor. The image of the ship at sea recalls the crescent boat of the moon goddess which she has sent to carry her followers from the flood to the warmth and light of the sun. This action, according to M. Esther Harding, means that psychologically the woman becomes, as the goddess, "one-in-herself," that is, not dependent upon someone or something outside her own psyche.[8] She thus reaches a stage which Erik H. Erikson calls "the self-containment of pure being,"[9] or as Harding puts it, "She is what she is because that is what she is," adding, "This sounds, perhaps, unattractive" (p. 148). I think Constance emerges with much of this quality of one-in-herself; it is comparable to the self-sufficiency which abandonment to Providence creates.

The general pattern of the progression as described by Harding may be detected in Constance. Her destructive side, her "coldness," brings death to the Sultan, but her destructive aspect is only suggested in her own characterization; it is seen largely in the Sultaness as Constance's *alter ego.* After she is adrift, she is exposed to another form of destructive egotism in the attentions of the young knight. His lust, as the Sultaness' hate, is ultimately self-destroying. Constance's faith in God enables her to triumph over the knight, and then it is Jesus Himself Who arranges for her marriage to Alla (690–91). Constance now assumes the role of physical life force and bears a son. The full impact of the destructive side of the Feminine may be seen in both the Sultaness and Donegild, both of whom reveal the connection of egotism and selfishness to uncontrolled instinct, and thus help to define more precisely Constance's role as Feminine. She demonstrates a lack of egotism when she is willing to give up her child to the care of the constable (858–59), reflecting Harding's distinction between the "love of the object as such" and "love of the object because it brings her satisfaction" (p. 228). We might also note that she seems to accept fully her role as wife, for she does not identify herself to her father until after she has reestablished her identity as Alla's wife; moreover, it is she who takes the first step towards reconciliation by sending Maurice to stand before Alla at table (1013–15). Her initiative is thus important in establishing her independence of, yet willing responsiveness to, those around her. It gives a psychological basis for the sense of detachment which the philosophical/theological pattern of abandonment to Providence leads to. While the outline of this psychological pattern does exist in the poem, it is hazy, because this is not Chaucer's central interest. It does help us understand her detachment, however, for it is this quality which makes her somewhat suspicious as a human being and, as Harding suggests, perhaps unattractive. But not passive.

Despite all these possible implications, however, Constance does not emerge in strong colors, partly due to the failure of the Narrator to understand her active/passive role. He succeeds best when her emotions conflict with her sense of constancy, for this harmonizes both the cosmic and the human: although her emotions betray her humanity, her humanity gives point to her virtue and defines its heroic scale. In Part III, although under Mary's governance, she is stripped of most of her cosmic nature and becomes, curiously, less interesting. Perhaps throughout this section we feel too strongly her detachment, her being one-in-herself without sufficient theological or psychological underpinnings. We do not, at any rate, see her respond with emotional control as in Part II: despite her swooning and tears, we do not get a very keen sense of her presence at the reconciliation, let alone of her emotion. There is a nice human touch when she accuses her father of forgetting her, and when she requests not to be sent to any more heathen lands

(1106, 1112). We are not touched by Alla's death, nor do we sense much reaction to this, her last trial. If anything, there seems a sense of relief as she returns to Rome with cosmic holiness again, and with a strong sense of an anagogical return to her Father's house. The tale ends as it began with active virtue and almsgiving. Nearly all suggestions of psychological/theological depth are passed over; the Narrator, for instance, seems unwilling to have her play too large a role in bringing about the reconciliation with Alla—one of the few events not attributed wholly or in part to Providence. His comments suggest a similar technique in *Troilus:*

> Som men wolde seyn at requeste of Custance
> This senatour hath lad this child to feeste;
> I may nat tellen every circumstance,—
> Be as be may, ther was he at the leeste.
>
> (1009–12)

After the comparative success of Part II with its frequent closeups, Part III seems even more distant by contrast. Even the joy-sorrow motif is perfunctorily handled. The Narrator, moreover, grows weary, begging off until tomorrow to continue his story of woe. The remark could be made thematically significant, playing off a pedestrian Narrator who can only weary with describing sorrow, against Constance, who has the strength to endure it without complaint. But the possibilities are not followed through; the tone jars because it reinforces our sense that the Narrator is less involved than previously, and the very scene itself, part of the reconciliation, hardly calls for this much anguish before the truth is discovered and all turns to joy. It is not even one of Chaucer's better jokes.

The Narrator's overindulgence in woe leads to a second problem. As Chauncey Wood observes, the Narrator is "more intense both emotionally and intellectually about Constance's sufferings than she is herself."[10] His attitude towards her seems instinctively protective: he is her champion at all times. He sees immediately her discomfort in leaving home for Syria, and he chides her father for not checking out the astrological implications for her voyage (309–15). This stanza and the preceding two serve both to show concern for Constance and to raise the possibility of divine intervention in a world apparently guided by chance. Once Constance is at sea, however, the Narrator is convinced that everything that happens, happens through Divine Providence. John A. Yunck has collected the instances—a considerable and depressing lot.[11] For instance, it is Jesus rather than Constance who converts Hermengild (538–39), and it is He Who sees to it that Alla marries her and makes her a queen (690–94). As if being a queen should matter to one who yields to whatever Providence sends! Yunck observes further, "In Chaucer's tale second causes fade into nothing in the majestic ubiquity of the great First Cause" (p. 259), but such fading also raises questions about Constance's free will—the active part of the *agere et pati* topos—and indeed tends to cancel out some of her awareness of the emotional cost of yielding to the divine will. Finally, it also raises questions about the analysis of the entire problem of Providence: the treatment is warmed-over Boethius, the point is naively reiterated over and over and over, and no aspect of it seems pursued very far. Both Constance and the poem suffer as a result when intensity is substituted for analysis.

Such over-involvement on the part of the Narrator leads elsewhere to a sense of naiveté and even of pomposity. His astrological forays in Part I illustrate the latter; the vehemence with which he chides the various characters and sins throughout, of the former. In neither case is there really enough substance in the situation itself to support so much rhetoric; the rhetoric always seems superimposed. But when the Narrator turns his attention directly to Constance, his apostrophes and protective instincts are nearly always supported by what Constance says or does immediately following: thus his analysis of Constance's situation upon leaving home is followed by her own (267–87), which includes a more penetrating comment about husbands than the Narrator's; when he commends her to Christ, she follows with her own prayer (446–62); when he is distressed by her lack of a champion, she again prays for divine aid (631–44). One of the best examples of his effective handling of rhetoric in a context involving Constance directly is the much-admired stanza beginning "Have ye nat seyn somtyme a pale face" (645–51). Here we as audience are invited to bring an instantly recognizable emotion from our own experience and apply it to the situation at hand, and transferring the emotion to the events in the poem makes us feel we understand those events and thereby brings us close to them. In the next stanza the Narrator addresses queens and other ladies living in prosperity; it is a variation of the preceding stanza, but it fails to work because the Narrator has taken himself away from the scene and stands between it and us. Whenever he detaches himself so completely from the scene, his rhetoric seems overblown. An example with rather disastrous results is the second rape scene. The Narrator points out the moral in line 924, "And thus hath Crist

unwemmed kept Custance," so that the three stanzas of commentary
which follow add nothing to our understanding of, or our feeling for,
the situation. When neither is engaged, we remain aloof.[12] The scene
is so brief that it cannot bear the weight of so much rhetoric. Surely
Constance's physical strength is the correlative of her spiritual
strength, and surely this late in the poem there is not much point in
wondering where she got that. The first time that the Narrator used
the "help of God" motif (470–504), the passage worked because the
penetration of all time with a sense of God's eternal present does
contribute to our understanding of Providence. But the Narrator's
insistence on driving home his point suggests only that he is even more
anxious for Constance to preserve her chastity than she is. This, in
turn, is suited to his superficial response to Constance as Feminine.

What emerges then is a sense that the Narrator's emotional and
intellectual intensities cover up a lack of depth. Perhaps they are com-
pensation as well for holding Constance's activity in check. The potentialities of Constance as a character tend to pull her in certain theological and psychological directions, but the Narrator seems determined to
hold her within the limits of some rather simplistic notions he has
about the Feminine and what constitutes the soul's relation to God.
This, in turn, probably rises from Chaucer's philosophical, rather than
religious or psychological, interests. He seems to explore only those
aspects of her character which conform to Boethian stoicism. As an
illustration of a philosophical attitude, Constance is difficult to believe
in as a human being, and those human touches which Chaucer does
give her seem to rise out of immediate contexts rather than from any
overall design. As in the hagiographic romance, we are invited to
marvel, and are allowed to recognize the human element in the abstraction just enough so we can recognize that the theme applies to our
lives. What satisfaction there is from such a work comes from the
completion of narrative and thematic patterns and from a recognition
that familiar values are being validated.

Whatever the achievement in blending the cosmic and the human in
Constance in Part II, Part III fails dismally. Chaucer seems to rely
merely on the plot to establish Constance's humanity; his Narrator, in
fact, fails to establish her as either cosmic or human, and the tone of
wonder becomes one of relief that all loose ends will now be finally
tied. Chaucer's adoption of a literally primitive narrative technique
contributes to the tedium throughout the poem and to Part III in
particular. For instance, Constance cannot merely meet her uncle as he
returns from Syria: first her father has to have heard of what happened,

then send the senator, who then slays the Sultaness and then returns, and only now can Constance meet him. No detail in the sequence can be omitted or subordinated. Moreover, all the rhetorical embellishment seems arbitrary in part because there seems no overall plan for it, either; hence it does not often crop up in Part III. This, of course, is characteristically medieval—to make the most of individual scenes in relationship to one another rather than in relation to a whole. Constance is a receptacle for a theme, and this is an aspect of the Feminine that emerges strongly. What is missing from her character is missing also from the theme, yet it too is Boethian. Much as the Romans praise Constance, any love they have for her is more implicit than stated; the Northumbrians, however, love her, especially Hermengild, who "loved hire right as hir lyf" (530–35). Nowhere do we feel strongly Constance's return of love. The Narrator seems to feel as little of it as we do. At any rate it remains for another Narrator and another poem to find the heroine loveable.

NOTES

1. See, e.g., for characterization of the Man of Law, Walter Scheps, "Chaucer's Man of Law and the Tale of Constance," *PMLA,* 89 (1974), 285–95; for an excellent discussion of narrative mode, Morton W. Bloomfield, "The Man of Law's Tale: A Tragedy of Victimization and a Christian Comedy," *PMLA,* 87 (1972), 384–90; for objection to the passive philosophy of life, Sheila Delany, "Womanliness in the Man of Law's Tale," *Chaucer Review,* 9 (1974), 63–72. All Chaucer quotations in this essay are taken from the edition of F. N. Robinson.
2. *Chaucer and the Making of English Poetry* (London: Routledge and Kegan Paul, 1972), II: 114.
3. For a discussion of the "isolating" tendency in medieval art, see D. W. Robertson, *A Preface to Chaucer* (Princeton: University Press, 1962), pp. 149–50.
4. *The Gothic Image,* tr. Dora Nussey (New York: Harper, 1958), p. 121.
5. For a discussion of this topos, see Georgia Ronan Crampton, *The Condition of Creatures* (New Haven: Yale U. Press, 1974), esp. pp. 1–44. Perhaps the most relevant formulation of this topos is Reginald Garrigou-Lagrange's notion of a harmony between the activity of fidelity and the passivity of abandonment to Divine Providence, or, as he heads a section, "Trusting Abandonment and Unwavering Fidelity," *The Three Ages of the Interior Life* (St. Louis: Herder, 1948), II: 195, 460.
6. *Summa Theologica* II–II: 136, 137; the reference to Luke 21:19 is made in 136.2. Joseph Pieper glosses the active rather than the passive aspect in

Aquinas' concept thus: "Enduring comprises a strong activity of the soul, namely, a vigorous grasping of and clinging to the good; and only from this stout-hearted activity can the strength to support the physical and spiritual suffering of injury and death be nourished," *The Four Cardinal Virtues* (Notre Dame: University Press, 1965), p. 128. Pieper also comments on the modern misconception of the virtue of patience, which Aquinas makes a necessary component of fortitude:

> Patience . . . is something quite other than the indiscriminate acceptance of any and every evil. . . . To be patient means to preserve cheerfulness and serenity of mind in spite of injuries that result from the realization of the good. Patience does not imply the exclusion of energetic, forceful activity, but simply, explicitly and solely the exclusion of sadness and confusion of heart. Patience keeps man from the danger that his spirit may be broken by grief and lose its greatness. Patience, therefore, is . . . the radiant embodiment of ultimate integrity. (p. 129)

7. See Albert C. Labriola, "The Doctrine of Charity and the Use of Homiletic 'Figures' in the *Man of Law's Tale*," *Texas Studies in Literature and Language,* 12 (1970), 5–14.
8. *Woman's Mysteries* (New York: Bantam, 1973), p. 146.
9. *Identity: Youth and Crisis* (New York: Norton, 1968), p. 283.
10. "Chaucer's Man of Law as Interpreter," *Traditio,* 23 (1967), 149.
11. "Religious Elements in Chaucer's *Man of Law's Tale,*" *ELH,* 27 (1960), 258–59.
12. See Wayne C. Booth's discussion of types of literary distance (intellectual or cognitive; qualitative, which Booth prefers to "aesthetic"; practical, which he prefers to "human"), *The Rhetoric of Fiction* (Chicago: University Press, 1961), p. 125.

3

ZACHARIAS P. THUNDY

Matheolus, Chaucer, and the Wife of Bath

It is unfortunate that Chaucer critics, whose major concern has always been the study of sources and influences, have generally ignored the *Lamentations* of Matheolus,[1] an important immediate source of Chaucer. Chaucer read it and used it with profit and delight in many of his works, especially in his discussions of sex, marriage, and women in the Wife of Bath's Prologue, the Merchant's Tale, and the Nun's Priest's Tale.[2] Chaucer's portrait of the Wife of Bath in the General Prologue in certain details was also influenced by Matheolus. A close comparative study of Chaucer and Matheolus will help solve several Chaucerian cruces as well as answer the question of the literary relationship between Chaucer and Deschamps.

Matheolus—alias Matheolulus, Mathieu, and Mahieu—was a French cleric who lived in the thirteenth century. He gave up his clerical status to marry Petronilla, a widow. Because of his marriage to a widow, he was considered a "bigamist" by medieval canon law though he was married only once.[3] According to the husband's testimony, soon after the marriage, the merry widow became a nagging wife and life with her changed from paradise to hell (288–91). Petronilla made life miserable for her husband in bed and at board (541–60, 561–70, 575–90, 657, 2315–24). The arrival of children did not change the pattern of misery. The shrewishness of the wife, the churlishness of the nurse, the anxieties of parenthood, and the constant cries of children increased Matheolus' suffering. Alas, the poor bigamist became the most wretched of all men! However, Matheolus, the artist, decided to sublimate his misfortune and misery by writing a misogynous poem of complaint. So he wrote his Latin *Lamentationes*.

The poem is divided into four books. The first book (1–654) contains the author's introspective analysis of his own bigamy and a devastating critique of womankind. The second book (655–2328), a systematic satire against marriage, is often interrupted by authorial lamentations and frequent attacks on the poet's wife. In the third book (2329–3767) the author describes his dream-vision in which God appears to him, comforts him, and explains the superiority of married life over celibacy in the heavenly kingdom. The fourth book (3768–5614) is an estates satire, a reform-oriented criticism of various social states, like Chaucer's own General Prologue in *The Canterbury Tales.*

Jehan Le Fèvre of Paris,[4] the author of the Middle French versions of *Disticha Catonis, Theoduli Ecloga,* and *Ovidii Vetula,* translated Matheolus' *Lamentationes* into French in 1371 or 1372.[5] The translator was quite faithful to the original. Only rarely did he modify the Latin text by amplifying the original—rather generously in certain places.[6] Gaston Paris even claimed that "John Le Fèvre translated the *Liber Infortunii* of Matheolus into French verse clearer than the Latin verse of the original."[7] In 1373, Le Fèvre made a sudden turn-around and wrote *Le Livre de Leësce,* a systematic refutation of Matheolus and a defense of marriage and women. This work is a dramatic monologue and an eloquent defense of marriage, bigamy, and womankind by a woman, Dame Leësce. She argues that women are more chaste, more honest, more virtuous, and more trustworthy than men.

Soon after publication, Matheolus' *Lamentationes* became widely known in England and Europe. Two manuscripts survive in England, two in Germany, and one in Holland. Toward the end of the fourteenth century, Eustache Deschamps and some of his close friends read it along with the *aureolus liber* of Theophrastus.[8] Without acknowledging his indebtedness to Matheolus, Deschamps used the *Lamentationes* as a source for his *Miroir de Mariage.*[9] In later years Le Fèvre's French translation became more popular than the Latin.[10] Thirteen manuscripts of the French work are extant, and of these two are preserved in the British Library. The fact that only eight manuscripts of *Leësce* survive suggests that this work of Le Fèvre was copied less frequently than his *Lamentations.*

Since these three works were fairly popular in fourteenth-century Europe and England, it is possible that Chaucer consulted them for his discussion of marriage and women in *The Canterbury Tales.* Scholars such as F. N. Robinson, J. M. Manly, and A. K. Moore suspected the possible use of Matheolus by Chaucer. Robinson wrote: "A number of parallels in the *Lamentations* of Matheolus . . . were noted years ago by the editor. . . . But it is not clear that Chaucer had read either of these works [Latin or French]."[11] Manly noted four references in the Wife of Bath's Prologue.[12] Moore pointed out six more parallels and wrote in 1946: "Whether the *Lamentations* . . . was even known in England during the fourteenth century has not been determined. . . . The fact that the Latin original has been preserved only in a University of Utrecht

Library manuscript favours the supposition that the work . . . was read in Le Fèvre's popular version."[13] It is worthwhile to repeat here that there are two Latin manuscripts of Matheolus, Cotton Cleopatra C.IX of the fourteenth/fifteenth century and Harleian 6298 of the fourteenth century, in the British Library, in addition to the two French versions of Jehan Le Fèvre: Add. 30985 and Royal MS. 20 B XXI.

Robinson, Manly, and Moore have pointed out only a few Chaucerian references to Matheolus and have not fully recognized the importance of Matheolus for a closer study of Chaucer's works, though they have left the door open for further research. Manly observes: "Whether Chaucer knew the even bitterer and more extensive satire entitled in Latin *Lamentationes Matheoluli* or the French version of it by Jehan Le Fèvre entitled *Les Lamentations de Matheolus* is not known, as no one appears yet to have investigated the subject."[14]

For some time, I have been investigating the subject of this literary relationship and have discovered over two hundred parallels of words, phrases, exempla, arguments, characters, and ideas in Chaucer and Matheolus. These are distributed as follows: (1) the Wife of Bath's Prologue and Tale: total number of parallels, 122; verbal parallels, 88; (2) the Merchant's Tale and Prologue: total number of parallels, 45; verbal parallels, 33; (3) the Nun's Priest's Tale: verbal parallels, 7; (4) the General Prologue: total number of parallels, 24; verbal parallels, 18; (5) others: total number of parallels, 17; verbal parallels, 13.

Because the Wife of Bath parallels are too many to be quoted in this study, I must limit myself to citing line numbers of verbal parallels only (Table One). I shall, however, follow with quotations of the *first* twelve verbal parallels from the Wife of Bath's Prologue to indicate Chaucer's familiarity with the works of Matheolus–Le Fèvre (Table Two). Then I shall give a list of topics which are found in both Chaucer and Matheolus–Le Fèvre (Table Three). A discussion of some of the important parallels, finally, will demonstrate how Chaucer made use of his sources in his portrait of the Wife of Bath and her Prologue.

In Table One the first and third columns contain references to Jehan Le Fèvre's French version of Matheolus' *Lamentations* and *Le Livre de Leësce*, in no special order. The second and fourth columns give parallels from Chaucer's Wife of Bath's Prologue, her tale, and her portrait in the General Prologue, in linear order.[15]

The verbal parallels show only that Chaucer was familiar with the works of Matheolus and Le Fèvre. They do not prove to what extent or for what purpose Chaucer used these works. A brief paradigmatic analysis of the main topics of both authors is necessary to illustrate how

much Chaucer depended upon Matheolus in his composition of the
Wife of Bath's Prologue, how much Chaucer borrowed, and how much
he omitted. For the sake of easy reference, this analysis is done in
parallel columns (Table Three) that will show which ideas of the *Lamentations* Chaucer incorporated in the Wife's Prologue and which he did
not.

The Wife of Bath's Prologue combines the medieval traditions of
complaint against women and marriage and defense of both women and
marriage. The inspiration for combining these two literary forms came
to Chaucer from Matheolus and Jehan Le Fèvre. The first two books of
the *Lamentations,* in fact, are a systematic attack on women and marriage while the third book, a dream-vision, is a lame defense of the
superiority of the sacrament of matrimony to a life of celibacy. *Leësce*
includes also a vindication of women by a woman, Leësce, who refutes
all the calumnies of Matheolus against womankind with suitable exempla and by arguments from scriptural, classical, and contemporary
authorities. Following the example of Leësce, the Wife of Bath also lists
complaints against marriage and women and refutes them. In the
Wife's Prologue, Chaucer used not just isolated lines from Matheolus
but often adapted long passages. For example, the Wife's discussion of
bigamy (III: 1–58) is a close adaptation of *Lamentations,* I: 1–564; the
comparison of married life with virginity (III: 59–183) is found in its
entirety in the French source (I: 2057–3246). The Wife of Bath is cruel
towards her old husbands (III: 194–223) in almost every way Petronilla
is towards Matheolus (I: 1257–1362); above all, Chaucer (III: 235–
665) compresses Matheolus' long treatment of the vices of women (II:
1–2806) into 430 lines.

It is necessary to demonstrate to some extent at least why Matheolus
is indeed a source of Chaucer and not an analogue and how Chaucer
made use of this source. The verbal parallels given above show that
several words and phrases are common to both authors; likewise, the
analysis of the topics of the authors given in parallel columns indicates
that Chaucer has numerous ideas on women and marriage in common
with Matheolus. It is, of course, possible that both authors might have
borrowed them from other available sources like Jerome's *Adversus
Jovinianum,* Walter Map's *Dissuasio Valerii, Le Roman de la Rose,* and
florilegia, or from oral tradition reflected in sermons, proverbs, and
folklore. Such arguments can be directed against almost all claimed
literary sources of Chaucer. However, because Chaucer was a literate
poet who composed his poems in writing, because traces of identifiable
literary sources remain in his works, and because he himself referred to

TABLE ONE

Matheolus–Le Fèvre	Chaucer, III	Matheolus–Le Fèvre	Chaucer, III
II: 47–48	3	II: 3140–41	248–49
I: 329	26	II: 3142–44 \ II: 3120–21 /	250–52
II: 1116–17	30–31		
II: 4077–83	32–43	II: 3142–44 \ II: 3394–99 /	253–55
II: 3246	46		
I: 418	53–54	II: 3099–3101	257
II: 4086–89	57–58	II: 2951–53	258
II: 1908–10	69–70	II: 3009–10	259–61
III: 2879–89	71–72	II: 2984–85	263–64
II: 3243	73	II: 3270–72	265–66
II: 1827–28	75–76	II: 3213–14 \ II: 3435–36 /	274–75
II: 3241–49	93–94		
II: 1877–1910	115–32	II: 2927–28 \ II: 68–71 /	278–80
III: 2795–2802 \ L: 831–36 /	126–28	III: 267–68 \ III: 285–88, 291 /	{ 285–87 \ 290
I: 1337–39	129–31	II: 2987–92	290–92
I: 1337–39	152–53	II: 2969–70	293–96
III: 955–56	{ 154–59 \ 376–77	I: 1373	299
		I: 1476	300
II: 1237–38	155	II: 3167–73	310–14
III: 1865	175	II: 3039–46	337–39
L: 3429	182–83	II: 3071–77	348–56
I: 1349–51	197–200	II: 928–32	352–56, 552
I: 1427–28	233–234	II: 2979–80	358
II: 1455–68	235–38	III: 3268–69	373–75
II: 147–52	242–45	I: 822	400–402

TABLE ONE (CONT'D)

Matheolus–Le Fèvre	*Chaucer, III*	*Matheolus–Le Fèvre*	*Chaucer, III*
I: 713–15	433	L: 1130–33	677–78
III: 1837–40	435–37	L: 3874–77	688–89 706
L: 2063–64	441		
L: 2981–84	437–42	III: 102–103 III: 217–19	715–18
II: 4152–54	446		
II: 1916 II: 1829–30	447,510	III: 1013–17 II: 682–86	721–23
		III: 929–32	727–28
II: 184	456 IV: 1848	II: 165–69	732
II: 2735	464	II: 1589	733
III: 1685–90; *Le Resolu en mariage,* 98	489–90	II: 95–97	775–76
		I: 165	781
		II: 3618	800
II: 2973–74	513–14 630	II: 1460	804
II: 1289	519	L: 3470–73	811–12
		I: 809–10	813–14
II: 3312–14 II: 949–50	551–53 555–56	II: 320 III: 2101	1038–40 (WBT)
I: 1415–16	583–84	I: 1167–73	I: 446 (GP)
II: 847–52 II: 594–601	587–92 593–99	II: 1431–51	I: 449–52
II: 1748–49	608	II: 3031–32	I: 453
II: 1020–21	617–18	L: 3202–03	I: 460 III: 196–97
II: 973–75	622–25	II: 1004–06	I: 465
I: 811–15	638	II: 1004–05	I: 467
I: 453–55	674	II: 1945–49	I: 475
II: 3519	677	II: 1831–36	I: 474–76

TABLE TWO

Matheolus—Le Fèvre	*Chaucer, III*
1. Ma femme les tenebres chante, "*Ve*" et lamentacios hante. (II: 47–48)	To speke of *wo* that is in mariage. (3)
2. Et trop plus doit faire la *glose.* (I: 329)	Men may devyne and *glosen,* up and doun. (26)
3. "Car, si comme Dieu le tesmoingne, *Pour femme laisse pere et mere.* (II: 1116–17)	Eek wel I woot, he seyde myn housbonde *Sholde lete fader and mooder,* and take to me. (30–31)
4. *Qui des femmes a un millier,* *Lors ne le puet on essillier;* *Franchement vit, tousjours est siens* *Par la franchise de ses biens.* Nature ne te crea mie Pour faire seule compaignie A une femme seulement. (II: 4077–83)	*But of no nombre mencion made he,* Of bigamye, or of octogamye; Why sholde men thanne speke of it vileynye? *Lo, heere the wise kyng, daun Salomon;* *I trowe he hadde wyves mo than oon.* As wolde God it were leveful unto me *To be refresshed half so ofte as he!* Which yifte of God hadde he for alle his wyvys! No man hath swich that in this world alyve is. *God woot, this noble kyng, as to my wit* *The firste nyght had many a myrie fit* With ech of hem, so wel was hym on lyve. (32–43)
5. *Certes, tu ne pues vivre chastes.* (II: 3246)	*For sothe, I wol nat kepe me chaast in al.* (46)
6. *Que diray je donc de Lameth?* (I: 418)	*What rekketh me,* thogh folk seye vileynye

TABLE TWO (CONT'D)

Matheolus–Le Fèvre	*Chaucer, III*
6.	*Of shrewed Lameth* and his bigamye. (53–54)
7. *Toutes pour tous, et tous pour toutes.* *Salemon* assés le nous preuve. *Des sains peres* aussi l'en treuve, *Qu'aucuns pluseurs femmes eslurent,* Et que trop mieulx que nous valurent. (II: 4086–89)	*And ech of hem hadde wyves mo than two* *And many another holy man also.* (57–58)
8. Et d'autre part, c'est fort a croire *Que Dieux,* qui est pere de vie *Condampnast l'amant pour l'amie.* (II: 1908–10)	For hadde God comanded maydenhede, *Thanne hadde he dampned weddyng with* *the dede.* (69–70)
9. *Se les peres et leur lignie* *N'eüssent charnel compaignie* En saint mariage jadis, Tout seul demourast paradis. Car qui tel fait point ne feroit, Ne vierge n'autre ne seroit. (III: 2879–84)	*And certes, if ther were no seed ysowe,* *Virginitee, thanne wherof sholde it growe?* (71–72)
10. Pour ce *saint Pol,* discret et sage. (II: 3243)	*Poul* dorste nat comanden, atte leeste. (73)
11. Quand elle sçot qu'enfant avroit, *Dart de leësce* la navroit. (II: 1827–28)	*The dart is set up for virginitee:* Cacche whoso may, who renneth best lat see. (75–76)
12. D'autre part, il convient mesure *Encontre l'ardeur de luxure.* Pour ce saint Pol, discret et sage, Loe en ses dis le mariage. (II: 3241–44)	And for to been a wyf he yaf me leve Of *indulgence.* (83–84)

TABLE THREE

Matheolus –Le Fèvre	*Chaucer*
1. Matheolus discusses his woes in marriage (I: 1–82).	The WB talks about her woes in marriage (1–3).
2. Matheolus attacks bigamy (I: 83–564).	The WB takes the opposite point of view and defends bigamy (4–58).
3. Marriage is superior to virginity (III: 2057–3246).	The WB disagrees: Virginity is superior to marriage (59–163).
4. No parallel	The Pardoner interrupts (164–88).
5. How Petronilla treats her old husband in matters of food and sex (I: 1257–1362).	How the WB behaves towards her three old husbands in bed and board (194–223).
6. Matheolus discusses his domestic troubles with the nurse who, in collusion with the wife, makes his life miserable (*Leësce,* 1363–1522).	Chaucer develops the same idea (224–34).
7. Women's vices are exposed and illustrated with exempla (II: 1–2806).	The WB refutes these charges while acknowledging the presence of some of these vices. Chaucer does not follow the same order as Matheolus in the treatment of feminine vices. He often uses the behavior of the WB as his illustrative example (235–665).

For example,

a. Women are quarrelsome (41–76)	156–57, 173–76, 638.
b. Women are unfaithful (77–144)	255–56, 265–68.
c. Women will not stay home; they roam abroad (146–54).	316–22, 348–56.
d. Remarriage is instant (847–79).	194–97.
e. Women are envious (1413–82).	235–38, 449–52
f. Women are superstitious (1993–2120).	609–18
g. Women are proud (2483–2520).	337–56

TABLE THREE (CONT'D)

Matheolus–Le Fèvre	*Chaucer*
7. *h.* Women are cruel (2525–88).	215–25
i. Women are gluttonous (2709–52).	194, 464–67
j. Women are incapable of keeping husbands' secrets (1107–1238).	531–42
8. The different motives for marriage are analyzed and rejected (II: 2807–3602).	Some motives for marriage are discussed (248–75).
9. Matheolus talks about more woes in marriage (II: 3603–4158).	No parallel.
10. Matheolus laments his marriage (II: 1–32).	No parallel.
11. Matheolus discusses his dream in which God appears to him and reveals the path of salvation for married men; the married and the bigamists will enjoy greater joy and glory in heaven (III: 33–3246).	No parallel.
12. God reveals that marriage is a purgatory to purify married persons of their sins and prepare them for heaven (III: 1673–1720).	Chaucer condenses the teaching of the dream into two lines (489–90).
13. Matheolus gives as exempla stories of wicked wives: II: 1565–1662; II: 2507–92; III: 990–1052.	Chaucer talks about Jankyn's book of the stories of wicked wives. The stories found in Matheolus and Chaucer are not all the same (627–787).
14. A wife, Berta, beats up her husband, Clemens (II: 2393–2432).	The WB hits her husband with her fist (788–93).
15. Peace follows battle. God comforts Matheolus, blesses him with peace, and promises him a great reward in heaven (III: 1–3246).	Peace comes after the battle of sexes. Chaucer, like Matheolus, ends the prologue with an intimation of the heavenly reward of the last husband of the WB (794–828).

some of his written sources, the problem of literary sources cannot altogether be dismissed. It may be objected, of course, that references to St. Paul, St. Jerome, the Bible, Adam and Eve, Samson, Delilah, Trotula, Heloïse, Pasiphaë, Socrates, and so on were so commonplace in medieval lore that Chaucer did not have to read Matheolus for these references. It is true that such commonplace names and ideas on marriage and women by themselves do not provide sufficient supporting evidence for my case. Yet there are several unique verbal parallels and important ideas in Chaucer which seem inexplicable without reference to Matheolus. If, then, Chaucer drew these ideas, words, and phrases from Matheolus, it could be argued that Chaucer's study of Matheolus was also probably responsible for the presence of several, if not all, commonplace names and ideas in the Wife of Bath's Prologue.

In Chaucer's development of the Wife's main ideas on marriage and women, Matheolus' influence can be clearly detected. In lines 1–150 the Wife defends bigamy and marriage and discusses the role of sex in human reproduction and the place of virginity in Christian teaching. For this section Chaucer used not only Jerome's *Epistola adversus Jovinianum*[16] but also Matheolus. Chaucer's indebtedness to Jerome has been clearly shown by Skeat, Robinson, and Whiting.[17] Matheolus and Le Fèvre also follow Jerome in their discussion of the very same ideas. In the following details Chaucer shows greater indebtedness to Matheolus than to Jerome.

Chaucer talks about Solomon's many wives and the pleasure Solomon had with them (32–41). Jerome does not refer to Solomon. Matheolus writes about the fun a man with many wives can have and refers to Solomon:

> Salemon assés le nous preuve.
> Des sains peres aussi l'en treuve,
> Qu'aucuns pluseurs femmes eslurent.
> (II: 4087–89)

> [Solomon proves it to us well enough; one finds that some holy fathers also had many wives.]

Chaucer's reference to Lamech: "What rekketh me, thogh folk seye vileynye / Of shrewed Lameth and his bigamye?" (53–54) is closer to Matheolus than to Jerome. Matheolus writes:

> Ergo de Lamech quid vobis dicere possim
> Nescio, . . .

Primus enim bigamus fuit iste miserrimus, unde
Mors, pestis, strages, maledictio sunt oriunde.
Ve! Lamech! bigamus. . . .

(161–65)

[Therefore, I do not know what to say about
Lamech; . . . that most wretched man was the first
bigamist. Through him perforce there arose death, pesti-
lence, carnage, and curse. Woe to Lamech, the bigamist.]

Jerome, on the other hand, writes: "Primus Lamech sanguinarius et
homicida, unam carnem in duas divisit uxores: fratricidium et di-
gamiam, eadem cataclysmi poena delevit" (23: 233) [Lamech, the first
bloody murderer, divided one flesh between two wives; the very
punishment of the Deluge blotted out both fratricide and bigamy].
While Jerome makes only a statement about Lamech, Chaucer, following Matheolus, formulates a rhetorical question about the first
bigamist.

In Chaucer's expression: "The dart is set up for virginitee" (75),
dart, "spear," is often taken to mean "prize," as in Jerome: "Pro-
ponit . . . *praemium,* invitat ad cursum, tenet in manu virginitatis
bravium: ostendit purissimam fontem" (23: 228) [He promises reward,
invites (men) to the race; he holds in his hand the reward for virginity
and points out the most pure spring]. Probably, *dart* in the sense of
male sexual organ, as used by Matheolus, makes more sense here:
"Quand elle sçot qu'enfant avroit, / *Dart de leësce* la navroit" (II:
1827–28) [When she knew that she might have a child, the dart of joy
would disappoint her]. The piercing action of the dart in sexual intercourse not only destroys virginity but also creates virgins, as the Wife
argues in lines 71–72: "And certes, if ther were no seed ysowe, /
Virginitee, thanne wherof sholde it growe?"[18]

When Chaucer writes "Al were it good no womman for to
touche,— / He mente as in his bed or in his couche; / For peril is
bothe fyr and tow t'assemble" (87–89), he seems to be referring to
Jerome: "Quomodo igitur qui ignem tetigerit, statim aduritur" (23:
219) [He who touches fire is at once burnt]. It is possible that Chaucer
also has Matheolus in mind when he talks about the incompatibility
between man and woman: "Droit canon dit, que mal s'acorde / La
harpe o le salterion, / Si fait Robin a Marion" (II: 1264–66) [Canon
law says that harp and psaltery just do not go together, as Robin said to
Marion].

Neither Chaucer's statement about the celibacy of Christ, "Crist was a mayde" (138), nor Matheolus' "Que tu ne voulsis femme prendre / Ne toy en mariage rendre" (III: 181–82) [You did not want to take a woman or get married] is found in Jerome.

Jerome, Matheolus, and Chaucer discuss at length the purpose of sex in marriage. In certain details Chaucer follows Matheolus and La Fèvre more closely than Jerome. Corresponding to Le Fèvre's "Il voult que propacion / Venist par delectacion (Leësce, 835–36) [He wanted that procreation should come through delectation] and Matheolus' "Pour le plaisir Dieu accomplir" (III: 2802) [to do the will of God], Chaucer writes:

> I sey this, that they maked ben for bothe,
> This is to seye, *for office, and for ese*
> Of engendrure, *ther we nat God displese.*
>   (126–28)

Further, Matheolus' *beauls instrumens* (II: 1879) becomes *sely instrument* (132) in Chaucer; in the same passage Matheolus' "Se le clergié en fait deffense" (II: 1883) [if the clerics indeed object] becomes Chaucer's "So that the clerkes be nat with me wrothe" (125). It should be added in this connection that the earliest known literary source for Chaucer's use of *bele chose* (447, 510) and *quoniam* with the sexual connotation is Matheolus: "Ceste *chose* est moult favourable" (II: 1916) [This thing (sexual intercourse) is very good]; "Vieille rit quant elle suppose / Qu'on li fera la *bonne chose*" (II: 1829–30) [The old woman laughs when she thinks this good thing is going to happen to her]: "Pour faire charnelment congnoistre / Leur *quoniam* et leur *quippe*" (II: 1748–49) [To know carnally their *quoniam* (female genitals) and their *quippe* (male genitals)]. Matheolus uses *chose* for coitus, but Chaucer uses it for female genitals.

Though both Chaucer and Matheolus refer to procreation and delectation as the double function of sex—Matheolus speaks rather of procreation through delectation—and develop the same ideas on marriage and virginity, they differ in their assessment of the relative superiority of one over the other. Matheolus argues at length in Book III of his *Lamentations* that marriage is in every way superior to virginity. But Chaucer professes the orthodox view that virginity is a more excellent way of life than matrimony (91–92, 95–96, 135–44). Both authors, however, approve of bigamy or remarriage after the death of a spouse. Of course, the readers of the Wife of Bath's Prologue will remember the Wife's side: "For myn entente is nat but for to pleye" (192) and will be careful about attributing misogynous ideas to Chaucer.

After the interruption of the Pardoner (164–93), the Wife of Bath talks about some of the woes in marriage which her first three old husbands had to endure (194–233). This section is almost entirely derived from Matheolus (I: 1257–1522). Matheolus describes in detail how badly his young wife treats him in bed and at table. Being an old man, he is impotent and unable to meet the excessive demands of his young wife:

> Mon impotence est anoncie,
> Et dit, se la bourse froncie
> Ne puet payer le droit pour elle.
> (I: 1349–51)

[My impotence is made known. And she says that if the purse is closed he cannot pay her his debt.]

> Quinze fois *de nuit et de jour*
> Avra passion sans sejour
> Et sera tormentés forment.
> (I: 759–61)

[Fifteen times *night and day* she would make her demands without ceasing and will torment (her husband) very much.]

> Ma femme veult, et je ne puis,
> Ses drois requiert souvent depuis,
> Que je luy refus a payer.
> (I: 1337–39)

[My wife wants and I cannot. Since then she demands her rights often, but I refuse to pay her.]

According to the testimony of the Wife, her three old husbands "unnethe myghte . . . the statut holde" (198); "Ye woot wel what I meene of this, pardee" (200). Like Matheolus' wife, she torments them in bed: "How pitously a-nyght I made hem swynke!" (202). There is a clear echo of Matheolus' phrase, *de nuit et de jour,* in the Chaucerian lines "Myn housbonde shal it have bothe eve and morwe / Whan that hym list come forth and paye his dette" (152–53).

Not only does Matheolus allude to the story of the accused chough

(II: 3084–94) like Chaucer (231–32), but he alludes also to the wife's collusion with the maid of the house for tormenting her husband. Chaucer exploits the potential of the cooperating maid not in the Wife of Bath's Prologue but in the Reeve's Tale. The miller untied the horse of the clerks, Aleyn and John, and chased it to the fen among the wild mares; the clerks then had to run after their horse (I: 4057–4106). According to *Le Meunier et les deux clers,* which is the closest analogue of the Reeve's Tale, it is the clerks themselves who turn the mare into a meadow.[19] In the *Lamentations,* according to the instructions of the wife, the maid unties the horse of Matheolus and makes him chase it into the woods (I: 1409–16).

Since, as shown above, Matheolus appears to be Chaucer's source for details on the ill treatment of husbands, it is probable that Chaucer's expression, "The bacon was nat fet for hem, I trowe, / That som men han in Essex at Dunmowe" (217–18), could simply mean that the husband was not given bacon when he asked for it. Therefore, these lines are not necessarily a reference to the custom of offering a flitch of bacon to any married couple who lived a year without quarreling. Chaucer would reinforce this idea later:

> And yet in bacon hadde I nevere delit;
> That made me that evere I wolde hem chide.
> For thogh the pope hadde seten hem biside,
> I wolde nat spare hem at hir owene bord.
> (418–21)

Matheolus says that his wife offered him bad meat instead of good meat and beer instead of wine (I: 1257–90). Moreover, both Chaucer and Matheolus treat the husband's imposed abstinence in food and sex one after the other in the same respective sections.

Chaucer and Matheolus describe womanly envy toward neighbors in matters of dress by using almost identical terminology. Chaucer's Wife complains:

> Sire olde kaynard, is this thyn array?
> Why is my neighebores wyf so gay?
> She is honoured over al ther she gooth;
> I sitte at hoom, I have no thrifty clooth
> (235–38)

Matheolus' wife chides her husband:

> "Chetif mari," ce dit la femme,
> "Tu as grant honte et grant diffame,

> Quant tu me tiens ainsi vestue
> Que je n'os aler par la rue."
>   (II: 1455–58)

> "certes, sire, j'ai bien raison;
> Je demeur nue en la maison,
> Et mes voisines sont ornées,
> Bien et noblement ordonnées."
>   (II: 1463–66)

["You weak man," the woman says, "You should have great shame and sorrow when you keep me dressed in such a way that I dare not go in the street. . . . Certainly, sir, I am right. I stay naked in the house when the women of the neighborhood are well adorned and well dressed."]

Chaucer condenses Matheolus' lengthy discussion of the motives of marriage, such as noble birth, high estate, wealth, beauty, and fair shape, in twenty-five lines (248–73) and concludes: "And that no wys man nedeth for to wedde, / Ne no man that entendeth unto hevene" (274–75). These lines echo Matheolus:

> Je te pri, pour sauver ton ame,
> Que tu n'espouses jeune femme.
>   (II: 3213–14)

[I beg you, to save your soul, do not marry a young woman.]

> N'espouses, car cil quiert sa mort
> Qui a prendre femme s'amort.
>   (II: 3435–36)

[Do not marry, for he who falls in love with a woman seeks his own death.]

Among the many reasons that men marry, Chaucer mentions *richesse* (257) just as Matheolus does:

> Qui prent femme pour ses deniers
> Ne pour les biens de ses greniers,
> Ne pour sa richesce briefment
> Je di, que il peche griefment.
> Contre la loy des mariages.
>   (II: 3099–103)

[He who marries a woman for her money—unless it is for
her goods in her attic and for her wealth for a short
time—I say, sins grievously against the law of marriages.]

Though Jerome, the common source, gives *liberalitas* as a motive for
marriage, Chaucer prefers to follow Matheolus by changing *liberalitas*
to *richesse* as a reason for marriage. Jerome puts it: "Alius liberalitate
sollicitat" (23: 277) [Another one seeks (her hand) by a display of
generosity].

The theme of trial marriage or the suggestion of testing women
before marriage is found in Jerome (23: 177) and Matheolus (II:
399–418, III: 265–91). Though there are several verbal similarities
between Matheolus and Chaucer (285–92), there is no overwhelming
evidence to conclude that here Matheolus is the only source of Chaucer;
it is more than likely that Jerome also was consulted by Chaucer for
this section.

The idea that both husband and wife have equal rights on family
wealth, which Chaucer indicates in line 310: "It is my good as wel as
thyn" is found only in one known written source, Matheolus: "Nos
biens deüssent communs estre" (II: 3167) [Our goods must be in
common]. Probably implied in the Wife's assertion: "Thou shalt nat
bothe, thogh that thou were wood, / Be maister of my body and of my
good" (313–14) is the truth that the woman is not a slave but a free
person. Matheolus develops this idea of the free status of the woman as
follows:

> Nos biens deüssent communs estre,
> Et tu en veulx faire le maistre
> Et mettre tout a ton usage.
> Quant je te pris en mariage,
> Se j'avoye peu de finance,
> Toutesvois ma personne franche
> Valoit trop plus que ta richesce.
>   (II: 3167–73)

[Our goods should be in common. But you want to be the
master of it and put everything to your own use. Of course,
when I married you, I had very little money. However, my
free person was worth much more than your wealth.]

Among the vices of women, vanity in dress with its concomitant
danger to chastity receives special mention and censure in both authors.
Chaucer alludes to a *rubriche* (346)—perhaps an exemplum—which is
supposed to illustrate the view that women who go out to show off

their "precious array" imperil their chastity. He also compares women to cats. To keep a cat at home one must singe its skin; but if its skin is "slyk and gay," it will go caterwauling. "This is to seye, if I be gay, sire shrewe, / I wol renne out, my borel for to shewe" (355–56). Before the time of Chaucer only Matheolus has developed the figure of the cat the way Chaucer does. Matheolus writes:

> On suelt brusler du chat la pel
> Pour ce que, s'il vient a l'appel
> De ceulx qui les chas embler seulent,
> Que pour la peau point ne le veulent.
> Qui des femmes ainsi feroit
> Et leur peliçons brusleroit,
> Leurs queues, leurs dras et leurs cornes
> Assés en seroient plus mornes,
> A bien faire plus curieuses
> Et assés moins luxurieuses.
> (II: 3071–80)

[They singe the skin of the cat so that those who would steal him may not want him because of his skin, especially if it goes out to them at their call. Whoever would do that to women and burn their coats, tails, clothes, and horns, may feel rather sad about it; but they will make them (the women) more grotesque and less attractive.]

Matheolus illustrates this idea of keeping women at home for their own protection with the exemplum of Dinah, the daughter of Jacob, who went out to the city of Shechem for sightseeing and thereby lost her virginity (II: 3054–70). It is probable that Chaucer is referring to the Dinah episode by his *rubriche* (346). Further, Chaucer points out that women go to the towns, shrines, festivities, and pilgrimages "for to pleye, / And for to se, and eek for to be seye / Of lusty folk" (551–53). According to Matheolus, women wear jewels and fancy clothes to show themselves off, and therefore they cannot remain chaste:

> Tousjours veult aler et venir;
> Jamais ne la tendroit close hom
> Ne en chambre ne en maison
> Par tous lieux veult estre veüe.
> (II: 928–31)

[She always wants to go and come and is never willing to stay close to her husband either in the bedroom or in the house; everywhere she wants to be noticed.]

> Femme qui veult souvent aler
> Aux jeux, caroler et baler,
> No puet estre longuement chaste,
> Car Venus de trop pres la haste.
>   (II: 3055–58)

[The woman who often wants to go to the games, to carol, and to dance cannot remain chaste very long, because Venus pressures her too much.]

Though the medieval view that "a wyf destroyeth hire housbonde" (377) [his body] is found in Jerome (23: 249), he does not talk about woman there as bringing sexual ruin on the man through emasculation and impotence. On the contrary, Chaucer (149–160, 197–202), following Matheolus, gives the idea of ruining a sexual twist. Matheolus writes:

> Aussi la femme en mariage
> Contre la char de l'omme estrive.
> Tant est la femme corrosive
> Que la char de l'omme degaste,
> Quant par mariage la taste.
> Il semble que les noces nuysent,
> Car les vertus d'omme amenuysent.
>   (II: 346–52)

[Also the woman in marriage fights against the flesh of man. The woman is so corrosive that the flesh of the man rots when he enjoys her in marriage. It seems that marriage is man's curse, for it diminishes his powers.]

The first recorded use of the verb *ba* (kiss) in English is in Chaucer: "Com neer, my spouse, lat me *ba* thy cheke!" (433), and "com *pa* me" (I: 3709). Among Chaucerian sources, only Matheolus uses this word: "Se je di *bo*, elle dit *beu* / Nous sommes comme chien et leu" (I: 713–14) [If I say *bo*, she says *beu*; we are like dog and wolf]. Likewise, the riming of *conscience* with *pacience* in the reference to Job's suffering is common to both authors. Christ preaches to Matheolus, the dreamer, in the dream vision:

> Chier fils, remembre en *conscience*
> De Job et de sa *pacience*.
> Se souffreras legierement
> Ce qui te trouble amerement.
>   (III: 1837–40)

[Dear son, if you recall in your conscience Job and his patience, you will suffer less from what troubles you much.]

And Chaucer writes:

> And han a sweete spiced *conscience*
> Sith ye so preche of Jobes *pacience*
> Suffreth alwey, syn ye so wel kan preche.
>   (435–37)

Also, the Wife of Bath's claim that "in erthe I was his *purgatorie*" (489) is a direct borrowing from Matheolus who is the first recorded author to develop the idea that woman as well as marriage is man's purgatory on earth. In Book III, Christ appears to Matheolus in a dream and reveals to him that, by enduring the sufferings of marriage on earth, a man can reach heaven right after death, because he has already endured his purgatory on earth:

> Pour amender leur conscience
> Et pour prouver leur pacience
> Et leurs vertus et leurs victoires,
> Leur ay fait pluseurs *purgatoires*
> Plains de tourmens et plains d'orage
> Entre lesquels est mariage.
>   (III: 1685–90)

[To purify their conscience and to prove their patience, their virtues, and their victories, I created for them many purgatories full of torments and full of storms, among which is marriage.]

The poem, *Le Resolu en Mariage* attributed to Matheolus, also refers to purgatory: "Moy, Resolu, je dy que telz meschans / En ce bas lieu font ja leur *purgatoire*" (97–98) [I have made up my mind: I say that such miserable people are already in their purgatory on earth here below].[20]

The Wife of Bath says that at the death of her fourth husband she cried but little and that she was looking for a fifth one when her late husband was still lying in the coffin (587–99). The resemblances between Matheolus and Chaucer here are so remarkable that we are persuaded to infer that Chaucer used Matheolus for this passage. For easy comparison the quotations are given in parallel columns.

Quant le mari gist en la biere,
La femme et avant et arriere
Pense tousjours en son courage
De ravoir autre a mariage
C'est coustume, quant elle pleure;
Après trois jours n'attent que l'eure.
(II: 847–52)

Whan that my fourthe housbonde
was on beere,
I weep algate, and made sorry
cheere,
As wyves mooten, for it is usage,
And with my coverchief covered my
visage,
But for that I was purveyed of a
make,
I wepte but smal, and that I
undertake.
(587–92)

Mais Dieu scet, quant les lermes
queurent,
Que par dehors mainent tristesce,
Comment les cuers ont grant leësce.
Ja soit que femme par dehors
Pleure de son mari le corps,
Par dedens s'esjoïst et chante,
Et de nouveau mari se vante,
Quant de noirs draps porte
l'enseigne.
(II: 594–601)

To chirche was myn housbonde
born amorwe,
With neighebores, that for hym
maden sorwe;
and Jankyn, oure clerk, was oon of
tho.
As help me God! whan that I saugh
hym go
After the beere, me thoughte he
hadde a paire
Of legges and of feet so clene and
faire
That al myn herte I yaf unto his
hoold.
(593–99)

[When the husband lies in his coffin, the woman thinks in
her heart—before and after (his death)—about having
another one in marriage. It is customary that she weep. But
after three days she waits only for her new joy!

But God knows that, when the tears fall, sorrow is displayed only on the outside and that great is the joy that the
hearts have. I know that a woman who on the outside weeps
over the body of her husband rejoices and sings in the
inside. She would not hesitate to brag about her new husband even when she is wearing her black dress.]

The alleged source of Chaucer's lines:

I ne loved nevere by no discrecioun,
But evere folwede myn appetit,
Al were he short, or long, or blak, or whit;
I took no kep. . . .
(622–25)

is *Le Roman de la Rose,* 8516–17: "Ne vous chaut s'il est courz ou lons, / Quant sui touz seus lez vous presenz" [It does not matter to you if it (the woman's wimple) is short or long when I am alone near you]. Here Jean de Meun is referring to the wimple the woman is wearing rather than to partners in sex whom the Wife of Bath has in mind; further, no source explains what *blak* and *whit* signify. Matheolus indicates that *blak* and *whit* stand for members of the religious orders: Dominicans and Carmelites who corrupt women and who are corrupted by them (II: 965–99). Chaucer's *short* could stand for *Friars Minor* and *long* for *Canons Regular;* or, *short* and *long* could indicate the clergy in minor orders and major orders. Matheolus writes:

> Les freres des religions,
> Venans de pluseurs regions,
> De l'ordre noire, blanche et bise.
> (II: 973–74)

> [From different places they come, friars of the religious orders: Black, White and Gray.]

"Hec nostras dominas corrumpunt parisienses" (1005) [They corrupt our women from Paris].[21]

Chaucer also borrowed from Matheolus several details for his portrait of the Wife of Bath. The name *Alys* bears a strong resemblance to La Fèvre's Dame Leësce, the articulate defender of women and marriage. Le Fèvre calls her: "Leësce l'amoureuse" (L: 2667) after Leësce, the accomplished singer and dancer of *Le Roman de la Rose,* 730, 832. It is more than coincidental, I believe, that the British Library Royal MS. 20 B XXI carries the notation on f. 1^V "Here I sit myselfe Alys." There is no external evidence to show that this manuscript ever belonged to Chaucer or was ever consulted by him. A "signature" in the manuscript—I was tempted to read it as "Geoffrey Chaucy"—is illegible even under ultraviolet-ray treatment. The only certain thing we know about the manuscript is that it carries the signature of Wyatt and that it belonged to George Boleyn in 1526. If, however, there is any manuscript that has a claim to having been used by Chaucer, then it is this one, which contains both *Lamentations* and *Leësce.*

The figure of the Wife as a rider on horseback—"He yaf me al the bridel in myn hand" (813)—especially in the General Prologue (I: 469), may or may not have been influenced by Matheolus' description of the dominating wife in debate: "Femme fu chevalier, et l'omme / Fu le cheval portant la somme" (I: 1147–48) [The woman was the rider and the man was the horse carrying the burden]. In any case, the idea behind it—with several verbal resemblances—that "Wommen desiren to have sovereynetee / As wel over hir housbond as hir love / And for to been in maistrie hym above" (1038–40) is found in Matheolus: "Du mari voult estre maistresse" (II: 320) [She wishes to lord it over her husband]; "La seigneurie veult avoir" (III: 2101) [She wishes to have sovereignty].

No literary source accounts for the deafness of the Wife of Bath (I: 446, III: 636) except Matheolus, who says that women pretend deafness to torment their husbands:

> Afin que femme puist troubler
> Son mari, elle fait doubler,
> Voire repeter d'une pose
> Dix fois une meïsme chose.
> La chose trois fois recitée
> Veut encore estre repetée
> Semblant fait que point ne l'entende.
> (I: 1167–73)

> [In order to trouble her husband she knows how to make him say the same thing twice and even repeat it ten times after a deliberate pause. Even if something has been recited three times, she wants him to repeat it, pretending she cannot hear him.]

Though a commonplace, the Wife's "haunt" of cloth-making (I: 447, III: 401–402) has also a witness in Le Fèvre: "Mais la femelle plus desire / Lin, laine, estoupes filer" (Leësce, 3763–64) [The woman prefers to spin linen, wool, and flax].[22]

Chaucer's description of the strife over precedence at the Offertory during Mass has an excellent parallel in Matheolus:

S'il y a une coustumiere	In al the parisshe wif ne was ther
De seoir au moustier premiere	noon
Ou d'aler devant a l'offrande,	That to the offrynge bifore hire
Il convient qu'ele soit bien grande,	sholde goon,
Se son fait vouloit frequenter	And if ther dide, certeyn so wrooth
Sans rioter ne tourmenter.	was she,
Souvent grans batailles en sourdent;	That she was out of alle charitee.
Celles qui d'envie se hourdent	(I: 449–52)
Ne veulent pas ainsi souffrir	
Que premiere deüst offrir.	And if that any neighebor of myne
Et qui veult paix, si se pourvoye	Wol nat in chirche to my wyf
Que, quant femmes vont par la	enclyne,
voye,	Or be so hardy to hire to trespace,

Que son salut ne rende a une,
Mais salutacion commune
Face a toutes en audience,
Avec signe d'obedience;
Car qui toutes ne les salue,
Mauldit sera de fievre ague.
Il n'est femme qui soit en vie
Qui sur pareille n'ait envie;
A ce nature les encline
(II: 1431–51)

Whan she comth hoom she rampeth
in my face,
And crieth, 'False coward, wrek thy
wyf!
By corpus bones, I wol have thy
knyf,
. . . .
Thou darst nat stonden by thy
wyves right!'
(VII: 1901–12)

[If a woman is accustomed to have the first seat in the church or is used to go first during the Offertory procession, it is necessary that she be a prominent lady, especially if she wants to continue doing so without causing a disturbance. Often great strife stems from that, for those who are envious do not want to allow her to go to the offering first. Whoever want peace will take care that, when they meet several women on their way, they do not greet only one but do obeisance to all in front of him (Christ in the Eucharist), because he who does not greet all of them will be damned of high fever. There is not a woman alive who does not envy her peers; nature inclines them to this.]

Chaucer's Wife of Bath, like Matheolus' women (II: 3031–32), likes to wear kerchiefs (I: 453–55), though Manly notes that the kerchief was not in style since the middle of the fourteenth century.[23] The dress of the Wife is elegant and extravagant (I: 447–58): Matheolus also dwells at length on the elegant and extreme clothing habits of women (II: 2483–520).

In contrast to the amiable, polite, sentimental Prioress (I: 118–62), the Wife is independent, aggressive, and overwhelming in speech and actions. The Wife's behavior exhibits certain characteristics traditionally associated with men rather than women. One wonders whether Chaucer intended to caricature her also as a hermaphrodi'e as Matheolus does on account of women's extravagance in dress, which takes monstrous proportions with horns and tail (II: 4127–29).

The Wife is also typical of Matheolus' censured women in her love of pilgrimages. She had been to Jerusalem, Rome, Boulogne,[24] Galicia, and Cologne (I: 463–66); "she hadde passed many a straunge strem" (I: 464); "she koude muchel of wandrynge by the weye" (I: 467). Chaucer's "wandrynge by the weye" seems to echo Matheolus' complaint of women's search for distant goals of pilgrimage and sexual aberrancy from the "straight and narrow" path:

Mieulx leur plaist le pelerinage,
Quant *la voye est un peu longnete,*
A saint Mor ou a Boulongnete,

. . . .

Mais nouveles voyes procurent
En obeïssant a Venus.

(II: 1004–21)

[A pilgrimage pleases them better when the journey is a
longish one, to St. Maur or to Boulogne. . . . They find
new ways to obey Venus.][25]

The Wife's being "gat-tothed" (I: 468) is usually associated with her
lust and wanderlust.[26] Matheolus, however, seems to support Curry's
suggestion that it is also a sign of gluttony and vinosity (III: 456–68):

Tant sont gloutes et dissolutes
Que par outrage sont polutes,
Qui leur fait puïr dens et bouche.
En femme n'a plus grant reprouche
Que de soy par vin enivrer.

(II: 2715–19)

[They are so gluttonous and dissipated that they are defiled
with excessive food. It makes their teeth and mouth stink.
In a woman no reproach is greater than to be inebriated
with wine.][27]

Chaucer's statement about the Wife's casual knowledge of the "remedies of love" (I: 475) appears to be an obvious allusion to Ovid's
work, *Remedia Amoris,* which provides an antidote for inordinate
love.[28] Chaucer's familiarity with Matheolus suggests, however, that
these remedies are rather specific drugs for foolish love, namely, con-
traceptives:

La vieille quist pluseurs racines
Et herbettes et medicines;
A Galatee en fist buvrage,
Afin que par son fol ouvrage
Ne peüst enfant concevoir.

(II: 1945–48)

[The old woman gathered many roots, small herbs, and
medicines. She made a potion for Galatea in order that by
her foolish act she might not get pregnant.][29]

Matheolus' description of old women provides another close parallel to Chaucer's "In felaweshipe wel koude she laughe and carpe" (I: 474), "For she koude of that art the olde daunce" (I: 476), and "teche us yonge men of youre praktike" (III: 187):

> C'est coustume de vieille femme,
> Que, puis que vieillesce l'entame
> Elle seult les jeunes induire
> Et au jeu d'amours introduire.
> Par ses dis et par sa parole
> Les fait dancer a sa karole.
>   (II: 1831–36)

[This is the practice of old women: as old age creeps in, she loves to teach the young and introduce them to love-play. Through her words and speech she makes them dance to her song.][30]

Of course, Chaucer does not create his Wife of Bath in the image and likeness of the duenna exclusively. He presents her also as an attractive young woman (at least in the eyes of her husbands, if not in the eyes of some readers) after Le Fèvre's Dame Leësce (*Leësce,* 127–35). In fact, there is no single viewpoint governing the physical and moral portrait of the Wife of Bath. She is a composite of several attitudes and positions which are often contrary but not necessarily contradictory. Such a variety of approaches enables Chaucer to exploit the comic possibilities inherent in the incongruity and impropriety of the Wife's estate, appearance, behavior, speech, and intention.

Now I should like to discuss briefly the various sources of the Wife of Bath's Prologue in order to discover the relationship between these sources and Matheolus. First, there is sufficient evidence that Chaucer used Jerome's *Adversus Jovinianum* as a source for the Wife's Prologue. According to Lounsbury, "to it the prologue to the Wife of Bath's Tale owes not only numerous passages, but even its existence."[31] The *Lamentations* of Matheolus also owes its existence to Jerome. Second, Chaucer probably borrowed the story of Arrius and Pacuvius—though Pacuvius becomes Latumius in Chaucer—from Walter Map's *Dissuasio Valerii ad Rufinum philosophum ne uxorem ducat.* Third, there is no doubt whatsoever about the pervasive influence of *Le Roman de la Rose,* especially since Chaucer himself translated the *Roman* into English.[32] Fourth, Eustache Deschamps' *Miroir de Mariage* is not a source of Chaucer for the reasons given below.

Eustache Deschamps was born in 1346 and died in 1406, six years after Chaucer's death.[33] On the basis of the only available internal evidence, Gaston Raynaud, the editor and biographer of Deschamps, argues that the *Miroir* was not begun before 1382 and the last lines of this incomplete poem were composed not before 1385, though not later than 1396.[34] There is, however, no evidence to suggest that the manuscript of the incomplete *Miroir* was made public before 1406, the year of the death of the poet. Concerning the oldest surviving manuscript of the *Miroir*, MS. Fr. 840 of the Bibliothèque Nationale, dated between 1406 and 1414, Raynaud writes:

> For whom was this manuscript made? The presence in this large volume of a great number of pieces of very personal nature and above all of two incomplete works—*la Fiction du Lion* and *le Miroir de Mariage*, certainly not having seen the light of the day before the death of the poet—proves adequately that the assembling and editing of the poems had to be accomplished under the direction of a close associate of Deschamps, himself a poet and capable of understanding the works of his friend and overseeing the posthumous publication of his works. None other than Arnaud de Corbie, the old colleague of Deschamps, could do a better job. . . . This assumption allows the dating of the manuscript and its execution between 1406, the probable date of the death of Deschamps, and 1414, the year of the death of Arnaud de Corbie.[35]

The only other surviving manuscript of the *Miroir* was copied from this fifteenth-century manuscript and is found in the Bibliothèque de l'Arsenal.[36] There is no evidence at all that any other manuscript of the *Miroir* ever existed or was ever in England during the time of Chaucer in spite of the conjectures of J. L. Lowes to the contrary.

Lowes writes: "The negotiations of 1393 [negotiations in Picardy towards peace between England and France] afforded, in one way or another, the amplest opportunity for the *Miroir de Mariage* to come into Chaucer's hands."[37] Yet there is no document to prove that a meeting between Lewis Clifford and Deschamps took place in 1393 and that Deschamps sent a manuscript of the *Miroir* to Chaucer through Clifford. Nor is there any evidence to suggest that Chaucer had the occasion to read the *Miroir* or meet Deschamps while Chaucer was in France, though Deschamps knew of Chaucer as the translator of *Le Roman de la Rose* and sent him by the hand of a common friend one of his 1200 ballades. According to Crow and Olson, an early meeting between the two poets is also ruled out: "It is a fairly well established fact that Guillaume de Machaut and Eustache Deschamps were in Reims during this siege [campaign of 1359–60], but that there could have been any contact then between Chaucer and the two French poets is most improbable."[38] Lowes himself admits that Chaucer and Deschamps never met.[39] Carleton Brown says that "in any case, Chaucer could hardly have become acquainted with Deschamps' poem [*Miroir*] until the early 90s, that is, during the later period of *The Canterbury Tales.*"[40] If that were the case, how could Chaucer ever have used *Miroir* 3376–81 as a source of lines 449–52 of the General Prologue, written, according to critical consensus, in or about 1387?[41]

Lowes's claim that Deschamps is a source of Chaucer has never been accepted unanimously by Chaucerian scholars. Though Carleton Brown accepted Lowes's position, he wrote: "The evidence of these parallels [between the Wife of Bath's Prologue and the *Miroir*], while convincing, is not so impressive as that in the case of the Merchant's Tale. Professor Lowes, with unerring intuition, presented his strongest case first, knowing that his first article would have the effect of breaking down the reader's power of resistance."[42] Tatlock has reservations about the *Miroir* as a source of the Merchant's Tale: "Lowes' phrase 'the approach of old age' might easily suggest the wrong idea of Franc Vouloir's personality; he indicates and I find in all the matrimonial discourse of *Mir. de Mar.* nothing as to the marriage of an old man to a young wife. The scene at the beginning of Deschamps' poem reminds one very much less of anything in *Merch. T.*"[43] French concurs: "The parallels, however, may well derive rather from identity of theme or common sources than from direct borrowing, and it seems hardly safe to accept the French poem as a source of the *Marchantes Tale.*"[44] Marian Lossing rejects Lowes's view that Deschamps' *Lai de Franchise* is a source of Chaucer's *Legend of Good Women*: "Certainly the *Lai de Franchise* exhibits no phrases which would oblige us to suppose that Chaucer borrowed precisely from it and no other. At most one might remark inconclusively that he might have used it. . . . As for the parallels in literary structure . . . they too fail to stand the test of examination. . . . Point by point they can be dismissed from consideration."[45]

The following synoptic table shows that not only all the Chaucer-Deschamps parallels but also other Chaucer passages can be accounted for by Matheolus. For our purpose it is enough to provide line numbers.[46] From this synopsis it is obvious that for the Wife of Bath's Prologue we need not resort to Deschamps. Matheolus has all the Deschamps material and more. In fact, I have not come upon a single passage in Chaucer which needs to be explicated by Deschamps. Therefore, if all the Chaucer-Deschamps parallels are found also in Matheolus–Le Fèvre, we can infer that Matheolus is the common source of both Chaucer and Deschamps.

There is evidence that Deschamps himself used Matheolus. The

TABLE FOUR

Matheolus – Le Fèvre	Chaucer, III	Deschamps
I: 1–82	1–3	
I: 83–564	4–58	
III: 2057–3246	59–183	
I: 1305–61	198–202 ⎫	
II: 1508–29	204–14 ⎬	1576–84
I: 1257–90	215–16 ⎭	
II: 3084–94	222–32	3644–856
I: 1415–16	233–34	3634–35, 3644–45
II: 1449–82 ⎫ II: 1080–82 ⎬ II: 3466 ⎭	236–37	1589–91, 1596
II: 3229–32	239–40	
Leësce: 3769–70	246–47	1610–11
II: 3140–3200	248–49	1758–59
II: 147–52	242	
II: 3142–44	250–52	1755–57, 1732–33
II: 2951–3010 ⎫ II: 3995–4002 ⎭	253–64	1625–48
II: 3101–09	257	
II: 2979–80	263–64	
II: 3403	265–72	1736–41
II: 3213–14	274–75	
II: 68–76 ⎫ II: 2927–28 ⎭	278–80	
III: 265–91	285–92	
III: 267–91	290–92	1570–75
I: 1476 ⎫ I: 1374–90 ⎭	293–302	1760–77
II: 3167–78	311	3225
II: 947–1030	316–22	3520–25
II: 3167–78	309–14	
II: 3027–80	337–39	1878–84, 8672–91
II: 947–1030 ⎫ II: 3071–77 ⎬ II: 928–32 ⎭	348–56	3207–15

TABLE FOUR (CONT'D)

Matheolus – *Le Fèvre*	*Chaucer, III*	*Deschamps*
II: 2979–80	357–58	
III: 3268–72	373–75	
II: 4135–58 } II: 4060–70 }	387–92	{ 3600–08, 3620–23, { 3629–32
II: 3229–32	393	3920–25
II: 3312–14 } II: 949–50 }	551–52	Title of chap. XLIII
II: 597–601 } II: 847–52 } II: 867–71 }	593–99, 627–31	1966–77
I: 165	782–83	2943–48

name of Matheolus occurs twice in Deschamps' works: in a ballade and in a letter dated May 16, 1403.[47] Further, Gaston Raynaud's study of the sources of Deschamps shows extensive influence of the *Lamentations* on the *Miroir*.[48] Since there is no internal or external evidence to claim Deschamps as a source of Chaucer and since Matheolus appears to be the common source of both Deschamps and Chaucer, we can conclude that Deschamps is only an analogue of Chaucer. Therefore, any statement on the chronology of the Chaucerian canon based on the influence of Deschamps' works on Chaucer is unreliable.

I may also add that any similarity found in the works of Chaucer and Deschamps should be explained as an influence of Chaucer on the younger French poet. This perception, I think, can be confirmed by a careful reading of the famous ballade of 1386 which Deschamps sent through Lewis Clifford as a tribute to Chaucer.[49] This ballade shows that Deschamps regarded Chaucer with great esteem:

> O Socratès plains de philosophie,
> Seneque en meurs et Auglus en pratique,
> Ovides grans en ta poëterie,
> Briés en parler, saiges en rethorique.
> (1–4)

[O Socrates full of philosophy, Seneca in morals and Aulus Gellius in practical affairs, a mighty Ovid in your poetic skill, concise in expression and artful in rhetoric.]

The poem also indicates that Deschamps had read or was familiar with several works by Chaucer such as *The Legend of Good Women*: "Enlumines le regne d'Eneas" (6), "Tu es d'Amours mondains Dieux en Albie" (11) [You illumine the kingdom of Aeneas; you are the earthly god of love in Albion]; *The House of Fame*: "Aigles treshaulz, qui par ta theorique" (5) [O lofty eagle who by your theoretical knowledge]; *The Romaunt of the Rose*: "Et de la Rose, en la terre Angelique" (12), "En bon anglès le Livre translatas" (16) [And you have translated the Book of the Rose into good English in that Angelic land]; and *Troilus and Criseyde*: "Aux ignorans de la langue Pandras" (9) [For the benefit of those ignorant of the language of Pandarus].[50] Deschamps' "L'isle aux Geans, ceuls de Bruth" (7) [The isle of giants, the people of Brutus] could be a veiled reference to the Wife of Bath's Tale as well as the Franklin's Tale and his "un vergier" (17) [an orchard] could be regarded as an allusion to the Merchant's Tale. It is possible, then, that Deschamps also read or heard about the Wife of Bath's Tale (with the Prologue?) and the Merchant's Tale. The ballade also informs us that Deschamps would willingly and humbly submit his work to the judgment of his English confrère (28) and that he would like to receive one of the authentic works of Chaucer (21–26). If indeed Chaucer honored the request of this worthy *escolier* (28) [student] with a gift of the Wife of Bath's Prologue and the Merchant's Tale, it would solve the problem of the literary relationship between Chaucer and Deschamps. We do not know, however, whether Chaucer granted that request. In future studies I shall show that Chaucer used Matheolus and not Deschamps in the Merchant's Tale and that Matheolus' influence on Chaucer is so pervasive that a few more Chaucerian cruces can be solved with the help of Matheolus.

Finally, I would like to point out that Jill Mann, in an independent study limited to Chaucer's estates satire in the General Prologue to *The Canterbury Tales*, supports my conclusion: "There is evidence that Chaucer was acquainted with this work [*Lamentations*]."[51] I believe that I have provided in this paper additional evidence. My research has convinced me that the two major sources of the Wife of Bath's Prologue are Jerome's *Adversus Jovinianum* and Matheolus–Le Fèvre's *Lamentations*. I have also shown that Chaucer in all probability could not have used Deschamps' *Miroir de Mariage*. Further, the presence of the fourteenth-century Latin and French manuscripts of Matheolus and Le Fèvre in England supports the view that Chaucer read these works in England.

NOTES

1. See A.-G. Van Hamel, ed., *Les Lamentations de Matheolus et le Livre de Leësce de Jehan Le Fèvre*, 2 vols. (Paris: Emile Bouillon, 1892–1905), II; clvii–clix. Arabic numerals stand for the line numbers of the Latin text; Roman numerals plus arabic numerals stand for the French text with the four-book division; L followed by arabic numerals represents *Le Livre de Leësce*.
2. All Chaucer citations are from F. N. Robinson, ed., *The Works of Geoffrey Chaucer*, 2nd ed. (Boston: Houghton Mifflin, 1957).
3. Du Cange, *Glossarium Mediae et Infimae Latinitatis* (Paris: Firmin Didot, 1840–1850), I: 679: "Bigamus dicitur, qui contrahit sive de facto, sive de jure cum vidua vel corrupta. Item Bigamus dicitur religiosus vel monachus, qui castitatem promissam violat. . . . Bigamia triplex est, una videlicet, quando quis duas vel plures habet uxores, alia est cum quis contrahit cum corrupta, tertia est quando quis castitatem promissam per votum solemne violat."
4. See Van Hamel, II: clxxv–clxxix, on the career of Jehan Le Fèvre.
5. Van Hamel, II: clxxix–clxxxii.
6. Van Hamel, II: cxc.
7. Gaston Paris, *Medieval French Literature*, tr. Hannah Lynch (1903; rpt. Freeport, N.Y.: Books for Libraries, 1971), p. 123.
8. Eustache Deschamps, *Œuvres Complètes de Eustache Deschamps*, ed. Le Marquis de Queux de Saint-Hilaire and Gaston Raynaud, Société des Anciens Textes Français, 28 (Paris: Firmin Didot, 1878–1903), V: 73–74.
9. Ibid., XI: 227–28.
10. Van Hamel, II: clx–clxxiv.
11. Robinson, *The Works of Geoffrey Chaucer*, p. 698.
12. J. M. Manly, ed., *Canterbury Tales* (New York: Holt, 1928), pp. 579–81.
13. A. K. Moore, "Chaucer and Matheolus," *Notes and Queries*, 190 (1946), 246.
14. Manly, *Canterbury Tales*, p. 574.
15. It seems unnecessary to quote the Latin original of Matheolus, and to do so would take up too much space. Besides, as a rule Chaucer used the French translation rather than the Latin original. Exceptions are noted. The italics added to words in quotations throughout this essay indicate words, phrases, and verbal echoes common to both Chaucer and Matheolus. To save space I have refrained from quoting long passages. "Matheolus" is used in this essay to refer to the work *Lamentations*, whether in Latin or French.
16. See *Patrologia Latina*, 23: 211 f.; henceforth abbreviated as 23: 211, etc., in the body of the paper.
17. W. W. Skeat, ed., *The Complete Works of Geoffrey Chaucer* (Oxford: Clarendon Press, 1900), V: 291–313; see Robinson, pp. 698–99, and W. F. Bryan and Germaine Dempster, *Sources and Analogues of Chaucer's Canterbury Tales* (New York: Humanities Press, 1958), pp. 208–10.

18. Jean de Meun, *Le Roman de la Rose*, 20704–21742, combines the martial and nature images in his description of the lover's conquest of the Rose. Chaucer probably had in mind both Jean de Meun and Matheolus when he wrote this passage. It must be noted, however, that Jean uses *bourdon* (pilgrim's staff) for the male genitals in lines 21605, 21640, 21646 and not *dart*.

19. Bryan and Dempster, p. 130: "Après ont mis en un prael / La jumant, joste lo choisel" (63–64). See also Germaine Dempster, "On the Source of the *Reve's Tale*," *JEGP*, 29 (1930), 473–74: "Of all the fabliaux stories in the *Canterbury Tales* only one can be studied in connection with an analogue close enough for a reasonable claim to the rank of source: the *Reve's Tale* is closely related to the French fabliau 'le Muenier et les deux Clers.' . . . Chaucer's great superiority is the creation of more living and more humorous characters, by means, first of introductory portraits, then of a few different details in the plot: the 'courteous' stealing, the untying of the horse, the girl's revelation of the theft."

20. Van Hamel, II: 132.

21. Robinson, p. 701 and Skeat, V: 307 refer only to the *Roman*.

22. See E. Talbot Donaldson, *Chaucer's Poetry* (New York: Ronald, 1975), p. 1054.

23. Manly, *Some New Light on Chaucer* (New York: Holt, 1926), pp. 230ff.

24. Is Chaucer's allusion to Boloigne a veiled reference to Matheolus, the bigamist cleric of Boulogne?

25. Jill Mann, *Chaucer and Medieval Estates Satire* (Cambridge: University Press, 1973), pp. 123–24.

26. See Robinson, p. 663.

27. Walter C. Curry, "More About Chaucer's Wife of Bath," *PMLA*, 37 (1922), 45–46.

28. Manly, *Canterbury Tales*, p. 528, and J. Koch, "Chaucers Belesenheit in den römischen Klassikern," *Englische Studien*, 57 (1923), 43, think that Chaucer's "remedies of love" are to be taken rather in a general sense than as a reference to the title and substance of Ovid's poem. See also R. L. Hoffman, *Ovid and the Canterbury Tales* (Philadelphia: U. of Pennsylvania Press, 1966), pp. 34–36.

29. One wonders why Chaucer fails to talk about the children of the Wife of Bath in spite of her claim: "I wol bistowe the flour of al myn age / In the actes and in fruyt of mariage" (113–14). Did she practice contraception?

30. See Skeat, V: 45, and James I. Wimsatt, *Allegory and Mirror* (New York: Pegasus, 1970), pp. 61–90.

31. *Studies in Chaucer*, (New York: Russell, 1962), II: 292.

32. See Bryan and Dempster, pp. 207–15; Robinson, passim; Skeat, V, passim; D. S. Fansler, *Chaucer and the Roman de la Rose* (Gloucester, Mass.: Peter Smith, 1965), passim.

33. Gaston Raynaud, in *Œuvres Complètes de Eustache Deschamps* (Paris: Firmin Didot, 1878–1903), XI: 9, 99.

34. Ibid., p. 198: "En tenant compte de ces deux derniers événements [la bataille de Poitiers et la disparition du royaume d'Arménie (1375)], on peut fixer approximativement l'époque à laquelle Deschamps écrivait la *fin* du *Miroir de mariage;* ce ne saurait être avant 1385, année de la première contribution imposée aux Cypriotes par les Gênois; d'autre part, ce doit être avant 1396, année du désastre de Nicopolis, que l'auteur n'aurait certainement pas oublié de mentionner dans une énumération des victoires turques, s'il avait écrit après cette date."

35. Ibid., p. 105: "Pour qui ce manuscrit a-t-il été fait? La présence dans ce gros volume de bon nombre de pièces d'un caractère tout intime et surtout de deux morceaux inachevés, *La Fiction du lion* et *le Miroir de mariage,* n'ayant certainement pas vu le jour avant la mort du poète, prouve suffisamment que la réunion et la copie des poésies a dû s'effecteur sous la direction d'un familier de Deschamps, poète lui aussi et capable de dépouiller les papiers de son ami et de surveiller la *publication* posthume de ses œuvres. Nul mieux qu'Arnaud de Corbie, ancien collaborateur de Deschamps, ne pouvait s'acquitter d'un tel office. . . . Cette supposition permet de dater le manuscrit, et de'en placer la confection entre 1406, année probable de la mort de Deschamps, et 1414, année de la mort d'Arnaud de Corbie."

36. Ibid., p. 106: "Une copie de ce manuscrit, faite pour Lacurne de Sainte-Palaye, existe en trois volumes à la bibliothèque de l'Arsenal sous les n°s 3291 à 3293."

37. J. L. Lowes, "Chaucer and the *Miroir de Mariage,*" *Modern Philology,* 8 (1911), 329.

38. Martin M. Crow and Clair C. Olson, *Chaucer Life-Records* (Austin: U. of Texas Press, 1966), p. 27.

39. Lowes, *Geoffrey Chaucer* (Oxford: Clarendon Press, 1933), p. 77.

40. Carleton Brown, "The Evolution of the Canterbury 'Marriage Group,'" *PMLA,* 48 (1933), 1045.

41. Robinson, p. 650.

42. Carleton Brown, pp. 1049–50. John C. McGalliard, "Chaucer's *Merchant's Tale* and Deschamps' *Miroir de Mariage.*" *Philological Quarterly,* 25 (1946), 193–330, does not critically examine Lowes's position but accepts it by saying that his study "is predicated upon Chaucer's familiarity with the *Miroir,* as established by Lowes and Brown and recognized by Robinson and Dempster" (p. 193).

43. J. S. P. Tatlock, "Boccaccio and the Plan of Chaucer's *Canterbury Tales,*" *Anglia,* 37 (1913), 98.

44. Robert D. French, *A Chaucer Handbook* (New York: Appleton-Century-Crofts, 1947), pp. 315–16.

45. Marian Lossing, "The Prologue to the *Legend of Good Women* and the *Lai de Franchise,*" *Studies in Philology,* 39 (1942), 35.

46. Here I am giving the line numbers of the passages compared by Lowes and reproduced by Carleton Brown, p. 1049, with my additions in the

middle: III: 242, 257, 263–64, 274–75, 278–80, 285–92, 309–14—lines from the Wife of Bath's Prologue.

47. Deschamps, *Ballade* 888, *Œuvres Complètes*, V: 74; VIII: 11.
48. Raynaud, in *Œuvres Complètes de Eustache Deschamps*, XI: 164–99.
49. For the text and translation of the ballade, see J. A. Burrow, ed., *Geoffrey Chaucer: A Critical Anthology* (Harmondsworth: Penguin, 1969), pp. 26–28.
50. Eugen Lerch, "Zu einer Stelle bei Eustache Deschamps," *Romanische Forschungen,* 62 (1950), 67–68.
51. Jill Mann, *Chaucer and the Medieval Estates Satire* (Cambridge: University Press, 1973), p. 308.

4

MORTIMER J. DONOVAN

Chaucer's January and May: Counterparts in Claudian

In this study of the Pear-tree Story,[1] we examine Pluto and Proserpine as divine counterparts of January and May respectively,[2] and we depend on a text of Claudian's *De Raptu Proserpinae* enlarged[3] by various means—by an *accessus*, by glosses, and by association with poets like Avianus, Cato, Statius, Theodulus, and certain others[4] in an anthology widely read in the schools; because this anthology usually opened with the so-called *Disticha Catonis*, it became known as the *Liber Catonianus* or *Liber Catonis*. The *De Raptu Proserpinae* appeared also in MSS containing Claudian's opera—in all in over one hundred such MSS. Whatever form the transmission took, it has been possible for the most recent editor, J. B. Hall, to divide the MSS into three classes: Alpha, which do not show the three major lacunae at I: 141–214, II: 280–360, and III: 438–48; Beta, which show all three lacunae; and Gamma, which show parts thereof. It has been possible also, following Boas' classic study of the *Liber Catonis*, to pull from Class Alpha such examples of the *De Raptu Proserpinae* as Chaucer might have encountered in the text he used in school. These examples would be likely to show a Preface to Book III found elsewhere in Claudian's *Panegyricus de Sexto Consulatu Honorii Augusti*, but not included in their critical edition by Jeep, Birt, Koch, Platnauer, Paladini and Hall, who provide for the first two books only.

The MSS which this study depends on include the eight listed by Professor Pratt plus two others. Of these the following, ranging from heavily to slightly glossed, offer the most for present purposes.[5]

1. Cambridge, Peterhouse, MS. 215, ff. 72ᵛ–78ʳ (13th c.)=C2.
2. Lincoln, Cathedral Library, MS. 132, ff. 151ʳ–162ᵛ (13th–14th c.)=w.
3. Munich, Bayerische Staatsbibliothek, MS. Clm 391, ff. 43ʳ–69ᵛ (14th c.)=M3.
4. Vatican City, Biblioteca Apostolica Vaticana, MS. Vat. Lat. 1663, ff. 57ʳ–77ᵛ (13th c.)=R5.
5. Vatican City, Biblioteca Apostolica Vaticana, MS. Vat. Reg. 1556, ff. 37ʳ–55ᵛ (13th c.)=R7.

In the following pages I attempt to answer from the text of the "medieval" *De Raptu Proserpinae* questions arising from the so-called Pear-tree Story. (1) Does the Latin poem account for the transformation of Pluto and Proserpine into King and Queen of Fairies in a setting remarkably different from Hades? (2) Does it account for the multiplication of ladies following Proserpine—Chaucer's "many a lady"? (3) Does it account for the apparently mistaken notion that the reader of Chaucer's tale should read Claudian's "stories" (plural) for more on the abduction of Proserpine? (4) Does it account for the prominence given Pluto's *grisely carte* in an otherwise small-scale description of the two regal figures? (5) Does it represent Nature sufficiently to identify her as the deity whom January sins against?

In the first of two accounts of January's garden, we are struck by the appearance of Pluto and Proserpine changed from what the serious reader of the Classics would expect to find. No one could describe

> The beautee of the gardyn and the welle,
> That stood under a laurer alwey grene.
> Ful ofte tyme he Pluto and his queene,
> Proserpina, and al hire fayerye,
> Disporten hem and make melodye
> Aboute that welle, and daunced, as men tolde.
>   (IV: 2036–41)[6]

Whatever the models for details in the garden—the *Romance of the Rose;* Daniel 13:20, telling the story of Susannah; or a combination of garden, well, and a laurel tree, suggesting Parnassus, as in *Anelida and Arcite* (15–20)[7]—nothing like January's garden turns up in the apparatus of the *De Raptu Proserpinae.* Equally striking is the designation of Pluto and Proserpine as King and Queen of the Fairies—a transformation paralleled before Chaucer in English only in the narrative lay *Sir Orfeo,* where the royal couple are unnamed, yet pass clearly as Pluto and Proserpine.[8] The latter is connected elsewhere with Diana, who is associated with the moonlight huntress, the mid-day demon, the fates who guard a child's birth, and the sirens; a story is told of her in which she is depicted as the beguiling mistress of mortals whom she lures from their homes. In other words, she survived as a personality about whom stories clustered, and many of her permanent and persistent attributes are paralleled in the fays of northern Europe.[9] The variations of the Diana myth are reflected in a gloss of *Hecate ternis figuris* (I: 15): "respicit ad fabulam que dicitur luna in celo, diana in silvis, proserpina apud inferos" (R5, f. 57ʳ) Translated, *De Raptu Proserpinae,* I: 15,

would read: Diana looks back to the myth that she is called moon in the
sky, Diana in the forest, and Proserpine in the Lower World. A parallel
gloss of I: 27 in the same poem, treating the same queen, tends to
establish a common source for phrases and for ideas.

Later, in glossing *proserpina ferox* (I: 27), the same MS (f. 57ʳ)
preserves in part the girl turned queen: "non ad illum statum quem
habebat quando rapta est sed in illum quem modo habebat quando
regina est inferni" or, translated: "this does not refer to her status when
ravished, but to that which she enjoyed when Queen of Hades." This
characterization of Proserpine agrees with the logic of Jupiter's decree
permitting her to spend half of each year away from the Underworld in
the land of greenery and growing things. Here we meet her in the first
of two accounts of January's garden, which is the setting of the Pear-
tree Story. The question arises, by what change do the Roman deities
become identified with what appear to be Celtic *fayerye*? We are given
the derivation of *fee* from the plural form of Latin *fata*—a change
merely of words, or not. *Amadas et Ydoine* has been quoted:[10]

> Et puis se müent a mervelle
> Em beles figures de *fees*:
> Si se tignent a Destinees,
> Pour Clotos se tient le premiere,
> Pour Lachesis l'autre sorciere;
> Et la tierce pour Atropos. . . .
>   (2089–94)

> [They transform themselves marvelously into beautiful fees
> and reckon themselves Destinies; Clotho considers herself
> the first; Lachesis the second; and Atropos the third seer.]

In this quotation from the twelfth-century *Amadas et Ydoine,* the three
Destinies—Clotho, Lachesis, and Atropos—are identified with *fees,*
"fairies," whose role it is to regulate the span of life for mortals. At any
rate it should not surprise us if, by the end of the fourteenth century,
vernacular literature should express this identification as if it needed no
glossing (Foster, pp. 346–47).

In the second account of January's garden, the characters are placed
in a setting unlike any in Hades:

> And so bifel, that brighte morwe-tyde,
> That in that gardyn, in the ferther syde,
> Pluto, that is kyng of Fayerye,
> And many a lady in his compaignye,

Folwynge his wyf, the queene *Proserpyna*
Which that he ravysshed out of *Ethna*[11]
Whil that she gadered floures in the mede—
In Claudyan ye may the stories rede.
How in his grisely carte he hire fette—
This kyng of Fairye thanne adoun hym sette
Upon a bench of turves.
                                            (IV: 2225–35)

There is no need to repeat details which are conventional and are so accepted in descriptions of otherworlds. The time is *morwe-tyde*, "morning," when fairies appear; the day is bright, so unlike black night in Hades, according to both Claudian and glosses in most of the manuscripts (e.g., I: 281), a color unrelieved except faintly (I: 99). This setting in which we find Pluto and Proserpine reveals the brighter, happier phase of their life cycle; their dual roles must have needed no glosses beyond the familiar one that Pluto was both King of the Fairies and King of Hades, and Proserpine shared in his authority. Just as "that morwe-tyde" can be profitably explicated by recourse to tradition, so too other elements can be noticed, Classical and Celtic as such have been included in comparable studies of *Sir Orfeo*.[12]

Of the many characters in the *De Raptu* few are troublesome for the glossator, but among these few are Proserpine's companions, the counterparts of Chaucer's "many a lady" following the queen of Fairies. As these are identified in a gloss of *vulgus* (II: 71) as Venus, Pallas, and Diana, some doubt is expressed (R5, f. 64ʳ), for *vulgus* seems inappropriate:

> tres deas vel proserpinam et comites suas. que tot erant quod videbantur esse vulgus. vel vulgus ideo dicit quod non erant de nobili genere. scilicet progenie cereris. proserpina et tribus deabus.

> [three goddesses or Proserpine and her companions, who were so numerous that they seemed to be a crowd. Or: a crowd for the reason that states that they were not of the nobility: namely, of the progeny of Ceres, Proserpine, and the three goddesses.]

The first explanation of *vulgus* is that the three were so many that they seemed a crowd; the second explanation is that they were not well-born. Whatever prompted the choice of *vulgus*, Chaucer accepted the first. Elsewhere (II: 137), as Proserpine collects flowers in the Garden of Henna, she advances before her companions, *ante alias*, who are called *puelle*, "virgins" (w, f. 155ʳ). When Pluto seizes Proserpine, and her companions scatter, *nymphe* (II: 204) is glossed "Pallas et Diana comitantes Proserpinam" (R5, f. 66ʳ). Whatever their identity in Chaucer's imagination, his *ladies* have no single counterpart in the glosses of *vulgus;* and it is possible that these figures are supposed to be ladies attending a queen and contributing to the magnificence of her court, about which more will be said later in connection with the narrator's advice, "read Claudian" (IV: 2232).

But "read Claudian" is not clear advice, because we are not sent to the *De Raptu Proserpinae,* as we would expect, but to *stories,* only one of which could be reconciled with the facts of the Claudian canon. Commenting on *stories* (IV: 2232), Professor Robinson (p. 716) explained the plural as an "error of the first copy." A review, however, of the single word for "book" leads one to the three senses of *liber,* all familiar enough—*Liber Catonis* or *Catonianus* (the collection); *Liber Claudiani* (the *De Raptu* itself or *Claudianus minor*); libri I–III (the three divisions of the latter). Whether the Latin source for ME *story* (with OF intermediary) parallels this usage is not clear, since the glosses under study do not appear to use *historia,* "narrative," "historical narrative," or "legend," as the marginal *divisiones* indicate:

(R5. f. 57ᵛ) *dux herebi* (I: 32) facta proposicione et invocacione hic incipit narracio. continuacio narracionis talis est in hoc opere voluminis. Continetur conquestio plutonis de iove et neptuno eo quod ipse solus carebat de conjuge. secundo continetur sedacio ipsius conquestionis per lachesin.

[*Ruler of the Underworld* (I: 32). With the proposition and invocation completed, here begins the narration. The continuation of the narration is such in this work of the volume. It contains a petition by Pluto to Jupiter and Neptune for a wife because he alone lacked one. Second, it contains a satisfaction of this petition by Lachesis.]

(Thus in Book I as in II, a formal introduction occurs in eight parts, of which the matter in Book I is an example.) What is important for us is the identification of the parts of the whole narrative. Although Chaucer's word *stories* does not translate any single word in the glosses, still it may be loose usage for 1) *books,* as in Claudian's Books I–III, or for 2) narrative units smaller than *book* and ones "contained" in the narration, and numbering eight such in Book I and another eight in Book II. Since Claudian's Book III is incomplete, no formal division occurs in the glosses. At best, Chaucer's plural form *stories* is not easily explained; one wonders how it passed by generations of copyists apparently with ease; as an error, it is easily enough corrected.

As we find in the description of January's garden the four-line reference to Claudian, we are reminded of Pluto, who by force carried off the daughter of Ceres in his *grisely carte,* "his terrible chariot." Why the vehicle from Hades should be so called is explained by a gloss of the *De Raptu* (II: 188), "Apparet subitus celo timor" [A sudden fear was provoked in the sky]. The gloss reads (R5 f. 66ʳ): "*subitus* quod ex isto gressu repentino plutonis celum patuit et horruit. vel *quod currus plutonis facit superis timorem.*" [*Sudden* because from that sudden move by Pluto the sky opened and roughened, or: because Pluto's chariot provoked fear among mankind.] Of the two reasons, the second, attributing to Pluto's chariot the power to arouse sudden fear, is the more memorable. In fact, it serves to remind one of the sights and sounds of the abduction scene; it is remarkable, of course, that Claudian mentions the chariot in the first line of Book I, as his poem opens.

Yet another chariot, prominent elsewhere in the *De Raptu Proserpinae,* builds on a contrast of life and death, of Proserpine and Pluto, and serves as an opposite of the *grisely carte* in Chaucer's tale. The second chariot, which belongs to Ceres or to Triptolemus, is used to broadcast the seeds granted by Jupiter for the benefit of mankind (III: 52)—a lifegiving mission indeed and one contrasting with Pluto's, which is deadly. But by the time the reader encounters in the Merchant's Tale the reference to the *grisely carte,* Pluto is already surrendering power and fearsome reputation in response to Venus' work.

In tone, however, the Pear-tree Story is hardly the sober narrative we have made it. We find, in lines IV: 2225–35 and following, reason for thinking that Venus' tricks have worked; we are reminded by a gloss of I: 223: "proprium est quod multos dolos habet Venus" (R5 6. 60ʳ) [It is characteristic of Venus to have many tricks]. By now a subdued Pluto undertakes from a sitting position the defense of a subdued January and becomes himself comic by association. We see at the same time how difficult it is for Pluto to realize that his authority is now shared: when he asserts, "I am a kyng," Proserpine replies in kind, "And I . . . a queene of Fayerye" (IV: 2315–16), for the Parcae are her servants (II: 305) and will assist her, whatever May's needs, since both ladies profit from Venus' cunning. The action of the Pear-tree Story involves one counterpart assisting January and another assisting May in a conflict forecast in the lines leading up to the action in January's garden. Two aged lovers suffering from the itch that *libido* becomes are helped to varying degrees each by two brothers; each is visibly distressed and hopes for relief through the solace and offspring usually promised in marriage.

But each aged lover offends against Nature by so desiring. If January's offense "lies not only in his taking a young bride at his age but also in his entering into a union that is self-centered from beginning to end" (Economou, p. 256), Pluto's offense also is explained in similar terms. In the *De Raptu Proserpinae* and its glosses, in fact, Nature is prominent in the elaboration of I: 250–63, and III: 33–66, where the theme of man's natural gifts is developed according to a late medieval reading of the *raptus* told by Claudian. For Claudian, however, Nature is presented poetically through her tangible effects, as will be shown below, and becomes for the glossator synonymous with the deity.

In the first of these two passages Claudian describes the ending of chaos. He employs the device of a cloth embroidered by Proserpine to look backward in time to the ordering of Nature's elements—the lighting of the universe, the separation of the seas from the land, the depiction of the five geographic zones, contrasting extreme cold and heat somewhat prophetically, as the embroidery reaches, in time, the present, when the abduction will come. In clarification of the concept of order, *qua lege* [by what law] (I: 249), is explained (R5 f. 61^r). Claudian's term *semina* (I: 250) is glossed: "id est, elementa de quibus omnia sunt sicut de semine procedunt vel semina id est natura scilicet deus creator et pater est omnium." [That is, elements from which all things are, as if they proceed from a seed or seeds that is Nature, namely, God. He is Creator and Father of all things.] It is significant that Nature is another term for the deity viewed as creator, father of all things, including man.[13] It is significant also that certain glosses which seem to crowd irrelevant learning into the margins of the manuscript are there to explain various levels of order, as in the gloss for I, 173, which accounts for volcanic eruptions exemplified by Etna (R5 f. 60^r), or, as in a gloss for I, 60, "*materies* terra enim est materia cuiuslibet rei nam oritur moritur. unde illud 'cinus es et in cinerem reverteris'" (R5 f. 58^r) [for earth is the matter of whatever kind in which things are born and die. Whence the text "you are dust and into dust shall return"]; here we find illustrated the familiar thought that those who come later will gloss the ancient text and determine whatever additional meaning is observable in the modern age. In an ironic management of time a late reference to Proserpine's embroidery (R5 f. 72^r, on III: 157) finds Ceres at home observing the unfinished work, as the glossator says, the "divine work," because "ibi continebatur pictura de divinis rebus. . . . hic elementorum seriem sedesque paternas insigniebat acu." [There is contained within a picture of divine things . . . here she made out with a needle the paternal seat.]

In the second of Claudian's two passages in which Nature is prominent, she is pictured as she complains to Jupiter that man, victim of his own lethargy, has survived on a diet of wild acorns since the time of

Saturn (III: 33–63). Jupiter, therefore, decrees that grain should be made available to man through the office of Ceres; not knowing where Proserpine has gone, Ceres moves on and in her search scatters from her chariot the grain which man will plant and harvest according to the art of tillage. But before Nature's complaint is finished and Jupiter's decree pronounced, Nature draws on rhetoric to move Jupiter: she asks why man should be so endowed with talents, yet should be so neglected (III: 40–45). The glossator interprets her complaint (R5 f. 70^v):

> clamat natura dicens *quid mentem* mentem et materiam quam a deo traxit homo. corpus ab elementis. unde illud sidereus est animus etc. et illud ad ymaginem et similtudinem dei factus est homo rationalis. unde in tali animo alterum cum diis alterum commune cum bebus ad pascendum herbas. quasi dicat non deberet placere.

> [Nature calls out, saying, what thing has formed the mind? the mind and matter which man has drawn from God, the body from elements? whence the thought that the spirit is starry, and the further thought that with respect to the image and likeness of God is man made rational. whence in such spirit one with the gods and another with the beasts to eating herbs. as if to say he ought not to please.]

Nature's assertion is hardly original in the present work. Man's dignity rests on a recognition of himself as both rational and animal: in this context desire in old age would be not only contrary to divine plan, but also ridiculous, as satirical treatments of the aged lover make clear. However thin the theme of outgrown desire in the tale of old January and May, we are reminded of it to the end by the personal names and by the sin against Nature made concrete before our eyes. In fact, as we witness January's final expectation, we read ironically, since there is no hope of its fulfillment:

> He kisseth hire, and clippeth hire ful ofte,
> And on hire wombe he stroketh hire ful softe,
> And to his palays hoom he hath hire lad.
>   (IV: 2413–15)

Thus, of the five numbered questions which this study began with, two are answered in the glosses summarily. The *De Raptu Proserpinae* reveals not only Proserpine liberated from Hades according to Jupiter's decree (no. 1), but also a conventional Nature offended by January's sin (no. 5). The three remaining questions elicit detailed answers: Chaucer's erroneous "many a lady" attending Proserpine is explained

by Claudian's unfortunate choice of *vulgus* to designate her three followers, who, in the glosses, constitute either a "crowd" or a "group of
commoners" (no. 2); Chaucer's advice "read Claudian's stories" (plural,
according to all MSS) is not explained in the glosses except possibly in
the *divisiones,* which give large and small structural units (no. 3);
finally, Chaucer's "grisely carte" keeps alive the gloss "currus plutonis
fecit superis timorem" (no. 4) and renders Pluto as terrible as ever, yet
at the same time a comic figure.

There remains for comment now what Leonard Digges in his 1617
translation of the *De Raptu Proserpinae*[14] calls the "Naturall Sense of the
Storie" (B1): "By the person of *Ceres* is signified *Tillage.* By *Proserpine,*
the seedes which are sowed: by *Pluto,* the earth which receives them."
Some three centuries earlier, the copyist of Clm 391 wrote (f. 44ʳ):

> per plutonem intelligitur terra. per cererem maturitas frugum. per proser-
> pinam incrementum. pluto rapuit proserpinam et eam traxit ad inferos id
> est in yeme absconduntur fruges mature donec ceres eas reducit id est dum
> tempus maturandi adveniat. unde dicitur quod proserpina per medietatem
> anni apud inferos moratur, per medietatem anni apud superos. *secundum
> opinionem vulgi* annus dividitur per yemen et estatem.

> [By Pluto is understood earth. By Ceres the maturity of the fruits. By
> Proserpine increase. Pluto seized Proserpine and dragged her to Hades, that
> is, in winter are hidden the mature fruit until Ceres brings them back, that
> is, until the time of maturing arrives, whence it is said that Proserpine
> lingers for half of the year among those of Hades and for the other half
> among those of the Upper World. According to the opinion of the common
> people the year is divided into winter and summer.]

One would hardly treat the Merchant's Tale thus mechanically, yet the
gloss quoted seems to support the contrasts developed before January
and May as well as between their divine counterparts: youth and age,
life and death, fertility and sterility, and summer and winter (according to a popular division of the year into two seasons—in the glossator's
words, *secundum opinionem vulgi*).[15]

NOTES

1. For parallel treatment see Alfred L. Kellogg, "Susannah and the *Merchant's
Tale,*" *Speculum,* 35 (1960), 275–79; George D. Economou, "Januarie's Sin
against Nature: *The Merchant's Tale* and the *Roman de la Rose,*" *Comparative
Literature,* 17 (1965), 251–57.

2. The present study is a sequel to "The Image of Pluto and Proserpine in the *Merchant's Tale*," *Philological Quarterly*, 36 (1957), 49–60, but is limited to specific parallels with Claudian's *De Raptu Proserpinae*, especially ones which clarify Chaucer's thought. For an aesthetic treatment see Karl P. Wentersdorf, "Theme and Structure in *The Merchant's Tale*: The Function of the Pluto Episode," *PMLA*, 80 (1965), 522–27.

3. Robert A. Pratt, "The Importance of Manuscripts for the Study of Medieval Education, as Revealed by the Learning of Chaucer," *Progress of Medieval and Renaissance Studies in the United States and Canada*, 20 (Boulder: U. of Colorado Press, 1949), 43–51; and, by the same author, "Chaucer's Claudian," *Speculum*, 22 (1947), 419–29. Earlier studies of Chaucer and Claudian include Thomas R. Lounsbury, *Studies in Chaucer* (New York: Harper, 1892), II: 254–58; Edgar Finley Shannon, *Chaucer and the Roman Poets*, Harvard Studies in Comparative Literature VII (Cambridge, Mass.: Harvard U. Press, 1929), pp. 356–58.

4. Pratt, "Chaucer's Claudian," p. 419. On the medieval *accessus* see E. A. Quain, *Traditio*, 3 (1945), 215–65, and R. B. C. Huygens, "Accessus ad auctores," *Latomus*, 12 (1953), 296–311, 460–84.

5. "Chaucer's Claudian," pp. 419–20. See also M. Boas, "De Librorum Catonianorum Historia atque Compositione," *Mnemosyne*, 42 (1914), 17–46, where Boas describes the components of extant copies of the medieval anthology. For a recent and thoroughgoing catalogue of all known manuscripts of the *De Raptu Proserpinae*, see J. B. Hall, ed. *Claudian/De Raptu Proserpinae* (Cambridge, 1969), pp. 3–33. I adopt Hall's sigla, which he remarks on in note 1, page 3.

6. I quote from F. N. Robinson, ed., *The Works of Geoffrey Chaucer*, 2nd ed. (Boston: Houghton Mifflin, 1957), pp. 115–27.

7. See note 1, above; also "The Image of Pluto and Proserpine," pp. 54–57.

8. Laura Hibbard Loomis, "Chaucer and the Breton Lays of the Auchinleck MS," *Studies in Philology*, 38 (1941), 29; "The Image of Pluto and Proserpine," pp. 54–55.

9. Lucy Allen Paton, *Studies in the Fairy Mythology of Arthurian Romance* (rptd. and enlarged by R. S. Loomis, New York: B. Franklin, 1960), p. 279.

10. Brian Foster, "Fé, Fée and Maufé," *French Studies*, 6 (1952), 345. I quote from *Amadas et Ydoine* as presented in this article, p. 346.

11. See Pratt's discussion of the wording and rhyme of IV: 2229–32 in "Chaucer's Claudian," p. 428; and A. Brusendorff, *The Chaucer Tradition* (London: Milford, 1925), pp. 98–100.

12. Constance Davies, "Classical Threads in 'Orfeo,'" *Modern Language Review*, 56 (1961), 161–66; John Block Friedman, "Eurydice, Heurodis, and the Noon-day Demon," *Speculum*, 41 (1966), 22–29; and his *Orpheus in the Middle Ages* (Cambridge, Mass.: Harvard U. Press, 1970), passim.

13. C. S. Lewis, *The Discarded Image* (Cambridge: University Press, 1967), pp. 36–40, finds in Claudian's Natura "the demiurge who reduced primeval chaos to cosmos." For a discussion of January's offense see Economou, pp. 251–57; P. J. C. Field, "Chaucer's Merchant and the Sin against Nature," *Notes and Queries*, N.S. 17 (1970), 84–86.

14. Ed. H. H. Huxley (Liverpool: University Press, 1959). See Douglas Bush, *Mythology and the Renaissance Tradition in English Poetry*, rev. ed. (New York: Norton, 1963), pp. 331–32.

15. For a convenient collection of essays on the Merchant's Tale see Robert J. Blanch, ed., *Geoffrey Chaucer/Merchant's Tale* (Columbus: Ohio State U. Press, 1970). "The Image of Pluto and Proserpine" is reprinted herein, pp. 94–104. A recent book-length study should be mentioned: Alan Cameron, *Claudian/Poetry and Propaganda at the Court of Honorius* (Oxford: Clarendon Press, 1970), especially pp. 253–304, "Techniques of the Poet."

5

MORTON W. BLOOMFIELD

The Wisdom of the Nun's Priest's Tale

The Nun's Priest's Tale (NPT), however complex, and complex it certainly is, belongs to the genre of beast fable and its related beast epic. It is the only example of these popular medieval genres found among Chaucer's works. It is also one of the most learned of Chaucer's tales and one of the most delightful. One of my teachers, broadening the Arnoldian touchstone theory to include whole works, used to say that an inability to enjoy the tale should disqualify anyone from the study of literature. If he could not enjoy NPT, then he could be sure that literary study and literature were not for him.

Along with Pope's *Rape of the Lock* it is the greatest of all English mock-heroic or mock-epic poems, and in its magnification of the small and unimportant and in its parody of high-style, it is charming, witty, and wise. Chaucer has taken a relatively simple genre and endowed it with a complexity of satire and perspective that is almost unbelievable and without parallel. It is an exposé of human weakness in many forms and the mock-heroic tone suits it perfectly. As an example of virtuosity alone, of sheer brilliance of narrative technique, it is outstanding. As a comment on the human condition and on the human spirit, it combines awareness and acceptance in an especially Chaucerian way. It is the quintessence of Chaucer.

The beast fable belongs to the category of wisdom literature, which is extremely widespread but not widely recognized. Wisdom literature comprises a very large proportion of the preserved literature of the world; its manifestations in Western Civilization from Sumer, Egypt, and Israel, through Greece and Rome, down to the last century are many. It is an element in practically all literature and also appears in its own forms. The genres of this type of literature, the purpose of which is to teach the accumulated wisdom about and knowledge of the past and of nature, or to effect wise and satisfactory results in manipulating man and nature, are numerous: meditations, gnomes, dialogues, proverbs, anecdotes, exempla, riddles, charms, and so forth. A large part of the literature of the past is devoted to rules for conduct or for control of environment, or to information about nature and man. The purpose of wisdom and its literature is to promote a tested scheme of life, in the broadest sense of the word, and to ensure its continuance by controlling the unpredictable. It attempts to manage life by the imposition of some kind of order, to reduce the area of the unexpected and the sudden. Its general tone is pessimistic and worldly-wise.[1]

The animal fable is one of the most widespread of the forms of wisdom literature. It attempts to teach wisdom, usually most explicitly, through animal adventures and dialogue. It no doubt reflects an earlier stage of society when man and beast felt close to each other. One of its great attractions rests on the general curiosity that man has always felt towards animals. It combines philosophy (wisdom) with the grotesque (animal world).

Although in some measure the beast fable touches on the grotesque at least in its mingling of two realms,[2] the animal and the human, in mood it is the opposite of the grotesque, which stresses the strangeness of another realm. Animals are like us yet different. The beast fable stresses the likeness; a certain kind of grotesque, the difference. While the world of the grotesque is alienated and disoriented, the world of the beast fable is close to us, and we can easily orient ourselves in it. In the grotesque we are given either no clues or contradictory clues on how to read such a tale; in the beast fable we are given clear clues. We are not driven to discomfort by its strangeness. No dragons or griffins assail us, but beasts we know or know of, talking in our language and acting very much as human beings talk and act.

The literary and source problems of the classical beast fable are very great and complex, but those fables gathered together under the name of Aesop give us adequate exemplars so that we may recognize the type.[3] These fables are short, organized around one point, and begin or close with an explicit moral. "Ancient fables are terse. They stick to essentials; most of all they provide an unforgettable image."[4] The story "must purport to be a particular action or series of actions, or an utterance, that took place once upon a time through the agency of particular characters."[5] It must be told in the past and is similar to a kind of metaphorical proverb which is especially at home in Western Asia and Greece.[6] Not all fables are concerned with animals nor with instruction. Some may be of humans or gods; but most deal with animals. Amusement and entertainment are almost as important in fable collections as wisdom, although one may doubt that these were originally so very important except to capture attention. Dialogue is very common.

Although the fable pattern comes through clearly in the NPT, the remarkable thing is the tremendous complexity of the fable as it leaves

Chaucer's hand.[7] The tone of the tale is satiric, mock-heroic, and at the same time philosophical. As Helen Corsa says, one is left puzzled as to the point of the Chaucerian fable, or situation, which no true fable leaves its reader in. "Is the 'fruyt' of the tale the lesson that women's counsels are not to be trusted? Is it that flatterers are to be avoided? Is it that disaster is fated? Is it that Fortune is fickle? Is it that lust and pride bring their own punishment? Is it that wit matched against wit ensures survival?"[8] The normal fable is deepened and enriched to an extraordinary degree.

The chief factors making for the tale's complexity, leaving the problem of motivation to others, are the richness of characterization, especially of Chauntecleer and Pertelote, the links with the preceding tale, and the philosophical disquisitions of Chauntecleer. The Monk's Tale, which comes just before the NPT, consists of a number of "tragedies," telling the brief story of a fall of fortune. The NPT is partly written to contrast with the dolorous necessity of these stories. It is a story of how *virtù* can outwit fortune. It is especially paradigmatic because it is the intelligent rogue who is outwitted by his usual victim, the rooster. The philosophy is concerned with the subject of man's freedom and predestination. How can God foresee the future and yet allow us freedom of choice? It is concentrated on dreams. "In the fall and escape of Chauntecleer, the Nun's Priest shows that turns of Fortune are often contingent upon human will, and that a man can often escape the consequences of bad fortune even after it has struck."[9]

According to Chaucer's tale, one night Chauntecleer dreams he is assailed by a red monster, and he fears for his life. Pertelote, his favorite wife, tries to persuade him that one should not trust in dreams. He overwhelms her with his learning, showing how dreams can foretell the future. Chauntecleer is so pleased with his success in rhetoric that he forgets his own arguments and neglects normal precautions. He is captured through flattery by Dan Russell the fox. Taken to the woods by the fox, pursued by the small community,[10] he then persuades the fox to open his mouth and escapes. The explicit morals are two. The cock sees the episode as teaching man to keep his wits about him and not to be beguiled by flattery. The fox sees the lesson to be that one should not talk too much.

This double moral, rare in the beast fable tradition as far as I know, is characteristic of Chaucer's negative capability, of his power of perspectivism.[11] But it is only a small sign of this power. The tale is a disquisition on wisdom presented with a complex web of ironies about dreams, matrimony, and predestination; the morals themselves seem insignificant compared to these subjects of vast moment.

Perhaps the best way to see how Chaucer has complicated the Tale is to contrast it with Robert Henryson's *The Taill of Schir Chantecleir and the Foxe* which is essentially the same fable but in complexity and tone very different.[12] Henryson separates completely here, as in his other fables, the *moralitas* from the narrative. It is given in his own voice and directed to the reader, drawing the moral both from the cock and the fox. The reader should, we are told, avoid vanity (of the cock), otherwise he will fall prey to flattery (of the fox). In Chaucer's tale, the two main morals are spoken by each of the main actors and only the final admonition to learn that all that is, is written for our doctrine, comes from the voice of the priest, a very vague moral left for the voice of the teller.

The fable of Henryson is charming but somewhat disturbing, as we shall see. It contains absolutely nothing about dreams or predestination. The action begins when the fox, Lawrence, in search of a meal, runs into Chantecleir. The text begins with a traditional humility formula. The nature of beasts is so various that the poet says he cannot write of them. Yet, he will record a meeting which "fell this ather yeir" (409) between a fox and a gentle rooster. The stress is on the reality of the happening and the recording of it. Thereupon, we meet the poor widow (who is even poorer than Chaucer's), her hens and a rooster. We are then told about a fox, Lawrence, who lives in a thorny copse nearby, and who is a perpetual raider of the widow's goods.

The fox flatters Chantecleir and refers to his great friendship with his father, even claiming that he died in Lawrence's arms. He says that Chantecleir, however, seems degenerate compared to his father, who could crow most skillfully. The cock shows him he can crow too. Lawrence adds that the father could close his eyes and crow and turn around thrice, all at the same time. The cock falls for this further appeal and soon finds himself in the fox's mouth being carried to the wood.

Pertok, Sprutok and Toppok, Chantecleir's wives, cry out and arouse the widow, who falls into a swoon. Then follows an amazing scene among the three hens while the widow lies in a faint.

Pertok breaks out into a lamentation "With teiris grit attour [down] her cheikis fell" (496) for "our loved and our day's darling." Who will now be our sweetheart, who will lead us, how shall we live without him? Sprutok, however, will have none of that. To her Chantecleir's death is a liberation. Love comes and goes. He was a bully and jealous and besides he was a poor lover. Pertok changes her tune and joins Sprutok in castigating her husband and ceases her false lamentation. Her quick agreement seems to have been gained by Sprutok's attack against Chantecleir's powers of love-making, for she says he could not satisfy their sexual appetites, even twenty like him would not suffice and within a week it will be easy to get a much better lover.

Toppok closes the discussion by assuming a spiritual point of view. Chantecleir's death is a deserved punishment from heaven, for he was also, we learn, dissolute and lecherous and full of pride. Her emphasis on his adultery does not seem entirely consistent with Pertok and Sprutok's complaint; but we must not expect too much consistency, I suppose, from hens who are at last free of a tyrannical husband. This whole scene has close similarities with the "two married women and a widow" theme, which Dunbar treated so notably.

The widow awakes from her swoon and sends her dogs out at Lawrence. The rooster at the edge of the wood tells the fox to announce to the dogs that he and Lawrence are friends, upon which remark they will no longer run after them. The fox opens his mouth to do as he is directed and Chantecleir escapes to a tree. He refuses again to succumb to Lawrence's blandishments. "My bludy hekill and my nek sa bla [livid] / Hes partit freindschip for ever betwene us twa" (577–78). The cock flies away to the widow's house while the fox curses his own foolishness. Then the morality follows: the cock is the type of proud and vainglorious man; the fox is the type of flatterer. From this tale we learn to flee from flattery and vainglory.

The emphasis in this Tale is very different from that of Chaucer in the NPT. Besides the striking absence of the long discussions of philosophy and the mock-epic tone, we find a story of a fraud who by skill escapes his doom. Chantecleir is heartily hated by his wives. Pertok's attempt to preserve the amenities by breaking into a conventional lamentation is quickly punctured and the three wives unite in vilifying him.

This incident curiously undercuts the whole fable.[13] The sexual prowess of Chantecleir and his relation to his three wives have nothing whatever to do with the point of the fable. In fact its extremely vivid liveliness is in direct contrast to the rather staid story line of the fable. It distracts our interest and weakens the unity of the work. It is a fascinating episode but an upsetting one. The escape of Chantecleir at the end raises issues in relation to his wives which we cannot solve. Will they take him back? Do they care for him at all? These questions have no relevance to the moral of the story. This lively little discussion, as fascinating as it is, undermines the direct fabulistic quality of the story. We are left in a moral ambiguity and feel that the fable is not a fable but something else.

Chaucer transforms the fable too but in a very different way, heightening not undercutting (or rather undercutting in order to heighten) its effect and making it a model moral tale which at the same time wins us over by its humor and presents us with a strong sense of the ridiculousness of human life. Furthermore his Chauntecleer is a much more sympathetic character than Henryson's and creates thereby a more pleasant atmosphere to the tale.

The beast epic, a medieval development of the fable as well as a parody of the epic, probably provided Chaucer with the model for these transmutations. Although we have had several studies of the NPT as fable, as far as I know no one has discussed the effect of the beast epic genre on the Tale. It is not minor.

The Chauntecleer-fox episode in the medieval French *Roman de Renart* (or in its German counterpart *Reinhart Fuchs*) in one of its forms no doubt was a major source. Recently Professor Pratt has strongly argued that Marie de France's *Fables,* Pierre de Saint Cloud's *Roman de Renart,* Branch II, and *Renart le Contrefait,* Branch VI are Chaucer's sources.[14]

The mock heroic tone was, no doubt, suggested by the beast epic itself. The beast epic is by its very nature satiric and parodic, cynical and yet amiable. Besides specific comparisons to Paris, Helen, Tristan, and the like, and besides references to mock heroic battles between Isengrim and Renart,[15] a major point of the beast epic is to mock the pretensions of the serious epic and romance and to glorify the trickster over the hero—or perhaps make the hero a trickster. The beast epic of the Middle Ages is the picaresque romance of the period—the shadow side of the heroic-chivalric-establishment point of view.

Let us now return to our text. The mock-heroic quality of the beast epic no doubt was congenial to Chaucer's mind, and he took a famous episode from the Renart story and made an independent fable out of it (possibly aware that it also had an independent existence), but keeping and deepening its mock epic quality until it encompassed almost the whole of the human condition.

The general situation in NPT is parodic and mock-heroic and yet curiously sympathetic. We start with a very poor widow, a humble person, and move to her barnyard.[16] Then we find ourselves in the animal world. The hens are magnified into humans as in a good fable, but bemused by Chauntecleer's learning we need to be reminded on various occasions that we are dealing with barnyard animals. We are reminded that they sleep at night on a perch, which makes love-making impossible (VII: 3167 ff.), just after Chauntecleer praises Pertelote's scarlet red eyes. Pertelote earlier (VII: 2920) had referred to

Chauntecleer's beard. Various changes are rung on what Professor Pratt calls "comic anthropomorphism and zoomorphism." At the end these small creatures are again put into their proper perspective as we move back to the widow and her friends, to the Nun's priest, to the pilgrims, to the audience of man and finally to God—all falls into perspective. The NPT is veritably at once Chaucer's Voyages to Lilliput and Brobdingnag.

But further, the Tale parodies courtly love and philosophical dispute. The whole situation of the cock—he believes in dreams, he does not listen to his wife's wisdom on dreams, he is so pleased with his victory over a wife who does not believe in dreams that he ignores his own lesson and falls into the trap—is profoundly ironic. His quintessential male vanity is beautifully shown up. Pride leads to a downfall, and in Chauntecleer's fall Adam's tragedy is relived. Pertelote is the practical female *par excellence*. These animals with their human problems, human interests and human failures bring us close; but we are never allowed to forget that they are animals.

The tale is told by the Nun's priest who is a very shadowy character, as Charles Owen has pointed out.[17] He was employed by a woman and no doubt had his anti-feminist resentments which could find full expression in his exquisite descriptions of Chauntecleer putting his wife in her place. This is what a nun-dominated priest could well do. The anti-feminism of the tale, admittedly not a major theme, receives some reinforcement from the teller. Much more important, however, are his neutral personality and his mirror-like or window-like nature, which help us to look *through* the layers of the tale into the animal world—or at least to have the illusion of doing so. We stay in both the human and animal world. We are not, as in the Merchant's Tale, shifted into the realm of the gods or into the problems of the teller. There is no strong personality speaking to us as in the Wife of Bath's Tale or the Pardoner's Tale, to color the story.

Marriage, women, love, learning, philosophy, male pride, human pretensions are all targets of the NPT. But above all the style is a parody of the epic and epic manner. What are some of the epic features which are satirized? First of all I suppose are the dreams which are a regular feature of both Virgilian and Lucanic epic.[18] Dreams occupy a central place in the NPT, in the furthering of the suspense of the plot, in characterization, and in raising the philosophical issue of fate and man's freedom. The cock's dream and his learned discussion of the significance of dreams, with its overwhelming use of authority, are very amusing and rich in interest.

Epic dreams are usually not questioned, yet Pertelote is able to dismiss her husband's forewarnings as nonsense. Although Chauntecleer's defense is spirited, he too is able to dismiss them lightly in the crucial showdown.

Second, the changes of pace in the NPT are extraordinarily apt, paralleled in the skill with which they are managed in the CT, I think, only in the Pardoner's Tale. The slow moving philosophical disquisition contrasts vividly with the speedy chase the widow, her two daughters, Talbot, Gerland, Malkin, and the dog Colle give to the fleeing fox. The cow, calf, and even hogs—frightened by the barking of the dogs and shouting of the men and women—run madly. The ducks, geese, bees all join the merry throng. The shouting is like the noise of fiends in hell, and some of the participants make music on instruments as they run. "It semed as that hevene sholde falle" (VII: 3401).

The pursuit, though not so common a feature of epics as dreams, is none the less found in *The Aeneid* and other epics. It is no doubt being used here as a parody of the hunt or the pursuit of Turnus in the Virgilian epic, not to speak of other possible models. The comic chase as such is already to be found in the *Roman de Renart*.[19] The pursuit of the enemy in some of the *chansons de geste* also comes to mind as a parodic model for the *Roman*. The non-literary basis lies in law—the hot pursuit of a suspected thief. From the epic point of view, the chase is a parody, but from the legal point of view, it is a perfectly understandable action—if the thief had been a human.[20]

The stress on action is proper to a story which wishes to make the power of the individual to defeat bad fortune one of its major themes. The Renaissance emphasis in Machiavelli and others on the way in which *virtù* may overcome fortune already appears here in this tale.

Third and more specifically we find parodies of epic apostrophes and set pieces in the NPT, especially after the cock has been seized. The author breaks out into an apostrophic attack on Dan Russell just before he appears before Chauntecleer a "false mordrour, lurkynge in thy den! O newe Scariot, newe Genylon . . ." (VII: 3226 ff.). Again he addresses destiny "O destinee, that mayst nat been eschewed." (VII: 3338 ff.) (just before actually it is to be eschewed), Venus (VII: 3342 ff.), and Godfrey (of Vinsauf) the master rhetorician for the Middle Ages (VII: 3347 ff.), just before Chauntecleer is seized. We find an address to the hens on their grief when the dire deed is done (VII: 3402 ff.). These epic devices and features of high style are delightfully turned by Chaucer for purposes of parody.

Fourth are the suggestions of epic simile and catalogues of comparable heroes. We find among these the inevitable comparisons to Troy (VII: 3355 ff.) and the almost inevitable one to Carthage. Nero is also brought in as a burner of Rome and source of grief to the wives of Roman senators. Chauntecleer in his great speech on the importance of taking dreams seriously refers to Cato, Bradwardine, Boethius, Macrobius, the life of St. Kenelm, Andromache, Croesus, and the Bible.

Even these lists and similes have their bathetic turns, when the Nun's priest refers to the Romance of Lancelot of the Lake (VII: 3212) and the Peasant's Revolt (VII: 3394–3397). The philosophical language also carries its suggestion of high style. This is mostly confined to Chauntecleer's speech, but not entirely. The term "heigh ymaginacion forncast" (3217) referring to the fox episode about to follow is a scholastic term and used of the prophetic imagination.[21] In fact, the whole speech, which is a good example of argument by authority with exempla, suggests a sermon. Even more, the whole tale is an exemplum, or could be used as an exemplum which contains within itself exempla, suggesting indeed the barnyard world as within the wide world of man.

Finally, the tone of the vernacular language as always in medieval times is hard to define. The stylistic level of the vocabulary is often a matter of guess work, not to speak of ironic uses of words. However, the subject matter is a fairly reliable guide. When pathos is being expressed or philosophy is being discussed, it is clear, I believe, that the vocabulary is appropriate to these ends and purposes. The whole situation of the barnyard makes the parody of epic language inevitable.[22]

Donaldson has expressed the belief that rhetoric in the NPT "is regarded as the inadequate defense that mankind erects against an inscrutable reality."[23] In one sense this is very true but in another it is not, because the victim of rhetoric finally wins out. The world is not entirely inscrutable. Rhetoric also enables man to win over reality as well as to succumb to self-gratification. Finally rhetoric is what enables Chaucer to give us the NPT whereby art wins out over life—at least for a while.

Genetically and rhetorically, then, what we have in the NPT is a fable devoted to the teaching of wisdom being undercut and destroyed by its mock quality, by its characterization, by its scholastic reasoning, but finally leading us back, but on a higher level, to its original didactic purpose. A fable becomes a non-fable and finally, when we return to the widow, to the moral, to the Nun's priest and to God, a super-fable again in which the wisdom of humility is taught. The setting of the fable, its various perspectives, suggests that we not be fooled by the delights of this world, but see its humor and its ridiculousness in the proper perspective. The distance which is destroyed is reestablished at the end both physically, one might say, by a return to the Nun's priest and to God and morally by the open moral. A moral is always a distancing factor.

The NPT is about the subversion of wisdom and its reinstatement. As we move down the scale of the great chain of being from man to animal, we learn how knowledge can fool itself and pride conquer prudence. But out of foolishness, out of the mouth of foxes, wisdom can come and man can be free. Destiny may be eschewed and we can learn our lesson. The mock magnification of the small is actually not mock at all, but real. These little subrational creatures can win out over fate and are bigger not smaller than life. And as they fade back into smallness, we carry with us an awareness of human life which reaches up to the very heavens.

In a curious way, the mock-heroic mode elevates even as it denigrates. It arises from an endeavor to subvert by elevating but ends by elevating through subversion. We can admire all the more the petty beings who are briefly taken seriously even as we are aware of the author's presumption.

The charm of the NPT is transformed into profound wisdom without losing its attractiveness. The ironies of the NPT turn back on themselves, and we can be more at home in a world that seems alienated, for the NPT preaches courage and humanity and sheer delight in mankind's endless ingenuity which even self-deception cannot completely destroy. Truly an inability to enjoy the NPT is enough to disqualify one from the study of literature.

NOTES

1. Some phrases in the preceding paragraph are taken from my paper "Understanding Old English Poetry" *Annuale Mediaevale*, 9 (1968), 5–25.
2. See Wolfgang Kayser, *The Grotesque in Art and Literature*, tr. Ulrich Weisstein (Bloomington: Indiana U. Press, 1963), pp. 179 ff. (original German 1957).
3. For medieval Latin fables, see the great work of Léopold Hervieux, *Les fabulistes latins depuis le siècle d'Auguste jusqu'à la fin du Moyen Âge*, 5 vols. (Paris: Firmin-Didot, 1884–99).

4. C. Kerényi, "Man and Mask," *Spiritual Disciplines; Papers from the Eranos Year Books,* Bollingen Series XXX, 4 (New York: Pantheon, 1960), p. 151 (original German version in *Eranos,* 16 [1948]).

5. Ben Edwin Perry, ed., *Babrius and Phaedrus,* Loeb Classical Library (Cambridge, Mass.: Harvard U. Press; London: Heinemann, 1965), p. xx. I am much indebted to this edition.

6. The similarity of these short wisdom genres is reflected in the Hebrew and Greek semantic range of their words for fable. The word *mašal* (Hebrew) and *mathla* (Aramaic) for "parable" also includes the literary genres: "similitude, allegory, fable, proverb, oracular utterance, riddle, significant name, symbol, pseudonym, example (type), commonplace, argument, apology, refutation, jest. Similarly παραβολη in the New Testament has not only the meaning 'parable' but also 'comparison' and 'symbol'. . . . 'proverb' or 'commonplace'. . . . 'riddle'. . . . 'rule' " (Joachim Jeremias, *The Parables of Jesus,* tr. S. H. Hooke, revised ed. [New York: Scribner's, 1963], pp. 17–18). The common notions behind all these forms seem to be brevity, metaphorical or symbolic meaning, and wisdom. See also David Daube, *Ancient Hebrew Fables,* Inaugural Lecture of the Oxford Centre for Postgraduate Hebrew Studies, Delivered in Corpus Christi College May 1973 (Oxford, 1973). Daube stresses the underlying political meaning of fables and the frequent need of clothing such meaning in "allegory." The Russians use the word Aesopic for masked political tales or tales put to political use. It is not surprising that the NPT has been interpreted politically by some scholars.

7. R. T. Lenaghan in his valuable and perceptive "The Nun's Priest's Fable," *PMLA,* 78 (1963), 302, attempts to link the complexity of the NPT to the complexity of the notion of fable: simple moral tale, fictitious narrative (as in rhetorical handbooks), and sophisticated retelling of simple fable. Chaucer generally uses the term *fable* in the second sense and does not use it at all to characterize the NPT as opposed to other "fictitious" tales. One does not need this hypothesis to account for Chaucerian subtlety of development. To find an example of the sophisticated fabulist, Lenaghan has to turn to La Fontaine and a weak reference to Deschamps because outside of Chaucer it is hard to find in the Middle Ages sophisticated fabulists, although there are many sophisticated writers of beast epics, romance parodies, and the like. The article, however, is a very intelligent study of the NPT and its ambience in the *Canterbury Tales.*

Stephen Manning in "The Nun's Priest's Morality and the Medieval Attitude toward Fables," *JEGP,* 59 (1960), 403–16, gives a good brief summary of the medieval attitude toward fable, particularly in the sense of a fictitious narrative. I do not, however, agree with his interpretation of the NPT. See also William Nelson, "The Boundaries of Fiction in the Renaissance: A Treaty between Truth and Falsehood," *ELH,* 36 (1969), 30–58.

8. *Chaucer, Poet of Mirth and Morality* (Notre Dame: University Press, 1964), p. 212. Lenaghan, p. 306, also discusses intelligently the complexity of the moral or morals of the fable. Cf. "Unlike fable, the *Nun's Priest's Tale* does not so much make true and solemn assertions about life as it tests truths and

tries out solemnities." Charles Muscatine, *Chaucer and the French Tradition: A Study in Style and Meaning* (Berkeley and Los Angeles: U. of California Press, 1957), p. 242.

9. Thomas J. Hatton, "Chauntecleer and the Monk, Two False Knights," *Papers on Language & Literature,* 3, Supplement, Papers on the Art and Age of Chaucer (1967), 31. See also Corsa, p. 213, and F. Elaine Penninger, "Chaucer's Knight's Tale and the Theme of Appearance and Reality in the *Canterbury Tales,*" *South Atlantic Quarterly,* 63 (1964), 400.

10. This chase is what in Roman law is called a *vestigii minatio,* the hot pursuit of a thief, found also in Indo-European and ancient Semitic law (e.g., the pursuit of Jacob by Laban, of the brothers by Joseph's officers and of the Danites by Micah, in the Bible). In England, "hue and cry" had official legal standing. Neighbors were needed as witnesses and hence usually joined in with noises to attract more. See David Daube, *Studies in Biblical Law* (New York: Ktav, 1969), pp. 201 ff. (original Cambridge, England, 1947).

11. See Bloomfield, "The Gloomy Chaucer," *Veins of Humor,* ed. Harry Levin, Harvard English Studies, 3 (Cambridge, Mass.: Harvard U. Press, 1972), pp. 57–68.

12. I am using the text in the edition of Henryson's poems by Charles Elliott in the Clarendon Medieval and Tudor Series (Oxford, 1963), pp. 13–19. Although he does not analyze our fable, Denton Fox, "Henryson's *Fables,*" *ELH,* 29 (1962), 337–56, has perceptively discussed the literary value of the *Fables.*

Although there are pre-Western related versions, the tale of the fox and the cock does not seem to be preserved in classical times ("The fable proper [of cock and fox] seems in its entirety a special mediaeval growth," E. P. Dargan, "Cock and Fox, A Critical Study of the History and Sources of the Mediaeval Fable," *Modern Philology,* 4 [1906–07], 39), but it is certainly widespread in medieval times. See, e.g., Perry, pp. 525–26 (where he summarizes the fable from a Brussels MS in Hérvieux, II: 598 ff.) and the source material in W. F. Bryan and G. Dempster, *Sources and Analogues of the Canterbury Tales* (Chicago: U. of Chicago Press, 1941), pp. 645–63. Dargan, pp. 40–41, lists 15 medieval versions. The most recent work on the sources of the NPT is Robert A. Pratt, "Three Old French Sources of the Nonnes Preestes Tale," *Speculum,* 47 (1972), 422–44; 646–68. A new text of the relevant part of French *Renart* is available in Mario Roques, ed., *Le Roman de Renart: Branches II–VI,* Classiques Français du Moyen Age, 79 (Paris: Champion, 1951), pp. 16 and 26 ff. It shows a number of variations from that in Bryan and Dempster and needs looking into.

13. Harold E. Toliver in "Robert Henryson: From *Moralitas* to Irony," *English Studies,* 46 (1965), 302, says that Pertok's concern "in ingratiating despite its excess." I find Pertok ingratiating but not especially at this point in the fable.

14. Pratt, op. cit.

15. See e.g. Roques, p. 16. On the Renart romance in the Middle Ages, see John Flinn, *Le Roman de Renart dans la littérature française et dans les littéra-*

tures étrangères au Moyen Age, U. of Toronto Romance Series 4 (Paris: Presses universitaires, 1963). On pp. 678 ff., Flinn discusses the NPT from the point of view of its Renart source or sources.

A non-Renartian beast-epic of German origin is to be found in the Latin *Ecbasis cuiusdam Captivi,* easily available in the edition and translation of Edwin H. Zeydel in the U. of North Carolina Studies in the Germanic Languages and Literatures 46 (Chapel Hill: U. of North Carolina Press, 1964).

16. "The farmyard scene is a perspective on the human world that reduces the human world to its comical absurdities, thereby rendering it manageable and acceptable—acceptable because it can be mocked, playfully caricatured, and dwarfed," Charles A. Watkins, "Chaucer's Sweete Priest," *ELH,* 36 (1969), 464.

17. See "The Crucial Passages in Five of the *Canterbury Tales:* A Study in Irony and Symbol," *Discussions of the Canterbury Tales,* ed. Charles A. Owen Jr., Discussions of Literature (Boston: Heath, 1961), 86–88 (reprinted from *JEGP,* 52 [1953]). See also W. W. Lawrence, *Chaucer and the Canterbury Tales* (New York: Columbia U. Press, 1950), pp. 134–36. On other interpretations of the character of the Nun's Priest, see Arthur Broes, "Chaucer's Disgruntled Cleric: *The Nun's Priest's Tale,*" *PMLA,* 78 (1963), 156–62, and Charles A. Watkins, pp. 455–69. See also R. M. Lumiansky, *Of Sondry Folk: The Dramatic Principle in the Canterbury Tales* (Austin: U. of Texas Press, 1955), pp. 105–17.

18. On the tradition of dreams in epic going back to Homer and their frequent use in the *Pharsalia,* see M. P. O. Morford, *The Poet Lucan, Studies in Rhetorical Epic* (Oxford: Blackwell, 1967), pp. 75 ff.

19. Bryan and Dempster, pp. 655 ff. See also Pratt, pp. 438 ff., 664.

20. See note 10 above.

21. The term "heigh ymaginacioun" is the same as Dante's "alta fantasia" and refers to the prophetic role of the imagination, part of the internal sense of imagination rather than to ordinary or low imagination which occupies a subordinate role in the scholastic chain of knowledge from sense experience to full cognition. See Victor N. Hamm, "Chaucer: 'Heigh Ymaginacioun,'" *Modern Language Notes,* 69 (1954), 394–95, who was the first as far as I know to recognize the force of the phrase even if he did not stress its role in scholastic epistemology.

22. See John M. Steadman, "Chauntecleer and Medieval Natural History," *Isis,* 50 (1959), 236–44, who discusses Chaucer's use of the disparity between content and style, matter and manner in developing the NPT, and who shows how much Chaucer is indebted to medieval scientific doctrine not only in the learned discussion of dreams but in his portrayal of the cock itself.

Zeydel, pp. 13–15, speaks of the tendency of the beast epic to use quotations, another feature of the NPT.

23. "Patristic Exegesis: The Opposition" in *Critical Approaches to Medieval Literature: Selected Papers from the English Institute 1958–59,* ed. Dorothy Bethurum (New York: Columbia U. Press, 1960), p. 20.

6

PAUL G. RUGGIERS

Serious Chaucer: The *Tale of Melibeus* and the Parson's Tale

Some years ago, working through some considerations of aesthetics pertaining to Chaucer's *Canterbury Tales,* I found myself weighing questions which have not yet been finally resolved in my mind. The first had to do with the degree of didacticism in Chaucer: aside from the consideration of an artist committed to the production of a fiction, bringing to bear upon it the full forces of his intelligence, tradition, and years of experimentation and study, how much of Chaucer's utterance is that of a writer speaking more or less directly to his audience, bringing out of his own experience of life direct comment upon human morality, upon human failure, upon ultimate things? I was led to the question by my own personal response to certain passages in the *Canterbury Tales* in which, though the sentiments uttered were suited to the speaker and the occasion, yet there was a sententious, even overtly didactic, statement being made which remained in the mind after the total effect of the tale had diminished.

One remembers immediately the speech of Theseus at the close of the Knight's Tale and that of the hag in the Wife of Bath's Tale, speeches which occupy so substantial a place in the thematic development of the tales that only an insensitive mind could complain about their relation to the thematic statement being made. In a certain sense, they are essential to the tales seen as thought structures or as ethical ones. And in varying degrees of relationship to theme, the same may perhaps be said of the short disquisition on destiny and freedom in the Nun's Priest's Tale, of which Chaucer seems to have felt a certain attraction as evidenced by the strong position he gives to it in Book IV of *Troilus and Criseyde.* And one must add, because of their length, if for no other reason, the passage on class morality and that on the control of the tongue at the close of the Manciple's Tale, where the "morality" is given large emphasis. And I found myself thinking of such tales as the Physician's and Monk's, as well as the prose tales, which have tended to receive less scholarly attention, perhaps because they are less "artistic" or because their thematic statement is too explicit. Yet it seemed to me their didactic content merited serious consideration in the metaphor of pilgrimage.

A second question in my mind, not divorced from the first, has to do with the influence of book-authority on Chaucer. In a borrowing from Boethius, or Dante, or any other author, does that passage have a life of its own, guaranteed to it by its placement in the poem in which it originates, or does it take on a different coloration, being now interwoven with a thematic statement which is that of the new poem of which it is now a part? I was tempted to say that it was obviously both; though it seemed to me that to say this was an evasion of some fundamental considerations, namely that it is possible to accept some of the premises of a philosophical system but not necessarily the conclusions of them, to use some of the views of an authority without intending that the finished poem would support the same conclusions as the original. At this point I found myself back where I had started: does the part borrowed from Dante, for example, carry with it always its own integrity, so to speak, so that no matter what Chaucer's poem says, its meaning cannot be assessed apart from the influence and investment provided by the borrowing?

Such considerations led me to think first of the smallest pieces of the *Canterbury Tales* (single stanzas like that on time and tide, in the Man of Law's Tale, the proverbs strewn through Chaucer's work, etc.), and finally to think of the largest part, the prose tales themselves, which may stand in the same relationship to the total fabric of pilgrimage as the smaller parts bear to the tale in which they are contained. And I remembered the old German thesis that the two prose tales may constitute a summation of Chaucer's moral and spiritual life. Though this statement is a gross oversimplification of that position, it does raise a most interesting consideration of developing intention on Chaucer's part with regard to a moral structure for the *Canterbury Tales* as well as a deeper, prior consideration of the *kind* of moral structure that Chaucer may have been developing.

A third consideration, arising for the most part out of these two previous ones, is a more aesthetic one, a question of the dynamics of the long poem, the entire *Canterbury Tales.* There are mysterious processes in the experiencing of a poem, processes the poet confidently predicts, expects, manipulates. They arouse in the sensitive reader a range of feeling as well as a series of cognitions-recognitions; for in the *Canterbury Tales* we experience the gamut from comic laughter to tragic pathos, and in the process these feelings and recognitions demand a certain level of thought or intellection. We could not savor the artistry of the Friar's Tale, for example, without full consideration of a preacherly point—repentance is necessary to salvation; or that of the

Wife of Bath's Tale—the disquisition on manners and grace, occupying nearly half the tale. The Manciple's Tale would be vastly less suggestive if it lacked its plain-speaking on public and private morality and its long appendage on control of tongue; and the Physician's Tale would be drastically diminished without its allusions to Natura genetrix or its warnings to parents about the nurturing of their children.

The pageant-like structure of the *Canterbury Tales* aids and abets us here: a series of tableaux takes place before us; before each of them we stand in varying degrees of absorption and response, taking in what seems at first a mere alternation of voices and attitudes, which in retrospect have the capacity to cohere into a developing pattern, the larger aspects of which we are able to discern and later recall. To be sure, the *Canterbury Tales* is episodic and incomplete in execution, and these factors tend to predispose us to finding the thematic statement, its "thought," fragmented and discontinuous.

Chaucer must have known it would appear so; he compensates by giving large emphasis and exaggerated length at various junctures to the didactic element. His age wished it to be so. And it helps to see, as one of the main influences upon Chaucer, along with the *Roman de la Rose* and Boccaccio and Ovid among masters of the dynamics of the long poem, Dante's *Divine Comedy,* not merely as a series of reminiscences, but as the most coherent treatment of the traditions dealing with the ethical and moral relations of men both as social and spiritual beings.

We have here a possible clue to the placement and meaning of the two prose translations, the *Tale of Melibeus* and the Parson's Tale, if we deem their function to be peak statements in the more overtly serious and didactic aspects of the "plot" of the *Canterbury Tales.* As a setting-in-order each provides a summary, so to speak, of the backgrounds against which to view the tales, during which the reader has placed before him in the most detailed demonstration the medieval norms against which all human action becomes measurable, and out of which moral priorities may be restated and reinforced.

To the student of Dante I am stating the obvious: the norms for that poem are the cardinal and theological virtues under which the Purgatorial experience is carried on, and which inform the life of Paradise in an ordered succession. It was Chaucer's tradition too, and Dante was a part of his past, though the differences between them in capacity and moral rigor are vast indeed, and the encyclopedic structures of the poems are ordered in different ways. But it is worth our consideration, in our concern to see the relations of *Melibeus* and the Parson's Tale to the

Canterbury Tales, at least to state the possibility of a common informing principle.

As we contemplate the resemblances between Dante's great poem, so carefully structured accumulatively, and Chaucer's less coherent organization, we can test the degree to which Chaucer, while excluding himself from the comparison with the great Italian, yet achieves his own depiction of the Purgatorial experience. And if we do not take into account the function of the prose tales in the form of the *Canterbury Tales,* to that extent we deny ourselves insight into one aspect of Chaucer's seriousness as a medieval poet writing his version of the pilgrimage on which he, in his turn, had embarked.

II

If anyone has doubted seriously that there is a moral Chaucer who was a man of his time, he has not given full consideration to the *Tale of Melibeus* or to the Parson's Tale, either as sententious statements or as parts of the total theme of pilgrimage; both of them belong to a discussion of moral philosophy and theology, both of them reflect the long tradition of the study of man as a moral and spiritual being. As treatises they are different from each other, the *Melibeus* approximating the appearance of fiction, having a plot of sorts and an intellectual action involving allegorical persons; the Parson's Tale being a homiletic discussion of variously clearly distinguished aspects of sin, virtue, and the sacrament of penance.

The *Tale of Melibeus* is oriented to the cardinal virtues, of which prudence or practical wisdom of the world is the demonstrated virtue, while that of the Parson absorbs the cardinal virtues into deeper considerations of reconciliation with God and cooperation with grace. Both of them, of course, are Christian to the core, but the *Melibeus* has to do principally with the correction of the intelligence and the use of counsels in this world, while the Parson's Tale has to do principally with the corrections of the will. Both of them make their own point about salvation, namely that the right use of reason and the right use of the will are necessities *in statu viae.*

Whether the *Melibeus* is part of a long joke at the expense of the host depends upon a kind of refined analysis: we accept the view that in its position as a second tale told by the pilgrim Chaucer it derives much from the contrast it offers to the delicacies of the abortive *Sir Thopas* (damned by the host as "dirty" rhyming) and from the marked shift in the narrator's stance: earlier he had expressed the greatest scrupulosity towards the literal "word"; now his allegiance is to the larger truth. We are all familiar enough with scholarship on this question. More important to us is the fact that Chaucer was attracted to it by the same quality of mind that led him to translate Innocent III, the materials that make up the Parson's Tale, and the *Consolatio* of Boethius: a fondness for the moral and didactic, and a search for the means by which the poet's vision of the world may be reinforced. Those who used to maintain that Chaucer is interested only in the human heart, not in the progress of the soul, fail to estimate sympathetically the place these treatises must occupy.[1] It is not that Chaucer does not have other dimensions—his reputation with posterity depends upon them—but only that these frankly moral works contain many of the values that Chaucer himself held; and each in its own way has left its mark upon various stages of Chaucer's development.[2]

Philosophically, the *Tale of Melibeus* can and should be related to the history of the virtue of prudence as an intellectual virtue, a tradition stemming principally from Aristotle which posits a relationship of prudence to the other cardinal virtues. Indeed prudence seems to have what someone has called empire over the moral virtues and has as its aim the perfection of the intellect in its practical decisions. In the final analysis prudence and the other moral virtues have a special relationship in that, without the center of prudence, the others tend to fall into vicious extremes; the special function of prudence is to direct the activities of the other virtues, to define their goals and prevent lapses into mere craft or rashness or lack of circumspection. Hence the natural emphasis in the *Melibeus* upon taking good counsel, upon finding out how in a particular case one may react justly with regard to the virtue of justice, and with discretion with regard to the virtue of temperance, and how one may avoid foolhardiness with regard to fortitude.

This taking counsel has to do not merely with the good of the individual or with the good of the family, but also with the good of the social group or state and with military prudence within it.[3] Thus we are concerned with recognizing the rights of individual men, recognizing the necessity of peace and order brought about through the operations of justice; we are concerned with the right use of fortitude to control the action stemming from passions of anger, or fear, or audacity, and at the same time we are concerned with avoiding cowardice or mere daring. We are concerned with the acquisition of that quality of mind called magnanimity, but magnanimity without vanity; we are concerned with temperance and the avoidance of any of the lusts of the spirit, largely through rational self-control.

The function of prudence with regard to the other virtues is not merely to find the means by which the particular end of a moral virtue may be achieved but to urge the use of the means which prudence in a sense makes available. In the matter of taking counsel, we see that the good of the individual, or the family or the state, which is the object of prudence, posits an intimate connection between the prudence of this world—reason informing human actions—with supernatural prudence—human actions informed by the law of God. In the *Melibeus,* as we see, the actions of the chief agent under the guidance of his wife are not divorced from the notion of their acceptability to God.

It has seemed to me that disdain of the didactic *Melibeus* in the *Canterbury Tales* will lead us to neglect, not the obvious truths drawn from Aristotle and Aquinas about the role of Prudence with respect to the other moral virtues, nor even the possibility that the story of Prudence and Melibeus, who between them bring forth Sophia, wisdom, is the germ of the marriage group, and so of tremendous significance in the development of the whole form of the *Canterbury Tales;* but rather that it has a singular import for a whole range of meaning and structure of the tales. Chaucer to be sure does not tie in its special meaning in any overt way, nor does he do so with the Parson's Tale; rather he allows the Parson's Tale and the *Melibeus* to stand as the great pauses for definition with regard to the rest of the structure.

In spite of the "bathos, forced allegory, spiritless and interminable moralising," which Ker found in it,[4] Chaucer liked it well enough to translate it; whatever value he found in it as a means of amplifying the Canterbury comedy, that comedy does not preclude nor exclude the kind of statement the *Melibeus* has to make.[5] On the one hand it is tied in with the power of women at crucial moments to convert the austere cruelty of men, whether by persuasive argument or by tears, a notion which Chaucer seems to have found attractive. On the other hand in the larger context of comedy and pilgrimage it offers a way of life in which taking thought or counsel for the sake of acting justly and temperately, within the law of charity, and with regard to salvation, is an obligation amidst the vicissitudes of pilgrimage. As a serious piece it must be taken as a guide-post of moral philosophy dealing with the correction of the intellect and the practical decisions affecting action in this life.

It is well and good to assert that the *Melibeus* (along with the Parson's Tale) is an early piece from which Chaucer was gradually moving away, "coming out from the medieval crowd to stand apart by himself individual and free,"[6] if we also remark that it was the mature Chaucer that reserved it for its place in the larger developing structure. He seems to be speaking here (as he does in the Parson's Tale) across his audience on pilgrimage to another visible and listening audience with a steady and determined criticism which that world might heed. To be sure we can see looming over the comic horizon Prudence reduced to the level of the nagging virago and Melibeus reduced to that henpecked husband in the words of the Host about his own wife in the Prologue of the Monk's Tale immediately following. But in its dogged emphasis upon what Ker calls "the monstrous virtue of Prudence," it has affinities we cannot deny with other theological and moral truths in the *Canterbury Tales.*

III

When we come to the Parson's Tale, we are dealing not so much with the habits of Prudence by which a man is made morally perfect, as with the means and content of that perfection: penitence and the examination of vice and virtue, delivered to us by a man whom William Blake called "a real Messenger of Heaven, sent in every age for its light and its warmth."[7] The position of the Tale is terminal, a last "setting-in-order," which moves us to more unpalatable considerations of human defection and measures them in terms of doctrine pure and unadorned. It comes to us as a deliberate reaction to wretched fictions, fables and romance, all regarded as chaff beside the wheat of "moralitee and vertuous mateere," which is to provide the soul "plesaunce leefful" in the Aristotelian sense, a movement by which the soul as a whole is consciously brought into its normal state of being. Our sights are addressed to the comparison between "this viage" and "thilke parfit glorious pilgrymage that highte Jerusalem celestial."

The weight such a moral treatise must impose upon the structure by being so purposely didactic a work may be deliberated by recalling that it is the last act of a drama which now, in a sense, announces its theme, salvation; and by our recognition of its marked difference in subject matter and mode from anything else in the *Canterbury Tales.* The Clerk's Tale, for example, which comes as close to being the poetry of beatitude as anything Chaucer has produced, makes capital of its un-compromising, even inhuman burden by being a poem, and makes its point through agents acting out their joys and sorrows in a powerful fiction about the obedient will. Perhaps because the strictness of its theme threatens the limits of his larger comic intention, Chaucer re-dresses its alignment at its close by means of irony in the famous Envoy; but in the tale itself, nonetheless, poetry makes a powerful statement out of the materials of theodicy, translating it into a controlled lyri-cism. Even the *Melibeus,* with its burden of the prudential life, is distinguishable from the Parson's Tale by having agents, dialogue necessary to an *agon,* an intellectual plot of sorts, and an impulse, however feeble, in the direction of an obvious allegory.[8]

The Parson's Tale is of course not a tale at all, but a treatise of instruction for the priest dealing specifically with the sacrament of penance and containing within it, between the two parts of the discus-sion of confession, a long treatment of the seven deadly sins with the virtues that oppose them. Chaucer's version, whatever its precise sources,[9] is a reflection of the Church's reform regarding administra-tion of the sacrament, of which in particular the extensive work by St. Raymund of Pennaforte and that of Guilielmus Peraldus are the great models. It is useful to know that the sacrament of penance has as its aim the reconciliation of our sinful nature with Deity, that this recon-ciliation is accomplished through contrition, confession, and satisfac-tion for sin, and that from the priest's judgment of the gravity of the sins confessed flows his judgment of the penance to be performed by the absolved sinner. The result aimed at is, as the Council of Trent has it, "that reconciliation with God, upon which there sometimes follows, in pious and devout recipients, peace and calm of conscience with intense consolation of spirit."[10] It can be seen quite easily that central to this judgment of the gravity of sin is a knowledge of the sins with their divisions and variety, a natural and essential part of the informa-tion of the confessor priest and hence a natural part of any practical treatise on penance. Our attention is quite naturally drawn to those passages illustrating the sins and the virtues that oppose them (387–955), where the subject matter makes for a subtle change of style arising out of a certain lively interest generated by the defections of the moral life; but there is a note of a great, even a passionate spirituality, a heated concern, throughout the entire compilation.

In the beginning of his treatise, the Parson sounds much like a kindly pulpit master: God desires the salvation of all of us and has provided many ways by which man may come to the Kingdom. Of these, penance—sorrow for sin and desire for amendment—is a noble, proper, and unfailing way. Thereafter, the kindly tone remains, but something sterner, sturdier intrudes and becomes the dominant voice. After dividing the sacrament into three parts (contrition, confession, and satisfaction), and constructing a moderately elaborate metaphor in which penance becomes the tree of life (its root, contrition; the branches and leaves, confession; the seed, grace; the heat in the seed, the love of God; its fruit, reparation), the Parson offers us six reasons why a man should be contrite before he pleads for total contrition, reminding us that contrition is the means by which man becomes the heir of grace.

The modern reader, who has generally bogged down long before this point, should remember that what the Parson is doing is to define "one of the old ways" by which man finds rest for his soul; to remember one's sins, to acknowledge one's slavery to them, to fear the day of judgment, to fear the loss of grace through sin, to contemplate Christ's passion, to cling to hope of forgiveness, to seek the grace to prosper, and to look forward to salvation—all the necessary implications of contrition. The Christian must go farther; he must confess his sins, realizing that man participates in Adam's fall and is forever subject to the temptations of the flesh, the world, the pride of his heart.

Within this statement of the first two parts of the sacrament of penance are many memorable passages revealing the intensity and concentration of sentiment bearing upon salvation, a holy zeal thrusting aside delicacy in favor of a strong and sober concern for the destiny of the soul. The spirit of fervent questions and answers is evidence of a practical, hand-to-hand grappling with the recalcitrant soul of man, urging a continuous state of grace upon us lest we sing in the modern way, "Jay tout perdu mon temps et mon labour" (248). It patiently reminds us (260 ff.) of the dominion of God over man's reason and of man's reason over sensuality, relationships inverted by sin, which makes reason a rebel against God and sensuality, and makes man's body rebel against reason. It also patiently explains how Christ came to redress the order (275 ff.), and what it means for mankind to be redeemed (283 ff.).

In the priest's recounting of the sins with their many subdivisions—those twigs on the branches of the tree of sin—we discern a greater degree of liveliness, a trenchant humor,[11] along with the prevailing sympathy arising out of the conviction of the charitable relationship existing between God and His creatures, from whom a rational response is called forth. Needless to say, the priest's task of dealing with sinners day after day, of hearing confessions and meting out penance, necessitates a range of knowledge encompassing the whole of life, from the lowest affairs and inclinations and attitudes of humble men to the most exalted ones of princes and tyrants. Nothing would seem farther from grace and its operation than the recital of the defections that are proper to the human condition; but without the vices, the virtues have no real existence (and the literary artist loses much of his material). Yet it is in the recital of these defections, with the description of the virtues that help to expunge them, that we see the truth of the comment by Sister Madeleva, not merely that "every page is a chronicle of life actual and contemporary, in all its moral phases, from sanctity to superstition," but that "the whole treatise, though written in the letter of penance, is conceived in the spirit of love," and that "the sacrament of penance is . . . the glorious *deus ex machina* to avert possible final disaster, to catch up life and death into a divine, deific comedy."[12] It is in this spirit of love and in the making capital of the stuff of life for the sake of that other life that the Parson's Tale shares much with the writing of Rolle, of Hilton, and of Juliana.

To focus attention exclusively upon the sins—and the virtues—is to deny the form of the treatise itself, which terminates with a discussion of the requirements of confession and satisfaction, or expiation. We must remember that the subject of the treatise is penance, into which the section on the sins has quite naturally been inserted, and that the process of cleansing the soul with its necessary examination of conscience was, and is for many, a familiar and vital part of the Christian's spiritual life. Its value lies in what it is: the definition of a sacrament which enables man to repair a damaged relationship with his Creator, with its view, through the eyes of a spiritual counselor, of the battle taking place in the soul of man.

Whether the parson discusses sovereignty, or gentilesse, or marriage, or business, or any of the myriad forms of rascality that interested Chaucer as a literary artist, they are aspects of the pilgrimage of this life in which the form of this life is projected forward upon the form of that other.[13] While the treatise is frankly expository, frankly didactic, frankly moral in its goal of a corrected will, and while its length and style are somewhat daunting by comparison with most of what has gone before in the *Canterbury Tales,* it is not without qualities of vitality, of a theological humor, of high indignation, of fervent love that make for the literature of power. The goal towards which it would passionately urge us, the goal for the sake of which the penitential journey was undertaken, meritorious and grace-full, is the endelees blisse of hevene, / ther joye hath no contrarioustee of wo ne grevaunce; ther alle harmes been passed of this present lyf; ther as is the sikernesse fro the peyne of helle; ther as is the blisful compaignye that rejoysen hem everemo, everich of otheres joye; / ther as the body of man, that whilom was foul and derk, is moore cleer than the sonne; ther as the body, that whilom was syk, freele, and fieble, and mortal, is inmortal, and so strong and so hool that ther may no thyng apeyren it; / ther as ne is neither hunger, thurst, ne coold, but every soule replenyssed with the sighte of the parfit knowynge of God. / This blisful regne may men purchace by poverte espiritueel, and the glorie by lowenesse, the plentee of joye by hunger and thurst, and the reste by travaille, and the lyf by deeth and mortificacion of synne.[14]

Obviously Chaucer is not grand, in the manner of Aquinas or Dante, but the schema outlined by the Parson depicts that great drama of God and His creatures, and the better "way" by which man returns to Him.

IV

The way of Prudence and the way of Salvation are so solidly "there" in the structure of the *Canterbury Tales* that we would be remiss in our understanding of the dynamics of the long poem not to take them fully into account. In his own way, Chaucer vies with Dante in a certain boldness by making materials generally inimical to poetry the large stepping stones across which we walk more confidently into the poem as a whole, or which we may find to be the foundation stones on which the whole poem is built.

NOTES

1. John E. Wells, *A Manual of the Writings in Middle English, 1050–1400* (New Haven: Yale U. Press, 1926), p. 602. Wells writes: "Chaucer's work has no vision; it is scarcely at all interested in the human heart or the ways of the soul."
2. J. S. P. Tatlock, *Development and Chronology of Chaucer's Works,* Chaucer Society, Second Series, 21 (London: Kegan Paul, 1907), pp. 188–97. W. W. Lawrence, "The Tale of Melibeus," *Essays and Studies in Honor of Carleton Brown* (New York: University Press, 1940), pp. 100–10. Gardiner Stillwell, "The Political Meaning of Chaucer's *Tale of Melibee,*" *Speculum,* 19 (1944), 433–44.

3. W. W. Lawrence, "The Marriage Group in the *Canterbury Tales,*" *Modern Philology*, 11 (1914), 247–58, and "The Discussion of Marriage," in *Chaucer and the Canterbury Tales* (New York: Columbia U. Press, 1950), pp. 119–44. More recently, Germaine Dempster has advanced the view that when the *Melibeus*, the Clerk's Tale, and the Nun's Priest's Tale were written, "there was no thought of stressing the Marriage Group themes inherent in the plots—woman's submissiveness or sovereignty, her role as good or bad counselor—still less of relating these tales to one another or to others with regard to the teller's ideas about marriage; . . . it was only later that Chaucer thought of using the *Clerk's Tale* as an integral part of his newly conceived marriage group and of making the *Melibeus* and the *Nun's Priest's Tale* function as preparatory steps to the debate." "A period in the Development of the *Canterbury Tales'* Marriage Group and of Blocks B-2 and C," *PMLA*, 48 (1953), 1142.

4. W. P. Ker, in Henry Craik, *English Prose I* (New York: Macmillan, 1893), p. 40.

5. Paull F. Baum, *Chaucer: A Critical Appreciation* (Durham: Duke U. Press, 1958), p. 80, assesses its comic relevance.

6. Ker, p. 41.

7. Geoffrey Keynes, ed., "A Descriptive Catalogue" in *The Complete Writings of William Blake* (London: Oxford U. Press, 1957), p. 570.

8. See Lawrence, "The *Tale of Melibee*," p. 105; and more recently Paul Strohm, "The Allegory of the *Tale of Melibee*," *Chaucer Review*, 2 (1967–68), 32–42. Charles A. Owen, Jr., "The *Tale of Melibee*," *Chaucer Review*, 7 (1972–73), 267–80. Robert Christmas, "Chaucer's *Tale of Melibee*: Its Tradition and Its Function in Fragment VII of the *Canterbury Tales*," Diss. University of California 1968, p. 143, dismisses the allegory as negligible, but sees the theme of the tale as one of self-control standing in sharp contrast to the self-indulgence of the tales of Fragment VII.

9. Richard Hazelton, "Chaucer's *Parson's Tale* and the *Moralium Dogma Philosophorum*," *Traditio*, 16 (1960), 255–74, and Siegfried Wenzel, "The Source of the 'Remedia' of the *Parson's Tale*," *Traditio*, 27 (1971), 433–53.

10. "Penance," *The Catholic Encyclopedia* (New York: Robert Appleton, 1911), XI, 623.

11. John Finlayson, "The Satiric Mode and the *Parson's Tale*," *Chaucer Review*, 6 (1971), 94–116. A lively, sane piece.

12. *A Lost Language* (New York: Sheed and Ward, 1951), 75–76.

13. I am far from suggesting that Chaucer intended the tales to represent the sins or virtues or that the Parson's Tale is "keyed" in any precise way to individual tales. See my studies, "The Form of the *Canterbury Tales: Respice Fines*," *College English*, 17 (1955–56), 443–44, and *The Art of the Canterbury Tales* (Madison: U. of Wisconsin Press, 1965), pp. 249–52.

14. F. N. Robinson, ed., *The Works of Geoffrey Chaucer*, 2nd ed. (Boston: Houghton Mifflin, 1957), X: 1075–80.

Chaucerian Problems: Minor Works

7

EDWARD VASTA

To Rosemounde: Chaucer's
"Gentil" Dramatic Monologue

A scribe, and not Chaucer himself, is responsible for the words "Tregentil. Chaucer" at the end of *To Rosemounde.* In adding the phrase after the ballade, as he did again after the *Troilus* in the same MS (Rawlinson Poetry 163), the scribe apparently meant to record for posterity not only the poem itself but also his judgment of it and of the mind responsible for it; according to the general opinion of scholars the sense of the words is *"très gentil,* Chaucer."[1]

What the scribe saw in the poem that elicited this particular compliment is a thing to ponder. Modern judgments universally find the ballade's language incompatible with its courtly intention; the poem speaks of weeping a tubful of tears and of wallowing in love like a boiled fish submerged in a thick sauce. For C. S. Lewis, who takes the poem as serious, this incompatibility is its failure; for Davies, Donaldson, Robbins, and Reiss, who take the poem as comic, the incompatibility is its success.[2] In either case, whether expressed seriously or in a bantering mood,[3] words and sentiments are mismatched. Then how could the scribal critic call poem or poet "gentil"? No "gentil" sensibility, addressing matters of refined love, could write of weeping tears by the tubful or of wallowing in love like a pike in pickle-sauce.

Still, it is quite possible that the scribe understood Chaucer and his little ballade in a special way. The incompatibility of the tub metaphor and the fish simile in this love poem is obvious; Chaucer surely used the figures deliberately. Like Plato he believed explicitly in suiting the word to the deed (CT I: 742). He also composed the advice Pandarus gives to Troilus about how not to write of love—unless for a joke:

> "Ne jompre ek no discordant thyng yfeere,
> As thus, to usen termes of phisik
> In loves termes; hold of thi matere
> The forme alwey, and do that it be lik;
> For if a peyntour wolde peynte a pyk
> With asses feet, and hede it as an ape,
> It cordeth naught, so nere it but a jape."
> (Tr. II: 1037–43)

The judging scribe read and recorded this very passage. Indeed, all of Chaucer's works prove that Chaucer never deviated from such advice unless, as in Absolon's speeches in the Miller's Tale (e.g., I: 3698–3707), for comic purposes. We cannot assume, therefore, that the scribe overlooked Chaucer's obvious manipulations of language in *To Rosemounde*. More reasonable to assume that he saw their justification. His perception of Chaucer's achievement may have revealed the poem to be more complex than we find it, more delicate and graceful, and thus poetically more noble than we know it, more pleasing, more "gentil."

To expose the complexities of the poem, I wish to analyze it from three points of view: from that of the speaker, from that of Rosemounde—taking her as real and assuming that her reactions to the address will be standard—and from that of the author. First, let us get the entire text before us:

> Madame, ye ben of al beaute shryne
> As fer as cercled is the mapemounde,
> For as the cristal glorious ye shyne,
> And lyke ruby ben your chekes rounde.
> Therwith ye ben so mery and so jocounde   5
> That at a revel whan that I see you daunce,
> It is an oynement unto my wounde,
> Thogh ye to me ne do no daliaunce.
>
> For thogh I wepe of teres ful a tyne,
> Yet may that wo myn herte nat confounde;   10
> Your semy voys, that ye so smal out twyne,
> Maketh my thoght in joy and blis habounde.
> So curtaysly I go, with love bounde,
> That to myself I sey, in my penaunce,
> "Suffyseth me to love you, Rosemounde,   15
> Thogh ye to me ne do no daliaunce."
>
> Nas never pyk walwed in galauntyne
> As I in love am walwed and ywounde,
> For which ful ofte I of myself devyne
> That I am trewe Tristam the secounde.   20
> My love may not refreyde nor affounde;
> I brenne ay in an amorous plesaunce.
> Do what you lyst, I wyl your thral be founde,
> Thogh ye to me ne do no daliaunce.
>   Tregentil.   Chaucer.[4]

Complexities emerge with an attempt to define the speaker's intention, a problem which in the modest and sketchy scholarship on this poem is lost in ambiguity. Each of three objectives typical in love poetry has been cited for this ballade: to praise a lady,[5] to complain of a lover's pains,[6] and to profess a great love.[7] All three objectives are clearly evident in the speaker's address: he praises Rosemounde's appearance, her temperament, her speech, and her influence; he displays his wound, his tears, his heart's woe, his penance, and his burning; and he professes his uncoolable love, his utter enslavement. These lyrical objectives are integrated within this address to a lady, furthermore, by means of a single, conventional conceit: the notion that the lady is the very cure of the illness she causes.[8] Inherent in this notion is a compliment to the lady, a complaint by a suffering lover, and the profession of a desperate love. Additionally, overriding these lyrical ends is a conventional rhetorical purpose: to win his lady over. In the course of his lyrical expressions the speaker strives to present himself so appealingly that his lady will be moved to admiration, sympathy, affection, love and the final solace. Thus at least four standard intentions are combined in the address offered by the ballade's speaker.

The speaker's rhetorical strategy is that of a learned lover who means to attract his lady by a display of mental dexterity. His first utterance is a compliment which applies several principles of medieval esthetics. Rosemounde, he begins, you are the shrine of all beauty because, like the glorious crystal and the ruby, you shine. How does such shining justify the praise that of all beauty Rosemounde is the shrine? Because beauty is a transcendental, in the medieval view—a quality which, like unity, truth, and goodness, permeates all being and is, in itself, an aspect of being. One of the essential characteristics of beauty is radiance, or clarity, or splendor of form. (The other two essential characteristics are integrity and proportion.) Beauty can be properly attributed only to God, of course; but an earthly being can be Divine Beauty's shrine. The argument underlying the ballade's first compliment is this: the beauty that radiates from all things is a universal beauty, which radiates most perfectly from the most perfect things. Because the perfection of beauty evident in Rosemounde is like that which radiates from the most glorious gems, the Transcendental itself must be enshrined in her.[9] Thus the beautiful things of this world may worship in Rosemounde the very essence of their perfection.

The speaker's first compliment is also based on several conventions of love literature. Medieval proclamations of love frequently commend a lady by attributing to her the qualities of gems. The shining of crystal is commonly cited in praise of the lady's beauty and is usually compared to the radiance of her face, particularly of her eyes.[10] In medieval medicine, as today, the interior lens of the eye is in fact called "the crystalline lens."[11] A lady's complexion is frequently said to be the color of ruby. Although rubies range in color from crimson to pale rose, only the most complimentary shades are to be imagined here—and in view of the convention, the deep shades.[12] The total effect of these images in *To Rosemounde* is like that achieved, but without naming gems, in Chaucer's *Book of the Duchess* by a description of the shining beauty of Fair White, who:

> Was whit, rody, fressh, and lyvely hewed,
> And every day hir beaute newed.
>
> (905–06)

The description of Rosemounde's cheeks as round also invokes the medieval convention of feminine beauty which found unbecoming in a woman's body any visible outline of sinews, muscles, or bones.[13]

The poet-lover then continues. The sight of you dancing heals the wound of love, he says, thus evoking the scene from *The Romance of the Rose* in which all of love's folk dance inside the walled garden. In the *Romance,* dedicated to Guillaume de Lorris' rose, love's folk are personifications of the personal qualities that qualify one for love, and all are presented as companions of Mirth (521–1278). By praising Rosemounde for being merry and playful, the speaker names the principal characteristics by which Rosemounde, as in the previous sentence she is called the shrine of all beauty, is placed at the center of the mirthful society of love. Thus the speaker's praise of Rosemounde moves from the *mappa mundi* (a religious and symbolic, as well as geographic, document[14]) to the dance, from the shrine to the revel, from beauty to love. Heaven and earth meet in Rosemounde, as do heavenly beauty and earthly love; and thus she is praised, in effect, as a perfect agency on earth through whom beauty and love come united to men.

The combined ideologies of beauty and love in the first stanza then yield the lover-poet's central, paradoxical theme. Beauty and love come in through the eyes. Beauty is a radiance; it is that which, when seen, pleases. Love is a wound caused by the sight of a woman's beauty: the sickness of love begins when the rays of the lady's beauty radiate through the lover's eyes and descend to wound his heart. Thus, seeing Rosemounde dance, the speaker feels both joy and pain. The joy comes from beauty, the pain comes from love. Rosemounde's beauty wounds him with love, but the sight of that shrine of beauty is also healing.[15]

In the next stanza the speaker develops the terms of his central paradox to the extreme. First he metonymically replaces the wound with tears and woe, the ointment with joy and bliss. Then he redefines his paradox by evoking two more conventions of love poetry. One is that love is not an act of reason, is not a deliberate choice, but is rather an act of desire by which one is enthralled despite oneself. The other convention is that love is ennobling. It makes one "go curtaysly," as the speaker puts it, and this term refers to the total complex of courtly refinements of which love is the inspiration. By the end of the second stanza, tears have become the penance of bondage while joy and bliss have become that degree of refined breeding which makes one courteous.

In the last stanza, again, he develops the terms of his paradox to a still further extreme: love's bondage completely immerses the speaker in love while love's courtesy elevates him to true Tristan the Second. Thus the paradox now embraces the extremes of immanence and transcendence. Having brought his case to its climax, the speaker, in the second half of the last stanza, proclaims that his love will never diminish from that climactic point: it will never cool nor subside; he will always burn in amorous pleasure. No matter what Rosemounde does, he will ever be her thrall.

From the point of view of the speaker, then, *To Rosemounde* is a love poem that seeks to endear the poet-lover to his lady and thereby win her over. It is at once an argument, an encomium, a complaint, a proclamation, a play of doctrine, and an exercise in the manipulation of poetic convention. In its strict prosodic form but expansive argument, it places poetic craft on exhibition. In moving from the union of beauty and love to the conflicting emotional impact of joy and sorrow, then to the extremes of physical and moral change caused in the lover, the address offers a learned display of wit. The speaker's tone, finally, is one of verve and confidence with a distinct sense of self-satisfaction, even a certain pride.

Now let us imagine Rosemounde receiving such an address. If within the framework of the conventions we put ourselves in her place, the ballade yields still more complexities.

The structure of the poem gives the address, first of all, a movement which implies that while the lover's ostensible intention is to seduce Rosemounde only in mind: that is, gain only her attention, covertly he is also conventionally after her body. The first four lines praise Rosemounde as the shrine of all the beauty encompassed by the map of the world. Here the scope of reference is large, distant, abstract, and even holy. In the next four lines, in which Rosemounde is seen dancing at a revel, the scope narrows to the social, as if the speaker were watching from the periphery of a dance. The next four lines, which speak of the subtlety of Rosemounde's voice, bring her closer, within hearing, as in a conversation. The entire last stanza, finally, moves beyond the private to the intimate. The poet-lover speaks of wallowing in love like a fish in sauce, of being wound about by love; like the love of Tristan, his love is hot, he says, and may not grow cold; he burns always in amorous pleasure. One scholar has already suggested that the image of the pike is phallic,[16] and another that the poet may be experiencing, and enjoying, the pleasure of love in anticipation of his lady's favor.[17] Certainly the last stanza is replete with intimations of sexual union.

The poem's structure also gives the speaker's address the force of action. The speaker addresses his lady in the present; he is now in love—ennobled but languishing because his love is unrequited; but he reminds us of his initial beholding and falling in love with his shrine of beauty, and of his having seen her from time to time thereafter at a dance or in conversation. He also forecasts for us the consummation he longs for. This narrative pattern is the standard pattern of the process of love. In describing Rosemounde's beauty, in speaking of her dancing and of the effect of her beauty on his sorrow, in explaining how he goes courteously, with love bound, and burns always in amorous pleasure, the speaker evokes the conventional pattern of falling in love with a lady at first sight, suffering through the period of sickness because of her "daunger," being ennobled by love, eventually winning over the lady's regard, and at last enjoying her favors.

Learning about such a state of affairs might conceivably perk up Rosemounde's interest, but if she is the standard lady of medieval love literature, she will be put off, perhaps insulted, possibly shocked. In the end, however, she will laugh at the fool and dismiss him from her mind because his language, his logic, and his tone reveal such limitations of character and talent as to make his cause hopeless. His "unliklynesse" in love (Tr I: 16) is everywhere apparent, albeit he is himself unaware of his "unliklynesse."

The notorious statements of stanzas two and three—the declaration that he weeps a tubful of tears and wallows in love like a fish in sauce—are the most obvious instances in which the poet-lover betrays his incompetence by his language. The images are colloquial and bathetic; they imply a domestic, middle-class taste, the sort of pragmatic sensibility that taints the genuineness of romantic ardor. They suggest a confusion in the poet-lover between romance and realism. Each image undermines the credibility of the stanza it introduces and is only less fatal to his aspirations than his lack of awareness that these images are inappropriate for plaints of refined love.

As hyperbolic as it is, the first stanza also suffers, subtly, from the bourgeois hand of realism. Madame, he says, you are the shrine of all beauty—and then adds, as far as is encircled by the "mapemounde." Now a regular poet, as Chaucer himself does consistently in his other works (BD 820–24, 907–12; PhysT 9–29), proclaims his lady's beauty as the most perfect in all of nature, whose regions include earth and sky and all realms from here to the moon.[18] Rosemounde's poet confines her supereminence to Europe, the northern half of Africa, and the western parts of Asia—the areas encircled by the medieval T-O map.[19] Again, the "mapemounde," a term used nowhere else in Chaucer's works, evokes a context for Rosemounde which mixes romance and realism. On the romantic side the term suggests the world of romances, especially popular romances, in which much travel takes place to foreign lands. In this context Rosemounde is complimented as the very shrine of beauty among the beautiful women found throughout romantic lands. On the realistic side, speaking of lands known to cartographers and comparing Rosemounde's shining to that of jewels suggest the world of trade, pilgrimages, shrines, and jeweled offerings of thanks hung about as memorials. Real maps, geography, and travel evoke associations too mundane for love lyrics. In the Renaissance these references will be elevated to lyrical metaphor because history will have brought a new experience and a new sensibility; in the fourteenth century, before the discovery of the New World, their implications are inconsistent with refined expressions of love. Such references are for Canterbury pilgrims.

The statement that her round cheeks are like rubies is also ambiguous. The speaker implies that her round cheeks are the color of rubies and that her cheeks are round like the shape of a ruby. Rubies have no uniform shape, but roundness and redness taken together suggest that the speaker may be thinking of a woman whose beauty derives from proper nourishment. At a certain strategically diminishing moment in the *Troilus,* for example, Chaucer's ambivalent *persona* describes Criseyde as well-nourished (Tr V: 821). It even happens, according to the *MED,* that "cristal" is a term of cookery and refers to a shiny clear jelly or glaze, and that rubies, like other precious stones, were regarded as averse to poisons.[20] Perhaps it should be no surprise, if the speaker does have food on his subconscious mind, that he will later compare himself to a fish prepared in a jellied sauce.[21] In any case, the ballade's most high-flown passage carries an undertone of mundane, practical, middle-class taste.

More seriously: though crystals, rubies, and the world itself are rare and beautiful, they define Rosemounde, whose name means Rose of the

World, in earthbound terms. The details of a *mappa mundi* intensify the impression of earthiness. The Hereford *mappa mundi* (c. 1300), the largest and most interesting surviving example of the circular world map,[22] represents an area roughly covering the two empires of Rome and Alexander the Great. Ancient provincial boundaries are indicated and some groups of towns are named. Jerusalem is located at the center, thus giving the place of honor to the terrestrial paradise, and the area of Palestine is considerably enlarged. Rome, Antioch, and Paris are also drawn conspicuously.

> Other cities and towns are represented by conventional drawings of towers and gates; mountains and rivers are numerous, the former in a conventionalized profile. Most of the space, which would otherwise be empty, is filled with neatly executed drawings depicting themes from the popular histories and bestiaries of the time. Indeed the whole is as much an encyclopedia of medieval lore as a map, and provides fascinating material for study.[23]

For the modern reader, Chaucer's reference to the "mapemounde" is a charming image; and so, one would guess, for a medieval audience. But the audience of *To Rosemounde,* as Patricia Kean has noted,[24] also shared definite experiences and expectations regarding literary conventions. Aware of the conventions of love poetry, they are quite likely to wonder at Rosemounde's earthiness.

The central paradox developed confidently by the speaker as the thesis of his address also reveals his essential incompetence: it is not so clever as it first seems. He comes smoothly to it in the first stanza, but in the second, when he makes a distinction between heart and mind parallel to that between love and beauty, he begins to undermine the nobility of his idea. In medieval thought love is on the side of the heart while beauty is on the side of the mind. Thus the speaker can describe himself as woeful in heart because wounded by unfulfilled love, but blissful in thought because delighted by his lady's beauty. Yet such a distinction leaves beauty and love opposed rather than integrated. It makes the speaker victim of an interior disharmony caused, in the medieval view, when the will acts independently of reason.[25] As the speaker develops the dichotomy between head and heart into that between courtesy and slavery, then to that between transcendence to Tristan-like nobility and submergence into animal love, he unwittingly develops as well his own state of interior chaos. Nobility and animality are mutually exclusive values, the highest and the lowest. As the speaker rises in courtly stature, he sinks in moral stature. He also damns love while praising it, for love debases as it ennobles. Needless to say, Rosemounde, the cause of both states in the dreamer, is by implication also debased while she is praised.

Interior chaos resulting from the conflict of intellect and will is a state to which all mankind is subject; it is one of the consequences of Original Sin, one of the ways man has obscured his divine image and likeness. The chief consequence of Original Sin is pride, that love of self which keeps man remote from God.[26] The interior chaos of Chaucer's speaker is plainly rooted in the deeper reality of pride. His self-love emerges with the inadvertent revelation of his mediocrity. In the second stanza, having recalled the subtlety of Rosemounde's voice, he responds with his own voice—talking to himself, in fact—saying that the return of love by Rosemounde is actually unnecessary:

> That to myself I sey, in my penaunce,
> "Suffyseth me to love you, Rosemounde,
> Thogh ye to me ne do no daliaunce."

From this point on—half the poem—the speaker talks about himself exclusively. Indeed, he began the shift of attention to himself in the first stanza, and in the second stanza the attention devoted to Rosemounde amounts to only one line. He not only talks about himself, he thinks only about himself; and as his self-preoccupation grows, so grows his self-satisfaction. He is so bound in love, he says in effect, he has grown so courteous, that he is enough unto himself—he needs no "daliaunce" from Rosemounde. His very often "divining" himself to be true Tristan the Second is a larger piece of vanity. The speaker declares himself, in effect, a classical lover, the noblest kind of lover, one of Love's heroes and martyrs.[27] The climactic revelation of self-love comes in the last lines of the ballade when, entangled in the unfavorable implications of his simile of himself as like a pike in galantine—a cold, jellied dish in which the fish has sunk to the bottom—he protests that his love will not cool or sink; he will always burn in amorous pleasure.[28] The intended contradiction between burning and pleasure disappears into the dissolving passion of sexual love, which is both burning and pleasurable (Rom 2465–78), and the word *plesaunce* by now carries a freight of meaning: self-satisfaction, vanity, pride, and sensuality—even a suggestion of psychological auto-eroticism. Over all, covering like his love sauce, is the self-love which makes him naive about himself, unaware of the import of his words, and thinking that all of this should be flattering to Rosemounde. The final picture of him, as he tells Rosemounde to do as she pleases, is of one captivated not so much by Rosemounde, who has paid him no attention, but, Narcissus-like, by the self-excitation and self-image that are the products of his own sensuality and pride.

His paradox, finally, defeats his rhetorical purpose with its logic. It leads the speaker to increasingly stronger declarations which insist upon increasing indifference from Rosemounde. First she is an ointment to his wound, then she need not return his love, and finally she can just do as she pleases. The last two lines logically dismiss not merely her actions but even her concern. Intent on a display of clever learning, the speaker seems unaware that his rationality leaves him without a claim on Rosemounde's love; if unrequited love is so completely sufficient for him that Rosemounde can do as she wishes, then, to borrow a phrase from Our Host, Harry Bailly: "What amounteth all this wit?" (RvT I: 3901). Addressing her about the matter is unnecessary. The poet's logic renders irrelevant the poem's very occasion.

Lady Rosemounde would find here no humble, self-abasing lover, one whom her perfection renders worthless in his own eyes; nor any thwarted lover either, a man struggling against her indifference, toiling for a sign of acknowledgment. She would find instead a comfortable and confident suitor whose mediocrity makes him neither saint nor sinner. As a man he wishes to be high-minded, but his references unwittingly betray his own share in common humanity's sensuality and pride. As a thinker he wants to be clever, but his cleverness turns complexity of thought into contradictions. As a poet he wants to appear at home in the tradition, but his expressions betray his limited powers. As a lover he wants to be ardent and refined, but his passions only reveal mankind's common appetites. All such forms of mediocrity are confirmed in the general mediocrity of his self-satisfaction. Lady Rosemounde would find him as unlikely a suitor as can be found anywhere among the first-person speakers of Chaucer's works.

From the third point of view, that of the author, Chaucer's ballade is a multi-layered satire. It satirizes, first of all, the style of love poetry. In lyric form, in sentiment, and in tone the ballade captures the quality of straight conventionality. We could easily accept the poem at face value if Chaucer had not contrived, at the beginning of each of the last two stanzas, travesties of love-imagery and love-language. Their purpose is to roughen the poem's conventional surface so that our critical attention is invited. Then we discover the stylistic flaws already noted in scholarship: the mooing repetition of dark, back nasals in the rhyme scheme, which Reiss sees as unsuitable for praise of a lady and assertions of love; the rigid form and artificial pose, which according to Robbins underlie the poem's chattiness; and, of course, the exaggeration, which for Donaldson transfers the images and attitudes of the poem from the realm of the ideal to that of the real.[29] In addition, we find the failures of style analyzed above.

In a second way Chaucer's ballade is a satire of character; and as in his other works, the character here is Chaucer's own *persona*. Chaucer mocks himself, not by utterly denying in himself craft, or intelligence, or feeling, but by presenting himself as second rate. He presents himself as a middle-class mentality caught up in an upper-class experience; an aspirant to sophistication whose honest mediocrity betrays his common humanity. He allows us to catch him taking pains to counterfeit the skill, the genius, and the taste of true courtly poets.

Chaucer's ballade, finally, does more than mock himself; it also mocks the ideology of love. The poem reveals how the conventions of love are contradictory among themselves and incompatible with medieval esthetics and morality. The poem articulates a progression of paradoxes which emerge out of each other in three stages, doubling at each stage. The first paradox, beauty vs. love, is elicited by Rosemounde. The next two, ointment vs. wound and joy vs. sorrow, come directly from the manifest speaker. The last four are reason vs. will, courtesy vs. pride, idealism vs. sensuality, and nobility vs. animality; these are supplied indirectly by the author. All seven paradoxes can be summed up in one overriding opposition: heaven vs. earth. The matter of the poem moves downward, moreover, through mind, heart, body: from doctrines of beauty and love, to the passions of joy and sorrow and the virtues of courtesy, to the sensations and appetites of the flesh. The poem also mocks the experience of love for, rooted in worldly beauty, it is inherently narcissistic and as vulnerable to the effects of Original Sin as is any other sort of human experience. All told Chaucer's little ballade is a satire both comic and serious, banal and sublime.

From the point of view of the reader, *To Rosemounde* has the complexity of a dramatic monologue. Claud Howard long ago suggested that Chaucer's ballade takes a first step in the transition from lyric to dramatic monologue by addressing emotional expressions to an individual who is "visualized and spoken to directly." He concluded, however, that "this rudimentary form is the only element of the dramatic monologue, for its spirit is essentially that of the lyric."[30] This paper has attempted to show that *Rosemounde* is a dramatic monologue in the full definition of the genre: in the course of his address to someone "offstage" the speaker reveals his character and circumstances. The ballade's susceptibility to analysis from the standpoint of the speaker, listener, and poet in itself implies an intrinsically dramatic "deep structure," as it were, and therefore an essentially socio-psychological, hence rhetorical, experience as the poem's occasion. The poem's yield of character traits, personal tensions, and authorial stances also suggests the same genre for which Robert Browning and T. S. Eliot are famous. Chaucer had already learned from Deschamps that the ballade is adaptable to philosophical and satirical purposes.[31] The further introduction of his self-mocking sanity, embodied in the authorial *persona* so familiar and distinctive in his works, was a creative decision of radical originality. It transformed the ballade into a work of a new genre which proved felicitously adaptable in his CT prologues for the Reeve, the Wife of Bath, and the Pardoner, and whose potential as an independent literary form would be fully explored centuries later.

The dramatic mode in *Rosemounde* is not as dominant, of course, as in many monologues of the nineteenth and twentieth centuries; but mainly because Chaucer is given to understatement. The poem's spirit is more than lyrical; its tone and texture are the product of a concentrated variety of lyrical and rhetorical stances. This variety accounts for the poem's receiving the differing critical responses which have led Robbins to call it an "enigma."[32] All the responses are valid: the ballade is a complimentary poem[33] or *salut d'amour,*[34] a complaint,[35] a profession of love that is both noble and ridiculous,[36] an urbane version of noble love-talk,[37] mingled seriousness and irony,[38] a love lyric written in a bantering mood,[39] a ballade of lively wit and grace,[40] and a satire.[41] All critics except C. S. Lewis, on the other hand, agree that the ballade is distinctive and sophisticated, though a minor work. Marchette Chute regards it as coming after Chaucer's youthful period of imitation.[42] R. D. French ascribes it to the period of Chaucer's emancipation from the conventional school of love poetry.[43] Wolfgang Clemen dates it before 1380 and adds: "the humor appearing in *Rosemounde* points to an unmistakably new tone even in this lyrical genre."[44]

The ballade's tone and texture have provided scholars the only basis for dating, and ascriptions of date have ranged over all periods of the Chaucer canon.[45] Recently, Rossell Hope Robbins has made a case for a very late date of composition: 1396, four years before Chaucer's death.[46] His argument combines Cowling's suggestion that *Rosemounde* expresses an old man's playful affection for a young girl[47] with the suggestion by Edith Rickert that the poem is addressed to the seven-

year-old princess Isabelle of Valois on the occasion of her marriage to
King Richard II.[48] Robbins' view includes the arguments that in the
poem, Rosemounde's "round" cheeks could only refer to the cheeks of a
"sub-teenager" and that the usual sensual descriptions and sexual demands are not present in this love lyric. For my part, the marriage of
Richard and Isabelle seems an unlikely occasion for such a poem. The
ballade's argument is beyond the range of a seven-year-old, and its tone
and sentiment are uncomplimentary to a suitor. Conventional descriptions of a lady's round arms and round neck make round cheeks consistent, furthermore, as does the medieval style in painting, sculpture,
and literature which depicts feminine beauty in smooth and curving
surfaces. Chaucer adheres to this style completely in his description of
John of Gaunt's fair Duchess Blanche:

> But swich a fairnesse of a nekke
> Had that swete that boon nor brekke
> Nas ther non sene that myssat.
> Hyt was whit, smothe, streght, and pure flat,
> Wythouten hole; or canel-boon,
> As be semynge, had she noon.
> Hyr throte, as I have now memoyre,
> Semed a round tour of yvoyre,
> Of good gretnesse, and noght to gret.
>   (BD 939–47)

Suggestions of sensuality and expectations of sexual union, this paper
has argued, are also quite evident in *To Rosemounde*.

A case can be made, on the other hand, affirming an early date of
composition, c. 1369–1370, at about the time Chaucer wrote *The Book
of the Duchess* and some early lyrics and complaints of the French type
and also translated, if the work is his, the *Romaunt of the Rose*.
Rosemounde's formal and material derivations are totally French; its
standards of beauty are those which underlie the description of Fair
White in *Duchess;* and it connects with the *Romaunt* in many ways.
Reference to crystal as a precious stone is found nowhere else in
Chaucer's works except the *Romaunt*.[49] The image of Rosemounde
dancing, and her very name, also suggest the original *Roman* as well as
the Chaucerian translation. In the *Romaunt* the dreamer's dialogue with
the God of Love, whose arrows have just smitten the dreamer with love
for the Rose (Rom 1927 ff.), expresses the same new experience which
by implication is the background for the speaker's address in
Rosemounde. The ballade's central conceit, that Rosemounde is both

inflictor and ointment of love's wound, is expressed in the dialogue
when the dreamer says to the God of Love:

> Comfort of helthe how shuld I have,
> Sith ye me hurt, but ye me save?
> The helthe of love mot be founde
> Where as they token first her wounde.
>   (Rom 1963–66)

The God of Love informs the dreamer of his obligations, including that
of courtesy, encourages him to endure love's pains, enjoins him to
penance, and commands "That in oo place thou sette, all hool, / Thyn
herte" (2363–64). Chaucer's speaker expresses his state in just these
terms. He also ironically violates a serious commandment to all lovers:
to avoid pride. The God of Love's summary statement pretty well
encompasses the traits of character with which Chaucer deals:

> Whoso with Love wole goon or ride,
> He mot be curteis, and voide of pride,
> Mery, and full of jolite.
>   (Rom 2351–53)

Most of all, the speaker of the ballade resembles the *persona* of
Duchess more directly than the *persona* in any other of Chaucer's works.
He is mundane and bourgeois, has a lady who is his "only physician," is
languishing for love, and has no awareness of his own disqualifications as
a lover. None of the *personae* in Chaucer's later works is in love, and all
are expressly aware of themselves as limited poets who can only be
servants to the servants of love. Thus the speaker of *To Rosemounde*,
beyond whose characteristics all later *personae* go, appears to be the
earliest instance of the *persona* whom Chaucer presents in full dress in
The Book of the Duchess and develops in all subsequent major works.
This early conception is already so complex and original as to justify the
scribe's admiring *très gentil*.[50]

NOTES

1. W. W. Skeat, *The Complete Works of Geoffrey Chaucer* (Oxford: Clarendon
   Press, 1899), II: 81, took "Tregentil" as the scribe's name. Helge Kökeritz,
   "Chaucer's Rosemounde," *Modern Language Notes*, 63 (1948), 310–18, es-
   tablished the current view, adopted in this paper.

2. C. S. Lewis, *The Allegory of Love* (London: Oxford U. Press, 1936), p. 171;
R. T. Davies, *Medieval English Lyrics* (London: Faber and Faber, 1963), p.
328; E. T. Donaldson, ed., *Chaucer's Poetry*, 2nd ed. (New York: Ronald
Press, 1975), pp. 1124–25; Rossell Hope Robbins, "The Lyrics," in *Companion to Chaucer Studies*, ed. Beryl Rowland (London: Oxford U. Press,
1968), pp. 313–31, and also "Chaucer's *To Rosemounde*," *Studies in the
Literary Imagination*, 4 (1971), 73–81; Edmund Reiss, "Dusting off the
Cobwebs: A Look at Chaucer's Lyrics," *Chaucer Review*, 1 (1966), 55–65.

3. A. C. Baugh, ed., *Chaucer's Major Poetry* (New York: Appleton-Century-Crofts, 1963), p. 535.

4. The text is from F. N. Robinson, ed., *The Works of Geoffrey Chaucer*, 2nd
ed. (Boston: Houghton Mifflin, 1957), p. 583.

5. Robinson, p. 521; Robbins, "*Rosemounde*," p. 74.

6. Agnes K. Getty, "Chaucer's Changing Conceptions of the Humble
Lover," *PMLA*, 44 (1929), 209.

7. Davies, op. cit. Like virtually all readers except C. S. Lewis, Davies regards
the tone of this profession of love as one of eloquence mixed with ridiculousness.

8. Cf., for example, Chrétien de Troyes, *Cligés*, in the W. W. Comfort
translation (London: Dent, 1914), p. 131: "And if it can be that sickness
brings delight, then my trouble and joy are one, and in my illness consists
my health."

9. These concepts of medieval esthetics are easily accessible in *An Introduction
to the Metaphysics of St. Thomas Aquinas*, tr. James F. Anderson (Chicago:
Regnery, 1953), pp. 88–98. They are explicated in Jacques Maritain,
Creative Intuition in Art and Poetry (Cleveland: Meridian Books, 1954), pp.
122–28.

10. The larger context is the convention of describing ladies as white, bright,
clear, etc. See W. C. Curry, *The Middle English Ideal of Personal Beauty*
(Baltimore: Furst, 1916), pp. 52, 55–57, 80–86.

11. *MED*, s.v. *crystal.*

12. Curry, pp. 91–94.

13. Ibid., pp. 99–100. Cf. Chaucer, BD 939–44.

14. R. V. Tooley, *Maps and Map-Makers* (London: Batsford, 1949), p. 12.

15. The psychologizing passages in Chrétien's *Cligés* or in Chaucer's *Troilus*,
and the love story in *Book of the Duchess*, document virtually all conventions
of love cited in this paper; or one might simply consult William George
Dodd, "The System of Courtly Love," in *Chaucer Criticism II*, ed. R. J.
Schoeck and J. Taylor (Notre Dame: University Press, 1961), pp. 1–15.

16. Reiss, p. 64.

17. Thomas W. Ross, *Chaucer's Bawdy* (New York: Dutton, 1972), p. 159.

18. A rhetorical convention included in the manuals of Matthew of Vendôme
and Geoffrey of Vinsauf: see D. S. Brewer, "The Ideal of Feminine Beauty in
Medieval Literature," *Modern Language Review*, 50 (1955), 258.

19. So called because the common medieval *mappae mundi* are round like an
O and sectored into three by the superposition of a **T**. Jerusalem appears at
the center with the east at the head of the map. Thus Asia is depicted in the

top sector, Europe in the lower left, and Africa in the lower right. See Tooley, pp. 12–14, and G. R. Crone, *Maps and Their Makers* (New York: Capricorn Books, 1962), pp. 25–28.

20. Madame De Barrera, *Gems and Jewels* (London: Richard Bentley, 1860), pp. 242–43.

21. That "galauntyne" is a jellied sauce is demonstrated by Constance Hieatt in her contribution to this volume.

22. Tooley, illus. 9.

23. Crone, p. 26.

24. *Chaucer and the Making of English Poetry* (London: Routledge and Kegan Paul, 1972), I: 31–38.

25. Thomas Aquinas, *Summa Theologica,* I–II: 113 and II–II: 23.2, rep. obj. 3.

26. See Etienne Gilson, *The Mystical Theology of St. Bernard* (New York: Sheed and Ward, 1940), pp. 45–46.

27. A Tristan as frustrated, Alain Renoir points out in his contribution to this volume, as the pike wallowing in "galauntyne."

28. See Hieatt essay.

29. See the works cited in n. 2 above.

30. "The Dramatic Monologue: Its Origin and Development," *Studies in Philology,* 4 (1910), 44–45.

31. Robinson, p. 521.

32. "Chaucer's *To Rosemounde,"* pp. 73–74.

33. Robinson, p. 521.

34. Robbins, *"Rosemounde,"* p. 74. For discussion of the two categories of love lyrics, *Salut* and *Complaint,* see his contribution to this volume.

35. French, p. 93; Getty, p. 209.

36. Davies, p. 328.

37. Kean, pp. 36–38.

38. R. K. Root, *The Poetry of Chaucer,* rev. ed. (New York: Houghton Mifflin, 1922), p. 73.

39. Baugh, p. 535.

40. Marchette Chute, *Geoffrey Chaucer of England* (New York: Dutton, 1946), p. 82.

41. George H. Cowling, *Chaucer* (New York: Dutton, n.d.), p. 185; Getty, p. 209.

42. Chute, op. cit.

43. Cowling, op. cit.

44. *Chaucer's Early Poetry* (London: Methuen, 1963), p. 174.

45. For a quick summary of dates assigned to the poem, see Robbins, *"To Rosemounde,"* p. 73.

46. Ibid.

47. Cowling, p. 186.

48. "A Leaf From a Fourteenth-Century Letter Book," *Modern Philology,* 25 (1927–28), 255.

49. "Cristal Stones" in the PardT (CT VI: 347) is the only other use of "cristal"; but here it refers to "glass cases," according to Robinson (p. 729), and not to precious stones.

50. An early version of this paper was read at the Conference on Medieval Studies, 1973, at Western Michigan University.

8

R. E. KASKE

Clericus Adam and
Chaucer's Adam Scriveyn

Among Chaucer's short poems, perhaps the most immediately appealing is that entitled *Chaucers Wordes unto Adam, His Owne Scriveyn:*

> Adam scriveyn, if ever it thee bifalle
> Boece or Troylus for to wryten newe,
> Under thy long lokkes thou most have the scalle,
> But after my makyng thou wryte more trewe;
> So ofte a-daye I mot thy werk renewe,
> It to correcte and eek to rubbe and scrape;
> And al is thorugh thy negligence and rape.[1]

Though it is included in only one manuscript (Cambridge, Trinity College, R.3.20) and one early edition (Stowe's of 1561), the poem seems universally accepted as a genuine work of Chaucer, presumably addressed to an actual scribe—a conclusion supported implicitly by the reference to Chaucer's *Boece* and *Troylus* (2), as well as by the famous stanza in *Troilus* (V: 1793–98) expressing a similar concern about the copying of his text. The aim of the present article is to suggest a possible figurative overtone to this evident historical situation.

A short antifeminist poem sometimes entitled *Versus de femina*, possibly dating from the twelfth century and found in various forms in an extraordinary number of Continental manuscripts, usually begins with the lines,

> Arbore sub quadam dictavit clericus Adam,
> Quomodo primus Adam peccavit in arbore quadam.[2]

> [Beneath a certain tree, Adam the clerk wrote of how the
> first Adam sinned by means of a certain tree.]

The rest of the poem consists of a kind of litany in dispraise of women, each line beginning with the word *femina;* we may notice in passing that a frequent feature is a brief catalogue of famous men who were deceived by women, sometimes approximating the list of Adam, Sol-

omon, Samson, and David in *Sir Gawain and the Green Knight* (2416–
19).[3] In any case, this evidently popular picture of a *clericus Adam*
writing about the sin of the first Adam makes one wonder whether
Chaucer may not be playfully introducing a similar juxtaposition in his
warning to *Adam scriveyn:* "Look here, *clericus Adam,* you little bung-
ler, don't you disfigure *my* handiwork the way your namesake disfigured that of God!"

If some such comic allusion does indeed hover over the poem, it
would seem to rest ultimately on the parallel between the artist as
creator and God as Creator, summarized for example by Edgar De
Bruyne: "Considérons l'artiste lui-même. Certes, il œuvre à l'image de
Dieu. Comme Dieu, il se fait une représentation de la forme à réaliser."
[Let us consider the artist himself. Assuredly he creates after the likeness of God. Like God, he visualizes the form to be brought into
being.][4] This relationship between the artist and God, though less
fully developed in the Middle Ages than it was to become in the
Renaissance, does seem to have been popular enough to provide a basis
for the kind of allusion I am suggesting. As might be expected, it finds
its most emphatic expression in the Platonic tradition, beginning with
Macrobius' famous praise of Vergil in the *Saturnalia:*

"Quippe si mundum ipsum diligenter inspicias, magnam similitudinem
divini illius et huius poetici operis invenies. Nam qualiter eloquentia
Maronis ad omnium mores integra est, nunc brevis, nunc copiosa, nunc
sicca, nunc florida, nunc simul omnia, interdum lenis aut torrens: sic terra
ipsa hic laeta segetibus et pratis, ibi silvis et rupibus hispida, hic sicca
harenis, hic irrigua fontibus, pars vasto aperitur mari. . . ."
   Tunc Euangelus irridenti similis, "Bene," inquit, "opifici deo a rure
Mantuano poetam comparas."[5]

["Indeed if you carefully examine the world itself, you will find a great
resemblance between that divine work and this poetic one. For just as the
eloquence of Maro is perfect for the qualities of all things—now concise,
now copious, now jejune, now ornate, now all of them at once, at intervals
gentle or roaring—just so is the earth itself here pleasant with crops and
meadows, there rough with woods and rocks, here dry with sands, here
watered with springs, and part lies open to the boundless sea. . . ."
   Then said Evangelus like one mocking, "Well do you compare a poet
from rustic Mantua to God the creator."]

Still more explicit is a statement by Guillaume de Conches in his
commentary on the *Timaeus:*

Ut enim faber, volens aliquid fabricare, prius illud in mente disponit, postea, quesita materia, iuxta mentem suam operatur, sic Creator, antequam aliquid crearet, in mente illud habuit, deinde opere illud adimplevit.[6]

[For just as a craftsman wishing to fashion something first arranges it in his mind, then having obtained the material produces it according to his plan, so the Creator before he created anything had it in his mind, then completed it in deed.]

The idea is approximated by various other medieval writers, among them Ambrose and Aquinas.[7] The pattern I am suggesting might be supported in a more general way by the great medieval commonplace of God as author of the "book" of the world or nature.[8]

Further whimsical parallels between *Adam scriveyn* and his ultimate ancestor, though obviously not compelling enough to contribute much in the way of support, are perhaps worth mentioning as possible delicate extensions of the joke. For example the reference to Adam's *long lokkes* (3) might call to mind both fourteenth-century fashions and illustrations of the Fall; *the scalle* (3), literally "the scab," might suggest also the time-honored figure of the leprosy of sin bequeathed by the first Adam; and the phrase *after my makyng* (4), "in accord with my composing," might, I suppose, carry an overtone like "in accord with my creation (of you)." Finally, a tradition of Adam as the inventor of letters, though apparently far from a commonplace, seems to have had at least a sporadic currency in the Middle Ages; witness a thirteenth-century Saxon chronicle by Eike von Repgow, which reports in the original German, "Adam underdachte bochstave allererst" [Adam invented letters first of all], and in a Latin translation, "Adam primus adinuenit literas" [Adam first invented letters].[9] An awareness of such a piece of lore by Chaucer, if it can be admitted as a possibility, would add to the potential complexity of the overtone I have been suggesting.

It is of course difficult to propose a theme of this kind in scholarly form without seeming to load the little poem beyond what common sense tells us is its capacity. But if we can accept the possibility of a jocular identification of *Adam scriveyn* with *clericus Adam,* and through it a jocular though tradition-grounded comparison between the failures of this Adam and the original Adam, there seem to be two situations worth considering: one that Chaucer is addressing an unidentified scribe or perhaps scribes at large, and using "Adam" as a generic name; the other that he actually had a scribe named Adam and is capitalizing on the happy correspondence between his name and that of *clericus Adam*. Of the two possibilities, I strongly prefer the latter—partly because it seems implied by the title of the poem in the manuscript, but also because it produces still another example of Chaucer's comic tension between the actual and the typical or even symbolic, seen at its finest in the portraits of the General Prologue.[10]

NOTES

1. F. N. Robinson, ed., *The Works of Geoffrey Chaucer,* 2nd ed. (Boston: Houghton Mifflin, 1957), p. 534.

2. MS. Vat. Palat. lat. 719, f. 50^r. For further examples, references, and information, see Ludwig Bethmann, "Nachrichten über die . . . für die *Monumenta Germaniae Historica* benutzten Sammlungen von Handschriften and Urkunden Italiens, aus dem Jahre 1854," *Archiv der Gesellschaft für ältere deutsche Geschichtskunde,* 12 (1872), 341; W. Wattenbach, "Verse gegen die Weiber," *Anzeiger für Kunde der deutschen Vorzeit,* N.S. 20 (1873), 257–58; idem, "Mittheilungen aus zwei Handschriften der k. Hof- und Statsbibliothek," *Sitzungsberichte der philosophisch-philologischen und historischen Classe der k. b. Akademie der Wissenschaften zu München,* 3 (1873), 709; idem, "Nachricht von drei Handschriften in Eisleben," *Neues Archiv der Gesellschaft für ältere deutsche Geschichtskunde,* 8 (1883), 291; S. G. Owen, "A Medieval Latin Poem," *English Historical Review,* 2 (1887), 525–26; Carlo Pascal, *Letteratura latina medievale: Nuovi saggi e note critiche* (Catania: F. Battiato, 1909), pp. 107–10; and Paul Lehmann, *Die Parodie im Mittelalter,* 2nd ed. (Stuttgart: Anton Hiersemann, 1963), pp. 119–20. Versions of the poem are printed by Owen and Pascal.

3. See MS. Vat. Palat. lat. 719, f. 50^r, lines 6 ff.; Wattenbach, "Verse gegen die Weiber," cols. 257–58; Owen, "A Medieval Latin Poem," p. 525; and Pascal, *Letteratura latina medievale,* p. 109. A closer parallel, however, is an independent two-line tag quoted by Wattenbach, "Mittheilungen aus zwei Handschriften," p. 686: "Adam, Samsonem, si David, si Salomonem / femina decepit, quis modo tutus erit?" [If a woman deceived Adam, Samson, David, Solomon, who now will be safe?] For examples elsewhere, see R. W. King, "A Note on 'Sir Gawayn and the Green Knight,' 2414 ff.," *Modern Language Review,* 29 (1934), 435–36.

4. *L'Esthétique du Moyen Age* (Louvain: L'Institut Supérieur de Philosophie, 1947), p. 171; see also his *Études d'esthétique médiévale* (Bruges: De Tempel, 1946), III: 212–13, 316–17.

5. V: i, 19, and ii, 1, ed. James Willis, Bibl. Teubneriana, 2nd ed. (Leipzig: B. G. Teubner, 1970), p. 243. See also Ernst Robert Curtius, *European Literature and the Latin Middle Ages,* tr. Willard R. Trask (London: Routledge and Kegan Paul, 1953), pp. 443–45.

6. *Glosae super Platonem*, 32, on *Timaeus* 27d, ed. Édouard Jeauneau, Textes philosophiques du Moyen Age, 13 (Paris: J. Vrin, 1965), p. 99; note also his quotation from Guillaume's *Glosae super Macrobium*, I: ii, 14, ibid., p. 99 note c. For a discussion, see Winthrop Wetherbee, *Platonism and Poetry in the Twelfth Century: The Literary Influence of the School of Chartres* (Princeton: University Press, 1972), pp. 145–51; I am indebted to Professor Wetherbee personally for the quotation from Guillaume on the *Timaeus*, as well as for information on the subject generally.

7. Ambrose, *Hexaemeron*, I: vii, 27 (*PL* 14:137), answering the question of why God did not create and adorn the earth simultaneously: "Accedit illud, quod imitatores nos sui Deus esse voluit, ut primo faciamus aliqua, postea venustemus." [(This (reason) is added, namely that God wished us to be imitators of himself, so that first we make something and afterwards adorn it.] Aquinas, *ST* I, 14.8, *Opera omnia* Rome: S. C. de Propaganda Fide, 1882–1948), IV: 179: "Sic enim scientia Dei se habet ad omnes res creatas, sicut scientia artificis se habet ad artificiata. Scientia autem artificis est causa artificiatorum . . ." [For the knowledge of God is to all created things just as the knowledge of the artificer is to the products of his art. Now the knowledge of the artificer is the cause of his products . . .]; note also q. 17, a. 1 (ibid., IV: 218). A parallel between Chaucer the Creator and God the Creator in *Troilus* is suggested by Morton W. Bloomfield, "Distance and Predestination in *Troilus and Criseyde*," *PMLA*, 72 (1957), 22–23.

8. See for example Curtius, *European Literature*, pp. 321–22.

9. German, ed. Gesellschaft für ältere deutsche Geschichtskunde, *Sächsische Weltchronik*, in *Deutsche Chroniken und andere Geschichtsbücher des Mittelalters*, MGH: Scriptores qui vernacula lingua usi sunt, 2 (Hannover: Hahn, 1877), II: 69; German and Latin, ed. H. F. Massmann, *Das Zeitbuch des Eike von Repgow in ursprünglich niederdeutscher Sprache und in früher lateinischer Übersetzung*, Bibliothek des Litterarischen Vereins in Stuttgart, 42 (Stuttgart: Litterarische Verein, 1857), p. 15. I owe this reference to the generosity of Professor Arthur Groos of Cornell University. Note also Suidas, *Lexicon*, A 425, ed. Ada Adler, Lexicographi Graeci, 1 (Leipzig: B. G. Teubner, 1928), I: 44; and Augustine, *Quaestiones in Heptateuchum*, II: 69 (*PL* 34:620), who says that many people believe letters were begun "a primis hominibus" [by the first men], but concludes, "unde hoc probari possit, ignoro" [whence this is able to be proved, I do not know]. For summarizing accounts, see Theodor Bibliander, *De ratione communi omnium linguarum & literarum commentarius* (Zürich: Christopher Frosch, 1548), pp. 42–43; and Johann Albert Fabricius, *Codex pseudepigraphus Veteris Testamenti*, ch. I, "Adamus litterarum inventor" (Hamburg: Christian Liebezeit, 1713), pp. 1–2.

10. Since the completion of this article, a connection between *Adam scriveyn* and the original Adam has been suggested briefly by Russell A. Peck, "Public Dreams and Private Myths: Perspective in Middle English Literature," *PMLA*, 90 (1975), 467.

9

JAMES I. WIMSATT

Chaucer, Fortune, and Machaut's "Il m'est avis"

Though Amour is the predominating subject of Guillaume de Machaut's poetry, a substantial number of his works center on politics and morals, reflecting his public careers as courtier and clergyman. Among such poems is the vigorous and attractive balade, "Il m'est avis qu'il n'est dons de Nature," which decries the power held by Fortune and her friends in high places. Chaucer, it appears, knew "Il m'est avis" well, for he used it in five works in his presentations of Fortune and related discussion. He employed it successively in the *Book of the Duchess,* the translation of Boethius, the Merchant's Tale, *Fortune,* and *Lak of Stedfastnesse.* In identifying and elucidating Chaucer's use of "Il m'est avis," this essay provides fresh insight into the English poet's concept of Fortune and into his extraordinary ability to incorporate into his own work the images and expression of his predecessors. It also supports a point I have made before:[1] Chaucer did not turn his back on Machaut's work after he came to know the Italians; to the contrary, he continued to value and honor his French master's artistry right to 1400.

"Il m'est avis" is relatively prominent among Machaut's lyrics. It appears in eight of the best manuscript collections of his work, in five of them twice, both in the *Louange des dames* (an anthology which includes most of Machaut's lyrics not set to music) and among the *balades notées* with musical notation.[2] As is typical of the form the poem consists of three stanzas with the same rhyme sounds and with the last line of each stanza comprising the refrain. In accord with Machaut's practice, and in contrast to Deschamps's preference, there is no envoy. The lines are all decasyllabic except for the shorter fifth lines of the stanzas which have seven syllables; the rhyme scheme is ababccdD. The text of the poem and an analysis of its contents will provide a basis for discussing Chaucer's use of it:

> Il m'est avis, qu'il n'est dons de Nature,
> Com bons qu'il soit, que nulz prise à ce jour,
> Se la clarté tenebreuse et obscure

De Fortune ne li donne coulour;   4
   Ja soit ce que seürté
Ne soit en li, amour ne loyauté.
Mais je ne voy homme amé ne chieri,
Se Fortune ne le tient à ami.   8

Si bien ne sont fors vent et aventure,
Donné à faute et tolu par irour;
On la doit croire où elle se parjure,
Car de mentir est sa plus grand honneur.   12
   C'est .i. monstre envolepé
De boneür, plein de maleürté;
Car nuls n'a pris, tant ait de bien en li,
Se Fortune ne le tient à ami.   16

Si me merveil comment Raisons endure
Si longuement à durer ceste errour,
Car les vertus sont à desconfiture
Par les vices qui regnent com signour.   20
   Et qui vuet avoir le gré
De ceuls qui sont et estre en haut degré
Il pert son temps et puet bien dire: "Aymi!",
Se Fortune ne le tient à ami.   24

[I think there is no gift of Nature, however fine it may
be, that anyone esteems in this time unless the shadowy and
dark brightness of Fortune colors it, even though there is no
security in her, love nor loyalty. I never see a man loved nor
cherished if Fortune does not hold him as her friend.

Her goods are only wind and chance, given by mistake
and taken away in wrath. One should believe her where she
perjures herself, for lying is her greatest honor. She is a
monster covered with happiness, full of misery. No one is
valued, however much good he has in himself, if Fortune
does not hold him as her friend.

And I marvel how Reason allows this wrong to last so
long, for the virtues are discomfited by the vices who gov-
ern as lords. And he who wishes to have the favor of those
who are and will be in high station, he wastes his time and
may well say "Aymi!" if Fortune does not hold him as her
friend.]

A moralistic commentary in the tradition of the sirvente on the
shallowness of the current values of society, this balade is based mostly
on the first two books of Boethius' *Consolation of Philosophy*.[3] In other
poems, especially the long *Remede de Fortune,* Machaut makes broad use

of the *Consolation* and shows that he was conversant with the argument of the whole work;[4] therefore one cannot impute to Machaut the poet the incomplete reasoning of the balade's complaining narrator. The work is dramatically conceived; as with Boethius in Books I and II, so with the narrator, his emotional involvement in the situation makes him insusceptible to profound explanations.

In the first two stanzas the deceptions of Fortune provide the theme; the figurative language emphasizes the discrepancy between appearance and substance. In the first stanza the narrator claims that in order to be valued in the world one must color over his native gifts, those of Nature, with the attraction of Fortune's benefits. As with Alain de Lille's goddess Natura, "Nature" here signifies the force which creates and sustains the universe—the heavens and earth, and notably man. Fortune's "colors," of course, are imparted by such things as wealth, honor, power, luxury, and fame, whose transience and lack of worth Lady Philosophy treats particularly in Book II of the *Consolation* and Machaut's narrator proclaims in the second stanza. He further asserts there that it is only in lying that Fortune is true; this is a corollary to one of the more familiar commonplaces that originates in the *Consolation*, that it is only in changing that Fortune is constant (II Prose 1).

In the final stanza another cosmic abstraction is introduced with the narrator's marveling that Reason permits Fortune to control matters so that evil rules over good. One infers that like Boethius' Lady Philosophy and like Reason in the *Roman de la Rose*, Reason here represents truth itself as well as the faculty one uses to arrive at truth. The puzzlement of the narrator, then, concerns how the triumph of vice is conformable to the divine matrix of existence, and it is closely related to Boethius' questioning (I Meter 5) why God, who controls all things in due order and season, fails only to regulate the works of man. Lady Philosophy, of course, discusses at length the fallacy of this assumption, asserting the true situation definitively in the climactic Meter 9 of Book III: "O qui perpetua mundum ratione gubernas terrarum caelique sator" [O thou that dost the world in lasting order guide, Father of heaven and earth].[5] The focus of Machaut's balade, however, is on the ills of the world, not on theodicy, and his poem ends with no justification of God but with a reiteration of the refrain, which is a variation on the familiar Boethian theme of the friends of Fortune. In its assertion that Fortune's friendship is necessary if a person is to be loved and esteemed by the world, the refrain accords with Philosophy's statement, made in the course of applying her lighter remedies, that Fortune when she departs takes her friends with her and leaves her former favorite with only his true friends.

As with the ideas expressed, the images of "Il m'est avis" are mostly indebted to the *Consolation*. The "dark brightness" of Fortune (3) no doubt is inspired by the oxymorons that became part of the poetic baggage of the goddess,[6] which in turn reflect Boethius' characterization of Fortune, as when he identifies her as a "prodigy" (II Prose 1), a thing like an oxymoron incompatible with nature. The adjectives "tenebreuse" and "obscure" (3) are related to the epithet "cloudy" ("nubila") that Boethius applies to Fortune (I Meter 1) and recall the use of light and dark imagery throughout the *Consolation* to identify good and bad, truth and confusion. They also may be inspired by the originally bright clothes of Philosophy which have been, in Chaucer's words, "duskid and dirked, as it is wont to dirken besmokede ymages" (I Prose 1). Though used in the *Consolation* to describe Fortune's stable contrary, the figures both of colored cloth and the painted images presented in the passage reappear in Machaut's and Chaucer's depictions of Fortune elsewhere. The passage in Boethius that is the origin of Machaut's calling Fortune a "monstre" (13) also involves reference to color—dyes—suggesting a picture or a robe. Lady Philosophy speaks of the "manifold dyes" ("multiformes... fucos") of "that prodigy" ("illius prodigii"). Machaut's "monstre" evidently stems from "prodigii," and his Fortune's concealment under "boneur" from the deceptive dyes which cover her true nature.

Though Machaut's "Il m'est avis" of itself is a fine poem, and well illustrates that his lyrics are much better than is generally thought, the foregoing analysis particularly aims at making Chaucer's use of the balade recognizable and comprehensible. Chaucer drew on it both before and after he translated the *Consolation*, and his *Boece* as well reflects the balade's language. For the *Book of the Duchess* and the Merchant's Tale he makes use of its imagery of Fortune, and for *Fortune* and *Lak of Stedfastnesse* he also uses its thought content and social commentary.

In the *Book of the Duchess* the Black Knight's extensive portrait of Fortune and denunciation of her is drawn alternately from the *Roman de la Rose* and several works of Machaut, the *Remede de Fortune*, Motet VIII, the Latin Motet IX, and the balade "Il m'est avis," all of them previously identified except for the last.[7] Chaucer's use of the balade, contained in the following passage, is closely intertwined with his employment of Motet VIII:

> An ydole of fals portrayture
> Ys she, for she wol sone wrien;
> She is the monstres hed ywrien,
> As fylthe over-ystrawed with floures.

Hir moste worshippe and hir flour ys
To lyen, for that ys hyr nature.
(626–31)

The first line is directly translated from Motet VIII in which Fortune is said to be "Une ydole ... de fausse pourtraiture" (9), an image that seems to fuse Boethius' besmoked picture and his dyes of the unnatural prodigy. The couplet immediately preceding in the motet, moreover, is certainly related to Chaucer's image of flower-covered filth:

C'est fiens couvers de riche couverture,
Qui dehors luist et dedens est ordure.
(7–8)

[(Fortune) is a fiend covered with rich clothing, who gleams without and is filth within.]

This clothing which deceives in covering was no doubt suggested to Machaut in part by Philosophy's statement (II Prose 1) that Fortune, who "veils" herself yet to others ("sese adhuc velat aliis"), has revealed herself wholly to Boethius.

But the Black Knight's whited-sepulchre image (Matthew 23:24) also is indebted to the equally Boethian "monstre envolepé de boneur" (13) of "Il m'est avis," as is strongly suggested by his use of the word "monster," and is confirmed by the close correspondence of the previous line of the balade to the Black Knight's lines that immediately follow; "Hir moste worshippe ... ys / To lyen" clearly renders "Car de mentir est sa plus grand honneur" (12).

The use of "Il m'est avis" in the *Duchess*, while confined to these lines, seems quite certain and establishes that Chaucer knew the balade early in his career. As with the Black Knight's entire discussion of Fortune, the Boethian content of the passage is derived through Machaut with no apparent direct reflection of the *Consolation*. When Chaucer later came to translate Boethius, moreover, he again recalled and used Machaut's wording. Thus, echoing the balade's rendering of "multiformes illius prodigii fucos" (II Prose 1), Chaucer translates, "the felefolde *colours* and desceytes of thilke merveylous *monstre*" (italics mine). "Monster" in the sense "prodigy," evidently brought into the English language in the *Duchess*,[8] is repeated here; and Chaucer also adopts Machaut's poetical "colours" for "fucos," finding it desirable to add as gloss "desceytes," which conveys the prosaic sense favored by other translators.[9]

In the Merchant's Tale, no doubt much later, in a fine ironic apostrophe to Fortune Chaucer revives the monster with her deceptive colors. After elaborating the figure of the scorpion that he had first used in the *Duchess,* he makes Fortune explicitly a painter:

> O sodeyn hap! o thou Fortune unstable!
> Lyk to the scorpion so deceyvable,
> That flaterest with thyn heed whan thou wolt stynge;
> Thy tayl is deeth, thurgh thyn envenymynge.
> O brotil joye! o sweete venym queynte!
> O monstre, that so subtilly kanst peynte
> Thy yiftes under hewe of stidefastnesse,
> That thou deceyvest bothe moore and lesse!
>
> (IV: 2057–64)

As in the Machaut balade, where Fortune "gives color" to the "gifts" of Nature, here she "paints" her own "gifts." The similarity of the actions and the wording indicates that the balade as well as *Boece* and the *Book of the Duchess* lies behind these lines. "Monster," of course, is used in all three Chaucer works, with "Il m'est avis" the ultimate origin.

A second Machaut balade, "Langue poignant, aspre, amere, et ague," which in most manuscripts is separated from "Il m'est avis" only by a short rondel on Fortune, is a source for the scorpion image in the Merchant's Tale. In this poem the narrator states of a certain slanderous lady, using terms that identify her with the scorpion,

> Sa fausseté n'est pas bien congneüe,
> Car par semblant aucune fois elle oint;
> Mais elle point, envenime et partue
> Souvent celi qui près de li la joint.
>
> (15–18)[10]

> [Her deceit is not well known, for it always seems that
> she anoints; but she often stings, envenoms, and absolutely
> kills him who comes close to her.]

The scorpion's successive flattering, stinging, envenoming, and killing in the Merchant's Tale finds a complete counterpart in this passage.[11]

Machaut's phrase "donne coulour" in "Il m'est avis" evidently led to Chaucer's verb "paint" in the Tale, with the particular choice of words probably dictated by the exigencies of rhyme. The introduction of the word "paint" into the development described here perhaps helped suggest the usual manuscript title of Chaucer's triple balade *Fortune,*

"Balade de visage sans peinture," which has an interesting set of potential meanings and implications. Walter W. Skeat doubtless is right that the "visage" to be displayed is Fortune's "doutous or double visage" spoken of in *Boece* (II Prose 1), as well as the "doutous visages" of false friends (II Prose 8).[12] "Peinture," like "fucos," implies illusion or deceit, a meaning well attested in both cases,[13] so that to show the faces without "peinture" is to display them with no deception. "Fucus," however, has a potential meaning which Chaucer and Machaut had not previously drawn on that probably also enters into the title.[14] In origin a plant from which red dye is extracted, "fucus" by transference came to signify the dye itself. Since one of the uses of the dye was as a cosmetic, the word was early generalized into a term for face paint—rouge—just as in a different development it had become a generic term for deception.[15] In *Boece,* where "fucos" is rendered as the "doutous colours or deceytes" of Fortune, the notion of rouge is not suggested, nor is it in the images of color in Machaut's balade and the Merchant's Tale; in these it is a question of color imparted to gifts rather than put on the goddess herself. But with the "visage sans peinture" it is hard to avoid the inference that Fortune is a strumpet who is to be presented without her usual heavy application of face paint. This meaning is made the more likely by the use of the verb "paint" to signify rouging in Chaucer's time,[16] and by the fact that one may readily apply the sense "false complexion" to the word "color" when it is applied to the goddess in the body of the poem: "Thou knewe wel the deceit of hir colour" (21). The meaning "complexion" for "color" is found several times elsewhere in Chaucer's writings.[17]

The *Consolation* and Machaut's balade are not only important for the development of the title; they also are sources for the substance of *Fortune.* Boethius surely is the main source of the poem, as most scholars, despite Shirley's report that the work is translated from the French, have recognized.[18] But that is not to say that French works did not also supply basic precedents. The French title and rubrics—"Le Pleintif countre Fortune," "La respounse de Fortune au Pleintif," etc.—suggest a French background. There is even a French line in the poem, "Jay tout perdu mon temps et mon labour" (7),[19] to lend additional color to Shirley's claim. One certain important French influence is the *Roman de la Rose,* the source of several significant passages.[20] However, like the *Consolation* the *Rose* provides a lengthy, discursive treatment of the concept Fortune, and one looks for precedents to Chaucer's triple balade that supply nearer approaches to its compact statement.

Aage Brusendorff thought that two complementary balades by Deschamps comprised Shirley's "French source."[21] The first of these is a statement by Franche-Voulenté [Free-Will] asserting the individual's ability to counter Fortune through impassive fortitude, and the second is a reply by Fortune to Franche-Voulenté's complaints against her. There are notable similarities in general plan. Chaucer's first balade is, like Deschamps's, a Stoic declaration of self-sufficiency. The refrains in particular express this sentiment; compare Deschamps's "Franc cuer ne puet de son siege mouvoir" [(Fortune) cannot move the free heart from its place][22] with Chaucer's "For fynally, Fortune, I thee defye!" (8, 16, 24). With both sets of balades, moreover, Fortune's response concludes with an unexpected admission of the superiority of eternal good to Fortune. The statements in the final stanzas are particularly similar, with Deschamps's last three lines presenting the strongest likeness to Chaucer:

> Le bien parfait, souverain doit avoir,
> Car souvent font vains biens, dont c'est pité,
> Lasche et moul cuer de son siege mouvoir.
>   (22–24)

> [(The free heart) ought to have perfect, sovereign good,
> but it is a pity that useless goods often move the slothful
> and soft heart from its place.]

Chaucer's statement more dramatically but quite similarly deplores misguided souls, scorns the world's goods, and asserts the superiority of the heavenly:

> Ye blinde bestes, ful of lewednesse!
> The hevene hath propretee of sikernesse,
> This world hath ever resteles travayle.
>   (68–70)

Several factors suggest, however, that Chaucer's use of Deschamps's pair of balades is by no means certain: there are numerous other precedents for the dialogue with Fortune;[23] verbal parallels, generally found in Chaucer's sources, are lacking; and there is the lively possibility that, if there is a direct relationship, the line of influence goes from the English to the French, as it does in at least one notable case with Chaucer and Froissart.[24] The question, then, remains open.

Another Deschamps balade, appropriately entitled "Les amis de Fortune," is suggested as Chaucer's source by Howard R. Patch.[25] Again, however, there are no notable verbal correspondences, and, what is more, Deschamps is heavily indebted in this work to the Machaut balade, "Il m'est avis," which we have been discussing.[26] "Il m'est avis" itself is much more certainly a direct source for the first balade of *Fortune.* The dramatic situation admittedly differs; while Machaut's narrator complains about the times from the standpoint of an objective social commentator, Chaucer's speaker in the first balade flings down the gauntlet to Fortune, defying her to her face, apparently in reaction to a personal calamity. There nevertheless are specific parallels in phraseology which confirm a real relationship between the poems. One full line in *Fortune,* "And that hir moste worshipe is to lye" (22), reproduces even more exactly than the Black Knight does in the *Book of the Duchess* (630–31) Machaut's "Car de mentir est sa plus grand honneur" (12). Moreover, Chaucer chooses as his major rhyme in the first balade (for twelve of twenty-four lines) the sound -*our,* which duplicates an important rhyme in the French balade (six rhymes), the correspondence extending in three cases to full words: "honour," "errour," and "colour" (*Fortune,* 2, 4, 21; "Il m'est avis," 12, 18, 4). The like use of "colour," in the light of the discussion here, appears especially significant. It is perhaps indicative too that the "mirour" of Fortune supplies a fourth of these rhyme words in Chaucer's poem since this uncommon figure probably is derived from Machaut's *Remede de Fortune,* where it is employed in a similar Boethian context.[27]

Underlying the verbal parallel between the first balade of Fortune and "Il m'est avis" is a pervasive comparable indebtedness to the thought of Boethius, which is based on the narrator's sharing the misapprehensions about Providence that Boethius expresses in the first part of the *Consolation.* The poems similarly derive viewpoint, structure, imagery, and thought from Boethius. Particularly similar is their notion of Fortune's rule in the world, well epitomized in Chaucer's first four lines:

> This wrecched worldes transmutacioun,
> As wele or wo, now povre and now honour,
> Withouten ordre or wys discrecioun
> Governed is by Fortunes errour.

The idea of the ascendancy of Fortune is relevant to the whole of Machaut's balade, but we may particularly recall for comparison here the beginning of the last stanza:

Si me merveil comment Raisons endure
Si longuement à durer ceste errour,
Car les vertus sont à desconfiture
Par les vices qui regnent com signour.
(17–20)

In both cases the erring forces of Fortune are seen as ruling in defiance of order and reason; the only solution to such a situation is that proclaimed by Chaucer's narrator, Stoic defiance. Of course the solution is based on a mistaken notion of the cosmos, and Chaucer in his two subsequent balades rubs more paint off Fortune's face and goes on to assert eternal Providence, as Machaut does not; the French poem is not designed to probe further Boethian depths. The parallels mentioned nevertheless make "Il m'est avis" a candidate for the French model Shirley referred to, at least for the first balade.[28]

Taking all factors into account, *Fortune* has stronger connections with "Il m'est avis" than any other work of Chaucer; but there is a Chaucer poem that is more like the Machaut lyric in its limited aim of commenting on the times, *Lak of Stedfastnesse*. Although Fortune does not enter explicitly into this Chaucer balade, there is probably an indebtedness to the Machaut lyric. The debt is suggested in the refrain, "Al is lost for lak of stedfastnesse," which implies the rule of unstable Fortune proclaimed in the Machaut refrain, and it more specifically appears in the correspondences between the third stanzas in the two poems where man's injustice to his fellows, his attention to worldly goods, the failure of reason, and the discomfiture of virtue entailed by the reign of vice are similarly decried:

Trouthe is put doun, resoun is holden fable;
Vertu hath now no dominacioun;
Pitee exyled, no man is merciable;
Through coveytyse is blent discrecioun.
The world hath mad a permutacioun
Fro right to wrong, fro trouthe to fikelnesse,
That al is lost for lak of stedfastnesse.
(15–21)

Between the final stanzas there is a similarity in thought and viewpoint that extends to the manner and details of expression.

The *Book of the Duchess* was Chaucer's first long original poem. *Lak of Stedfastnesse* is entitled by Shirley, "Balade Royal made by our laureal poete of Albyon in hees laste yeeres." From the beginning to the end, then, Chaucer made use of Machaut's "Il m'est avis, qu'il n'est dons de

Nature." Along the way he drew on it for the translation of Boethius, the Merchant's Tale, and *Fortune*. He clearly apprehended the work at its various levels: its images appear especially in the *Book of the Duchess* and the Merchant's Tale, its philosophical language in *Boece,* and its viewpoint and social comment in *Lak of Stedfastnesse*. All of these aspects enter into *Fortune*. In all of his uses of it Chaucer puts "Il m'est avis" to meaningful employment. In the *Duchess* its imagery serves in the presentation of Fortune as a visual and moral foil to Fair White; in the Merchant's Tale it tellingly assists the irony; in *Boece* the terminology of Machaut aids definition of Fortune and her deceit; and in *Lak of Stedfastnesse* the indignant social critic finds in the Frenchman's words language expressive of his country's present distress. In *Fortune* "Il m'est avis" helps provide a firm basis for developing the philosophical statement of the second and third balades. Thus, while the influences on Chaucer's poetry obviously multiply tremendously from the 1360s to 1400, the persistent reappearance of this single poem as an influence in his work provides proof—limited but not negligible—that Chaucer knew well and never outgrew or disdained the poetry of his first master, Guillaume de Machaut.

NOTES

1. I have asserted Machaut's continuing influence recently in "Chaucer and French Poetry," *Geoffrey Chaucer,* ed. Derek Brewer (London: Bell, 1974), pp. 109–36; in "Guillaume de Machaut and Chaucer's *Troilus and Criseyde,"* *Medium Aevum,* 45 (1976), 277–93; and in "Guillaume de Machaut and Chaucer's Love Lyrics," *Medium Aevum,* 47 (1978).
2. My discussion of "Il m'est avis, qu'il n'est dons de Nature" is based on a full collation of the extant manuscripts. Since there are no manuscript variants that bear significantly on Chaucer's employment of the poem, the text presented follows the better and more available edition, *La Louange des dames,* ed. Nigel Wilkins (New York: Barnes and Noble, 1972), p. 74 (musical notation, pp. 139–41). The texts of almost all of Machaut's short poems are edited by V.-F. Chichmaref, *Guillaume de Machaut: Poésies lyriques,* 2 vols. (Paris: Champion, 1909). "Il m'est avis" is his CLXXXVIII.
3. Though we might expect a follower in the tradition of the *Roman de la Rose* like Machaut to employ Jean de Meun's long Boethian passage on Fortune, there is little if any debt in "Il m'est avis."
4. For the use of Boethius in RF see the discussion by Ernest Hoepffner, ed., *Œuvres de Guillaume de Machaut,* Société des anciens textes français, II (Paris: Firmin-Didot, 1911), xix–xxxii.

5. The Latin text of the *Consolation* is quoted herein from H. F. Stewart and E. K. Rand, eds., *Boethius,* Loeb Classical Library (Boston: Harvard U. Press, 1918), pp. 128–411. The translation is that of "I. T.," used in this Loeb edition. I later quote Chaucer's own *Boece.* All citations of Chaucer's works herein are from F. N. Robinson, ed., *The Works of Geoffrey Chaucer,* 2nd ed. (Boston: Houghton Mifflin, 1957).

6. See Howard R. Patch, *The Goddess Fortuna in Mediaeval Literature* (Cambridge, Mass.: Harvard U. Press, 1927), pp. 55–57.

7. For a summary of the sources, aside from "Il m'est avis," of Chaucer's portrait of Fortune in BD 618–78, see James I. Wimsatt, *Chaucer and the French Love Poets,* U. of North Carolina Studies in Comparative Literature, 43 (Chapel Hill: U. of North Carolina Press, 1968), pp. 158–59.

8. See the *Oxford English Dictionary,* ed. James A. H. Murray et al., 12 vols. (Oxford: Clarendon, 1933), s.v. *monster.* The only use of the word in any sense recorded in *OED* as occurring earlier than Chaucer's is in *Cursor Mundi* (c. 1300).

9. Chaucer's only uses of "color" elsewhere in *Boece* (I Prose 1; Meter 5) translate Latin "color." Were it not for Machaut's model Chaucer might well have rendered "fucos" as "deceytes" only, in line with I. T.'s (1609) "illusions" and the "wrenches and wiles" of John Walton (c. 1510; *De Consolatione Philosophiae,* ed. Mark Science, EETS, O.S. 170 [London: Oxford U. Press, 1927], p. 61).

10. *Louange,* ed. Wilkins, p. 80.

11. Machaut's Motet IX, which evidently is the primary source for the scorpion image in BD 636–41 (See George L. Kittredge, "Guillaume de Machaut and *The Book of the Duchess,*" *PMLA,* 30 [1915], 11), does not offer a comparable parallel to the imagery in the Merchant's Tale. Moreover, the word "envenime" in the balade (17), not found in Motet IX, suggests that the balade contributed to BD ("envenyme," 641) as well as to the Merchant's Tale.

12. *The Works of Geoffrey Chaucer,* 2nd ed. (Oxford: Clarendon Press, 1899), I: 542–43.

13. See Frédéric Godefroy, *Dictionnaire de l'ancienne langue française,* 10 vols. (Paris: Bouillon, 1881–1902), s.v. *peinture;* and Charlton T. Lewis and Charles Short, *A Latin Dictionary* (Oxford: Clarendon Press, 1879), s.v. *fucus,* III.

14. I assume that "fucus" was for Chaucer a conscious origin of the notion of Fortune the painter, an assumption which in the light of the tradition discussed and Chaucer's superlatively retentive mind seems fairly safe.

15. See Lewis and Short, s.v. *fucus,* II: B.

16. See *OED,* s.v. *paint,* 4, for examples of "paint" in the sense "to rouge" in *Cursor Mundi* and Wyclif. The same sense occurs in the Squire's Tale, V: 560–61; *Romaunt,* 1020; and perhaps in *Legend of Good Women,* 875.

17. See John S. P. Tatlock and Arthur G. Kennedy, *A Concordance to the Complete Works of Geoffrey Chaucer* (Washington: Carnegie Inst., 1927), s.v. *color.*

18. Tending to confirm its primary Boethian affiliations, *Fortune* occurs in the text of *Boece* after II Meter 5 in the manuscript most relied on by editors of the lyric, Cambridge University Library II.3.21.

19. The line evidently comes from a popular song; the Parson, I: 248, refers to the "newe Frenshe song, *Jay tout perdu mon temps et mon labour.*"

20. Cf. especially Skeat's notes, I: 544–46.

21. *The Chaucer Tradition* (London: Humphrey Milford, 1925), pp. 242–43.

22. *Œuvres complètes de Eustache Deschamps,* ed. Le Marquis de Queux de Saint-Hilaire (Paris: Firmin Didot, 1878–1903), II: 140–42.

23. Other works with such a dialogue include the *Consolation* itself, the *Roman de la Rose,* Boccaccio's *De Casibus,* and *Remede de Fortune.* For the last two, see Robinson's headnote, p. 860.

24. See James I. Wimsatt, "The *Dit dou Bleu Chevalier:* Froissart's Imitation of Chaucer," *Mediaeval Studies,* 34 (1972), 388–400.

25. Deschamps, *Œuvres complètes,* I (1878), 289–90. Patch, "Chaucer and Lady Fortune, *Modern Language Review,* 22 (1927), 381n.

26. The nearness of Deschamps's refrain, "Au jour d'ui n'est ami que de Fortune," to Machaut's refrain in "Il m'est avis" is indicative of the overall debt.

27. Hoepffner, ed., *Œuvres,* II: 2705–07; see also Hoepffner's Introduction, II: xxvii, for the origin of the idea.

28. Machaut does not present a formally connected series of poems on Fortune like Chaucer's and Deschamps's, but the rondel which follows "Il m'est avis" in most manuscripts of the *Louange,* "Helas! pour ce que Fortune m'est dure" (ed. Wilkins, *Louange,* p. 109), deals again with Fortune, and in it the theme of the friends of Fortune is prominent as it is in Chaucer's second and third balade in *Fortune.*

10

J. A. W. BENNETT

Some Second Thoughts
on *The Parlement of Foules*

I begin[1] with Chaucer's description of the *Somnium Scipionis:* "chapitres sevene it hadde, of hevene and helle."[2] In fact, neither Cicero nor Macrobius wrote in chapters or said anything about hell; classical texts were not divided into chapters in our sense until the seventeenth century; but it would be true to say that in the *Somnium* are seven main *capitula* or themes: (1) the common profit, (2) the afterlife, (3) the view of the present life *sub specie aeternitatis,* (4) the nine spheres and their music, (5) the immortality of the soul, (6) the punishment of the wicked, and (7) the restoration of all things—at the end of the Great Platonic year: a topic that attracted Christian readers, who found warrant for it in the Apocalypse and in St. Peter's reference to the restitution of all things (Acts 3:21). Cicero's reference to purgatorial pain (IX: 2, reproduced in PF 80) suggested hell to medieval readers; but the most that Macrobius does—expansive though he generally is—is to refer to the infernal regions (I: xi, 5), though in a sense rather different from Dante's. In his description of the *Somnium,* as in *The House of Fame* 918, Chaucer is actually following Jean De Meun:

> Si con fist Scipio [sic] jadis
> veit enfer et paradis[3]

[As Scipio did formerly, he sees hell and paradise].

Jean's mention of paradise is equally distant from Cicero's thought: Cicero's heaven had nothing material about it. But there was a real likeness between Cicero's view of the relation of this little earth to the vast heavens and the Christian or scriptural view which was determined at one point by the Psalmist: "When I consider the heavens . . . the sun, moon, and stars that man hast ordained. . . . What is man, that thou art mindful of him . . . ?" (Ps. 8:2) and at another point by St. Paul (2 Cor. 5:1): "If our house of this tabernacle be dissolved . . . we have a tabernacle immortal in the heavens"—which Chaucer alludes to in the Knight's Tale, I: 2809.

Dante had given sublime expression to the sense of perspective induced by this contrast between earth and the heavens by drawing on Lucan's account of the ascent of Pompey's soul.[4] Boccaccio had followed him—more decorously than he sometimes did when imitating his master—when he came to the death of Arcite. Chaucer, coming to the death of Troilus, followed all three; and when he passes over the fate of Arcite's soul in the Knight's Tale, he uses terms reminiscent of this reference to the *Somnium* in the PF:

> Therfore I stynte, I nam no divinistre;
> Of soules fynde I nat in this registre;
> (I: 2811–12)

i.e., there is nothing about souls in the register of contents—the chapter heads—of the book he is following: a metaphorical way of indicating that he does not intend to raise the question—though the metaphor is one more suitable for a scholar than a knight. The Knight continues:

> Ne me ne list thilke opinions to telle
> Of hem, though that they writen wher they dwelle.
> (I: 2813–14)

The allusion would cover just such writers as Cicero and Macrobius; *dwelle* is the very term that Chaucer uses of souls at PF 33 and 51.

Certainly the Knight's words are not to be construed as flippant or cynical. All his life Chaucer remained curious about the fate of the soul of the heathen, righteous or otherwise: it was in fact almost a preoccupation of many fourteenth-century thinkers, arising from their concern with the doctrine of predestination. In *Troilus* Chaucer will go out of his way, when describing the death of Hector, to say:

> The fate wolde his soule sholde unbodye
> And shapen hadde a mene it out to dryve.
> (V: 1550–51)

There is no equivalent to these lines in Boccaccio, and Chaucer seems to have invented the verb *unbody* for the occasion: it is only used again by his contemporary admirer Thomas Usk, of unhappy memory.

All Christian *auctores* agreed that the soul did not die; but they remained uncertain about the fate of the virtuous heathen, as readers of Langland and Duns Scotus know. Statius, in the *Thebaid*, had

suggested that the soul of a good man could at death immediately be
wafted up to the throne of Jupiter. Statius passed in one tradition for a
Christian;[5] and Statius' account of the death of Menaeceus in *Thebaid*
(x: 781) is indeed "strangely like" that of the death of Roland in
Chanson de Roland 2397: "Morz est Rollant, Deus en ad l'anme es cels"
[Roland is dead, God has his soul in heaven]. One of the difficulties
that medievals found in Virgil was just this difference between Christian and pagan views of the destiny of the soul. As Gavin Douglas put
it, Virgil "admittis that queynt philosophy / haldis sawlys hoppys fra
body to body,"[6] i.e., he saw Virgil as a Pythagorean. So when Douglas
comes to *Aeneid* VI, he extols him as a high philosopher but has to
admit that the Roman poet fails on this score:

> I say nocht all hys warkis beyn perfyte,
> Nor that sawlys turnys in othir bodeys agane,
> Thocht we traste, and may preif be haly write,
> Our sawle and body sal anys togidder remane.
>   (129–32)

Scipio's teaching in the *Somnium* became complete neoplatonism as
Macrobius developed it, almost approaching gnosticism. The body, in
this doctrine, is treated as the prison of the soul: which was never
orthodox Christian belief, though it can be found in some Christian
writers (not, however, in the Greek patristic tradition). Marvell's *Dialogue* expresses the resultant tension. I do not think Chaucer ever put
this semi-gnostic doctrine on Christian lips—though it comes to mind
when Theseus speaks of Arcite's death as an escape from "the foule
prison of this life." It must have been profoundly disturbing to a poet
so aware of the visible world as he was. Small wonder, then, that when
he found it, or thought he found it, in such a highly regarded text as
the *Somnium,* he put down the book "fulfild of thought and busy
hevinesse" (89)—"busy" implying a throng of disturbing reflections.
In chapters X to XII of Book I of the Commentary, Macrobius had
indeed given much attention to the various views of philosophers on
the nature and fate of the soul, noting that some thought souls went at
death to the "infernal regions" (considered to begin with the galaxy
mentioned by Chaucer at 56); whilst others ("the Platonists") said the
departed souls dwell in the region between the moon and the earth.
Neither view fitted easily into Christian belief. Hence, if the "certeyn
thing" that Chaucer was striving to learn was some satisfying doctrine
of the future life and the relation of this world to the next, he might

well have said, as he does at 90–91, that he "hadde thing that I nolde, and eke nadde thing that I wolde."

The question of the fate of heathen souls had always attracted intellectuals, notably Abelard, who quotes a large part of the relevant passage in Macrobius both in his *Theologia Christiana* and his *Sic et Non*. Neither Abelard nor his successors thought that Revelation had settled such questions once for all. They came up repeatedly (as in Macrobius) in any discussion of the ethics of self-murder, a matter of some concern to poets who treated of stories—abundant in Ovid—in which heroes or heroines regularly committed suicide, like Dido. Pyramus, Thisbe, and Cleopatra are listed in this very poem (228 ff., where Chaucer—unlike Boccaccio—is quick to remind us "in what plyt they dyde" 294). One of the reasons why Macrobius was acceptable to the medievals was that, like Cicero, he argued *against* suicide.

Thanks to the dominance of such weighty scenes in the *Somnium*, the mood of the opening passage of the *Parlement*, which paraphrases it, is a mood of unease, uncertainty, "heaviness." It is not the mood that a reading of Macrobius would necessarily produce; it results rather from the poet's preoccupation with the search for a doctrine that he has not found in his "olde bokes." But this makes for a sharper contrast with the compensatory dream that follows, which is of the earth earthy, though it yields paradisal sights and scenes and sounds. The initial mood is sober if not sad: when the dreamer closes his book, night is falling, the lifegiving sun has sunk, good things of day begin to droop and drowse, birds and beasts are forced to cease their activities (*besynesse* 86). But when at the end of the poem the scenes in Nature's garden are played out, all is changed. Now the birds are busy rejoicing that the reviving sun has driven away "the longe nihtes blake." We end in a springtime world, with birds in flight and eager song; the poet, refreshed by his sleep and heartened by his dream, turns eagerly and hopefully to study other books in the morning light. We have moved from a neo-platonic cosmogony to a scholastic world-view, tinged with all the exuberance of the Paris schools that generated the vision of Jean de Meun. The austere heavenly mentor of the opening is replaced by the benign and saintly—if shadowy—Valentine, who is like all saints a mediatory figure. He is present in heaven (accepted into the divine cosmogony): "that art ful *hye on-lofte*" (683), yet not removed from terrestrial concerns. In the Ciceronian-platonic view, the world was "ful of torment and of harde grace"; bliss was to be found solely in the heaven of the pure souls (76–77). In the waking scene at the close, the birds are blissful as they hymn the sun and the saint. The decorum of the poem, which is primarily classical in its reference, forbids any direct allusion to the Christian theogony. But the very shadowiness of Bishop Valentine permits the introduction of his name as a pointer to the heavenly bliss that the bird-song, however distantly, anticipates.

If this reversal of mood resembles the change that takes place between the end of Book I of the *House of Fame* and the middle of Book II, it is because the two poems share a common starting point: the *House of Fame* is in part a parody or offset of the *Somnium*. Scipio's celestial journey provides a model for the dreamer's own dream journey through the ethereal regions—though he gets no farther than Fame's temple. But the emphasis is very different. Whereas the lesson of the *Somnium*, as Chaucer construes it in the *Parlement*, is that we should not in the world delight, the *House of Fame* is flooded with ecstatic pleasure in the visible universe:

> "O God!" quod y, "that made Adam,
> Moche ys thy myght and thy noblesse!"
> (970–71)

This is the Christian God who looked on his creation and saw that it was very good. Chaucer's *sweven* stands in antithesis to Scipio's austere classical dream. But all was grist that came to his mill, or, as he says in the *House of Fame* 2139–40:

> For al mot out, other late or rathe,
> Alle the sheves in the lathe.

In the *Parlement* the poet professes to have found in the *Somnium* what he did not need, and to have failed to find what he looked for. But in due course he was to make use of the pattern of the *Somnium* for his different purposes in the longer poem.

His deep and patient scrutiny of the *Somnium* and its commentary is explicable if we bear in mind that it was one of the basic texts of the Christian Middle Ages. Long before St. Thomas had christianized Aristotle, ascetical writers had converted Cicero. The stoic elements in his philosophy, as in Seneca's, were particularly malleable: the despisal of worldly goods, the conception of divine rewards and punishments— these were wholly acceptable to Christian thought. In the eleventh century we find such a powerful spiritual writer as Gerbert alluding warmly to Cicero, as to Seneca. Macrobius ran second only to Boethius—and gave much more attention to natural phenomena. It is noteworthy that these are the only two philosophical texts that Chaucer chose to summarize or translate. And Macrobius kept his prestige till the sixteenth century—partly because of the Ciceronian base, for the Renascence favored Ciceronian style and Ciceronian themes; partly because the text could be fitted into the genre of textbooks for princes. It was one of the first books to be printed, in a handsome edition by Jenson (Venice 1472), and there was still a market for the printed text in 1535, when one appeared at Basle. I suspect it was still read in schools in the following century. Certainly the *Somnium* was, for it is the source of Pepys' motto, which whoso enters his library must read: *Mens cuiusque is est quisque* [the mind is the true self of each man (c. vii)].

II

I turn now to the structure of the main part of the poem—the dream. But the opening cannot be divorced from this structure. It represents a characteristic feature of the medieval dream poem, which regularly included (1) an introduction giving the occasion of the dream, (2) a description of initial disquiet or uncertainty, (3) the mention of weariness that induces sleep, and (4) an astronomical allusion that provides a true setting for the dream (here it is the planet Venus: 113–17).

All these features may be found either in the *Book of the Duchess* or the *House of Fame* or *Piers Plowman* or in the Scottish poem that derives much of its machinery and inspiration from the *Parlement*—the *King's Quair*. In these poems, however, the dreamer himself participates in the action. Here, after African has pushed him through the gate, he is a mere spectator, with a purely recording role. Much of the art of dream-poetry—and much of its appeal—lay in the manipulation of the dreamer's role. For comparison I take two examples: (1) The conclusion of *Confessio Amantis* (viii: 2440 ff.). There Amans falls into a swoon and has the vision of Cupid and a *parlement* of lovers, marshalled by Youth and Elde. He takes no part in the procession, but hears Elde's company pray to Venus on his behalf. Cupid leads the company to the prostrate dreamer, who *thinks* that he feels the God withdrawing the dart of love from his heart, while Venus shows him his hoary locks in a mirror. With that he wakes up—to find that Venus is still there. (2) Henryson's *Testament of Cresseid*. There Cresseid has her 'doolie dream' of the

Assembly of the Gods. She hears them discuss her case—as though she were not present. But when the sentence is given Saturn passes it down to "wher careful Cresseid lay" (310), and is followed by Cynthia, who

> Out of hir sait discendit doun belyve,
> And red ane bill on Cresseid quhair scho lay[7]

When Cresseid wakes she seizes a mirror and sees that what the gods had decreed had already come to pass—she is leprous. If one asks where Cresseid found her mirror, the answer is—if not in the *Confessio,* then in the Knight's Tale, where Arcite picks up a mirror in precisely the same situation: there (527 ff.) Mercury appears to him in a dream and bids him go to Athens. Arcite decides to do so at the risk of death; but the mirror shows him that his face is now so disfigured by woe that none will recognize him: he will be safe.

Henryson imagines the gods as actually descending from their spheres, just as they did in classical epic. One of the attractions of dream poetry was that it enabled the poet to incorporate classical mythology without giving it literal credence: it could be associated with astrological lore—and in any case the poet is not vouching for the truth of his dream. Hence the presence of Venus in the *Parlement* and Minerva in the *Quair,* and of Jove's eagle and Aeolus in the *House of Fame.*

As to the dream garden, it is archetypal and perennial, not least because it can often be associated with some childhood memory of a garden that one stumbles on by accident and alone and finds full of novelty. A modern analogue is in Forrest Reid's *Apostate*[8]—a very evocative passage, though Reid did not read any *sen* into his memories. Chaucer's picture undoubtedly contains suggestions of the true Earthly Paradise—to the location of which a Swedish scholar, L. I. Ringbom, has now devoted a whole book.[9] His early illustrations of the *paradaezza* show it as a fenced park (for preserving rams and deer) as well as a pleasure-garden: the wall links it with the biblical Eden of which the gate was locked and guarded.

I leave aside the arboreal catalogue, for it demands a survey of a theme that goes back to Ovid,[10] and that was to be taken up by Sidney, who in the *Old Arcadia* has a long series of hexameters that are so many glosses for the trees in Chaucer's list.[11] In *Teseida* vii (which Chaucer is here following) Boccaccio mentions only a myrtle. Chaucer has filled out the passage by resort to *Teseida* xi: 22—a stanza that he adapts to different effect in his notable display of *disjunctio* in the Knight's Tale

(2062–64). The significance of PF 176–82 lies in the almost total absence of botanic description. The trees are identified by their uses, as the birds will be by their functions and moralized activities: e.g., "the byldere ok," "the shetere ew," "the waker goos," "the cukkow ever unkynde."

Birds in groups have a part in the tradition of Persian manuscript illumination, and conceivably contact with this tradition through the Latin kingdom of Jerusalem (which developed its own distinctive art) encouraged the introduction of birds into the decorative schemes of Western manuscripts. The story of St. Francis preaching to the birds is illustrated in some manuscripts of the *Fioretti.* English art early fixed on naturalistic representations of birds, even when otherwise stylized. One of the first and finest arrays of English birds is found on the border of a Charter of 1291 (reproduced in the *Illustrated London News,* March 1957). Amongst them we find a merlin, a peacock, a kingfisher(?), and a "hobby." The English birds in the fourteenth-century Pepys pattern book are given English names by the artist or a user: and there is a long list of similar names on f. 216 of St. John's Cambridge MS. 120, a miscellany of twelfth- to fourteenth-century date—including redlag, merle, feldefare, snipe, teal, bunting, spink, wodewake, and others that I can not identify. It suggests that the English have always been a nation of bird-watchers. In the seventeenth century Topsell's *Fowles of Heven* catered to this interest. Chaucer's list constitutes a revealing fusion of traditional bestiary lore with an "organic" classification that goes back to Aristotle and is an outgrowth of the Aristotelian renaissance. In the *Natural History* 592–93[b], (as T. P. Harrison has noted) Aristotle classifies birds according to their *food,* a division that Vincent of Beauvais reduces to five categories. This is essentially the division that Chaucer has in mind at 323 and 500 ff. The birds of rapine (eagle and hawks) belong to class one, the turtledove (representing seed fowl) to class two, the cuckoos (wormfowl) to class four, and the goose (waterfowl) to class five. Chaucer specifically alludes to this ordering when he puts the "fowls of rapine" (324) first in the list and water-fowl last—they "sat lowest in the dale" (327).

This classification represents the more "scientific" side of traditional birdlore. But bestiary lore, which we tend to discuss as pseudo-science, often likewise derived from Aristotle or Pliny, via Isidore of Seville, Alexander Nequam, or Bartholomew the Englishman's *De Proprietatibus Rerum*[12] (which Trevisa was translating about this time). The scientific and pseudo-scientific were intermingled; and if even Dr. Johnson was quite sure that in winter swallows conglobulated together under water, it was because Nequam had said so. By the same token Chaucer's description of the crane as "the geaunt, with his trompes soun" (344) comes ultimately from Isidore, who says: "Quem nomen de propria voce sumpserint tali enim sono susurrant" [They take their name from their call, which is a kind of muttering sound]. This was repeated by Vincent and Bartholomew but also by Alanus, who gives Natura a robe crowned with all kinds of birds, each with its characterizing epithet. Chaucer was immediately following Alanus when he called the crane a giant, the chough a thief (345), the hawk a tyrant (334). Drayton will revert to Alanus' figured garment in *The Man in the Moon* (1606), where seafowl and waterfowl are catalogued as arrayed on Phoebe's mantle.

Chaucer's characterizing phrases or epithets, not always ornithological, contribute to the effect of density—each line is packed as the whole piece is packed, and the human attributes prepare us for the "parlement" in which the birds will speak. Most of these epithets are self-explanatory, but a few have eluded editors, e.g., the *raven wys* (362). I find the raven's wisdom alluded to elsewhere only in the York Play of Noah (where it sustains itself in flight, till the flood dries up). The lapwing (347) is false and treacherous because for all readers of Ovid he is identified with the false Tereus, the villain who raped Philomela. Gower, who retells the tale, concludes:

> And yit unto this dai men seith
> A lappewincke hath lore his feith [i.e., his trustworthiness]
> And is the brid falseste of alle.[13]

It is the same tale of Tereus that explains why Chaucer says the nightingale "clepeth forth the grene leves newe" (352). This is not a decorative allusion to spring, but a specific association of the bird with the tale of Philomela's shame. She appears, says Gower, only when Nature the Goddess ordains that

> the wodes and the greves
> Ben heled al with grene leves
> So that a bird hire hyde mai
> . . . .
> [And that] there is no bare sticke
> But al is hid with leves grene
> (CA V: 5960 ff.)

—then the nightingale hides in the woods and sings her sorrow. Chaucer tells this tale in the *Legend of Good Women*, but stops before the metamorphosis of Philomela and Procne. In Ovid as in Gower, Procne,

Philomela's sister, becomes a swallow—hence Chaucer's characterization of that bird in *Troilus* II: 64: "the swalowe Proigne, with a sorrowful lay." In *Troilus,* the swallow wakes Pandarus with her *chiteringe.* That is the very term used by Gower in the same context in the same tale (6011)—to describe both Procne's song and the sounds that issue from Philomela's mouth after Tereus had cut out her tongue (5700). Here (PF 353–54) the swallow is characterized as "mortherere of the flyes smale / That maken hony." *Murderer* is a strange term. Perhaps it retains overtones of the Philomela story: Procne *is* a murderess, for in revenge for Tereus' rape of her sister she kills his child (and heir) and serves it upon a plate for breakfast. Brewer and Robinson, following the Cambridge University Library MS, read *"foules* smale" (and gloss *foules* "birds"). But I cannot believe that either of them seriously thought flies could be called *birds.* The phrase has an exact equivalent in Nequam, who alludes to Ovid's tale and says the swallow is "culicum et muscarum et apecularium infestatrix" [the persecutor of gnats, flies, and bees];[14] bees were included in the genus *flies:* cf. *Ayenbite:* "þe smale uleze that maketh thet hony." Like the tree list, the bird catalogue is very much a set piece; and as such it caught the eye of Sidney, trained as he was in rhetoric. He copies it with variations in *The Old Arcadia:*

> The peacock's pride, the pie's pilled flattery
> Cormorant's glut, kite's spoil, kingfisher's waste,
> The falcon's fierceness, sparrow's lechery,
> The cuckoo's shame, the goose's good intent,
> E'en turtle, touched he with hypocrisy
> And worse of other more: till by assent
> Of all the birds, but namely those were grieved,
> Of foules there called was a parliament.[15]

When Spenser comes to adapt Chaucer's passage in the *Faerie Queene,* II: xii, 36 (describing the journey of Guyon and the Palmer to the Bower of Bliss) he selects from Chaucer's list only birds of ill omen, adding others to indicate that the Bower is evil:

> Even all the nation of unfortunate
> And fatall birds about them flocked were
> (Such as by Nature men abhor and hate)
> The illfaist owle, death's dreadful messengere, [cf. PF 343]
> The hoars night-raven, trump of dolefull dere,
> The lether-winged bat, days enemy [bats were treated as birds]
> The rueful strich, still waiting on the bere [a Bestiary touch]
> The whistler shrill, that whoso heres doth dy—

III

The central sequence of the appeals of the three bird-suitors may seem simple and undramatic. But it resembles the pattern of many a romantic novel, e.g., Meredith's *Diana of the Crossways*—where Emma Dunstane plays the part of Nature, and Diana (so aptly named) does eventually succumb to marriage. The formel's final plea for a year's *respite*—in which the rival suitors will strive to "do well"—is in accord with accepted medieval practice; indeed *respit* is used in a technical sense.[16] In the charming Anglo-Norman romance of *Jehan and Blonde*, Blonde (an Oxford girl), wishing not to marry the Earl of Gloucester but her squire Jehan, says to her father:

> "Sire," dit elle, "si feray
> Quant il vous plaist, je le prendrai
> Mais je vous demande respit." [for five months]
> (2321–23)

["Sire," she said, "I bow to your wish; I will accept him, but in due time."]

> "Ne me voel pas marier ore
> Pour Dieu vous en requei respit."
> (2229–30)

["I do not wish to marry now, and I ask delay in God's name."]

Entremes (665) has a similar technical flavour. It is usually translated "interval": yet *entremetyn* (515) means "intervene, meddle." Nature is referring not to the interval itself but to her *intervention:* she intervenes for the good of all concerned.

The suitors are to strive to "do well," to show themselves worthy of such a worthy mistress. All we have had so far is the expression of high-flown courtly sentiments of eternal fidelity. Nature tests these by requiring that they show love "in deed." "A year is not so longe to endure"; though in at least one romance (*Ywain and Gawain*) the hero forgets, before a year is out, his promise to his lady. In setting this condition Nature acts as a royal judge, not as the embodiment of a resistless life force. Shakespeare, in the play that comes closest to the "courtois" convention, uses the same device. In the last scene of *Love's Labours Lost* the matches are deferred for a twelve-month and a day. The Princess requires the King to remove himself to a hermitage. Rosaline bids Berowne purge himself by *good deeds* ("seeking the weary beds of people sick"); Dumaine promises that he will serve Katherine true and faithfully all the year.

I V

At the end of the poem the birds give out not native woodnotes wild but a song patterned by human art: their *note,* or tune, is *maked* in France (677): the France that in the fourteenth century produced the finest music and musicians, blending words and music as they had hardly been blended before. And the song itself is *roundel* or *roundeau,* a harmony, an earthly counterpart in miniature to the music of the spheres; strikingly similar in words and structure to the roundel that Arcite sings in the Knight's Tale (I: 510–12).

The lyric impulse cannot, of course, be tied down to any particular philosophy of nature. But the contexts of spring songs are always worth attention. In classical verse the occasion of such song is usually simple delight that the snows have fled—"diffugere nives." In the twelfth century the mood of delight is juxtaposed with the mood of the lover:

> Levis exsurgit zephirus,
> Et sol procedit tepidus,
> Jam terra sinus aperit,
> Dulcore suo diffluit.

[The gentle west wind rises, the soft sun begins its course, and the earth opens her bosom and diffuses her sweet fragrance.][17]

Birds build their nests and voice their joy among the blossoms, only the lover is sad—as he is in the lyric "Lenten is come with love to toun," which ends with the lover's threat to flee in self-pity to the woods as an outlaw. The absence of this note in Chaucer's roundel is noticeable: here the song-birds join in praise of Nature, their creator's vicar, doing to *her* honor and pleasance (676)—not praying for favor: in marked contrast to the suppliants in Venus' temple, victims of passion or unrequited love. This is the mild sun of spring, not the hot sultry sun of line 285. It suggests the temperate air of the garden that the dreamer first relishes on his first entering (204–205): "so attempre [it] was that nevere was ther grevaunce of hot ne cold." It may seem a difficulty that on St. Valentine's day, in mid-February, the birds should welcome *Somer*. But what the birds are singing is their theme-song. This is merely a rehearsal for their summer celebrations that rightly belong to April and May. It is in May that in LGW Prologue, F:170 the same "smale foules" (lark, thrush, blackbird, nightingale?) sing a song of welcome to "somer, oure governour and lord!" Dr. Brewer, in his note on the roundel, cites lines 131–32 of that prologue (G), in which they also sing

> "Blyssed be Seynt Valentyn
> For on his day I ches yow to be myn."

But *ches* (G), "choose," is surely an inferior reading to F's *chees:* i.e., "on St. Valentine's day I chose you"—months ago: cf. PF 386–88 and the *Complaint d'Amours* (another St. Valentine's day poem, made on that day "whan every foule chesen shal his mak").

Dr. Brewer (like Skeat) found a difficulty in the sense of *recoverede* (687), which he says must here mean simply "gained," not "recovered." Actually, examples of the sense "gained" are very rare; Chaucer may well have meant what the *OED* takes him to mean—"found again, got back": the suggestion being that they all separated while the *parlement* was in session; the sense "returned to" / "got back" would be particularly appropriate to the "newfangle" tidifs or sparrows, who in LGW F: 155 repent of their unfaithfulness to their "makes."

V

In some MSS of the *Parlement* there stands written above the roundel the words: "Qui bien aime a tard oublie" [whoso loves well is slow to forget]. This does indeed suggest that the "note" was *maked* in France, i.e., that the roundel was designed to fit the tune belonging to the French song that began with these words. The words are in fact sometimes ascribed to Machaut, whose influence is so pervasive in the early Chaucer and who was notable also as a musician—setting his own songs as well as a splendid mass (he was a canon of Rheims). But the French words themselves are much earlier than Machaut. They occur in a list of *diversa proverbia* in a twelfth-century MS (Bodl. Digby 53); and in another MS they are followed by some Latin verses that may represent the words of the lost French song:

> *Ki bien eimet tart le ublie.*
> Cuius amor verus sopor est in pectore serus

Verus amor, vera si mens, oblivio sera
Non absentatur cordi, vere quod amatur.

[Where love is true, it is a long time dying. True love, true
mind, challenge oblivion. A faithful love will never leave
the heart.][18]

The French line has eight syllables, the English ten: but the French
may well have been extended in its metrical form. Dunbar introduces a
similar bird-song in *The Thrissil and the Roiss,* but with it is a May
dawn-song, glancing at the Prologue to the *Legend of Good Women:*

O luvaris fo, away thou dully nicht
And welcum day, that confortis every wicht.
Haill May, haill Flora, haill Aurora schene,
Haill princes Nature, haill Venus lufis quene.

After this lyrical consummation to his dream, the dreamer on waking turns at once with refreshed spirits to find—another book.
Chaucer, unlike Wordsworth, found no dichotomy between literature
and nature, and did not believe that one impulse from the vernal wood
can teach more than all the sages can. As he says in the same Prologue
that Dunbar remembered,

Ther is wel unethe game anon
That fro my bokes maketh me to gon,
But it be other upon the holiday
Or elles in the joly time of May,
Whan that I here the smale foules sing . . .
Farwell my stodye, as lastynge that sesoun.
(LGW 33–39)

There is a time for all things. Chaucer's poetry is the poetry of
equipoise. He will not side with the Flower against the Leaf nor with
the sheaf against the corn, nor with tercel against formel. The same
balance of sympathies allows him to portray a Pandarus without scorn
and a Criseyde without sentimentality.

In this lyric close the mating birds typify the seasonal bliss, which is
good in its time, for creation is inherently good—if not the highest
good. And though the conclusion seems to outweigh the Prologue we
should not forget that Chaucer nowhere wholly rejects Macrobius or his
philosophy. It is after all to Africanus, Cicero's austere mentor, that the
dreamer owes his dreams of natural bliss and divine plenitude. There

were links and cross-webs between the most disparate medieval philosophies.

NOTES

1. These notes represent a reconsideration of passages or aspects of Chaucer's *Parlement of Foules* to which I hardly gave sufficient attention in my 1957 study of it. See *The Parlement of Foules: An Interpretation* (Oxford: Clarendon Press, 1957). I reserve a fresh study of the role of Venus and Nature for another occasion.
2. *The Parlement of Foules,* 32. Hereafter *The Parlement of Foules* will be abbreviated as PF. Quotations are from F. N. Robinson's edition (1957).
3. *Roman de la Rose,* ed. E. Langlois, Société des anciens textes français (Paris, 1914 ff.), 18367–68.
4. See my *Chaucer's Book of Fame* (Oxford: Clarendon Press, 1968), p. 48 n. 1 and p. 83.
5. See C. S. Lewis, "Dante's Statius," *Medium Aevum,* 25 (1956), 138.
6. Gavin Douglas, ed., Aeneid (Edinburgh: W. Blackwood, 1957), II, prol. 185–86.
7. *Testament of Cresseid,* in Robert Henryson, *Poems,* ed. C. Elliott (Oxford: Clarendon Press, 1963), lines 331–32.
8. *Apostate* (London: Faber and Faber, 1947), p. 73.
9. Lars Ivar Ringbom, *Paradisus Terrestris. Myt, bild och verklighet,* Acta Societatis Scientiarum Fennicae, N.S. C, I, 1 (Helsingfors, 1958).
10. *Metamorphoses,* X: 90 ff.
11. See Jean Robertson, ed., *The Countess of Pembroke's Arcadia (The Old Arcadia)* (Oxford: Clarendon Press, 1973), p. 86.
12. Over 100 MSS from c. 1296.
13. *Confessio Amantis* (CA), ed. G. C. Macaulay (New York: Oxford University Press, 1901), V: 6040–42.
14. *De nat. rer.,* II: lii; cf. *De laudibus,* 790–95.
15. Jean Robertson, p. 78. Equally pertinent is *The Parlement of Byrds* imprinted at London for Antony Kytson (?1550), which extended Chaucer's list and gives the parliament a topical and political color.
16. Compare an early example (not in *OED*) in Mannyng's *Chronicle;* the Earl Marshal is addressing the King in parliament: "Of þis we aske respite, our conceile to take" (ed. Hearne, p. 292, line 3).
17. *Die Cambridger Lieder,* ed. K. Strecker (Berlin, 1926), p. 95.
18. Serlo of Wilton, *Poèmes Latins,* ed. Jan Öberg (Stockholm, 1965), p. 145.

Chaucerian Perspectives

11

CONSTANCE B. HIEATT

"To boille the chiknes with the marybones": Hodge's Kitchen Revisited

The character of Chaucer's Cook has never been a matter of controversy. No one seems to have felt that there were complex mysteries here, for the characterization in the General Prologue and links, plus the nature of the tale Hodge begins, is sufficiently clear. The only questions really to excite scholarly curiosity have concerned the nature of the sore on his shin and his possible identification with a contemporary Roger of Ware, as the few notes to his portrait and the headlink of his tale in Robinson's edition testify.[1] Notes dealing with the food which is his professional concern are so sparse[2] that it may be suspected most Chaucerians know far less about the Cook's business than—thanks to the efforts of Father Beichner, and others—they know about the business of the Summoner and the Monk.

This situation may seem odd when we consider that cooking is an activity almost everyone knows something about, while few of us have any first-hand experience to instruct us in the nature of the work of a monk, let alone a summoner. It is true that the more insight we gain into the activities of a medieval monk the more we can understand the Monk as a character in a medieval poem, while the same may not be the case with a cook. Yet food and eating provide central images and activities in Chaucer's poetry. The poet whose *abstynence* was *lyt* was just as obviously interested in food as, say, Dickens. Readers of Dickens, however, unlike readers of Chaucer, have a very clear picture of the food so constantly and enthusiastically described, whether this is the Cratchits' Christmas dinner or the underdone mutton grilled before the fire (with mustard) by the resourceful Mr. Micawber. We have little trouble appreciating the savor of the delicacies in Mr. Wardle's hamper, or the lavish luncheons consumed by Mr. Guppy and friends, but few of us are likely to react enthusiastically to the idea of the Franklin's "poynaunt and sharp" sauce.

It is also true that Shakespeare's references to food seem more comprehensible than Chaucer's today, although Elizabethan cookery was nearer in time and nature to medieval practice than to modern. Those who doubt this might consider the festive shopping list of the clown in *The Winter's Tale:*

> ... what am I to buy for our Sheepe-shearing-Feast? Three pounds of Sugar, fiue pound of Currence, Rice: what will this sister of mine do with Rice? ... I must haue Saffron to colour the Warden Pies, Mace; Dates, none: that's out of my note: Nutmegges, seuen; a Race or two of Ginger ... Foure pound of Prewyns, and as many of Reysons o' th Sun.[3]

While these are familiar ingredients in the modern kitchen, all of them, except sugar, and perhaps rice, are more prominent in medieval recipes. Rice, an item more common in aristocratic kitchens than in rustic ones, was frequently ground into rice flour to be used as a thickening agent, and may have been intended here as an ingredient in a pie filling which could have called for all the items on this list.[4] Of course, what most of Shakespeare's readers (or auditors) recall are such meals as Falstaff's roast capon (*I Henry IV*, II, iv), which may sound much more palatable than the Monk's fat roast swan; but it should be noted that Falstaff consumed fourpennyworth of "sauce" with his capon. At that price (about a sixth of the value of the capon itself), this must represent a fairly ambitious sauce, and probably one not unlike those the Prioress was so careful to wipe from her lips.

It is clear, however, that while readers of Shakespeare (or even, sometimes, Dickens) may sometimes misunderstand the nature of the food mentioned, Chaucer's readers may miss points more essential to their comprehension of his poetry. *To Rosemounde* offers perhaps the most remarkable example. It will be recalled that the last stanza of the poem begins,

> Nas never pyk walwed in galauntyne
> As I in love am walwed and ywounde.

Robinson, following Skeat, glosses *galauntyne* as "galantine; a sauce."[5] Readers can thus see that the poet is comparing his (presumed) state to that of a fish in sauce, and, since the fish is "walwed," evidently a great deal of sauce. But what sort? One the fish appears to swim in, or one so thick he is immobilized? This may make a considerable difference to the impact of the simile. The only editor to suggest the nature of the sauce seems to be Baugh, who says it is "made of wine, vinegar, and spices, thickened with bread and boiled," and refers the reader to the recipes for pike in galentyne in the EETS *Two Fifteenth-Century Cookery-Books.*[6] But this summary still does not give a really adequate picture: the galantine used for fish appears to have been a cold, *jellied* sauce. Galantine is, in fact, a variant spelling for gelatine, though this may not be immediately apparent to those curious enough to check the recipes printed from medieval English sources.

Most scholars in search of Chaucer's cuisine have turned, naturally enough, to the most accessible collection, the EETS volume edited by Austin,[7] which includes two nearly identical recipes for "Sauce galentyne." To give the one from Ashmole 1439 (p. 108):

Take faire crustes of broun brede, stepe þem in vinegre, and put þer-to poudre canel, and lete it stepe þer-wyþ til it be broun; and þanne draw it þurwe a straynour .ij. tymes or .iij., and þanne put þer to poudre piper and salte: & lete it be sumwhat stondynge, and not to þynne, & serue forth.

Nothing here suggests gelatine. The sauce is simply to be on the thick side ("sumwhat stondynge"), as well it might be if it consists of only bread and cinnamon steeped in vinegar.

If we turn to a cookery book of Chaucer's own generation, *The Forme of Cury,* which is attributed in the manuscript, no doubt correctly, to the "chef Maister coks of kyng Richard the Secunde" and generally dated as ca. 1390,[8] we find almost the same recipe:

Take crusts of Brede and grynde hem smale, do þerto powdor of galyngale, of canel, of gyngyner and salt it, tempre it with vyneger and drawe it up þurgh a strayner & messe it forth. (FC 138, p. 65)

The principal differences between the two recipes are that the later version spells out the procedure in greater detail—we are to take *good* crusts of *brown* bread and strain the mixture *two or three times*—and varies the spices slightly, omitting galingale and ginger and adding pepper.[9] The expansion is typical of later recipes in general. Most of the *Forme of Cury* recipes are shorter than fifteenth-century versions, as Paul Aebischer has shown to be the case with later versions of the same recipes in the French collection known as the *"Viandier* of Taillevent."[10] The omission of spices is, however, not typical: fifteenth-century recipes are apt to add, rather than subtract, spices. In particular, the absence of galingale is notable, since that seems to be an invariable ingredient of earlier recipes for galantine. Pegge suggested that the sauce takes its name from the galingale, just as, he thought (and later writers have agreed), the name of the similar-sounding sauce called Cameline seems to be derived from the cinnamon (*canel*) it contains.[11]

However, the term *galantine* survives in modern cooking terminology as a kind of cold, jellied dish, defined by André Simon as "cooked meat . . . cased in or covered over with its jelly."[12] If we turn to medieval recipes for pike in galantine, as against galantine sauce, we generally find at least some suggestion that this is a dish to be served cold. One reads,

> Take browne brede, and stepe it in a quarte of vinegre, and a pynt of wyne for a pike, and quarteren of pouder canell, and drawe it thorgh a streynour skilfully thik, and cast it in a potte, and lete boyle; and cast there-to pouder peper, or ginger, or of clowes, and *lete kele* [italics added]. And þen take a pike, and seth him in good sauce [i.e., something like wine and water] and take him vp, and *lete him kele a litul;* and ley him in a boll for to cary him yn; and cast þe sauce vnder him and aboue him, that he be al y-hidde in þe sauce; and cary him wheþer euer þou wolt.[13]

That this is, then, essentially a cold, jellied dish is also indicated by the entry under "Galatina" in Du Cange (1840–50 ed., III, 461), which, citing a thirteenth-century MS, *inter alia,* and giving as alternate spellings *Galatio, Galentine,* says, "Jus concretum e piscibus vel carnibus elixis, vulgo *Gelée*" [solidified juices of fish or meat, commonly called jelly]. Further, the fourteenth-century Italian treatise *De saporibus* of Maino de' Maineri[14] gives a recipe for *gelatina* which contains the usual ingredients for galantine sauce—cinnamon, galingale, cloves, toasted bread, and vinegar—plus the water and wine in which the fish has been boiled, specifying that this is a way to preserve the fish for several days.

Some of the same sources give a quite different recipe for "Gele of fyssh,"[15] a simpler dish containing few spices and no bread; but, like some of the galantine recipes, these generally fail to instruct us that the dish is to be served cold.[16] Perhaps the point seemed too obvious to be spelled out. Any cook knows gelatine does not set until it is cold. Some of the galantine recipes seem to call for the dish to be served hot, as, for example, a recipe for "Lamprons in Galentyne" in Harl. 4016 (Austin, p. 100); and the later sources consulted by Furnivall[17] seem to agree that the term applied to a simple sauce much like the one first cited above, made from bread crumbs and spices steeped in vinegar. But these later traditions could easily have arisen as variants based on the seasonings used in the classical (and obviously persistent) jellied versions.

By this point, some readers may well be wondering why anyone would put bread crumbs in a gelatine dish. I suspect there were two reasons. One was that toasted brown bread gives a dark color to the sauce—a color which is specified as necessary in some of the recipes.[18] But also, an additional thickening may have been very helpful in achieving the desired solidity in an age when powdered gelatine from a package was not available to stiffen the jelly. One has but to read the recipes for "Fyssh in gele" to see that in making this dish, for which a light, clear jelly was desired, getting the jelly to set was a problem; we are told that if it will not "catch," stockfish pieces, especially skins, should be added. These would obviously increase the gelatine content.[19]

If we may, then, take it as reasonable that the reference in *To Rosemounde* is to a fish which is not merely immersed in sauce but in the midst of a murky variety of aspic, we can see that the hapless lover is, like the pike, completely immobilized in the thickest of all possible fishy milieux. A further cogency is apparent in the following line, "My love may not refreyde nor affounde" (21): though the lover is as trapped as that fish in jelly, he is, on the other hand, quite the opposite in that his love is so hot it cannot be cooled and cannot sink.[20] A fish in jelly sinks when the jelly is in its hot, liquid state, but of course is then cooled.

A kitchen-tested recipe for the kind of galantine Chaucer must have had in mind is included in *Pleyn Delit: Medieval Cookery for Modern Cooks,*[21] as are others; but it is to be doubted that a galantine recipe will sound appealing to most readers. It is just the kind of recipe which has convinced many people that our medieval ancestors were overly addicted to strange combinations of highly spiced food. Thus, for example, the standard work on English medieval food, William Edward Mead's *The English Medieval Feast,*[22] comments again and again on the "immoderate use of spices," and asserts that "most dishes were smothered in spices, whether needed or not" (p. 77). Like many such commonplaces, this simply is not fair. Much medieval cooking was, in fact, extraordinarily bland. The recipe for poached eggs in *The Forme of Cury* calls for a sauce which has none of the "poynaunt" quality we enjoy in the hollandaise of a modern Eggs Benedict:

Take Ayren [eggs] and breke hem in scalding hoot water, and whan þei bene sode [boiled] eynowh, take him up and take ʒolkes of ayren and rawe mylke and swyng hem togedre, and do þerto powdor gynger, safron, and salt, set it ouer the fire, and lat it not boile, and take ayren isode & cast þe sew onoward, & serue it forth. (FC 90, p. 46)

This bland sauce of milk thickened with egg yolks is hardly seasoned at all. Saffron is there, as in most uses of it in the period, mainly for the color; ginger is commonly called for where we would use a little pepper, no doubt in the same sparing quantities.

A similar, or identical, sauce appears many places and under various names. It must, for example, be the sauce called "dodine" commonly served in France with ducks and other water fowl. Godefroy's *Diction-naire de l'ancienne langue française* identifies this as a sauce "qui se faisait de blanc de chapon, amandes, ail et œufs" [made of the white meat of capons, almonds, garlic, and eggs], which might be an interesting mixture, but the source for that list of ingredients is seventeenth-century. The only *medieval* recipe cited is one from the Taillevent *Viandier,* which calls for milk thickened with egg yoks and seasoned only with a little ginger. It does not sound like a particularly exciting sauce for duck in comparison with such modern accompaniments as apple or orange sauce. Nor are we likely to wish to follow the fifteenth-century recommendation of the same milky sauce to go with roast leg of pork (Harl. 279 ii: 32, p. 40); most of us would no doubt prefer to eat our pork in the manner prescribed by Alexander Neckam in the twelfth century, foregoing condiments "aliud quam purum salem vel simplicem aliatam" [other than plain salt or simple garlic sauce], although Neckam does not give the recipe for that simple garlic sauce.[23]

Even the sweet dishes of Chaucer's time would be likely to strike us as singularly insipid. Mead was horrified at the recipes for fruit puddings; recounting one which calls for pureed strawberries, thickened and sweetened, with a little spice seasoning, he remarks, "then the mess should be made acid with vinegar and a little white grease put thereto" (p. 76). There is really nothing odd about this pudding. Modern equivalents frequently add lemon juice to a fresh fruit dessert in order to give it tartness, and "grease" appears in the form of butter, cream, or egg yolks. But we have the advantage of being able to use vanilla to give otherwise bland dishes character; our ancestors, lacking such flavorings, would naturally have had to make more uses of the spices available. What may seem peculiar is that they often did not do so. A great many recipes resemble one in Harl. 279 (13, p. 8) called "Creme Boyled," which is a sort of bread pudding made with bread, milk, eggs, butter, sugar, and no further seasoning except a little salt. We would surely prefer one like "Gaylede" (85, p. 22), a blancmange made with ground almonds, rice flour, sugar or honey, and dried fruits (raisins or chopped figs)—or cubes of bread—seasoned with ginger and galingale.

The word "blancmange" has been used here in the modern sense, of course, referring to a simple sweet pudding. One of the few facts about medieval food known to almost all students of Chaucer is that this is not the dish which Hodge of Ware made "with the beste." Dishes with the same names as familiar modern ones but actually quite different in nature seem to have been particularly dismaying to earlier readers. One remarked complacently, "Our custards are free from 'freche pork mynced smale,' and our blancmange is innocent of 'lamprey or other fysshe.' "[24] But what is so appalling about a dish of fish or poultry with rice and almonds? The real drawback of the fourteenth-century style of blancmange is that it is likely to be too bland to have much character. The seasonings called for are usually simply those which went into almost every dish, as we automatically add salt and pepper; ginger, salt, and sugar—the latter presumably in as modest quantities as the former two, as many cooks use it today in vegetables and other non-sweet dishes. The blancmange would be tastier with onions added, or a touch of vinegar or verjuice (the medieval equivalent of lemon juice),[25] but no recipe seems to call for either. One does call for saffron, which can add a pleasantly savory effect, but this is probably improper since the resulting dish can hardly be described as *blanc*.

Since many soups today, not least chicken soups, are on the bland side, modern diners might not find blancmanger of capon (or chicken) out of the ordinary if it were served as a soup course, and probably it was actually rather softer than the rice dishes usually served now. Some recipes say to cook the rice until the grains burst, and others say to serve it "in manner of mortrews," which evidently means "in a dish."[26] Both mortrews and blancmanger were classified as "pottages," all of which are more or less liquid, whether "running"—thin, or in broth—or "chargeant," thick, as is the case with blancmanger and mortrews, as against "leche meats," foods which are to be cooked until they are solid enough to be served in slices. There is, however, one difference between blancmanger and mortrews which may indicate a rather different degree of thickness. Several recipes call for blancmanger served "departed with" another pottage, Caudle Ferry (variously spelled), as a sort of sauce. "Leche meats" were often served with a sauce, but a more liquid pottage naturally called for no extra sauce. No sauce is ever specified for mortrews. It seems fair to conclude that blancmanger was the more solid of the two.[27]

Mortrews was, of course, another of the dishes which Chaucer notes among the Cook's outstanding achievements. This equally bland dish has a base of the same kind as a modern French mixture for quennelles or mousse of meat, poultry, or fish, for it is a puree, ground "al to dust" (FC 45) of flesh mixed with eggs in a sort of basic cream sauce.[28] The seasonings are, again, minimal, yet, as noted, it was never, as far as one can tell from either recipe collections or feast menus, served with the savory sauces which invariably accompany the modern varieties. The version given by the Menagier (II, p. 211) includes wine and verjuice and thus sounds more sprightly, but none of the English recipes calls for anything more exciting than saffron. If we agree to regard it as a thick soup, it is pleasant enough, but such a dish may cause modern cooks to welcome the suggestion found in some recipes that further spices be added before serving: "And loke þat þow caste Gyngere y-now a-boue," for example (Harl. 279, 13, p. 14).

Unfortunately, it is not always clear which spices are the appropriate ones. When we are told "blanke pouder is best" (Harl. 279, 69, p. 19), are we to understand the mixture of cinnamon, ginger, and nutmeg Furnivall reports as standard (p. 108 index)? Such a powder would hardly be white, unless mixed with a good deal of sugar or salt, but both of these are often separately specified.[29] Elsewhere we are directed to use spice powders with other names: powder "douce," powder "fort," "good powders," or the Cook's "poudre-marchant," but there are few clues to the composition of any of them. One recipe in the *Forme of Cury* does suggest ginger and white sugar as an alternative to *blanche* powder, and another suggests ginger, cinnamon, and mace—a combination hardly differing from the ginger, cinnamon, and nutmeg suggested elsewhere as a formula for blanche powder—in lieu of *fort* powder, which surely must be different in some way from *blanche* or *douce*. No one gives an alternative for "poudre-marchant."[30] Pegge thought powder *marchant* and powder *fort* were probably synonyms, and that *blanche* and *douce* were similarly interchangeable, which may or may not be correct. It may be suspected that these are variable formulations, according to the tastes of the cook (or vendor), though it seems reasonable to presume that *fort* powder would be stronger or sharper in flavor than the *douce* variety.[31]

We find no clue to the nature of the spices in Hodge's chicken boiled with marrowbones in the contemporary recipes which seem to be variants of that dish. No doubt, however, the cook was free to use his own judgment and add whatever "powder" he wished. Chaucer is apparently congratulating Hodge of Ware on his culinary taste here, for this dish is singled out for two full lines of description and is the first to be mentioned. Such a dish is represented in at least one English version, Harl. 279's "Schyconys with the bruesse" (144, p. 32), and one French one, the Menagier's "Trumel de Beuf au Jaunet" (II, p. 149). While one emphasizes the beef and the other the chicken, both call for boiling them together with herbs in what is obviously the same basic dish. And a really basic dish this is: its ancestry must run back to the stone age, and its descendants today include a variety of the celebrated French pot-au-feu known as "Potee Normand."[32] The recipe in Harl. 279 (144, p. 32) reads,

Take halfe a dosyn Chykonys, & putte hem in-to a potte; þen putte þer-to a gode gobet of freysshe Beef, & lat hem boyle wel; putte þer-to Percely, Sawge leuys, Sauerey, noȝt to smal hakkyd; putte þer-to Safroun y-now; þen kytte þin Brewes [slices of toasted bread] & skalde hem with þe same broþe; Salt it wyl.

This does not specify what cut of beef, but the Menagier calls for a shank, which means a marrow bone is included; he leaves the herbs to the cook's discretion, so we are free to opt for any potherbs which seem appropriate—onion, for example. The dish is a good one in any case, but one can do well to follow Hodge's example and add a judicious pinch of spice.[33]

Hodge's other culinary accomplishments are more general ones, and there may seem little need to explicate the arts of roasting, seething (boiling), broiling, frying, and baking. Yet even in these familiar categories there have been notable misunderstandings about medieval practices, such as the still widely circulated myth that roasted meats, aside from poultry, were rarely eaten in this period. This misconception goes back to Pegge, who interpreted the preponderance of stews over roasts in the manuscripts as meaning that fewer roasts were consumed. This is hardly a justifiable conclusion; roasting is a simple procedure which would have been well understood by anyone working in a medieval kitchen,[34] while stewed dishes are almost infinitely various.

The menus for contemporary feasts include a great many roasts. On these menus, which show a greater sense of order than is generally realized, the first course (at least in England) usually consists of plain roasts and boiled meats, served with simple vegetable dishes such as pease pottage. More elaborate roasts, featuring game birds, come later, along with more complicated pottages (such as blancmanger and mortrews), "leche meats," and fried dishes. There is usually some emphasis on sweeter dishes in the last course, and the indications are that the meal generally ended with sweet cakes or wafers, fruits, or cheese.[35] The roasts served no doubt included the "roast-beef of Old England" which Pegge (p. xxi) thought absent from British tables until Elizabethan times, though it is seldom (if ever) specified. It must have seemed too commonplace to deserve the featured billing of such courtly fare as venison and wild boar, and was thus disguised under such headings as the "gross char" served in the first course at Henry IV's wedding feast. And although no recipe tells us how to roast the beef, one does say what should be served with it: "To make sauce aliper for rostid bef take brown bred and stepe it in venygar and toiste it and streyne it and stampe garlic and put ther to pouder of pepper and salt and boile it a litill and serue it."[36]

Another widespread myth is that medieval people did not eat vegetables. The treatises on gardening list an astounding variety, and some differentiate between those to be eaten cooked and those to be used in salads.[37] Hodge no doubt "seethed" a good many vegetables along with meat, or in meat broths, to make pottages. Recipes of this type in *The Forme of Cury* include several for mixed greens, quite a few for cabbage, beans, and peas, and one or two each for mushrooms, leeks, and root vegetables, which pretty well covers the field. But vegetables were also served in other ways: parsnips appear in parsnip fritters, for example, while spinach could be braised in olive oil or used in an omelet, and beans might be fried with onions.[38] There were many other fried dishes, including various sorts of rissoles and fritters (especially apple fritters).

Fish was one of the foods frequently fried, but then as now, this was only one of the ways of cooking fish. The bream taken from the Franklin's "stuwe" would have been likely to end up poached in water mixed with wine or ale, or broiled on a grill. In either case, it would be served with a sauce not very different from those used with fish today. The most common accompaniment for fish was a sauce that is indeed "poynaunt and sharp": a "green sauce," or "sauce vert," made with at least one green herb (parsley, for example), ground with bread and mixed with vinegar. Often the sauce included garlic and a variety of green herbs, as in the earliest recognizable full recipe, one for just this sauce in Neckam's *De utensilibus* (ca. 1180):

Pisces . . . cum salsa coquantur composita ex vino et aqua; postmodum
sumantur cum viridi sapore, cujus materia sit salgea, petrosillium, costus,
ditanum, serpillum, et alia, cum pipere; non omittatur salis beneficium.[39]

[Fish . . . should be cooked in a broth of wine and water, then served with a
green sauce made of sage, parsley, costmary, dittany, thyme, and garlic;
salt should not be omitted.]

The Forme of Cury's "verde sawse" (140) is very close to this: "Take
persel, mynt, garlek, a litul spell and sawge, a litul canel, gynger,
piper, wyne, brede, vyneger & salt, grynde it small with safron &
messe it forth." But Ashmole 1439's version is even closer: "Take
percely, myntes, diteyne, peletre, a foil or .ij. of costmarye, a cloue of
garleke. And take faire brede, and stepe it with vynegre and piper, and
salt; and grynde al this to-gedre, and tempre it vp wiþ wynegre, or wiþ
eisel, and serue it forþe" (p. 110). And the recipe survived at least to
the seventeenth century, for it appears again in a version of 1599,
which calls for "sweete hearbes, as Betony, mint, Basill: also Rose
vineger, a clowe or two, and a little garlicke."[40]

Wynkyn de Worde recommended a similar green garlic sauce for
roast goose (Furnivall, p. 278), which may explain Harry Bailly's
comments on the ill effects of parsley eaten with Roger's goose (CT I:
4351–53). Goose was also served with more elaborate sauces, frequently containing grapes, but garlic and parsley are standard ingredients in all sauces for goose, plain or fancy. One would think that
swan, a bird which must have some culinary resemblance to goose,
might also be thus served, and indeed roasting directions say to roast
swan in the same way as goose (see Harl. 4016, p. 78), but the sauce
for it is invariably "Chawdon." This means that the Monk ate his fat
roast swan with a sort of giblet gravy, colored and enriched with the
swan's blood and toasted bread.[41] Blood is not a particularly frequent
ingredient in medieval recipes. It was used in sausages of the blood-
pudding type, as it is today, and as a coloring in such dishes as chawdon. The only "pasty" in which it is a notable ingredient is a pasty of
lamprey, reported in greatest detail in Harl. 279 (no. 23 of the "bake
metis" section, p. 52). Hodge would indeed have had to let a quantity
of blood (CT I: 4346) to make such pasties, for the cook is directed to
let the lampreys bleed to death in a basin, then use the blood in his
sauce.

Here we reach a favorite delicacy of our ancestors -which seems dis-
tinctly unappealing today. Lampreys are no longer the popular food

they were in an age when royalty could die of a surfeit, and contemporary cooks, especially non-professionals, are apt to be squeamish. Where the medieval cook routinely slaughtered his own poultry, our meats come trimmed and packaged, and some of us are too tenderhearted to wish to boil a live lobster. Thus it is hard to imagine a revival of medieval lamprey pasties. Yet no one would object to the alternate version given in Harl. 4016 (p. 100) if the other fish there suggested, salmon, were substituted for lamprey. In fact, most recipes of the period can be used with perfectly acceptable results by an experienced cook equipped with common sense, sound culinary instincts, and discretion.

This is even true of the notorious recipe for gingerbread, which omits ginger.[42] It is not at all unusual for a medieval recipe to omit (no doubt inadvertently) an essential ingredient. We have, for example, quite a few recipes for a sweet-and-pungent stew of meat or fish, but almost all recipes omit either the "sweet" or the "pungent" component. One should simply remedy such obvious omissions. In the case of the gingerbread, the result is a cake of slightly different consistency from any of the types we are used to, but the delicacy which refreshed Sir Thopas had a flavor which would be quite recognizable to today's gingerbread fanciers.

It may well be suspected that the revolution in tastes and cooking habits so often assumed by writers in this field[43] may be more a matter of emphases than of basic techniques and ingredients, which have not changed as much as many people think. During the period when this essay was in preparation, I spent an evening in a rural Oxfordshire pub chatting with a village ancient who was proud to inform me that he was a far better cook than the ones who were coming in from France these days ruining good British food. This sounded familiar, and I expected him to continue with complaints about sauces which make it impossible to know what you are really eating, and so forth. But I heard no such thing. My informant said there was nothing like a pot kept boiling on the back of the fire, into which one put various meats along with some parsley and . . . in effect, I was told how to *boille the chiknes with the marybones.*

NOTES

1. F. N. Robinson, ed., *The Works of Geoffrey Chaucer,* 2nd ed. (Boston: Houghton Mifflin, 1957), pp. 660 and 688–89 (all references to Chaucer's

works are to this edition); see also Muriel Bowden, *A Commentary on the General Prologue of the Canterbury Tales* (New York: Macmillan, 1949), pp. 185–91.

2. Robinson gives one to *mortreux,* concerned only with the pronunciation of the word, and one to *Jakke of Dovere;* the brief explanation of the nature of the cook's wares given by Bowden is fuller than most but still inadequate.

3. IV: iii, in the spelling of the first folio (facsimile ed. H. Kökeritz and J. Prouty).

4. See, e.g., the tart of apples and wardons (pears) from a fourteenth-century MS appended to *The Forme of Cury* (hereinafter designated in notes as FC), ed. S. Pegge (London, 1780), p. 119; cf. also "Charwardon," a tart filling thickened with rice flour, in *A Noble Boke of Cookry,* ed. Mrs. Alexander Napier (London, 1882), pp. 81–82. This book, printing a fifteenth-century MS, is hereinafter referred to as Napier.

5. Donaldson's note is no more helpful. He glosses the phrase as "rolled in galantine sauce" and does not include *galantine* in his vocabulary.

6. Thomas Austin, ed. (London, 1888), EETS O.S. 91: 101. Hereinafter cited as Austin, or simply with page numbers of relevant MS.

7. This is the source of all the recipes given by Edith Rickert in *Chaucer's World* (New York: Columbia U. Press, 1948), pp. 88–90, and Bowden, pp. 186–87.

8. See FC, esp. pp. xi–xii and 1.

9. Galingale is, according to André L. Simon's *Guide to Good Food and Wines,* rev. ed. (London: Collins, 1963), pp. 27 and 431, made from the roots of a plant of the snowdrop family, and is not to be confused with "galangal," a mild form of ginger which is rare today but obtainable. The two are, however, similar, and many recipes give galingale and ginger as alternatives. The "galingale" provided by a New York firm turned out to be somewhat more aromatic than ginger.

10. See "Un manuscrit valaisan du 'Viandier' attribué à Taillevent," *Vallesia* 8 (Sion, 1953), 73–100; the MS concerned is said to be much the earliest of its kind, dating from no later than the first decade or so of the fourteenth century. Aebischer compares successive versions of two recipes, showing in both cases more elaboration in the later fourteenth-century or early fifteenth-century versions, and considerably more in a version from a later fifteenth-century MS.

11. See Pegge's glossary, and cf. Simon, p. 431; this information is probably derived from Pegge, directly or otherwise.

12. Ibid.; cf. Simone Beck, Louisette Bertholle, and Julia Child, *Mastering the Art of French Cooking* (New York: Knopf, 1963), p. 569. This book is hereinafter referred to as *French Cooking.*

13. Harl. 4016, Austin, p. 101 (corrected to agree with Douce MS 55); cf. Napier, p. 79.

14. Ed. Lynn Thorndike, "A Medieval Sauce-Book," *Speculum* 9 (1934), 183–90.

15. FC 101; Harl. 279 110, p. 26.

16. In his ed. of FC (*Antiquitates Culinariae,* London, 1791), Richard Warner

glossed the phrase "cole the broth" as "cool . . . ," but incorrectly: *cole* means "strain," from Lat. *colare*.

17. F. J. Furnivall, ed., *The Babees Book . . .* , EETS O.S. 32 (London, 1868), pp. 156 and 216. Hereinafter cited as Furnivall. Still later, "galantine" was confused with "chawdon" (discussed below), as is evident in Gervase Markham's *The English Housewife* (London, 1649), pp. 97–98.

18. For example, the recipe for "Lamproie a la galentine" in the early *Viandier* MS (Aebischer, 92–93) ends, "doit estre noir." Toasted bread is specifically advised for coloring in a number of medieval recipes.

19. See recipe in Harl. 279 cited in n. 15 above.

20. Baugh, following Helge Kökeritz ("Chaucer's Rosemounde," *Modern Language Notes*, 63 [1948], 316), glosses *affounde* as "grow cold," giving it the same meaning as *refreyd*. I would rather follow Donaldson, Robinson, Skeat, and the *MED* in assuming the proper definition here to be "sink, founder," since that adds an extra depth to the line in question.

21. Constance B. Hieatt and Sharon Butler (Toronto: University Press, 1976).

22. (New York: Barnes and Noble, 1967), p. 74; hereinafter cited as Mead.

23. In *A Volume of Vocabularies*, ed. Thomas Wright (Privately printed, 1857), p. 102. The garlic sauce may have been similar to the sauces just described, but with garlic added; cf. Ashmole 1439's "Sauce gauncile," Austin, p. 110.

24. Napier, p. vi. *Custard* (more properly, *crustard* < *crust*) is a tart which usually has a filling made basically from beaten eggs, with variable added ingredients, such as pork. It is, thus, what we usually call a *quiche*, something which, happily, never died out in England, whatever it may be called.

25. "Verjuice" was generally the juice of sour grapes or crabapples, used with little fermentation, and, to judge by the comments in the *Menagier de Paris* (ed. Jerome Pichon, Paris, 1846), never kept for more than half a year or so. The Menagier recommends orange juice as a substitute, but of course he had bitter oranges in mind—Seville oranges, which are rarely obtainable in North America.

26. See, e.g., Harl. 4016's "Mortreus de Chare," pp. 70–71.

27. A version of the late sixteenth-century which is still a dish of rice and capon (although by then becoming a more pronouncedly sweet dish) calls for the "Maunger Blaunche" to be allowed to grow cold and then sliced and laid in dishes, which may or may not be indicative of the consistency of the earlier version. See *The Good Hus-Wifes Handmaide for the Kitchin* (London, 1594), pp. 16–17.

28. Cf. *French Cooking*, pp. 184 and 187. Similar dishes have also remained current in Scandinavia, such as Norwegian *fiskefarce* (fish pudding).

29. A recipe for "fine powder" given by the Menagier does include sugar (see vol. II, p. 247), but it does not necessarily represent standard ingredients.

30. Bowden gives Harl. 279, 10's mixture of ginger, cinnamon, and galingale as a type of poudre-marchant (p. 186), but the term is not used in the recipe; presumably she saw it in the preceding recipe and somehow confused the two.

31. Certainly "douce" and "fort" powders were not the same, since some recipes call for both separately. Experience in grinding spices in the kitchen leads to one other tentatively advanced hypothesis: since it is difficult to grind some spices (saffron, for example) in a mortar unless one adds salt or sugar, it is possible that one produces a "douce" powder with sugar as the abrasive element but a "fort" one with salt.

32. Cf. *French Cooking,* pp. 306–09.

33. The spices suggested in *The Good Hus-Wifes Handmaide* (pp. 4–5) for capon boiled with marrow bones and/or beef (still much the same dish, served with "brewes," though considerably elaborated) are mace, pepper, and ginger. A similar recipe in Markham's *English Housewife* calls for ginger and cloves.

34. We are thus told to roast "Yrchouns" (an elaborate type of large sausage) on a spit "as men don piggys"; Austin, p. 38.

35. For a statement on the order of service which seems to bear some resemblance to custom both in England and in France throughout the period, see the *Modus Cenendi,* in Furnivall, Part II, pp. 34–57. Feast menus will be found in Austin, Furnivall, Mead, Warner, and most other works in the area.

36. Napier, p. 77. The same garlic-pepper sauce appears in sources which neglect to say what it is to accompany, and a more elaborate version is indicated to go with roast beef in Wynkyn de Worde's *Boke of Kervyng;* see Austin, pp. 77 and 108, and Furnivall, p. 274.

37. E.g., Sloane MS 1201, cited by C. Anne Wilson, *Food and Drink in Britain* (London: Constable, 1973), p. 339. Warnings against eating salads and raw fruits, sometimes cited as proof that they were not eaten, would seem to prove the opposite: no one condemns unheard-of practices.

38. See FC 5, 6, 10, 80, 149, 180, 181, *inter alia.*

39. Page 102. An Anglo-Norman gloss translates some of the words; e.g., "verde sause" appears over "viridi sapore."

40. Henry Buttes, *Dyets Dry Dinner* (London, 1599), p. 116.

41. E.g., in *Liber Cure Cocorum,* ed. R. Morris (London, 1862), p. 29.

42. Cf. Mead's comment, p. 65. The recipe is Harl. 279, II, 4, p. 35. Gingerbread was still made by this method in the seventeenth century; cf. Markham, pp. 124 and 127.

43. Such as Mead, p. 53.

12

EDMUND REISS

Chaucer's *deerne love* and the Medieval View of Secrecy in Love

When Chaucer describes "hende" Nicholas at the beginning of the Miller's Tale, he first cites his "fantasye" for astrology, then writes significantly of the clerk as lover:

> Of deerne love he koude and of solas;
> And therto he was sleigh and ful privee,
> And lyk a mayden meke for to see.
> (I: 3200–3202)[1]

Whereas it would seem that Nicholas' desire to know the secrets of the natural world extends to the realm of love, the lines state a motif, *deerne love*, that is at the heart of the Miller's Tale and is very much in evidence throughout the whole of the *Canterbury Tales*. *Deerne*, leading immediately in this passage to *privee*, extends the moral stated by the drunken Miller at the outset of his tale—"An housbonde shal nat been inquisityf / Of Goddess pryvetee, nor of his wyf" (3163–64)—and reinforces the play on *privee* so much in evidence in the tale.

Although *deerne love* would appear to represent love-longing—love in mind as opposed to *solas*, love in deed, the successful consummation of love-longing[2]—Nicholas is never presented as a suffering lover, one who, like Palamon and Arcite in the previous Knight's Tale, languishes for years in love, or one who, like Aurelius in the Franklin's Tale, brings himself only after years of concealing his feelings to ask his lady for mercy. To the contrary, as the action of the Miller's Tale begins, Nicholas "ful subtile and ful queynte," catches Alison "prively . . . by the queynte," and says to her, "Ywis, but if ich have my wille, / For deerne love of thee, lemman, I spille" (3275–78). In this context *deerne love* would seem to refer as much to a certain kind of love as to a state of suffering. But it is not the love which Chaucer has Pandarus describe in *Troilus and Criseyde* as felt by mankind in general:

> For this have I herd seyd of wyse lered,
> Was nevere man or womman yet bigete

164

> That was unapt to suffren loves hete,
> Celestial, or elles love of kynde.
>
> (I: 976–79)

What Nicholas feels is clearly not "celestial" love, nor is it the proper "love of kynde." In fact, it would seem to be more artificial than natural.

Although Chaucer uses the term *deerne* twice at the beginning of the Miller's Tale and once a bit later when Alison warns the clerk that if he plans to deceive her husband, he "moste been ful deerne" (3297), it is not one of his favorite or even customary terms. As E. Talbot Donaldson has noted, Chaucer does not even use this "common adjective to modify other words besides love," apparently feeling that the reputation of the word was such that it connoted something sinful— that the term *deerne love* "was already in potentiality what it became in actuality in Nicholas, a device for getting away with adultery, if not really a sort of excuse for indulging in it."[3] In medieval love literature—at least that found in Latin, Provençal, French, Italian, Spanish, and German—contrary to what one might expect, "secret love" does not exist as any kind of formulaic or fixed phrase: there is no *amor celé* or *amor secret* comparable to *bon amor* or *fin amor*. Although it is probably too much to say that *deerne love,* as an expression describing a kind of love, is an English original, the phrase itself apparently does not represent a translation of a term previously existing in a fixed form in another language, as, for instance, does English "fyn love," translating "fin amor."

From its earliest uses in English, the adjective *deerne* is ambiguous, as Donaldson states, "reflecting sometimes justified secrecy and sometimes secret sin."[4] But the first meaning of the term given in the *Oxford English Dictionary* is in reference to that which is "kept concealed, hence, dark, of evil or deceitful nature";[5] and references in Old English amply justify this connotation. Beowulf, for instance, is praised for not acting with "dyrnum cræfte" (2168),[6] that is, with secret cunning. The pejorative nature of this expression is reinforced later in *Beowulf,* when the thief of the dragon's treasure is said to have acted with just such "dyrnan cræfte" (2290). And earlier, Grendel is said to have possibly been the offspring of "dyrnra gasta" (1357), probably best understood as evil spirits. This usage is echoed in *Genesis B,* where the tempting fiend is described as "dyrne deofles boda" (490),[7] the secret messenger of the devil; and later Adam wonders whether this messenger has come with "dyrne geþanc" (532), that is, secret or evil intention.[8]

Along with this sense of *deerne* is that showing the term to be an innocuously descriptive adjective or adverb as in the early Middle English Harley lyric "Lenten ys come wiþ loue to toune," where the animals are described as telling secrets; "deores wiþ huere derne rounes, / domes forte deme."[9] The term even appears in reference to the incarnation of Christ and to divine love. As the early-thirteenth-century *Ormulum* phrases it, Christ was born "Swa dærnelike onn eorþe" (3325);[10] moreover, the thirteenth-century lyrical praise of Mary, "Edi beo þu, heuene quene," states that there is no maiden on earth "þat swo derne louiȝe kunne";[11] and the *Assumption of Our Lady* (c. 1300), speaks of the "derne priuete" of Christ.[12]

The more customary sense of *deerne* in Middle English, however, is "stealthy, insidious, crafty; dishonest, deceptive; immoral, evil."[13] The *Ormulum* speaks of man's sinning in thought and also in "dærne dedes" (396); the thirteenth-century *Bestiary,* describing the nature of the eagle, expands the application to describe the unbaptized man as "old in hise sinnes dern" (90);[14] and the *Vices and Virtues* of the same century refers to the "derne senne" of *tristicia,*[15] a usage in accord with that in the Old English translation of Gregory's *Pastoral Care* referring to the secret envy ("dierna aefst") that can corrupt calm judgment.[16] Similarly, the poem "Glade in god, call hom ȝoure herte" links "synne, morþere, derne tresoun";[17] *Piers Plowman B* speaks of the sins of adultery and usury—"auoutrie . . . and dirne vsurye" (II: 175);[18] and the *Cursor Mundi* joins the "traitur dern and priue theif" (7234).[19] The term is the basis of some notable wordplay in the Harley lyrics, in "Middlelerd for mon wes mad," for instance, with its criticism of those who secretly commit sinful deeds—"þat derne doþ þis derne dede" (8).[20] Though these sins "ben derne done" (9), they will necessarily be revealed. Similarly, in the Harley lyric "Ichot a burde in a bour ase beryl so bryht" (also known as "Annot and John") Christ is said to help man "when derne dedis in day derne are done" (36).[21] Along with such usage linking *deerne* with sin is that which employs the term to describe the activities of the devil. The *Ormulum* refers to his "dærne wiless" (11446), the early-thirteenth-century *Ancrene Wisse* describes the devil's tempting of man as something done "dearnliche,"[22] a description found also in the *Bestiary* (428). The term is likewise appropriate to death which, as Friar William Herebert admonishes in a fourteenth-century lyric, will come "with derne dunt . . . and smyte þou nost whare."[23]

It is in the phrase *deerne love,* however, that the term most frequently occurs in Middle English; and apparently from its earliest appearances this secret love contains connotations of the illicit and the sinful.[24] The

Harley lyrics record this sense explicitly. In "A wayle whyt ase whalles bon" the poet writes that there is no fire in hell so hot as that felt by the man whose love is secret: "nys no fur so hot in helle / al to mon / þat loueþ derne ant dar nout telle / whet him ys on" (41–44).[25] And a full understanding of the real nature of this love may be found in the two complementary poems—both on the same leaf of the Harley manuscript—beginning "Lutel wot hit any mon." The first, generally called "The Way of Christ's Love," uses the opening lines to say that man does not understand the way of Christ's love, which "vs haueþ ymaked sounde" and which has defeated death (5–6).[26] The companion piece, known as "The Way of Woman's Love," reads "Lutel wot hit any mon / hou derne loue may stonde" (1–2).[27] No matter whether the secular poem is a parody of the religious, or the religious one an adaptation of the secular,[28] it seems clear that at least as set down in the Harley manuscript the two poems are designed to be read together and that what is called "derne loue" in the second is being contrasted with the ideal love of Christ described in the first. The implication is clearly that this "derne loue" is *de facto* less than the other love.

The medieval views of "secret love" may be traced back to classical antiquity. Terence, for instance, refers to illicit love as hidden love, "dissimulatum amorem et celatum."[29] Ovid refers several times in his *Ars Amatoria* to secrecy as both pleasant and necessary to love.[30] As he presents it, love is a furtive sport ("furtivos . . . iocos," III: 640); and the secret doings of lovers ("furtis . . . nostris") belong to darkness and dim shadow (II: 615–20).[31] In the *Heroides* Ovid also links secrecy to love: he shows Helen telling Paris to keep on with his seduction of her yet be secret about it (XVII: 153);[32] and he suggests that Leander's tragic ending comes about, at least in part, because of the need to conceal his love of Hero (XVIII: 13–14).

A similar attitude toward the secrecy of illicit love is found in the twelfth-century *De Amore* of Andreas Capellanus. Like Ovid in his *Ars Amatoria,* Andreas states the apparent need to keep love secret, twice listing secrecy as a rule of love,[33] and even making it the essence of love. In the Seventh Dialogue the man defines love as "an inordinate desire to receive passionately a furtive and hidden embrace" ("immoderata et furtivi et latentis");[34] though, in something of a contradiction to this, Andreas in Book II says that love will increase if it lasts after it has been made public (II: ii). And in Book III, with its overt criticism of love, Andreas criticizes women for being deceptive and suggests the illicit nature of that which is concealed: the woman who is slave to her belly seeks out hidden places where she indulges herself.[35]

This secrecy is like the "furtiuum . . . amorem" expressed in the twelfth-century *comoedia elegiaca Pamphilus* (555);[36] it is obviously different from a chaste love ("amor castus") such as that which reigns in Amphitryon's heart as he returns to his wife in the *Geta* of Vital of Blois, another twelfth-century *comoedia* (133).[37] The evaluation of secret love as sinful love is seen even more clearly in the medieval Latin lyric, especially in the poems comprising the *Carmina Burana*. Speaking of the hidden fire ("ignem . . . tacitum") of his love, one narrator states that his perverse desire longs for forbidden fruit.[38] Along with showing the need to keep the lady's name secret and hidden from others ("secretum . . . et celatum")[39] and the delight that love takes in secret places ("letatur amor latebris"),[40] as well as apparently approving of the secret affairs of Venus ("res archana Veneris / virtutibus habenda"),[41] these poems also offer criticism of love and its secrecy. Although love may be regarded as hidden and secret—"Amor est interius / latens et occultus"[42]—one speaker emphasizes that his love is different: it is not secret ("noster amor non furtiva").[43] This same speaker refers to the secret yoke of Venus ("iugum secretum Veneris" st. 13), though another poet is even more outspoken when, in talking about the need to flee love, he refers to it as secret poison ("venena secreta").[44]

The same attitudes toward secrecy are found in the early Provençal lyrics. Guilhelm IX swears that if his lady will grant him her love, he will keep it secret ("celar").[45] Bernart de Ventadorn, who speaks of the secret signs ("cubertz entresens") of lovers,[46] also presents a narrator who worries that his lady has another secret love, "autr' amic privat";[47] in response to these feelings he urges the lady to love his rival in public and him in private: "a prezen amat / autrai, e me a celat" (57–58). On another level Bernart reveals that love is something which cannot be covered or hidden: "mas l'amor qu'es en me clauza, / no posc cobrir ni celar."[48] Peire Vidal is fond of citing the secrecy of love. He begins one poem with a statement of how he found a secret love in a foreign land—"En una terra estranha / Trobei amor privada"[49]—and elsewhere refers to "amics privatz."[50] Whereas secret love in these instances might appear to be innocuous, the early troubadour Marcabru makes clear that it is really an expression of false love. In "Al son desviat, chantaire," he speaks of her to whom "fals' amistat"—which knows how to practice guile (7)—is sweet and secret ("douss' e privada," 11).[51] He, moreover, laments the old times when the qualities of "fin' amors"—as opposed to those of "falss' amors"—were perpetuated both secretly and openly, "a celat et a sabuda" (40).

The apparent praise of secrecy continues in the thirteenth-century

French lyric. Gace Brulé, for instance, gives a full statement of the need to hide one's love in "De bone amour et de loial amie";[52] and Adam de la Halle writes not only that one should love secretly but that those who do otherwise are wrong.[53] Such praise continues in the Italian lyric, from Giacomo da Lentino in the Sicilian school[54] to Dante, whose *Vita Nuova* is in one sense the account of one who has gone beyond hidden love and "lo secreto del mio cuore,"[55] and beyond using "screen-ladies" to hide his love and deceive others,[56] to an affirmation of a higher love.

At the same time secrecy is overtly associated with that which is unworthy and shameful. In the highly influential *Roman de la Rose,* La Vielle speaks of the privacy needed for the pleasures of illicit love;[57] the Lover is praised for being wise and secret ("mout sages et celez," 12405); and La Vielle is asked to conceal him so that he may proceed in his lovemaking without causing suspicion of villainy. In this sense "amor privé" seems to be related to Faus Semblant in the *Roman,* who needs to be hidden (10977–84).[58]

Although secrecy is frequently thought to be associated with the love found in courtly romances, it may not actually be a major concern or motif in these narratives. In the writings of Chrétien de Troyes, for instance, only *Cligés* presents characters concerned with maintaining the secrecy of their desires.[59] When secrecy is insisted upon, it is often because the love is adulterous—as in the various versions of the story of Tristan and Iseut; or the secrecy functions to cause loss of love and even death—as in the thirteenth-century *Chastelaine de Vergi,* and, perhaps, Chaucer's *Troilus and Criseyde.* It should be emphasized also that the secrecy of illicit love, for all its courtly associations, conflicts with feudal and Christian ethics requiring "that nothing be withheld from a liege-lord or husband."[60]

Concealed love does not escape the critical eye of medieval theologians. St. Augustine had warned in his *De civitate Dei* that "lust requires for its consummation darkness and secrecy,"[61] and, citing Cicero—"the greatest master of Roman eloquence"—he points out that to the contrary of secrecy, "all right actions wish to be set in the light, *i.e.* desire to be known."[62] In the definitive discussion of friendship given in his *De amicitia,* Cicero had insisted on the need for frankness and openness—a frank man does not conceal his feelings with a false expression[63]—and had spoken of that true and perfect friendship,[64] not private love but the tie among all people, the accord of all things human and divine joined by mutual good will and love.[65] This view is echoed in the twelfth century by Aelred of Rievaulx, who speaks of friends' opening their hearts and revealing their secrets.[66]

The ideas of both Augustine and Cicero are also restated in the
twelfth century by Hugh of Saint Victor, who writes in his *De sacramentis* that "he who truly loves God, loves everywhere."[67] More to
the point, Hugh says of secret marriages that "concealed agreements
are not marriages but adulterous cohabitations or defilements";[68] and,
speaking of hidden sin, he writes citing Proverbs 28:13 that "He that
hideth his sin shall not be justified."[69] Related to this Old Testament
statement is the New Testament idea that "God is light, and in him
there is no darkness at all" (I John 1:5-7). Likewise pertinent is the
Johannine admonition that "Only the man who loves his brother dwells
in light" (I John 2:10-11). Speaking of the love of God and Nature,
Hugh writes in his *De substantia dilectionis* that by love the rational
creature is brought into fellowship with his maker.[70] This love, as
Hugh elsewhere makes clear, is charity, which gladly shares its own
blessings with all.[71] As he writes, "by the love of God all might come
together into one, while by the love of their neighbour all might be
joined to each other."[72] Such love allows each of us to "possess more
fully and completely in another that which he could not lay hold of in
himself of the One to whom all adhere, the good of all becoming in this
way the sum of individual possession."[73] One should rejoice in his
neighbor's salvation and wish to have him "as a fellow-traveller on the
road to God and a companion when the goal is reached."[74]

That which is secret and private would seem to be opposed to the
public or common good and contain a hint or suggestion of sin. Such is
the sense of the term *deerne* in Middle English, as seen, for instance, in
Richard Rolle's comment on the phrase "nouit abscondita cordis" of
Psalm 43:23 (Vulgate): "God . . . knaws all the dern in oure hert."[75]
And desire would seem by definition to be *deerne*. As Amans says in
John Gower's *Confessio Amantis*, "loue is of himself so derne, / It luteth
[lurks] in a mannes herte."[76] The loue that is *deerne* is opposed to
marriage and to lawful love. The Middle English version of Cato's
Districha, called the *Great Cato*, links "derne loue," and the "fflessches
wille";[77] and the fourteenth-century *Aȝenbite of Inwyt* of Dan Michel of
Northgate, like Ovid and Andreas Capellanus, criticizes those in love
for always seeking remote corners and secret places, "þe halkes and þe
derne stedes."[78]

Although the secret love of maidens and friends, at least as expressed
in such Middle English romances as *Horn Childe* and *King Horn*,[79]
might seem to be innocent, *deerne love* as expressed in other English
writings is clearly culpable. The *Gest Hystoriale of the Destruction of Troy*
describes Medea's falling in love with Jason as "Dissyring full depely in

her derne hert, / As maner is of maydons þat maynot for shame"
(478–79);[80] and in the *Earl of Toulouse,* because the lovers are so
affected by "dèrne loue . . . to dethe they were nere dyght" (492–93).[81]
Moreover, criticizing women's love, the Thrush says to the Nightingale in the debate between these two birds that for a little reward
women will do this "sunfoul derne dede," even at the cost of losing
their own souls (65).[82] And in the *Owl and the Nightingale* the Nightingale, defending her song, says she is not to be blamed if women wish
to "luuie derne" (1357).[83]

In other cases the *deerne love* of women is blatantly sinful. In the
Middle English *Jacob and Joseph* Potiphar's wife asks Joseph to love her
secretly: "ʒif þou canst in boure louie me derne."[84] And in the *Tale of
an Incestuous Daughter* a girl possessed by the devil works so assiduously
to win her father's love that one day in "a pryde stede / Hur fadur
prayed hir of luf derne" (33–34).[85] The outcome is that father and
daughter love together "priuely & stille, / þei were wondur wylde!"
(38–39). This sin of incest leads to further sins as the daughter kills the
child she bears and then murders her mother when she discovers the
incest. Such unforeseen results of *deerne love* are frequent. In Laʒamon's
Brut, for instance, Ascanius' son Silvius loves a maiden "deorneliche
swiþe," that is, very secretly.[86] This illicit union results in the conception of Brutus, who causes the death of both his parents.

The term *deerne* is also properly used by the seducer. In the *Avowing
of Arthur* the king comes to the lady's bed "in derne for to play"
(824).[87] A similar description occurs in *Sir Gawain and the Green
Knight* when Bercilak's wife, acting as seductress, enters Gawain's bedroom "ful dernly and stylle" (1185).[88] And in the dramatic poem *Dux
Moraud,* when the lord demands love from a maiden, the term seems
appropriate to the occasion. He says his desire is so great that he must
show *deerne love:* "Loue so deryn me most schewe to þe, / My loue to þi
body is castyn so bryth, / My wyl me most oue of þe" (62–64).[89] The
kind of love referred to here is emphasized by the repetition of the
term: "Derne dedys me most do by day & by nyth" (69); and "Now wyl
I makyn solas, / For my deryn loue xalt þou be" (76–77). The "derne
dedys" of lovers are clearly not to be condoned. Speaking of lovers'
being together in bed, *Piers Plowman* A affirms that only husband and
wife should be so: "that deede derne do no mon scholde," except those
who are married (X: 199).[90]

The evidence would seem to indicate strikingly that *deerne love* is not
noble, not an expression of *fin amor,* but, rather, a low love, one illicit
and sinful, and more appropriate to fabliaux than to accounts of noble

and proper love. In the earliest English fabliau, the late thirteenth-century *Dame Siriȝ,* the lover protests to his lady that he does not intend shame or villainy, only "derne loue": "Same ne vilani / Ne bede I þe non; / Bote derne loue I þe bede, / As mon þat wolde of loue spede" (128–31).[91] In spite of his protestations of innocence, however, the term "derne loue" acts here to identify his lust and allow it to be seen for what it is. Earlier the lover had said, "Dame, if hit is þi wille, / Boþ dernelike and stille, / Ich wille þe loue" (85–87). The repetition, as in *Dux Moraud,* reinforces the irony that the love is to be associated with the shame and villainy disclaimed by the lover.

Although giving the impression of belonging to the world of courtesy, *deerne love* is actually more pertinent to the bawdy, coarse activities detailed in the fabliaux and in the various *contes à rire* of the Middle Ages. These stories frequently allude to the "moult grande privauté" of illicit love,[92] and contain as a stock situation the lady's hiding her lover.[93] In the fourteenth century this fabliau tradition is continued in such works as Juan Ruiz' *Libro de buen amor* and Boccaccio's *Decameron,* both of which contain several references to hidden love. For instance, in the *Libro de buen amor* the narrator reproaches Amor for acting in his false ways like a brigand. From hidden places, he says, love springs out to ambush the unwary: "de lugar encobierto sacas celada fiera" (393).[94] And in the *Decameron* secret love is invariably associated with trickery and deception, as the stories of the third and seventh days amply reveal with their many accounts of intrigue, disguise, and deceit. These loves are hardly the open and generous expression of "magnificenza" represented in the tales of the tenth day. Defined as the clearness and light ("chiarezza e lume") of all virtue,[95] "magnificenza" provides the ideal lacking in the earlier accounts of deception and hidden lust.

It is ironic that such a fabliau-like tale as the *Lai d'Ignaure* of Renaut de Beaujeu should begin with the affirmation that "He who loves should never hide it."[96] Such a view, though wholly in accord with that of medieval theologians, is diametrically opposed to that ostensibly stated by the lyric and narrative writers of the Middle Ages. But the secrecy, even when it would appear to be taken seriously, is too frequently a cause of destruction of love and lovers. So at the end of the *Chastelaine de Vergi* secrecy has been responsible for the deaths of two lovers and for a lord's killing his own wife. Ironically, however, the poet says that the tale should serve as an "example" teaching the need to conceal love, for disclosure gains nothing while secrecy has everything to commend it.[97]

Chaucer's use of *deerne love* in the Miller's Tale is wholly in accord with the sense of secrecy found in the fabliaux, the *Libro de buen amor,* and the *Decameron,* though, as in the romances, the term gives the impression of being something noble. But it is not merely that the term "is used to emphasize Nicholas' quasi-aristocratic ways," or that it is a term "comically out of place."[98] Rather, by referring in this tale to *deerne love,* Chaucer first of all projects an equivalent to what might be termed the "deerne lore," the secret prophecy of a new Deluge used by Nicholas as the means of deceiving John the carpenter. This *deerne love* is emphasized by being juxtaposed against the open love of Absalon. In his courtship of the married woman Alison, Absalon openly serenades her, even while she is lying in bed with her husband, and expresses his "love-longynge" (I: 3349, 3679) in ludicrously incongruous and public ways. He woos her through go-betweens ("by meenes and brocage"), he assumes the conventional posture of the courtly lover (he "swoor he wolde been hir owene page"), he sings to her, sends her food and drink, and, "for she was of town," even offers her money (3375–80). Such public expression—culminating in the most ludicrous maneuver to call attention to himself, his playing Herod "upon a scaffold hye" (3384)—functions as a parody of the ideal open expression of love advocated by medieval Christianity. But although Absalon, who "rometh" through the town (3694), provides a contrast to his private counterpart, Nicholas, who, "sleigh and ful privee" (3201), stays home pursuing his *deerne* concerns, neither of these lovers is to be seen loving properly. The point of Absalon's blatantly public courtship would seem to be to highlight Nicholas' *deerne* doings.

As Nicholas is first encountered, he is in his chamber in Alison's house, "allone, withouten any compaignye" (3204)—an ironic echo of an identical line in the Knight's Tale (I: 2779) when Arcite on his deathbed describes man as being alone in his grave. Nicholas is then seen "still in his chambre" all day long (3420) as he initiates the deception of John. And his ultimate bedding down with Alison is likewise a *deerne* act. While John is asleep in his tub in the rafters, the two lovers slyly sneak down to John's chamber: "Doun of the laddre stalketh Nicholay, / And Alisoun ful softe adoun she spedde" (3648–49).[99]

The progress, as well as the climax, of the Miller's Tale may also be seen in terms of the revealing of that which has been *deerne.* When Nicholas first makes his *deerne love* known to Alison, he addresses one who has been kept *deerne* by her jealous husband—John "heeld hire narwe in cage" (3224)—and his words are intended to include her in his secret. Likewise, when Nicholas makes his secret vision known to

John, his ostensible purpose is to include him in that secret. In contrast, at the end of the tale all that had been *deerne* is made public with great commotion and outcry. After Absalon, through his misplaced kiss, becomes familiar with what might be termed Alison's *deerne* or *privetee,* he responds with rage and a *deerne* of his own. He goes "a softe paas" to a smithy (3760) and, with the hot iron, steals back "ful softe" to Alison's house (3786). It is then Nicholas who feels the revelation of Absalon's *deerne* as, attempting another *deerne* of his own—and at the same time, ironically, revealing himself—he opens the window and "out his ers he putteth pryvely" (3802). This revelation in turn causes John to fall from the rafters and leads to his realization of what had previously been *deerne* to him. At this point all the action becomes public. Both Alison and Nicholas cry out in the streets and attract the neighbors who run in to "gauren" on the fallen John (3827) and to "kiken" and "cape" at the tubs in the rafters, and, furthermore, to "laughen" at John and turn "al his harm unto a jape" (3840–42). Such a transformation is also what happens to the *deerne.* Although it had seemed serious or even, to John, supernatural, it is now revealed to be only folly. Made public and put into the light, it is now seen as "fantasye," as something unreal and foolish, something like John's "ymaginacioun" (3612), which had caused him to weep and wail in fear of the coming Deluge.[100]

With the removal of the *deerne* the Miller's Tale comes to an end. No overt evaluation of it or its expression in love has been offered, nor has the illicit been replaced by the virtuous, though with the purging comes a sense of fulfillment. While functioning to direct Chaucer's narrative, *deerne love* acts to suggest comically the true nature of the passion at hand as well as to provide a comment on the love previously described in the Knight's Tale, where Palamon and Arcite had kept their love of Emilye hidden for years. It finally links the Miller's Tale to a tradition of love stories that both provided *mirthe* for medieval audiences and served to show the inadequacy of that which is illicit and hidden.

NOTES

1. *The Works of Geoffrey Chaucer,* ed. F. N. Robinson, 2nd ed. (Boston: Houghton Mifflin, 1957), p. 48. The reference to Nicholas' appearing meek as a maiden may be a comic echo of the line in the General Prologue describing the Knight as "meeke as is a mayde" (I: 69).

2. Although critics have neglected *deerne love* in Chaucer, at least two articles have focused on the "solas" of the Miller's Tale: Fletcher Collins, " 'Solas' in the *Miller's Tale,* " *Modern Language Notes,* 47 (1932), 363–64; David Brown, " 'Solas' in the *Miller's Tale,* " *Modern Language Notes,* 48 (1933), 369–70.

3. "Idiom of Popular Poetry in the Miller's Tale," in *English Institute Essays* 1950, ed. A. S. Downer (New York: Columbia U. Press, 1951); rpt. in *Explication as Criticism: Selected Papers from the English Institute* 1941–1952, ed. W. K. Wimsatt, Jr. (New York: Columbia U. Press 1963); rpt. in *Speaking of Chaucer* (London: Athlone Press; New York: Norton, 1970), pp. 19–20.

4. Ibid., p. 19.

5. *OED,* D: 231.

6. *Beowulf and the Fight at Finnsburg,* ed. Friedrich Klaeber, 3rd ed. (Boston: Heath, 1950). The dragon's treasure room is also described as being a secret hall, "dryhtsele dyrnne" (2320).

7. *The Junius Manuscript,* ed. G. P. Krapp, Anglo-Saxon Poetic Records, I (New York: Columbia U. Press, 1931), p. 18.

8. See also Joseph Bosworth and T. N. Toller, *An Anglo-Saxon Dictionary* (Oxford: Clarendon Press, 1882), p. 222, who also cite a similar meaning for the term in Old Saxon and Old Frisian.

9. *The Harley Lyrics,* ed. G. L. Brook, 2nd ed. (Manchester: University Press, 1956), p. 44; see also *English Lyrics of the XIIIth Century,* ed. Carleton Brown (Oxford: Clarendon Press, 1932), p. 146; hereafter cited as Brown, *XIII.*

10. *The Ormulum,* ed. R. M. White, rev. R. Holt (Oxford: Clarendon Press, 1878).

11. Line 45; ed. Brown, *XIII,* p. 117.

12. B. M. Add. MS, 10036; in *King Horn, Floriȝ and Blauncheflur, the Assumption of our Lady,* ed. George H. McKnight, EETS O.S. 14 (London: Oxford U. Press. 1901), p. 135.

13. *MED,* II: 1006.

14. *Bestiary,* in *An Old English Miscellany,* ed. Richard Morris, EETS O.S. 49 (London: Trübner, 1872), p. 4. See also *Early Middle English Verse and Prose,* ed. J. A. W. Bennett and G. V. Smithers, 2nd ed. (Oxford: Clarendon Press, 1968), p. 356, n. 38.

15. *Vices and Virtues,* 7–9; ed. F. Holthausen, EETS O.S. 89 (London: Oxford U. Press, 1888), p. 3.

16. *King Alfred's West-Saxon Version of Gregory's Pastoral Care,* ed. Henry Sweet, EETS O.S. 45 (London: Trübner, 1871), pp. 78–79.

17. Line 94; in *Twenty-Six Political and Other Poems,* ed. J. Kail, EETS O.S. 124 (London: Kegan Paul, Trübner, 1904), p. 53.

18. *Piers the Plowman,* ed. W. W. Skeat (London: Oxford U. Press, 1886), I: 54.

19. *Cursor Mundi,* ed. Richard Morris, EETS O.S. 59 (London: Oxford U. Press, 1875), pp. 418–19. This is the reading in all four versions.

20. Brook, p. 29; Brown, *XIII,* p. 134.

21. Brook, p. 32; Brown, *XIII*, p. 137, follows the MS reading, "when derne dede is indayne [unworthy], derne are done."

22. *Ancrene Wisse*, ed. J. R. R. Tolkien, EETS O.S. 249 (London: Oxford U. Press, 1962), p. 124.

23. Herebert, "Soethþe mon shal hoenne wende," 32–33; in *Religious Lyrics of the XIVth Century*, ed. Carleton Brown, 2nd ed. rev. G. V. Smithers (Oxford: Clarendon Press, 1952), p. 26.

24. *MED*, II: 1007, sect. 5.

25. Brook, p. 41. The poem is not included in Brown, *XIII*.

26. Brook, p. 70; Brown, *XIII*, p. 161.

27. Brook, p. 71; Brown, *XIII*, p. 162.

28. See Brown, *XIII*, pp. 236–37.

29. Terence, *Andria*, I: i, 105; in *The Comedies of Terence*, ed. Sidney G. Ashmore, 2nd ed. (New York: Oxford U. Press, 1910), p. 9.

30. *Ars Amatoria*, I: 33, 275; in *The Art of Love, and Other Poems*, ed. and tr. J. H. Mozeley, Loeb Classical Library (Cambridge, Mass.: Harvard U. Press, London: Heinemann, 1939), pp. 14, 32.

31. Ibid., II: 615–20; Mozeley, pp. 108–109. See also II: 639–40; Mozeley, ibid.

32. *Heroides and Amores*, ed. Grant Showerman, Loeb Classical Library (London: Heinemann; New York: Putnam's Sons, 1925), p. 234.

33. *De Amore*, I: vi, dialogue 5, rules 6, 10; ed. Amadeu Pagès (Castelló de la Plana: Soc. Castellonense de Cultura, 1930), pp. 61–62; tr. J. J. Parry, as *The Art of Courtly Love* (New York: Columbia U. Press, 1941), pp. 81–82; see also II: viii, rule 13 (Pagès, p. 178; Parry, p. 185); and I: vi (Pagès, p. 8; Parry, p. 34).

34. Ibid., dialogue 7 (Pagès, p. 83; Parry, p. 100).

35. Pagès, pp. 199–200; Parry, p. 203.

36. *Pamphilus*, in *La "Comédie" latine en France au XIIe siècle*, ed. Gustave Cohen (Paris: Belles-Lettres, 1931), II: 214. Pamphilus says that when one loves, he can scarcely hide the secrets of the heart: "Vix celare potest intima cordis amor" (506; Cohen, II: 212).

37. *Geta*, in Cohen, I: 40.

38. "Clauso Cronos et serato," st. 5; in *Carmina Burana*, ed. Alfons Hilka and Otto Schumann, I: 2; *Die Liebeslieder* (Heidelberg: Winter, 1941), p. 44.

39. "Si linguis angelicis," st. 2; Hilka-Schumann, p. 53.

40. "Rumor letalis," st. 1, line 15; Hilka-Schumann, p. 200.

41. "Dum curata vegetarem," st. 11; Hilka-Schumann, p. 174.

42. "Anni parte florida," st. 9; Hilka-Schumann, p. 95.

43. "Estatis florigero tempore," st. 5c; Hilka-Schumann, p. 37.

44. "Axe Phebus aureo," st. 7a; Hilka-Schumann, p. 40.

45. "Mout jauzens me prenc en amar," 39; in *Les Chansons de Guillaume IX, Duc d'Aquitaine (1071–1127)*, ed. Alfred Jeanroy, 2nd ed., Classiques français du Moyen Age, 9 (Paris: Champion, 1967), p. 24.

46. "Can l'erba fresch' e·lh folha par," 47; in *Bernart von Ventadorn. Seine Lieder*, ed. Carl Appel (Halle: Niemeyer, 1915), p. 222.

47. "Era·m casselhatz, senhor," 6; Appel, p. 32.

48. "Amors, e que·us es vejaire?" 43–44; Appel, p. 24.

49. "En una terra estranha," in *Les Poésies de Peire Vidal,* ed. Joseph Anglade, 2nd ed., Classiques français du Moyen Age, 11 (Paris: Champion, 1966), p. 19.

50. "Son ben apoderatz," 39; Anglade, p. 44.

51. "Al son desviat, chantaire," in *Poésies complètes du troubadour Marcabru,* ed. J.-M.-L. Dejeanne, Bibliothèque Méridionale, I, 12 (Toulouse: Privat, 1909), p. 19.

52. *Chansons de Gace Brulé,* ed. Gédéon Huet, Sociéte des anciens textes français, 45 (Paris: Firmin Didot, 1902), pp. 16–19.

53. "On doit d'amour goïr secréement; / et qui ne le fait ensi il mesprent," in "Adan, mout fu Aristote sachans," 51–52; *Adam de la Halle, Œuvres complètes,* ed. E. de Coussemaker (Paris: 1872), p. 169.

54. Giacomo da Lentino, "Maravigliosamente," st. 4; in *Le Rime della scuola siciliana,* ed. Bruno Panvini, Biblioteca dell'Archivum Romanicum, I, 65 (Florence: Olschki, 1962), I: 8; see also the words of Jacopo Mostacci, "Amor si de' celare / per zo che più fine ene / ca nulla gioi c'a esto mondo sia," in "Mostrar vorria in parvenza," 29–31; Panvini, p. 153.

55. *Vita Nuova,* XVIII; in *Le Opere di Dante,* ed. Michele Barbi, 2nd ed. (Florence: Soc. Dantesca Italiana, 1960), I; on the narrator's wish to conceal his love, see IV.

56. On the narrator's using ladies as a screen (schermo) of the truth, see *Vita Nuova,* V.

57. "Et facent en leur priveté / tretoute leur joliveté" (14305–306); in Guillaume de Lorris and Jean de Meun, *Le Roman de la rose,* ed. Félix Lecoy, Classiques français du Moyen Age, 92, 95, 98 (Paris: Champion, 1966–70).

58. Ironically, just as the lover begins to tell his "granz privetez" to Bel Acueil (3947), Amour robs him of everything.

59. *Cligés,* e.g., 626, 1040, 3021; ed. Alexandre Micha, in *Les Romans de Chrétien de Troyes,* Classiques français du Moyen Age, 84 (Paris: Champion, 1970).

60. Robert Harrison, *Gallic Salt* (Berkeley, Los Angeles, London: U. of California Press, 1974), p. 8.

61. *De civitate Dei,* XIV: xviii; *PL* 41: 426; tr. Marcus Dods, *The City of God,* Modern Library (New York: Random House, 1950), p. 466. Augustine speaks further of wrong loving and of "honestos amores" in his *Sermo, 385* (I: 2; *PL* 39: 1691).

62. *De civitate Dei,* XIV: xviii; *PL* 41: 426; tr. Dods, pp. 466–67. On Augustine's view of frankness in friendship, see Marie A. McNamara, *Friendship in Saint Augustine,* Studia Friburgensia 20 (Fribourg: University Press, 1958), pp. 207–10; on man's instinct of sociability, see Bernardo A. Pereira, *La Doctrine du mariage selon saint Augustin,* 2nd ed. (Paris: Beauchesne, 1930), pp. 18–21.

63. *De amicitia,* XVIII: 65; in Cicero, *De senectute, De amicitia, De divinatione,* ed. and tr. W. A. Falconer, Loeb Classical Library (London: Heinemann; New York: Putnam's Sons, 1923), pp. 176–77.

64. Ibid., VI: 22; Falconer, pp. 132–33.

65. Ibid., VI: 19–20; Falconer, pp. 128–31.

66. *De spirituali amicitia*, III; *PL* 195: 689.

67. *De sacramentis*, II: xiii, 6; tr. Roy J. Deferrari, as *On the Sacraments of the Christian Faith* (Cambridge, Mass.: Mediaeval Academy of America, 1951), p. 380.

68. Ibid., II: xi, 6; Deferrari, p. 334. Although a recent book by Henry A. Kelly (*Love and Marriage in the Age of Chaucer*, Ithaca and London: Cornell U. Press, 1975) presents secret love, especially secret marriage, as being without blame, some medieval authorities obviously assert otherwise.

69. Ibid., II: xiv, 1; Deferrari, p. 402.

70. *De substantia dilectionis*, III; in *Hugues de Saint-Victor. Six opuscules spirituels*, ed. and tr. Roger Baron, Sources Chrétiennes, 155 (Paris: Cerf, 1969), p. 88.

71. *De laude caritatis*, VII; in *The Divine Love*, tr. by a Religious of C.S.M.V. (London: Mowbray, 1956), p. 22.

72. *De substantia dilectionis*. III; Baron, p. 88; tr. by a Religious of C.S.M.V. as *Of the Nature of Love*, in Hugh of Saint-Victor: *Selected Spiritual Writings* (London: Faber and Faber, 1962), p. 189.

73. Ibid.

74. Ibid.; *Nature of Love*, p. 190.

75. Richard Rolle of Hampole, *The Psalter of Psalms of David and Certain Canticles*, ed. H. R. Bramley (Oxford: Clarendon Press, 1884), p. 162.

76. *Confessio Amantis*, I; 1932–33; in *The English Works of John Gower*, ed. G. C. Macaulay, EETS E.S. 81 (London: Oxford U. Press, 1900), I: 88.

77. *Great Cato*, II; 281–84; in *The Minor Poems of the Vernon MS*, ed. F. J. Furnivall, EETS O.S. 117 (London: Kegan Paul, Trench, Trübner, 1901), II: 576.

78. *Dan Michel's Ayenbite of Inwyt or Remorse of Conscience*, ed. Pamela Gradon, EETS O.S. 23 (London: Oxford U. Press, 1965), I: 143.

79. *Horn Childe and Maiden Rimnild*, 313–15; in *King Horn*, ed. Joseph Hall (Oxford: Clarendon Press, 1901), p. 182. *King Horn*, O (Laud) MS, 1382–83; ed. Hall, p. 76.

80. *The "Gest Hystoriale" of the Destruction of Troy*, 478–79; ed. G. A. Panton and D. Donaldson, EETS O.S. 39 (London: Oxford U. Press, 1869).

81. *Earl of Toulouse*, 492–93; in *Middle English Metrical Romances*, ed. Walter H. French and Charles B. Hale (New York: Prentice Hall, 1930), p. 398.

82. "Somer is comen wiþ loue to toune," 65–66; ed. Brown, *XIII*, p. 103.

83. *The Owl and the Nightingale*, 1357; ed. Eric G. Stanley (Edinburgh and London: Nelson, 1960), p. 88.

84. *Iacob and Iosep*, 214; ed. A. S. Napier (Oxford: Clarendon Press, 1916).

85. *A Tale of an Incestuous Doughter*, 33–34; in *Altenglische Legenden*, neue Folge, ed. C. Horstmann (Heilbronn: Henninger, 1881), p. 334.

86. *Laȝamon: Brut*, Otho MS, 131; the Caligula MS reads "mid darnscipe" (131); ed. G. L. Brook and R. F. Leslie, EETS O.S. 250 (London: Oxford U. Press, 1963), I: 6–7.

87. *The Avowing of Arthur;* in *Sir Amadace and The Avowing of Arthur,* ed. Christopher Brookhouse, Anglistica, 15 (Copenhagen: Rosenkilde and Bagger, 1968), p. 85.

88. *Sir Gawain and the Green Knight,* ed. Israel Gollancz, EETS O.S. 210 (London: Oxford U. Press, 1940), p. 43.

89. *Dux Moraud,* ed. W. Heuser, *Anglia* 30 (1907), 183.

90. *Piers Plowman A,* ed. Skeat, I; 282.

91. *Dame Siriʒ;* in *Middle English Humorous Tales in Verse,* ed. George H. McKnight (Boston and London: Heath, 1913), p. 6.

92. See, e.g., *Lex Deux changeors,* 23–25; in *Recueil général et complet des fabliaux des XIIIe et XIVe siècles,* ed. Anatole de Montaiglon and Gaston Raynaud (Paris: Librairie des Bibliophiles, 1872–90), I; 246; *La Dame qui aveine demandoit pour morel sa provende avoir,* 33–34, 58; Montaiglon-Raynaud, I: 319–20; *Guillaume au fauçon,* 247, 255; Montaiglon-Raynaud, II: 97–99.

93. See, e.g., *La Borgoise d'Orliens,* Montaiglon-Raynaud, I; 117; *Aloul,* Montaiglon-Raynaud, I: 255; Jean de Condé, *Le Pliçon,* VI: 260.

94. Juan Ruiz, *Libro de Buen Amor,* ed. and tr. Raymond S. Willis (Princeton: University Press, 1972), pp. 112–113.

95. Giovanni Boccaccio, *Il Decameron,* ed. Charles S. Singleton, Scrittori d'Italia 98 (Bari: Laterza, 1955), II; 237–38.

96. "Cors ki aimme ne doit repondre," l; Renaut de Beaujeu, *Le Lai d'Ignaure ou Lai du prisonnier,* ed. Rita Lejeune, Académie Royale de Langue et Littérature Françaises de Belgique, Textes Anciens, 3 (Brussels: Palais des Académies, 1938), p. 45; tr. Paul Brians, *Bawdy Tales from the Courts of Medieval France* (New York: Harper and Row, 1972), p. 37.

97. "Li descouvrirs riens n'avance / et li celers en toz poins vaut" (954–55), *La Chastellaine de Vergi,* ed. Gaston Raynaud, rev. Lucien Foulet, Classiques français du Moyen Age, 1 (Paris: Champion, 1972).

98. Gardiner Stillwell, "The Language of Love in Chaucer's Miller's and Reeve's Tales and the Old French Fabliaux," *JEGP,* 54 (1955), 694.

99. Father Beichner noted several years ago the basic association of Nicholas' epithet, "hende," with what is near or at hand; "Chaucer's Hende Nicholas," *Mediaeval Studies* 14 (1952), 151–53.

100. See the recent study by E. D. Blodgett, "Chaucerian *Pryvetee* and the Opposition to Time," *Speculum,* 51 (1976), esp. 482–84.

13

ALAIN RENOIR

The Inept Lover
and the Reluctant Mistress:
Remarks on Sexual Inefficiency
in Medieval Literature

With due apologies for proclaiming the obvious, I should like to suggest that one may perhaps best approach medieval love literature by recalling that sexual frustration was a perfectly acceptable subject for the narrative art long before the producers of *Bonnie and Clyde* decided to edify mankind by broadcasting on the screen their apparent conviction that shooting a few people may prove a satisfactory substitute for copulation. From a puristic point of view, my statement clearly calls for censure as a misleading generalization, for the annals of medieval love literature abound with protagonists who exhibit no intention of submitting to the external pangs and internal delights of sexual frustration. Students of English will think of a well-known Harley lyric usually printed under the title of *When the Nightingale Sings:* here, after four lines of conventional amorous complaints reminiscent of Jaufré Rudel, Bernart de Ventadorn, and a host of other more or less frustrated Provençal lovers, the speaker devotes an additional fifteen lines to his eagerness to experience the end of his beloved's quaint reluctance, and he brings the poem to a close with a sudden about-face which implies a rather cavalier rejection of the courtly ideal of unrequited love.[1] Whereas Jaufré submissively concludes a poem with the passive observation that his sorrow is sharper than a thorn ("que pus es ponhens qu'espina / la dolors")[2] and Bernart composes an envoy in which he owns to being too scared to dare approach his lady ("del anar vas midons sui temens"),[3] with a love complaint the Middle English poet bluntly sums up his recriminations with the very unfrustrated assertion that he fully intends to play the field rather than put up with any kind of sexual starvation: "Y wole mone my song / on wham þat hit ys on ylong."[4] Likewise, one need not be a professional medievalist to recall how the conclusion of the triple roundel *Merciles Beaute,* sometimes attributed to Geoffrey Chaucer, makes a clean sweep of the fooleries of love and its never-fulfilled expectations:

Sin I fro Love escaped am so fat,
I never thenk to ben in his prison lene;
Sin I am free, I counte him not a bene
(27–29)[5]

I have admittedly been somewhat less than ingenuous in citing exceptions which do not fundamentally detract from my original statement. Yet, the very presence of poems belittling the theme of sexual frustration both bears witness to the existence of that theme and suggests its importance in the literature of the period. Just as Thomas Rymer could expect his audience to accept his summation of *Othello* as a play designed to teach young ladies to be careful with their linen,[6] so a literal-minded reader with the foregoing assumptions in mind might conceivably look upon the *Nibelungenlied* as the story of a sexually frustrated woman who massacred 10,000 Burgundians because an over-eager relative had killed her bed-companion, and upon Chaucer's *Troilus and Criseyde* as the story of a man who went to Heaven because it took him an unconscionably long time to get to bed with his mistress.[7]

From the story-teller's point of view, the theme of sexual frustration presents at least one substantial advantage: whether one wishes to concentrate its impact within a few brief lines like William IX of Aquitaine in *Ab la Dolchor del Temps Novel*[8] or to drag it endlessly through the nooks and crannies of a shooting estate like D. H. Lawrence in *Lady Chatterley's Lover,* its basic components are simple and permanent. Somehow, someone is not getting what someone wants or should be getting. This simplicity enables the author of the *Nibelungenlied* to summarize the first half of his epic in eight lines and the second half in one and a half,[9] and Chaucer to do the same thing for *Troilus and Criseyde* in five lines (1–5). Simple themes, however, usually make for variations, and the topic under discussion presents us with at least two fundamental alternatives since the victim of frustration may obviously be either male or female.

Ever since the publication of Claude Fauriel's *Histoire de la Poésie Provençale,* in 1846, much attention has been given to the former alternative,[10] and the chances are that Gaston Paris' fortuitous coining of the term *courtly love,* in 1883,[11] did much to lend a formidable impetus to the assumption that every medieval lover must by definition suffer sexual frustration for the gratification of a reluctant mistress. The most influential expression of this view in the twentieth century occurs in C. S. Lewis' *Allegory of Love,* where we read that the lover "is always abject. Obedience to his lady's lightest wish, however whimsical, and silent acquiescence in her rebukes, however unjust, are the only virtues

he dares to claim. . . . he is no light-hearted gallant: his love is represented as a despairing and tragical emotion."[12] In other words, the
medieval mistress is assumed to display a determined reluctance to
admitting her lover to her bed before she has taken him through his
paces. The logic behind this kind of behavior was already expounded in
the late-twelfth-century *De Amore,* where Andreas Capellanus argued
that easily acquired amorous favors are never taken seriously, while
difficulty of attainment adds value to the prize,[13] and it was only with
the fifteenth century that John Lydgate pointed out the masochistic
nonsensicality of a convention which must surely prove as frustrating to
the mistress herself as to the lover toward whom it was directed.[14]

Nonsensical or otherwise, the theme of the reluctant mistress and
the frustrated lover pervades the high Middle Ages. Students of French
will recall the case of *Yvain,* in which Chrestien de Troyes has Laudine
banish Yvain from her sight because he has inadvertently missed a
deadline. Such is the impact of her summary judgment that the knight
immediately falls prey to amnesia, goes mad, and takes to the woods,
where he survives on venison which he kills like a wild man and
devours without benefit of cooking:

> Por ce mesne li sovenoit
> De nule rien qu'il eüst feite.
> Les bestes par le bois agueite,
> Si les ocit et si manjue
> La veneison trestote crue.

[But of what he did, he remembered nothing afterwards.
Then he lay in ambush in the forest for wild animals and
killed them and ate their flesh raw.][15]

Chrestien makes it a point to emphasize his hero's wildly deranged
state of mind when he specifically shows him acting "com hon forsené
et sauvage" (2828) ["like a lunatic or a wild man" (p. 48)], but we
must turn to Hartmann von Aue's Middle High German adaptation for
a categorical statement to the effect that Yvain's complete intellectual
and physical collapse is a tribute to the power of Love:

> doch meistert vrou Minne
> daz im ein krankez wîp
> verkêrte sinne und lîp.

[Yet Lady Love brought it about that a frail woman over-
turned both his body and his mind.][16]

The theme of the reluctant mistress and the frustrated lover almost necessarily brings up—at least in the male reader's mind—the question of efficiency. Notwithstanding the regrettable error in timing already mentioned, Ivain may be rated a fairly efficient lover: I, for one, can think of no adjective more suitable to a man who can talk himself into the bed of a bereaved widow whose husband he openly admits having recently killed. Sîvrit, in the *Nibelungenlied,* is in certain respects even more efficient despite his quasi-total innocence, as one may infer from the amazing ease and speed with which he publicly conducts his progress from a first hesitant look at Kriemhilt to the point where he secures her love over more than five thousand ("fünf tûsent oder mêre," 271:3) lusty knights.[17] When considered statistically, on the other hand, Tristan seems rather less efficient in amorous matters than his popular reputation would suggest. Notwithstanding the incomparable resourcefulness with which he usually eludes those who would interfere with his romantic assignments, the tangible results can only be described as meager when contrasted to the formidable output of energy behind them, and there is something decidedly inefficient about a hero who proves emotionally incapable of making love to his beautiful bride on their wedding night.[18] It may not be entirely coincidental that, when Chaucer decides to expose his own failure to get a prompt return on his romantic efforts, in *To Rosemounde,* he first emphasizes his pathetic inefficiency by comparing himself to a "pyk walwed in galauntyne" (17) and then goes on to call himself "trewe Tristam the secounde" (20). The ultimate in amorous inefficiency has been conveniently illustrated on a grand scale in Ulrich von Liechtenstein's *Frauendienst.* Here, because the lady whose love he has been seeking dislikes the shape of his mouth,[19] we find Ulrich submitting to painful surgery followed by the humiliation of having a foul-smelling, bright-green ointment ("ein salbe noch grüener denn der klê / ... diu stanc alsam ein fûler hunt" [st. 103]) smeared all over his lips. When, a number of weeks later, he screws up his courage to show his reconstructed mouth to the lady in question and offer to be her knight, her answer leaves no doubt about the total ineffectiveness of his methods: "Swîget! ir sît gar ze kint" [shut up! you're nothing but a boy] (st. 151). This disaster, incidentally, seems to have left Ulrich unshaken in his conviction that the scalpel is the quickest way to a woman's heart, so that another section of the book shows him turning once again to the surgeon to have a finger chopped off and sent to the same lady as a token of love. Not altogether surprisingly, the gift merely convinces her of her suitor's madness and draws her loud protest that his service would be in

vain ("der dienst wære gar verlorn" [st. 454]), even if he were to carry
on for a thousand years. Considering that this sort of antics goes on for
1850 eight-line stanzas with results reminiscent of those cited above,
we may point to the *Frauendienst* as illustrative of the respective ways
of inept lovers and reluctant mistresses.

Chaucer, whom one should always call in as a technical consultant in
amorous matters, paints a relatively clear picture of the elements which
yield respectively efficiency and inefficiency in love. In the Miller's
Tale, he presents us with two competitors for the sexual favors of
Alisoun, the young and concupiscible small-town belle whom he considers equally worthy of a night in bed with a lord or of marriage to
"any good yeoman" (3269–70) and whose sex appeal more than war-
rants this realistic assessment:

> For she was wylde and yong . . .
> . . . .
> As any wezele hir body gent and smal.
> . . . .
> And sikerly she hadde a likerous ye.
> . . . .
> There nys no man so wys that koude thenche
> So gay a popelote or swich a wenche.
> . . . .
> Hir mouth was sweete as bragot or the meeth,
> Or hoord of apples leyd in hey or heeth.
> (3225–62)

One of the competitors is the parish clerk, Absolon, who is in dead
earnest about his project and spares no time or effort to woo the object
of his desire. To this end, he short-changes the Sunday collection,
makes token gestures at sleepless nights, and even composes pathetically bad poetry. Yet, the final reward of this elaborate production is a
particularly sensual kiss which the would-be lover is permitted to
apply, not on Alison's sweet lips, but, alas, on what Chaucer
graphically chooses to call her "nether ye" (3852):

> This Absolon gan wype his mouth ful drie.
> Derk was the nyght as pich, or as the cole,
> And at the wyndow out she putte hir hole,
> And Absolon, hym fil no bet ne wers,
> But with his mouth he kiste hir naked ers
> Ful savourly, er he were war of this.
> Abak he stirte, and thought it was amys,

For wel he wiste a womman hath no berd.
He felte a thyng al rough and long yherd,
And seyde, "Fy! allas! what have I do?"
"Tehee!" quod she, and clapte the wyndow to,
And Absolon gooth forth a sory pas.

(3730–41)

I hope not to be accused of overstating my case if I suggest that this passage argues at least a certain amorous inefficiency on Absolon's part.

The other competitor is a student named Nicholas. Unlike his rival, he wastes no time on unnecessary niceties, and he gets his way within precisely fifteen lines (3276–90). His approach is simple and direct: "And prively he caughte hire by the queynte" (3276). The means whereby he pursues his initial advantage are likewise devoid of the various time-consuming adornments of courtly love so convincingly recommended by Andreas:[20] we see him hold "hire harde by the haunche-bones" (3279) and moving straight on to the request, "Lemman, love me al atones" (3280). Considering that Nicholas succeeds in getting the operation going while carrying on a conversation with his mistress' husband (3638–39), I feel relatively secure in venturing the opinion that we are here provided with an instance of high-level sexual efficiency.

The foregoing discussion should not lead us into thinking that Chaucer concerns himself exclusively with the ludicrous aspects of sexual behavior. His *Troilus and Criseyde,* which he himself labels a "litel . . . tragedye" (V: 1786) reveals on a serious level a sexual pattern similar to that of the Miller's Tale. Some relevant differences and similarities between the casts of these poems are worth noting here. In each case, we have a triangle composed of one woman and her two suitors; but, whereas the protagonists of the Miller's Tale are students, craftsmen, and other people of little consequence who act accordingly within the context of their small provincial town, those of the *Troilus* are members of the highest nobility upon whom depends the outcome of a great war and who act accordingly in and about the renowned capital city whose survival is at stake. Turning once more to Andreas' testimony, we see from this disparity in social status that the latter are ideally suited for the intricacies of courtly love while the former are hardly removed from those peasants who can at best rush into the simplest forms of mating like a horse and a mule ("naturaliter sicut equus et mulus" [p. 272]).[21] This fundamental difference, however, is matched by equally significant similarities between the principal characters. Whereas Alison is a delightfully oversexed carpenter's wife and looks every inch the part, Criseyde is a great lady, and everything about her proclaims the aristocrat:

> Criseyde mene was of hire stature,
> Therto of shap, of face, and ek of cheere,
> Ther myghte ben no fairer creature.
> And ofte tyme this was hire manere,
> To gon ytressed with hire heres clere
> Doun by hire coler at hire bak byhynde,
> Which with a thred of gold she wolde bynde.
> . . . .
> She sobre was, ek symple, and wys withal,
> The best ynorisshed ek that myghte be,
> And goodly of hire speche in general,
> Charitable, estatlich, lusty, and fre.
>
> (V: 806–23)

Yet, just as we are told of Alison that "she hadde a likerous ye" (3244), so we are told of Criseyde that ". . . trewely, they writen that hire syen / That Paradis stood formed in hire yën. / And with hire riche beaute evere more / Strof love in hire ay, which of hem was more" (V: 816–19). Considered as invitations to love, the difference between the provincial wench's lecherous eye and the paradise in the great lady's eyes is one of literary tone and social level, but the promise is the same to the would-be lover as long as he belongs to the appropriate class. From the opposite point of view, one may note the same relationship in the means used by both women when they play the part of the reluctant mistress: Alison delays Nicholas for nearly thirty seconds by pretending to spring away from his embraces "as a colt dooth in the trave" (3282) and chirping out such enticing interdicts as "lat be . . . , lat be / Or I wol crie 'out, harrow' and 'allas'! / Do wey your handes, for youre curteisye" (3285–87), while Criseyde's haunting concern for her "estat" (II: 465) and "honour" (e.g., II: 468, 472, 480) leads her to keep a despairing Troilus at a chaste distance month after month although she has seen "noon unryght" (II: 453) in his prayer from the start.

Similar negative and positive comparisons may be drawn between the two sets of rivals. Whereas Absolon is a ridiculous hick who comes equipped with a ruddy complexion, dresses ostentatiously in a provincial counterpart of today's loudest rock-festival fashions, enjoys singing "a loud quynyble" (3332) while accompanying himself on a fourteenth-century precursor of the electric guitar, and sports an impressive head of curly hair which "strouted as a fanne large and brode" (3315), Troilus looks like a prince and acts accordingly:

And Troilus wel woxen was in highte,
And complet formed by proporcioun
So wel that kynde it nought amenden myghte;
Yong, fressh, strong, and hardy as lyoun;
Trewe as stiel in ech condicioun;
Oon of the beste entecched creature
That is, or shal, whil that the world may dure.

And certeynly in storye it is yfounde
That Troilus was nevere unto no wight,
As in his tyme, in no degree secounde
In durryng don that longeth to a knyght.

(V: 827–37)

The two men are worlds apart. Yet, just as Absolon comically stumbles through his rudimentary version of the book of love, so does Troilus movingly suffer through every page of the entire book; just as Absolon expresses his emotion with a grotesque poetic effort in which he compares his yearning to that of a "lamb after the tete" (3704), so does Troilus express his love in a fine English adaptation of *Sonnet CXXXII*[22] from Petrarch's *Il Canzoniere:*

If no love is, O God, what fele I so?
And if love is, what thing and which is he?
If love be good, from whennes cometh my woo?
If it be wikke, a wonder thynketh me,
When every torment and adversite
That cometh of hym may to me savory thinke,
For ay thurst I, the more that ich it drynke.

And if that at myn owen lust I brenne,
From whennes cometh my waillynge and my pleynte?
If harm agree me, wherto pleyne I thenne?
I noot, ne whi unwery that I feynte.
O quike deth. O swete harm so queynte,
How may of the in me swich quantite,
But if that I consente that it be?

And if that I consente, I wrongfully
Compleyne, iwis. Thus possed to and fro,
Al sterelees withinne a boot am I
Amydde the see, bitwixen wyndes two.
That in contrarie stonden evere mo.
Allas! what is this wondre maladie?
For hete of cold, for cold of hete, I dye.

(I: 400–20)

Just as Absolon consistently mishandles the details of his courtship, so Troilus plumbs the depth of sexual ineptitude when he faints in his beloved's bedroom, has to be dumped into her bed by her uncle, and proves in no shape to perform his part until she has brought him out of his swoon and practically raped him:

> Therwith his pous and paumes of his hondes
> They gan to frote, and wete his temples tweyne;
> And to deliveren hym fro bittre bondes,
> She ofte hym kiste; and shortly for to seyne,
> Hym to revoken she did al hire peyne.
> And at the laste, he gan his breth to drawe,
> And of his swough sone after that adawe. . . .
>
> . . . .
>
> And therewithal hire arm over hym she leyde,
> And al foryaf, and ofte tyme hym keste.
>
> (III: 1114–29)

Just as the hilarious reward of Absolon's amorous antics is a misdirected kiss, in addition to which the foolish parish clerk receives full in the face, as a kind of tactile and olfactory afterthought, "a fart / As greet as it had been a thonder-dent, / That with the strook he was almoost yblent" (3806–3808), so the sorrowful reward of Troilus' faithful and unselfish adherence to the code of chivalric love is the loss of his mistress to a rival, soon followed by his own heroic death on the battlefield. Finally, just as Absolon's misadventure momentarily teaches him to despise the treacherous pleasures of the flesh, "For fro that tyme that he hadde kist hir ers, / Of paramours he sette nat a kers, / For he was heeled of his maladie" (3755–57), so Troilus' disappointment teaches him to despise the vanity of earthly passions as he indulges in a moment of posthumous contemplation:

> And down from thennes faste he gan avyse
> This litel spot of erthe, that with the se
> Embraced is, and fully gan despise
> This wrecched world, and held al vanite
> To respect of the pleyne felicite
> That is in hevene above; and at the laste
> Ther he was slayn, his lokyng down he caste.
>
> And in hymself he lough right at the wo
> Of hem that wepten for his deth so faste;
> And dampned al oure werk that foloweth so

> The blynde lust, the which that may nat laste,
> And sholden al oure herte on heven caste.
>
> (V: 1814–25)

The difference between the parish clerk's misadventure and the nobleman's total undoing is the difference between comedy and tragedy, but the lesson of either is surely the same, provided of course that each tale be recited before the appropriate audience.

The same kind of parallelism occurs between Nicholas and Diomede. Whereas the former is a poverty-stricken student, the latter is a great knight and the heir apparent to two mighty kingdoms:

> This Diomede, as bokes us declare,
> Was in his nedes prest and corageous,
> With sterne vois and myghty lymes square,
> Hardy, testif, strong, and chivalrous
> Of dedes, lik his father Tideus.
> And som men seyne he was of tonge large;
> And heir he was of Calydoigne and Arge.
>
> (V: 799–805)

Yet, just as Nicholas knows all about "deerne love" (3200) and is "sleigh and ful privee" (3201) as well as "ful subtile and ful queynte" (3275), so Diomede is described as "he that koude more than the crede" (V, 89) in the game of love and a man who conducts his amorous adventures "as he that koude his good" (V: 106) as well as "with al the sleghte" in the world (V: 773). Just as Nicholas goes after Alison for the fun of it and in a spirit which Chaucer characterizes with the word "pleye" (3273), so Diomede goes after Criseyde in a spirit of totally irresponsible gamesmanship. We are told that "to fisshen hire, he leyde out hook and lyne" (V: 777), and we hear him delight in the thought that "whoso myghte wynnen swich a flour / . . . He myghte seyn he were a conquerour" (V: 792–94) and callously conclude that he has nothing to lose in the attempt: "I shal namore lesen but my speche" (V: 798). Although Nicholas never actually states the fact, he also is in Diomede's enviable position of having nothing to lose in the chase, for each man is an outsider to the world of his would-be mistress and need accordingly not worry about the consequences of his actions.[23] Just as Nicholas moves into immediate action by grabbing Alison by the most intimate part of her anatomy, so Diomede moves into action "with shortest taryinge" (V: 774). The first twenty-seven lines of his initial conversation with Criseyde (V: 108–34) are all the space and time he needs to assure her that the Greeks make as satisfactory lovers as the Trojans (V: 125–26) and pull the old gag of offering to love her as a brother (V: 134–40); and it takes him only another thirty-five lines to ask for her love: "and mercy I yow preye" (V: 168). Just as Nicholas gets what he wants in record time, so Diomede gets what he wants in record time. Admittedly, the rituals which carry each man to his respective victory assume different outward manifestations. Unlike Nicholas, for instance, Diomede feels early in the game the need to apologize for the celerity of his proceedings: "And wondreth nought, myn owen lady bright / Though that I speke of love to yow thus blyve" (V: 162–63). But, here again, the difference is one of social level and literary tone: within their respective bailiwicks, the two men act on similar impulses and use similar methods to get what they want. In other words, both may be offered as illustrations of complete sexual efficiency.

Chaucer's testimony in the Miller's Tale and the *Troilus* points to a distressingly negative correlation between earnestness and sexual efficiency. Only the man who moves in for the fun of it is likely to deliver prompt and efficient service, while the sincere lover seems doomed to unhappiness and failure. Those of us who have gained a modicum of experience outside the protective walls of the cloister will probably not find this paradox very paradoxical. What probably seems much more paradoxical to the twentieth century, however, is the implied lesson which we read in Chaucer's insistence upon presenting himself as the most inept of all inept lovers. In the introduction to the *Troilus*, we may recall, he blames his own romantic inefficiency for his hesitation to invoke the God of love:

> For I, that God of Loves servantz serve,
> Ne dar to Love, for myn unliklynesse,
> Preyen for speed, al sholde I therfore sterve,
> So fer am I from his help in derknesse.
>   (I: 15–18)

In *The Legend of Good Women*, he must ask for the help of men with actual experience in love—those "lovers that kan make of sentement" (F: 69)—in order to compose his poem, and his unwarranted boldness in approaching the God of Love's favorite flower earns him a humiliating tongue-lashing:

> What dostow her
> So nygh myn oune floure, so boldely?

> Yt were better worthy, trewely,
> A worm to neghen ner my flour than thow.
>
> (F: 315–18)

Again, toward the end of his often-quoted introduction to *The Parliament of Fowls,* he specifically denies any first-hand knowledge of the fleeting joys of love:

> The lyf so short, the craft so long to lerne,
> Th'assay so hard, so sharp the conquerynge,
> The dredful joye, alwey that slit so yerne:
> Al this mene I by Love, that my felynge
> Astonyeth with his wonderful werkynge
> So sore, iwis, that whan I on hym thynke,
> Nat wot I wel wher that I flete or synke.
>
> For al be that I knowe nat Love in dede,
> Ne wot how that he quiteth folk here hyre,
> Yit happeth me ful ofte in bokes reede
> Of his myrakles and his crewel yre.
>
> (1–11)

As often with Chaucer, the reader may easily be puzzled by the mixed tone of humor and earnestness, but we cannot overlook the fact that the emphasis upon the transitory nature of love and the sufferings normally attendant upon its servants finds a sharp echo in the conclusion of the *Troilus:*

> Swich fyn hath, lo, this Troilus for love!
> Swich fyn hath al his grete worthynesse!
> Swich fyn hath his estat real above,
> Swich fyn his lust, swich fyn hath his noblesse!
> Swich fyn hath false worldes brotelnesse!
> And thus bigan his lovyng of Criseyde,
> As I have told, and in this wise he deyde.
>
> O yonge, fresshe folkes, he or she,
> In which that love up groweth with youre age,
> Repeyreth hom fro worldly vanyte,
> And of youre herte up casteth the visage
> To thilke God that after his ymage
> Yow made, and thynketh al nys but a faire
> This world, that passeth soone as floures faire.
>
> (V: 1828–41)

If we accept the evidence presented above, we must also lend an ear to my contention that Chaucer the poet not only recognizes the problem of sexual efficiency and inefficiency but that he casts his own vote on the side of the latter.

We have thus far considered only one of the two alternatives which I proposed earlier—that of the reluctant mistress and the frustrated lover—and we have examined works in which the reluctance of the mistress is in direct proportion to the ineptness of the lover and vanishes as soon as a more efficient entrepreneur pops up on the scene. Furthermore, because this essay began with a consideration of principles outlined in Lewis' *Allegory of Love,* I have thought it appropriate to remain within the general context of that work and accordingly limit my observations to texts which illustrate what might be called the French way of making love. By crossing the seas and glancing at the Scandinavian way of making love, I should now like to illustrate the other alternative: that of the frustrated mistress and the reluctant lover. The work which I propose to discuss here is the *Gunnlaugssaga Ormstungu,* composed in Iceland a century or more before *Troilus and Criseyde* but dealing with events which must have taken place around 1000 A.D.[24]

As already mentioned above, the very simplicity of the theme of sexual frustration makes for easy summary, and the anonymous author of the *Gunnlaugssaga Ormstungu* needs less than a printed page in a modern edition to summarize his story at the outset:

Þat dreymði mik at ek þóttumk heima vera at Borg ok úti fyrir karldurum, ok sá ek upp á húsin ok á mœninum álpt eina væna ok fagra, ok þóttumk ek eiga ok þótti mér algóð. / Þá sá ek fljúga ofan frá fjǫllunum ǫrn mikinn. Hann fló hingat ok settisk hjá álptinni ok klakaði við hana blíðliga, ok hon þótti mér þat vel þekkjask. Þá sá ek at ǫrninn var svarteygr ok járnklœr váru á honum; vaskligr sýndisk mér hann. / Því næst, sá ek fljúga annan fugl af suðrætt. Sá fló hingat til Borgar ok settisk á húsin hjá álptinni ok vildi þýðask hana. Þat var ok ǫrn mikill. Brátt þótti mér sá ǫrninn er fyrir var ýfask mjǫk er hinn kom til, ok þeir bǫrðusk snarpliga ok lengi, ok þat sá ek at hvárumtveggja blœddi. Ok svá lauk þeira leik at sinn veg hné hvárr þeira af húsmœninum, ok váru þá báðir dauðir. En álptin sat eptir hnipin mjǫk ok daprlig. / Ok þá sá ek fljúga fugl ór vestri; þat var valr. Hann settisk hjá álptinni ok lét blítt við hana, ok síðan flugu þau í brott bæði samt í sǫmu ætt, ok þá vaknaða ek.

[In my dream, I seemed to be at home at Borg, standing outside and in front of the main doorway, and up on the roof-ridge of the house I saw a swan, a fine and lovely pen; I felt she was mine and I prized her highly. /

Then I saw a big eagle flying down from the mountains. He flew towards us and settled beside the swan and chattered gently to her, and at that she seemed well pleased. Then I saw that the eagle had black eyes and claws of iron; he looked active and bold. / Next, I saw another bird flying from the south. He flew here to Borg and landed on the house beside the swan and tried to win her favour; this bird was a big eagle too. Now, it seemed to me that the first eagle soon got very angry when the other arrived, and they had a long fierce fight, and I saw that both of them were bleeding. The struggle ended with both of them falling off the roof, each on his own side; and they were both dead. The swan stayed there, very sad and dejected. / And then I saw a bird flying from the west; it was a falcon. He landed beside the swan and was gentle with her, and by and by they flew away together in the same direction. Then I woke up.][25]

The first eagle is Gunnlaug himself. His bold appearance ("vaskligr sýndisk mér hann") may be considered the key to his character, especially when taken in conjunction with a subsequent statement to the effect that he was very arrogant in every respect of his temperament ("hávaðamaðr mikill í ǫllu skaplyndi" [p. 6]), for *boldness* and *arrogance* are indeed the two terms which best describe his behavior. While still a youngster,[26] for instance, he makes a bold though unsuccessful attempt at tricking the father of the girl whom he already loves into promising her to him before witnesses. A few years later we find him acting so obstreperously around home that he forces his own father to help his matrimonial plans under the most adverse conditions, and he thinks nothing of beating senseless a man who had ridden his horse into a sweat. As an adventurer and roving retainer, he shows himself the bravest of men and wins all the honors most coveted by the warriors of his time and culture. The second eagle is Hrafn, who marries the same woman whom Gunnlaug has been wanting since childhood, with the result that the two men must eventually kill each other in single combat. The falcon who flies away with the swan is Thorkell, the pathetically nondescript man who becomes the woman's husband after the death of Gunnlaug and Hrafn. Finally, the swan is Helga, the dreamer's lovely daughter, for the possession of whom two brave and handsome warrior-poets have killed each other, so that she must bear the children of a well-meaning and reassuringly wealthy man in whose unadventurous bed she finds little pleasure while her sorrow for the loss of Gunnlaug slowly drives her to her own death.

If we consider that the several protagonists whose undoing has been summarized here belong to families of some wealth and importance and that the historical Gunnlaug and Hrafn have won more than honorable mentions on the roll of Icelandic poets, we may see that the story is a tragedy in the medieval sense of the word as Chaucer has conveniently glossed it for us in the prologue to his Monk's Tale:

> Tragedie is to seyn a certeyn storie,
> As olde bookes maken us memorie,
> Of hym that stood in greet prosperitee,
> And is yfallen out of heigh degree
> Into myserie, and endeth wrecchedly.
>
>   (1973–77)

More specifically, it falls, like the *Ajax* of Sophocles, within the category of what Aristotle calls "pathetic tragedy," in which it seems that a grave error on the hero's part brings about a drastic change from happiness to unhappiness.[27] In the present case, the error is one of judgment on Gunnlaug's part: unlike Troilus, he never admits to himself the deplorable fact that his boldness on the battlefield and in the making of poetry is not matched by his boldness in the bedroom,[28] and his failure to do so brings about the series of events which culminates in the death of the principal characters of the story. Indeed, we may assume that everything would proceed peacefully except for Gunnlaug's deliberate failure to claim his promised bride on the appointed date and his subsequent refusal to recognize Hrafn's right to move into the bed which he has thus declined to occupy.

From the point of view of the present analysis, however, the tragedy is that of Helga, for it is she who must suffer through the antics of the man she loves. Ever since their first meeting at the age of twelve,[29] she has returned Gunnlaug's love: "Lagði hvárt þeira góðan þokka til annars bráðliga" ["they quickly took a strong liking to each other"] (p. 7). Her ordeal begins when it becomes obvious that her promised husband will not appear to claim her and that she may consequently have to marry another man: "Ok frestaðisk tilkváma Gunnlaugs, en Helga hugði illt til ráða" ["and still Gunnlaug's return was delayed. Helga loathed the thought of this marriage"] (p. 23). Her subsequent wedding to Hrafn holds so little attraction for her that even the guests at the ceremony notice "at brúðrin væri heldr dǫpr" ["that the bride was somewhat dejected"] (p. 27), and the life which henceforth lies ahead of the couple proceeds accordingly. The drooping state of their matrimonial activities is graphically suggested with the statement that "Helga vakir, en Hrafn svaf" ["Helga was awake . . . . Hrafn was asleep"] (p. 27), thus uncomfortably reminding the modern reader of Emma Bovary's creeping into bed "contre Charles que dormait" [against a sleeping Charles].[30] Helga's sentiments toward Hrafn become unequivocally clear when he tells her of a premonitory death-dream which has troubled his sleep, and she succinctly answers, "þat mun ek aldri gráta" ["I will never weep over such a thing"] (p. 27), before bursting into tears at the mere thought of Gunnlaug: "Ok grét Helga þá mjǫk" ["Then Helga wept bitterly"] (p. 27). After Gunnlaug finally reenters her ken, she becomes so cold toward her husband—"svá stirð við Hrafn" (p. 27)—that he must give up keeping her at home, and their sexual relations come to an end: "ok nýtti Hrafn lítit af samvistum við hana" ["He enjoyed little intimacy with her"] (p. 27). As suggested at the outset of this essay, the situation outlined above is by no means unique: one may recall the female character of Lydgate's *Temple of Glass,* who bitterly complains about having to endure a husband while longing for the presence of her lover,[31] or the woman speaker of *Wulf and Eadwacer,* who also suffers anguish for the wandering man with whom she knows full well that she will never be united.[32] The quiet death of Helga, which brings the saga to an end, is a fittingly moving conclusion to the long sexual frustration which she endures throughout the narrative.

Although the *Gunnlaugssaga* begins with a prediction of the birth of Helga and ends with her death, her part is purely passive: she endures the results of the action, but the action itself is carried out by others and brought about by Gunnlaug's failure to come to terms with reality. His amorous ineptitude controls the action, and the passion that urges him on against all reason yields the emotional tension which makes the saga one of the most powerful works of literature ever written. Gunnlaug wants Helga with all the might of passion, but he wants her only when he knows he cannot have her: whenever he perceives the slightest opportunity of sharing her bed, his interest dies off to return to life only when the bed in question is again safely out of reach. The following analyses of some of the episodes already mentioned will bear out my contention.

Early in the saga, the boy Gunnlaug proves brash enough to try obtaining Helga's hand through the shameless device of asking her father to teach him the proper procedure for betrothal and allow him to go through the ceremony with Helga under the pretense of wishing to see how it is performed. The boldness of the act, however, seems somewhat less excessive if we realize that Gunnlaug can entertain absolutely no hope of success. Because Helga is the loveliest woman in Iceland—"fegrst kona ... á Íslandi" (p. 7)—her father naturally expects to make a profitable match, and the fact that Gunnlaug has just

run away from home in protest against parental discipline hardly qual-
ifies him as a worthwhile prospect, even if one were to take seriously
the matrimonial aspirations of a mere child. Furthermore, it is
noteworthy that Gunnlaug does not go through the actual mock-
betrothal until Helga's father has declared before witnesses that "þetta
skal vera sem ómælt" ["this is to be counted as unsaid"] (p. 7).

The same principle applies to the occasion when Helga's hand is
actually promised to Gunnlaug. Six years have elapsed since the
juvenile attempt discussed above, and the saga offers no indication that
he has given any further thought to the matter. Now, he receives his
father's permission to sail abroad and acquires half-interest in a ship for
an expedition that will last at least twelve months. No sooner has he
settled the details of the journey and thus assured that half an ocean
will soon separate him from Helga's bedchamber than his interest in
her revives with a new burst of energy, and he will not rest until she has
been promised to him. As may be expected, everybody else realizes the
inconsistency of his intentions, and Helga's father answers his urgent
request with the sober statement, "Ekki sinni ek hégóma þínum" ["I'm
not pandering to your fancies"] (p. 10). His own father likewise tells
him, "þú ert óráðinn maðr" ["you are an unsettled fellow"] (p. 11),
and argues with him the blatant inconsistency in his decision both to
acquire a bride and to set off immediately on a long and hazardous
journey. Gunnlaug, however, is not one to listen to reason: he bullies
his father into making arrangements for a betrothal, and he stubbornly
asserts, "Ek ætla þó útan allt eins" ["I still intend to go abroad just the
same"] (p. 11). The conclusion of the episode is that Helga will be
betrothed to Gunnlaug if he returns to claim her within three years. I
have already said enough to make it clear that he does not come back in
time to make good his intransigent intentions.

The circumstances under which Gunnlaug succeeds in failing to
return home in time to claim Helga's hand, and his subsequent behavior, will illustrate the point which I have been attempting to make.
The end of his third year abroad finds him at the court of Norway.
Since the voyage between Iceland and the Continent was then possible
during the warmer months only, he has already missed two opportunities to sail home and must either go now or give up the right to
claim his bride-to-be, who has recently been conditionally promised to
his rival Hrafn in the all-too-probable event that her wandering suitor
should fail to meet the deadline. Yet, Gunnlaug manages to reach the
port of Thrándheim so late in the season that he must discover the
predictable fact that all the ships for Iceland have already sailed. As

luck would have it, a belated ship is lying at anchor a few miles up the coast although it left Thrándheim five days before Gunnlaug decided to make the return voyage, so that he can find absolutely no excuse for delaying another year. No sooner has he come aboard than the captain inquires whether he shares the now-common knowledge that Helga will be given to Hrafn under the conditions outlined above. The brief and matter-of-fact statement which describes Gunnlaug's reaction to the question is more revealing than a detailed analysis: "Gunnlaugr kvezk frétt hafa" ["Gunnlaug said he had heard"] (p. 25). In other words, he has been wasting time in full awareness that only hurry could insure his possession of the woman he loves.

As things turn out, the ship makes Iceland a few days before the appointed date for Helga's marriage to Hrafn, so that Gunnlaug has ample opportunity to challenge his rival if he wishes to do so. Ever resourceful, however, he succeeds in wasting some more time by helping unload the cargo before proceeding with his own business. Even so, he reaches his home district on the weekend of the wedding and announces his plan to attend the event: "Gunnlaugr kvazk þá þegar vilja ofan ríða til Borgar" ["Gunnlaug said he wanted to ride down to Borgar at once"] (p. 26)—presumably to stop it, but a sore foot prevents him from acting upon his stated intention. The impediment is legitimate but revealing when considered within context: a few days before, while helping unload the ship, he has taken part in a wrestling bout and thrown his foot out of joint, with the result that it has to be reset and bound up before he may ride to his father's homestead. Nothing in the text indicates that the pain makes the journey especially difficult or heroic: "þeir Hallfreðr riðu tólf menn saman ok kómu suðr á Gilsbakka í Borgarfirði . . ." ["Gunnlaug and Hallfred with ten companions rode off together and arrived in the south at Gilsbakki in Borgarfjord"] (p. 26). Nevertheless, he who has never been known to accept unpleasant advice before now yields to his father's opinion that the condition of his foot would make it ill-advised to proceed a few more miles to the place where Helga is to be married. In contrast, we have seen him earlier in the saga suffer with another sore foot so badly maimed that "freyddi ór upp blóð ok vágr er hann gekk við" ["blood and pus oozed up out of it when he put his weight on that foot"] (p. 13). Yet, when Earl Eric of Norway noticed the blood spurting from his shoe and marvelled at his walking as though he felt no pain, he haughtily dismissed the matter with the assertion, "Eigi skal haltr ganga meðan báðir fœtr eru jafnlangir" ["a man mustn't limp while both his legs are the same length"] (p. 13).

The juxtaposition of the two episodes outlined here underscores the fact that Gunnlaug will endure much greater hardship for the sake of his personal reputation as a brave warrior than to secure possession of the woman whom he has loved since childhood. Even when he again meets Helga alone after her separation from Hrafn, he makes no attempt at bringing about any sort of sexual relationship between them, although her behavior makes it almost impolite not to proposition her: "þá stóð Helga ok starði á Gunnlaug lengi eptir" ["Helga stood and gazed for a long time after Gunnlaug"] (p. 32). Nor may his reluctance to take the hint and act accordingly be attributed to a relaxation of his love, for her sight has moved him a few moments earlier to compose two poems whose intensity of sentiment reveals the extent of his passionate yearning for the woman whom he refuses to possess, and blatantly exposes his utter blindness to his own responsibility in losing her to another man:

> Ormstungu varð engi
> allr dagr und sal fjalla
> hœgr, síz Helga in fagra
> Hrafns kvánar réð nafni;
> lítt sá holðr inn hvíti,
> hornþeys, faðir meyjar,
> gefin var Eir til aura
> ung, við minni tungu.

[For Snake-Tongue no whole day, under the hall of the mountains, was easy, since Helga the Fair had the name of Hrafn's wife; / the white man, the girl's father, paid little heed—the goddess of the horn-thaw was married young for money—to my words.]

And again:

> Væn, ák verst at launa,
> vín-Gefn, fǫður þínum—
> fold nemr flaum af skaldi
> flóðhyrs—ok svá móður,
> því at gerðu Bil borða
> bæði senn und klæðum,
> herr hafi holðs ok svarra
> hagvirki, svá fagra.

[Beautiful wine-goddess, I have the worse injury to repay your father and mother—the land of the sea-fire takes joy

> from the poet— / because both together under the bed-
> clothes they made the goddess of woven bands so fair: the
> devil take the craftsmanship of that man and woman!] (pp.
> 28–29).[33]

These illustrations of Gunnlaug's passion and his error of judgment are
important in more ways than one, for his passionate inability to assess
reality provides the mechanism which brings about the catastrophe of
the action. Indeed, when Gunnlaug challenges Hrafn to the duels
which will take both their lives, he does so with the accusation, "þat
veizt þú at þú hefir fengit heitkonu minnar" ["you know . . . that you
have married my promised bride"] (p. 30). But *we* know, of course,
that Hrafn has merely picked the option which his rival never claimed.

The motive of the prospective or actual husband who fails to meet
his deadline is well-known to historians of literature, and we have
already seen Yvain perform a similar breach of etiquette in the romance
that bears his name. Yvain, however, is guilty of a mere oversight in
respect to the calendar rather than of chronic sexual reluctance, and he
submits to his punishment without deluding himself into thinking
that he has been deceived by the machinations of a double-crossing
rival. Nor is Gunnlaug the only reluctant lover in Old Norse literature:
in the *Kormákssaga,* for example Kormák loses interest in the woman he
loves the moment they are formally engaged, proves emotionally incapable of attending his own wedding, and concludes their relationship by
turning her down when she is actually offered to him.[34] The thing
which sets the *Gunnlaugssaga* apart from the other works discussed
here, however, is that the mixture of boldness and sexual reluctance
which characterizes him may not be regarded as a mere decorative motif
or an interesting insight into human nature added to an adventure story
for good measure: quite the contrary, it is the central controlling
element for the structure of the entire saga. Were he not so brash as he
is, Helga would never have been promised to him; and were he not so
reluctant, he would have married her instead of going abroad, thus
terminating the narrative at the very point where it becomes psychologically interesting. Could Gunnlaug bring himself to return home on
time, Hrafn would never marry Helga; and were he not so passionately
bold, he would never challenge his rival to a duel. It is his every action
and failure to act that bring about each successive episode in the
narrative, and his last act brings about not only his death and that of
Hrafn but that of Helga as well.

I have waited until now to discuss Helga's death because it affords a
ready-made conclusion to my analysis insofar as it seems to bring

together all the elements of the saga. Sometime during Gunnlaug's stay abroad, King Sitrygg of Ireland has rewarded his poetic skill with a splendid scarlet cloak, and Gunnlaug has eventually given it to Helga. Now that the two rivals have killed each other and she has remarried, she must endure life with an honorable man in whom she finds no pleasure, and she spends her days thinking of her dead love. Her only joy is to spread out the scarlet cloak before her and gaze endlessly upon it: it is the symbol of Gunnlaug's love and of his poetic skill, as well as of the wanderings which have kept him from her forever, and it is her only tangible token of the passion that was both too much and not enough to unite them through life. The last chapter of the saga shows her sitting by her husband and calling for the scarlet cloak: "Ok einn laugaraptan sat Helga í eldaskála ok hneigði hǫfuð í kné Þorkatli, bónda sínum, ok lét senda eptir skikkjunni Gunnlaugsnaut. Ok er skikkjan kom til hennar, þá settisk hon upp ok rakði skikkjuna fyrir sér ok horfði á um stund. Ok síðan hné hon aptr í fang bónda sínum ok var þá ørend" ["One Saturday evening, Helga sat in the living-room resting her head on her husband Thorkel's knee. She sent for Gunnlaug's gift, the cloak, and when it was brought to her, she sat up and spread the cloak in front of her and gazed on it for a while. Presently she sank back into her husband's arms and was dead"] (pp. 39–40).

Thus, Helga dies as she has lived, passively holding the symbol of the passionate ineptitude that has killed her. No other conclusion is necessary. After a few lines to the effect that the still-nondescript Thorkel utters the proper words of mourning and continues to exist, the narrative comes to an end in the laconic manner typical of Icelandic sagas: "Ok lýkr þar nú sǫgunni" ["And there the saga ends"] (p. 40).

The three works which we have examined in some detail belong to three different literary categories: the Miller's Tale is a *fabliau* and treats copulation in accordance with the conventions of this genre; *Troilus and Criseyde* is a courtly romance and treats love in accordance with the conventions of this genre; the *Gunnlaugssaga Ormstungu* is a would-be biographical tale which relates an occurrence involving real people who lived and suffered, and it treats a particular instance of sexual relationship as it has supposedly come down to the author.[35] From the point of view of realism, we may accordingly wish to oppose the Icelandic saga to the two English poems, since the latter must treat their subject matter within the framework of conventions which may or may not suit the reality of the action, while the former purports to concern itself only with the transmitted facts of the situation. We must not, however, rush to the conclusion that the former is necessarily more realistic than the latter, for every work of literature worthy of the name creates its own world, and realism develops within the context of that world. The difference is that the two English works, as one expects with Chaucer, present us with a sharp psychological realism of detail, while the Icelandic work presents us with an equally sharp realism of the whole. Though the overall action of the Miller's Tale may intentionally stretch the limits of the credibility gap, Absolon's reaction to his own misdirected kiss is a piece of superb psychological realism, and any man who thinks he would react differently ought to make an emergency appointment with his analyst. The same thing may be said of the *Troilus* and Diomede's incentive for working himself into Criseyde's bed, or Troilus' terror at the thought of approaching it; and these illustrations are typical of the poems from which they are drawn. On the other hand, Gunnlaug's reluctance is not merely the direct cause of every detail of the action but indeed the very subject matter of the entire story, and anyone who ever hesitated a half-second before taking what he most wanted will feel the full impact of the powerful psychological realism which pervades the entire action of the saga.

If the foregoing views about realism be not thoroughly mistaken, I should like to conclude by returning to the beginning of this essay and to my remarks on the basic simplicity and permanence of the theme of sexual frustration. Under the pen of a master, these characteristics make for the sort of narrative which can occasionally escape the tyranny of time: they allow a Geoffrey Chaucer or an anonymous saga writer to portray an Absalon, a Troilus, or a Gunnlaug in such manner that their misadventures, their joys, and their sorrows are as real for the modern reader as they must have been for their original audiences many centuries ago. Paradoxically, the most earthly of all subject matters thus becomes a quasi-Boethian tool in the endless human struggle to emulate divinity.[35]

NOTES

1. For Provençal sources, see e.g. Jean Audiau, *Les Troubadours et l'Angleterre* (Paris: Vrin, 1927), pp. 42–45. Arthur K. Moore, *The Secular Lyric in Middle English* (Lexington: U. of Kentucky Press, 1951), discusses the relationship of *When the Nightingale* to Northern French counterparts of the poets mentioned here (pp. 62–64) and notes the English poet's "happy faculty of disengaging himself at will from his literary background" (p. 72).

2. Jaufré Rudel, *Quand lo Rius de la Fontana,* 26–27, in Frederick Goldin, ed. and tr., *Lyrics of the Troubadours and Trouvères* (New York: Anchor, 1973), pp. 102–104.

3. Bernart de Ventadorn, *Can l'Erba Fresch',* 58, in Goldin, *Lyrics,* pp. 136–40.

4. *When the Nyhtegal Singes,* 20–21, in George L. Brook, ed., *The Harley Lyrics* (Manchester: University Press, 1948), p. 63.

5. All quotations from and references to Chaucer are from Fred N. Robinson, ed., *The Works of Geoffrey Chaucer,* 2nd ed. (Boston: Houghton Mifflin, 1957).

6. Thomas Rymer, *A Short View of Tragedy,* in Curt A. Zimansky, ed., *The Critical Works of Thomas Rymer* (New Haven: Yale U. Press, 1956), p. 132.

7. These simplistic interpretations seem to have been partially shared by predecessors of both the *Nibelungenlied* poet and Chaucer: e.g., in *Guð-rúnarkviða I* (in Sopphus Bugge, ed., *Sæmundar Edda* [Christiania: P. T. Malling, 1867]), the wrath of the yet-to-be avenger of the *Nibelungenlied* partly stems from her frustration at having been deprived of her man in bed ("i sęingo" [st. 20]); in the proem to *Il Filostrato,* which Nathaniel E. Griffin, ed. and tr., *The Filostrato of Giovanni Boccaccio* (Philadelphia: University Press, 1927), believes to have been composed before Maria d'Aquino granted its author "the final favors" (p. 18), Boccaccio first regrets having wasted time on the assumption that merely thinking about one's beloved ought to be no small part of a lover's pleasure (". . . non essere picciola parte della beatitudine dell' amante" [p. 116]) and then states that no man ever experienced amorous misadvantures so similar to his own as did the valiant young Troilus (". . . che il valoroso giovane Troilo" [p. 126]).

8. The speaker of *Ab la Dolchor* (Goldin, *Lyrics*) complains that love longing keeps him from sleeping or laughing ("mos cors non dorm ni ri" [9]), but he willingly endures his frustration since the object of his desire has given him her affection and her ring ("sa drudari' e son anel" [22]) and he hopes for more tangible tokens in the future: "enquer me lais Dieus viure tan / c'aia mas manz soz so mantel" ["God let me live long enough / to get my hands under her mantle"] (23–24).

9. *Das Nibelungenlied,* ed. Karl Bartsch, rev. Helmut de Boor (Leipzig: Brockhaus, 1949), 13:1–14:4, and 2:3–4.

10. Claude C. Fauriel, *Histoire de la Poésie Provençale,* ed. Jules Mohl (Paris: Labitte, 1846), discusses what he calls a very strange system ("un system fort étrange" [I, 497]) in which women demanded and received a quasi-religious kind of worship ("le culte qu'elles exigeaient et obtenaient comme dames de chevaliers" [I, 499]). Since the printed text was the posthumous publication of university lectures presumably delivered about 1831–1844, the discussion in question reached a limited audience before 1846.

11. Gaston Paris, "Études sur les Romans de la Table Ronde: Lancelot du Lac," *Romania,* 12 (1883), e.g., p. 534.

12. C. S. Lewis, *The Allegory of Love* (Oxford: Clarendon Press, 1958), pp. 2–3.

13. Andreas Capellanus, *Trattato d'Amore: Andreae Capellani Regii Francorum "De Amore" Libri Tres,* ed. Salvatore Battaglia (Rome: Perrella, 1947): "Facilis perceptio contemptibilem reddit amorem, difficilis eum carum facit haberi" (rule xiv, p. 358).

14. John Lydgate, *Lydgate's Temple of Glass,* ed. Joseph Schick, EETS, E.S. 60 (London, 1891), 339–61. I have discussed the details of Lydgate's handling of this problem in "Attitudes Toward Women in John Lydgate's Poetry," *English Studies,* 42 (1961), esp. p. 12.

15. Chrétien de Troyes, *Yvain,* ed. Wendelin Fœrster, rev. T. B. W. Reid (Manchester: University Press, 1948), 2822–26, tr. Robert W. Ackerman and Frederick W. Locke, *Ywain* (New York: Ungar, 1957), p. 48.

16. Hartmann von Aue, *Iwein,* ed. Georg F. Benecke and Karl Lachmann, rev. Ludwig Wolff (Berlin: de Gruyter, 1968), I, 3254–56; my translation.

17. In "Levels of Meaning in the *Nibelungenlied:* Sifrit's Courtship," *Neuphilologische Mitteilungen,* 61 (1960), 353, I have argued that Sîvrit conducts his courtship like an object lesson to illustrate ahead of time Jehan le Maire de Belges' outline of the five steps of love.

18. Not only does it require a mighty potion to make Tristan woo Isolde, but Gottfried von Strassburg, *Tristan und Isolde,* ed. Wolfgang Golther (Berlin: Spemann, 1880) describes the result as an endless heartache ("endelôse herzenôt" [11679]) rather than satisfaction, and he devotes only 595 lines (16683–17278) to an unimpaired period of potential love during which they waste unconscionable time gazing at each other ("si sâhen beide ein ander an" [16819]), playing the harp while singing sad songs (they "liezen danne klingen / ir harphen unde ir singen / senelîchen" (17209–11]), and proving generally very pure ("sô lûter" [17240]), while much of the total 19554 surviving lines show Tristan indulging in such exhausting activities as fighting a fierce Irishman, killing a dragon, undoing an evil dwarf, or wading through water to deceive his king. Thomas, *Les Fragments du Roman de Tristan,* ed. Bartina H. Wind (Geneva: Droz, 1960), has Isolde of the White Hands embrace, kiss, and hold Tristan near her on their wedding night before realizing that she wants "iço qu'il ne desire" [That which he does not desire] (Fragment *Sneyd*[1], 592).

19. Ulrich von Liechtenstein, *Frauendienst,* ed. Reinhold Bechstein (Leipzig: Brockhaus, 1888), st. 80. Following a tradition apparently dating back to Ludwig Tieck's modernization, significantly entitled *Frauendienst, oder: Geschichte und Liebe des Ritters und Sängers Ulrich von Lichtenstein* (Stuttgart: Cotta, 1812), Bechstein accepts the general historicity of the poem (e.g., p. ix ff.), while John W. Thomas, ed. and tr., *Ulrich von Liechtenstein's Service of the Ladies* (Chapel Hill: U. of North Carolina Press, 1969), sums up the principal views in this respect and presents a tightly-knit argument for reading the work as a satirical parody on contemporary love poetry. Both positions are compatible with my use of the *Frauendienst* as illustrative of amorous inefficiency in medieval literature.

20. Andreas, for whom uprightness alone is worthy of the crown of love ("Sola ergo probitas amoris est digna corona" [*De Amore,* p. 22]), devotes nearly

the entirety of a long chapter (ch. vi, pp. 24–254) to various dialogues illustrating the acceptable ways of conducting a courtly love affair.

21. Whereas Andreas' intricate illustrations of courtly love proceedings (see n. 20) range from a dialogue between middle-class lovers ("Loquitur plebeius ad plebeiam" [p. 24]) to one between members of the higher nobility ("Loquitur nobilior nobiliori" [p. 180]), the rudimentary sexual practices of peasants are dispatched in a brief paragraph ("De Amore Rusticorum" [p. 272]) in which the male reader interested in seducing one of their women is urged to waste no time on courtly niceties and to proceed straightaway to action, since they are not normally won unless the timely remedy of a little compulsion be applied to their bashfulness ("nisi modicae saltem coactionis medela praecedat ipsarum opportuna pudoris" [p. 282]). As noted by John J. Parry, tr. and ed., in his introduction to Andreas' treatise, *The Art of Courtly Love* (New York: Ungar, 1959), the social classes here considered eligible for love correspond to the French "*bourgeoisie* (not the peasants), the *simple noblesse,* and the *noblesse titrée*" (pp. 35–36, n. 13). In view of my own argument, it might be well to add that the French *bourgeois* of the late twelfth century, when Andreas is assumed to have written (see Parry, *Art,* pp. 20–21) were presumably better suited to courtly amenities than the craftsmen of fourteenth-century Oxford, as suggested by the term *gnof,* which Chaucer uses to describe Alison's carpenter husband and which the *Middle English Dictionary* glosses as "ill-mannered fellow."

22. Number in Alberto Chiari's edition of *Il Canzoniere* (Rome: Curcio, 1968), but the sonnet ("S'amor non è che dunche è quel ch'io sento?") is also numbered LXXXVIII (e.g., in Robinson's note to *Troilus,* I: 400–20).

23. If we go outside the Miller's Tale for a context presumably available to Chaucer's audience, Nicholas becomes not only an outsider but as much of an enemy to Alison's people as Diomed is to Criseyde's, for we recall that the hostility between the university and the town of Oxford was so bitter that the inhabitants staged a riot and massacred several students in 1354–5.

24. Sigurður Nordal and Guðni Jónsson, eds., *Borgfirðinga Sǫgur: Hœnsa-Þóris Saga, Gunnlaugs Saga Ormstungu, etc.* (Reykjavik: Hið Islenka Fornritafélag, 1938), give the chronology of the historical Gunnlaug as 984–1009 (p. lix) and place the time of written composition about 1270–80 (p. lx). Jan de Vries, *Altnordische Literaturgeschichte* (Berlin: de Gruyter, 1941–1942), also argues in favor of 1280 (II, 391). L. M. Small, ed., *Gunnlaugssaga Ormstungu* (Leeds: T. Wilson, 1935), dates Gunnlaug's life as 987–1010 and suggests the first half of the thirteenth century for written composition (p. 16). An oral version may have existed as early as the eleventh century; see, e.g., Matthew H. Scargill and Margaret Schlauch, tr. and ed., *Three Icelandic Sagas* (Princeton: University Press, 1950), p. 5.

25. *Gunnlaugs Saga Ormstungu,* ed. Peter G. Foote and tr. Randolph Quirk (London: Viking Society, 1957), p. 3.

26. The events mentioned here occurred the year "when the whole country became Christian" ("at landit varð allt kristit" [p. 8]), which we know from

the *Brennu-Njáls Saga* to have been 1000 A.D., so that Gunnlaug must have been about thirteen or sixteen, depending on whether he was born in 987 or 984 (cf. n. 24).

27. Aristotle, *Poetics,* in S. H. Butcher, *Aristotle's Theory of Poetry and Fine Art* (London: Macmillan, 1911), 1455b:35–1456a–1 (passion as motive for pathetic tragedy), 1453a:12–16 (major error or weakness as central point of effective tragedy), and 1452b:9–13 (inclusion of painful action or death on the stage).

28. Even before Troilus' display of a "wrecched mouses herte" (III: 736) upon approaching Criseyde's bedroom, his misgivings about his own amorous qualifications are evident when he refers to himself as the "refus of every creature" (I: 570) and fears the very possibility that his intentions may suggest to her anything "that toucheth harm or any vilenye" (I: 1033).

29. Gunnlaug is twelve years of age ("Gunnlaugr var tólf" [p. 67]) at the time of his first meeting with Helga, and "they were much the same age" ("þau váru mjǫk jafnaldrar"] (p. 7).

30. Gustave Flaubert, *Madame Bovary,* ed. Roger Tisserand (Paris: Larousse, 1936), I, 103.

31. See n. 14.

32. Not all scholars share this view of *Wulf and Eadwacer,* which I have discussed in "*Wulf and Eadwacer:* a Noninterpretation," *Franciplegius: Medieval and Linguistic Studies in Honor of Francis Peabody Magoun, Jr.,* ed. Jess B. Bessinger, Jr., and Robert P. Creed (New York: University Press, 1965), pp. 147–63.

33. Discrepancies between Quirk's translation of these poems and translations by other scholars reflect the near-impossibility of translating skaldic verse into English. In Scargill's words, these verses "had an elaborate use of metaphors and a complicated meter with a highly involved sentence structure . . . [which] cannot be imitated" (*Three Icelandic Sagas,* p. 6); cf. Scargill's own translations of these poems (p. 36), and those by Lee M. Hollander, in *The Skalds* (Princeton: University Press, 1947), p. 141.

34. Einar Ó. Sveinsson, ed., *Vatnsdæla Saga, Hallfreðar Saga, Kormáks Saga, etc.* (Reykjavik: Hið Íslenka Fornritafélag, 1939), tr. Lee M. Hollander, *The Sagas of Kormák and the Sworn Brothers* (Princeton: University Press, 1949): Kormák loses interest "at síðan þessum ráðum var ráðit" (p. 223) ["after all arrangements had been made" (p. 24)]; he "sœkir eigi brullaupit eptir því sem ákveðit var, ok leið fram stundin" (p. 224) ["he did not come to the marriage on the day agreed upon, and the time agreed upon went by without his coming" (p. 24)]; and, when his beloved's husband offers to withdraw "Kormákr bað Steingerði fara með bónda sínum" (p. 298) ["Kormák had Steingerd stay with her husband" (p. 70)]. Although the saga states specifically that Kormák's reluctance is the work of the witch Thorveig (pp. 221–22 and 223), his behavior is clearly similar to Gunnlaug's.

35. For such relationship as may be established between the narrative and actual history, see Foote's introduction to the edition used here, pp. xiv–

xvii; see also Hollander, *Skalds,* pp. 137–44. Scargill, *Three Icelandic Sagas,* p. 4, notes that the historical evidence concerning Helga and her second husband is at best nebulous.

36. To Boethius, *Philosophiae Consolatio,* ed. Ludwig Bieler, Corpus Christianorum, series latina, 94 (Turnhout: Brepols, 1957), a fundamental difference between man and God is that, whereas the former must regrettably live in the present ("in tempore" [p. 101]), reason must assume the latter to be eternal ("æternum esse" [p. 101]) and to remain unaffected by time, since eternity is by definition the total, perfect, and simultaneous possession of endless life ("Æternitas igitur est interminabilis uitae tota simul et perfecta possessio" [p. 101]). In view of the paradoxical coincidence suggested here, one might wish to keep in mind that Chaucer translated the *Consolatio* into English and that Howard R. Patch, who devoted two solidly packed chapters of *The Tradition of Boethius* (New York: Oxford U. Press, 1935), to medieval translations and imitations of this treatise (pp. 46–113), has pointed out that the influence of Boethian concepts over a millennium of European culture was so pervasive that it "is beyond our power to estimate" (p. 87).

14

DOROTHY BETHURUM LOOMIS

Constance and the Stars

It has been frequently claimed recently that the Man of Law's Tale, saint's legend and *Märchen* though it is, is highly appropriate to its teller, an astute, highly successful member of a profession not notably inclined to piety or to folklore.[1] On the face of it this contention seems highly dubious. The Man of Law's Tale, constituting Fragment II of the *Canterbury Tales,* together with the tales of Fragments VII, III, and VI, about whose order in the *Tales* there is the least certainty, illustrates Chaucer's changing purpose and conception of his characters as he worked on the tales. There seems little doubt that Chaucer originally intended to have the Man of Law tell the *Tale of Melibeus,* since the Man of Law says plainly that he is to speak in prose (96) and so will not compete with Chaucer. *Melibeus* would have been not inappropriate to him, and Chaucer's assignment of the tale to himself is a part of the joke of his whole performance in the pilgrimage.

It is the purpose of this article to deny that the story of Constance is an especially appropriate one for the Man of Law and to claim that Chaucer was attracted to it because in the first place it is a good piece of fiction and in the second because it offered him the perfect opportunity to set forth and justify his belief in astrology. To be sure, Chaucer has done something to adjust the tale to the Man of Law. The best illustration was pointed out by Father Beichner in his discussion of *disparitas cultus* in which he shows the lawyer familiar with both canon and secular law.[2] But neither the trial in Part III of the tale[3] nor the rhetoric added by Chaucer to Trivet's story[4] offer proof of the teller's skill. The treatment of astrology in the story, therefore, can scarcely be interpreted as the lawyer's misunderstanding of destinal forces.[5]

Chaucer's principal additions to Trivet's tale of Constance are of two kinds: those that enhance Constance's piety, suffering, and maternal feeling; and those that offer an astrological explanation for her adventures. The first are paralleled in the Clerk's Tale by Chaucer's treatment of Griselda, and in neither case, it seems to me, can we argue that the additions were necessitated by the tender sensibilities of the tellers. If one should make such a case, the Man of Law would emerge as a very

different person from the portrait drawn by recent critics. The astrological additions are of a different kind, and again this is not the first time
Chaucer has changed his source to give an astrological explanation of
events. In the Knight's Tale he elaborates Boccaccio's simple encounter
of Mars and Venus[6] and adds the powerful figure of Saturn to explain
the outcome of the tournament.[7] The gods in Chaucer's story are the
planets whose influence controlled Palamon, Arcite, and Emily. In
Troilus and Criseyde Chaucer again changed Boccaccio's gods of the
usual mythological pattern into the planets that shaped the destiny of
the characters. Troilus was under the protection of Venus, which was
well situated when he rode through Troy in all his martial glory and
made a favorable impression on Criseyde (II: 680–87), and Venus was
apparently sufficiently powerful at his birth to insure his success in love
(III: 712–15), though her influence was not strong enough to enable
him to keep Criseyde's love. The rare conjunction of Saturn and Jupiter
in Cancer that caused the downpour on the night of the consummation
of Troilus' and Criseyde's love is a cause out of proportion to its effect.
The rain would have been assured by the inferior conjunction of Saturn
and the moon, and it is this that Pandarus counted on. But the stanza
that explains the operation of the heavens (III: 617–24) leaves no doubt
that Chaucer intended the astral determinism that operates in the
poem. Not the rain that detained Criseyde in Pandarus' house is
foretold by the heavens but the fall of Troy,[8] to which Troilus and
Criseyde are inevitably linked. A third case of Chaucer's adding an
astrological explanation to the story told by his source is the legend of
Hypermnestra. Hypermnestra was the only one of the fifty daughters of
Danaus who failed to carry out her father's command to slay her
husband on her wedding night. (Chaucer has exchanged Danaus and
Aegyptus.) What could account for her courage and her tragedy?
Chaucer adds to the account of his sources, principally Ovid's *Heroides,*
an elaborate nativity which explains Hypermnestra's nature and her
unhappy doom.[9] Venus and Jupiter, two propitious planets, bestowed
beauty, compassion, integrity, and modesty upon her; and Mars, who
might have made her ruthless enough to obey her father's command, is
in such an unfavorable position at her birth that he could exert no
influence. All might have been well had not Saturn, the most malign of
all planets, come into a position of such power that he brings about her
death in prison. The passage on Hypermnestra's nativity (1580–98)
shows Chaucer familiar with and concerned about the influences of each
of the planets and able to use astrology artistically in a rather wooden
tale.

There can be no doubt about Chaucer's interest in astrology, nor of his competence as an astronomer. *The Astrolabe* may have been child's play to a fourteenth-century man of scientific interest, as it is addressed to a child, but it was still being praised by Gabriel Harvey in the sixteenth century and by Thomas Hearne in the eighteenth for its accuracy.[10] And it has been called by a contemporary scientist "the earliest first-class scientific work in our language—and even as a textbook it is still unrivalled for the lucid description of a scientific instrument."[11] If indeed Chaucer was the author of *The Equatorie of the Planets*, as its editor claims,[12] he appears there not as a casual amateur but as a serious student of astronomy. Astrology was an interest that came to him rather late in his career. He read the mythographers before he began a study of astronomy, and the pagan pantheon in his poems before he wrote *Troilus* or the Knight's Tale is at first from Ovid and Vergil (*Book of the Duchess, House of Fame*) and then takes on the iconographical features of the mythographers (*Parliament of Fowls*). Around 1385 he began to be interested in both astronomy and astrology, and it may have been that about that time he gained access to the astrological and astronomical texts he subsequently made use of. The Merton College library at Oxford received in 1385 from William Rede, Bishop of Chichester, an important gift of books on science and philosophy, among them, apparently, works of Aristotle and commentaries on them, and the writings of Averroes and John of Lignano. The list of Rede's books is lost, but he was known to have had a strong interest in astronomy and must have had astronomical texts in his collection.[13] Professor Roland Smith has suggested that the books in the Merton College library before 1385 "would go a good way toward accounting for Chaucer's sources, whether scientific or philosophical."[14] When we add the fact that *The Astrolabe* is calculated for the meridian of Oxford[15] and that the Merton College library had, and still has, a planetary equatorium antedating *The Equatorie of the Planets*,[16] it is easy to believe that Chaucer had access to the library. Whether he did or not, it is not until after 1385 that he began to use astrological material in his work.

It is time to ask whether or not Chaucer believed in astrology, and the answer is, Of course he did. What alternative was there? Astrology after a long lapse attributable to the early hostility of the church had returned to prominence on the Continent in the twelfth and thirteenth centuries and by the fourteenth was a strong interest of the intelligentsia. The question was to what degree man's destiny was controlled by the stars, and that resolved itself into the question of the degree to

which mind was under the control of body, for it was almost universally accepted that the body was influenced by the stars.

The Neoplatonic astronomy cultivated at Chartres in the twelfth
century developed quite logically from the relation of Providence and
Destiny which Boethius stated in the *Consolation of Philosophy*. God,
whether Plato's or Boethius', has the whole plan of the universe in one
simple, timeless act of cognition. Destiny, as the late Middle Ages
understood it, working out the divine plan, operates through Neoplatonic intermediaries, which may be divine spirits, Nature, angels, or
devils, but principally the stars.[17] At a considerable remove from
Destiny is another agent, Fortune, whose capricious and erratic force
governs the gifts allotted to man in his mundane existence. It is the
stars that engaged the study of medieval man, a study half religious,
half scientific, and Chaucer was no exception. In fact, he more than any
other writer was responsible for bringing English literature, belatedly,
to be sure, into the current of interest in astrology which was flowing
strong on the Continent.

According to Aristotle the stars, incorruptible and powerful, are the
cause of all motion and therefore of all generation and corruption in
inferior things. They determine the composition of the four elements in
every created thing. Moreover, they reveal the purposes of God and his
perfection, which are accessible to reason.[18] Eternal and forever carrying out the plan of God and of Destiny, they contain all the secrets of
the future if only they could be read correctly. The modern parallels to
this are the sciences of genetics and of meteorology. The modern
melancholic man is so because he inherited the genes of his dour father
and because he is susceptible to climatic variations. The medieval man
was melancholic because Saturn was powerful in his horoscope.
Granted the premises on which it was based, astrology was a logical
theory. It probably retained throughout the thirteenth and fourteenth
centuries, in the eyes of its most enlightened practitioners, something
of the tentativeness that Platonic theories about the natural world
always had, rather than the firmness of Aristotle's assumption that
causes could be known from repeated instances.[19]

Astrology's strong appeal rested on the fact that it gave a unified
view of the cosmos, a philosophical as well as a scientific one. It
revealed the pre-established harmony of the universe which in the
Timaeus, in Macrobius, and in Boethius rested on numbers. (One is
reminded that a recent astronomer has said that if there is a God one
thing can be said of him, that he is a great mathematician.) The sacred
number seven blazes in the heavens. There are seven planets, seven stars

in the Big Dipper, in the Pleiades, in Orion, and there are seven days for each phase of the moon. Twelve also occurs in mystical significance. There are twelve signs of the zodiac and twelve months of the year. There are (approximately) thirty days in a lunar revolution and thirty years in Saturn's. And the product of twelve and thirty is the number of the days of the year.[20] Thus the stars are the living witness to man that the universe is not ruled by blind fate but by eternal and intelligible laws. The inequities of actual life find a correction in the universal operation of the stars on all things. Though the horoscope of a princess could be expected to be more certainly known than that of a serf, the latter's was equally decisive for his career. The Wife of Bath no less than Constance belonged to that perfect order.

If, then, as Thorndike has claimed, there were in the Middle Ages no complete disbelievers in astral influence, it is easy to understand why that is true. There was no alternative. Before the development of the biological sciences there was no other explanation for differences in human temperament and behavior that was consistent with a belief in a God who has a concern for order. The question was not really whether the divine direction of affairs operated through the stars upon earthly creatures but the degree, as I noted above, to which the mind of man partook of matter and was controlled by them, and the degree to which the divine purpose could be discovered. Astrology had every *a priori* justification, and its practitioners needed the most stringent astronomical competency, which Chaucer had.

Though there may have been no outright disbelievers in the influence of the heavens, there were many shades of belief and careful limits to its area. For example, Robert Grosseteste, who had one of the best minds of the thirteenth century, whose lectures at Oxford early in the century established Oxford as a center of scientific interest, and whose early interest in astrology was responsible for furthering England's knowledge of the pseudo-science, in his book, *De prognosticatione,* used his full scientific equipment in favor of judicial astrology. But in later life he came to repudiate it on the ground that a belief in it deprived man of freedom.[21] Guillaume de Conches, the influential philosopher of Chartres in the twelfth century, distinguished in his classification of astronomers between the mythographers whom he called the fabulous (Aratus and Hyginus) and astrologers (Firmicus and Ptolemy), but does not recognize any pure astronomers. He himself believed the stars control nature and the human body but not the mind.[22] That is the position of most of the best minds from the twelfth through the fourteenth century, including Thomas Aquinas. But the matter does not end there, for the mind exists in a body and in universal experience is to a large degree influenced by it. Boethius and many others believed man was free to the degree that he freed himself of his body, but even Augustine, who in his early manhood thought it possible to escape the desires of the flesh, came in mature life to realize they never could be wholly subdued. And so the mind is in part under the domination of the stars. It is on the degree to which the future can and should be read in the heavens that opinion was divided in Chaucer's time, as well as on the extent of astral control. Judicial astrology was opposed by many churchmen on the familiar ground (which Milton repeats in *Paradise Lost*) that man should not attempt to know God's secrets. But it was tolerated by many churchmen also.

There is some indication that Chaucer's attitude toward astrology shifted from time to time and every indication that, like his stand on most problems, he never states outright what it is. It seems, however, that like his contemporaries he believed that the stars as instruments of Providence influenced human behavior; that the Wife of Bath, for example, was inclined to lust because Venus was powerful in her horoscope; that some of this pattern could be read by astute astrologers; that the influence was not absolutely decisive in human behavior; and that there were many charlatans in the field pretending to be sober scientists.

Chaucer's interest in astrology was in part purely scientific, and was based on his competence as an astronomer, as shown in *The Astrolabe* (and in *The Equatorie of the Planets?*), as well as in many astrological passages in his poems. These passages are not all clear and learned, but many are. The difficulty for modern critics is that few of us ever acquire astronomical learning sufficient to judge Chaucer's. Both Manly and Curry had it, and some others also. But we are better able, perhaps, to understand his philosophical interest in astrology, for it was at the center of the debate on freedom and determinism which so engrossed the fourteenth and fifteenth centuries.[23] Astrology provided the answer to that debate. It is in the Man of Law's Tale that Chaucer, it seems to me, makes his final statement on astrology, the orthodox answer to the question of the degree to which man is free.[24]

In the Man of Law's Tale Chaucer states the case for astral control in a stanza taken from Bernard Sylvestris' *De mundi universitate* (whose influence on him appears not only here but in the Knight's Tale):

> Paraventure in thilke large book
> Which that men clepe the hevene ywriten was

With sterres, whan that he his birthe took,
That he for love sholde han his deeth, allas!
For in the sterres, clerer than is glas,
Is writen, God woot, whoso koude it rede,
The deeth of every man, withouten drede.

In sterres, many a wynter therbiforn,
Was writen the deeth of Ector, Achilles,
Of Pompei, Julius, er they were born;
The strif of Thebes; and of Ercules,
Of Sampson, Turnus, and of Socrates
The deeth; but mennes wittes ben so dulle
That no wight kan wel rede it atte fulle.[25]

Bernard's lines read (I: iii, 33 ff.):

Scribit enim caelum stellis totumque figurat.
. . . .
Praeiacet in stellis series, quam longior aetas
Explicet et spatiis temporis ordo suis.
Sceptra Phoronei, fratrum discordia Thebae
. . . .
In stellis Priami species, audacia Turni,
Sensus Ulixeus, Herculeusque vigor.
. . . proelia Roma gerit.
In causas rerum sentit Plato, pugnat Achilles,
. . . .
Sic opifex ut in ante queant ventura videri
Saecula sidereis significata modis.[26]

[He inscribes the heaven with stars and shapes all things.
. . . He forecasts by means of the stars' course, which
unfolds the ages at length and explicates His order in space
and time. . . . The stars foreshadow the sceptre of Phoron-
ius, the discord of the Theban brothers, the race of Priam,
the boldness of Turnus, the cunning of Ulysses, the vigor
of Hercules. . . . Rome wages wars. Plato seeks the causes
of things, Achilles fights. . . . Thus the masterworker: in
order that the coming ages may be seen, marked in the
course of the stars.]

Sampson is Chaucer's only addition to Bernard's list, though he makes
proelia Roma definite in Pompey and Caesar and has Socrates utter
Plato's thought. The heavens as a book was by Chaucer's time a commonplace, but he might not have used it had he not read Bernard's

lines. The image recurs in *De mundi universitate*. At the beginning of Book II Bernard repeats that the heavens exhibit, if they can be read, the signs of the future (II: i, 23–26).

Chaucer's passage is perfectly clear. The future is there to be read, though no one can "rede it atte fulle." But certain things can be known, and his whole astrological addition to Trivet's story is an elaborate explanation of what of Constance's future might have been foretold if only the Emperor had used care in consulting his astrologers to make an election which, in consideration of Constance's nativity, would have been as favorable as possible for her journey into Syria. The Sultan's death, as the stanza quoted says, was foretold in the stars. Whether his astrologers might have warned him Chaucer does not say, but Constance's "roote" or horoscope was known (314), and a more favorable time for her voyage might have been chosen. But no election could have saved her marriages, for the stars at her birth had been unpropitious. "Crueel Mars hath slayn this mariage" (301).

Both Curry and Manly have explained in detail the astrological situation of 295–308,[27] as Skeat had done before them. They differ somewhat in their explanations, Curry thinking "the derkeste hous" of 304 to be the zodiacal house Scorpio, and Manly that it is the darkest of mundane houses, probably the twelfth. Manly's is the more likely explanation, for the action of the *primum mobile* (295) is not to control the position of the planets in the zodiac but to alter their passage through the mundane houses, which, unlike the zodiacal houses, are fixed areas through which the heavenly bodies move. Any celestial body takes a complete revolution through the mundane houses daily, carried by the diurnal motion of the *primum mobile*. The lines read:

> O firste moevyng! crueel firmament,
> With thy diurnal sweigh that crowdest ay
> And hurlest al from est til occident
> That naturelly wolde holde another way,
> Thy crowdyng set the hevene in swich array
> At the bigynnyng of this fiers viage
> That crueel Mars hath slayn this mariage.
>
> Infortunat ascendent tortuous,
> Of which the lord is helplees falle, allas,
> Out of his angle into the derkeste hous!
> O Mars, o atazir, as in this cas!
> O fieble moone, unhappy been thy paas!
> Thou knyttest thee ther thou art nat receyved;
> Ther thou were weel, fro thennes artow weyved.

The second stanza indicates that Aries, an unfortunate sign, is just rising above the horizon and is rising obliquely, and Mars, the Lord of Aries—Aries is the day mansion of Mars—has been thrust by the diurnal motion of the Primum Mobile from one of the four angles— houses 1, 4, 7, and 10—where he had power into one of the cadent houses—12, 3, 6, and 9—where he exerted no influence. The "derkeste hous" is 12, the most unfortunate of all, and it is adjacent to 1, a favorable angle. It appears that Constance's nativity was in Aries, and no enterprise in her life should have been undertaken when Mars was in an unfavorable position. Besides that, the moon that had special influence on voyages was in an unfavorable position, being, like Mars, "weyved" from a position of power into one where she is not well "received" by the planet with which she is in conjunction, in this case Mars. That is, Mars did not reinforce the moon's influence. She is therefore enfeebled, her beneficent influence cancelled out. The astrologers agree that these circumstances are sure to bring disaster to a marriage, and all of this the Emperor's astrologers could have known and avoided had he only consulted them.

The fact that Chaucer blames Constance's unhappy election on the Primum Mobile—"O firste moevyng! crueel firmament"—needs comment. Apparently in the late Middle Ages the Neoplatonic identification of the Primum Mobile with God was by no means universal, and perhaps a more purely astronomical reading of the heavens was supplanting the philosophical. Both Plato and Aristotle identified the east-to-west motion, induced by the Primum Mobile, with reason and the contrary motion from west to east, the "natural" motion of the planets, with *cupiditas;* Plato called the two "the same" and "the other."[28] But difficulties and contradictions arise. Calcidius in his commentary on the *Timaeus* emphasized the serenity of the heavens, which remain "the same," and the turbulence of the carnal appetites of the soul. Yet it is hard to identify serenity with the swift diurnal motion induced by the Primum Mobile, and turbulence with the slow annual motions of the planets from west to east.

Furthermore, there had been at least from the time of Macrobius an unwillingness to identify the outermost sphere with God. Cicero says in the *Somnium Scipionis,* "The outermost of these [the nine spheres] is the celestial sphere . . . itself the supreme god," but Macrobius comments: "When Cicero called the outermost sphere, whose motions we have just explained, the *supreme god,* he did not mean to imply the First Cause and All-Powerful God, since this sphere, they say, is the creation of Soul, and Soul emanates from Mind, and Mind from God, who is truly the Supreme."[29] Yet under the influence of Boethius and of Neoplatonic cosmology it became usual to refer to the Prime Mover as God, as Chaucer does in the Knight's Tale (2987 ff.) and in the *House of Fame* where he echoes the *Gloria patri* (81–82).

Fortunately perhaps Chaucer seemed not to know much about astronomy when he wrote the *House of Fame*. If he had he could not have been so vague about the location of Fame's palace nor about the scenery on his celestial journey. When he really began the study of the heavens that was deeply to engage him he read accounts of celestial motions that put a different light on the action of the outer sphere. Sacrobosco's *Sphere*, after Ptolemy's *Almagest* the most popular of astronomical texts, says of the movement of the outer sphere, in Thorndike's translation: "But the first movement carries all the others with it in its rush about the earth once within a day and night, although they strive against it."[30] The idea of the ninth sphere being in active opposition to those of the planets is even more strongly expressed in an anonymous commentary: "sed primum motus, scilicet primi mobilis motu sue influentie et sua virtute rapit secum violenter omnes inferiores ab oriente in occidentem infra diem et noctem circa terram semel." [But the first motion, namely that of the prime mover, by its influence and power drags violently with it all beneath from east to west around the earth once in the course of each day and night]. This is not far from Chaucer's lines:

> With thy diurnal sweigh that crowdest ay
> And hurlest al from est til occident,
> That naturelly wolde holde another way.

It is possible that between the time Chaucer translated Boethius and wrote the Knight's Tale he had accepted the idea of the Crystalline Sphere above the ninth and identified it with heaven and with God. To be sure, it filled no such function when it first appeared in astronomy but was posited to provide a sphere through which the sun could make an exact solar revolution within a year. This was necessary to the astronomers who worked out the Alfonsine Tables in the thirteenth century, for the sun does not complete his course through the zodiac in exactly 365¼ days, and the astronomers needed a constant for their computations. Some in the fourteenth century made the Crystalline Sphere the abode of the saints.

Dante's treatment of the Primum Mobile in *The Convivio* is as inconsistent as Chaucer's. Though he speaks in one place of nine spheres, in

Book II, ch. XIV, he says: "As was narrated above, then, the seven heavens that are first with respect to us are those of the planets; next come two moving heavens above them; and one above them all, which is quiet." Dante does not here mention the Crystalline Sphere or iden- tify it with the Primum Mobile; but it is the ninth sphere that moves. Then in the next chapter he compares the Crystalline Sphere, which he there identifies with the Primum Mobile, with moral philosophy be- cause it regulates the daily revolution of all the spheres beneath it. The interesting point is that just before this passage comes one in which he says the daily motion of the heavens signifies the corruptible things of nature, while the west-to-east motion signifies the incorruptible things of God and is to be compared with metaphysics. Chaucer, then, was not alone in disagreeing with the accepted view of the action of the Primum Mobile.[31] Nor do I think this passage is the Man of Law's perversion of accepted values but Chaucer writing as an astronomer and not as a philosopher.

Whether it is unorthodox or not to refer to the Primum Mobile as "crueel firmament," there can be no doubt whatever that the import of the story is highly orthodox. It might have had for its motto another quotation from Bernardus Sylvestris, this time from *Experimentarius,* a work Chaucer knew,[32] where he says that the planets control all things unless it please God, yielding to prayer, to change evil to good, or, offended by crimes, good to evil.[33] The story illustrates perfectly how a Christian could believe in astrology and not be a complete determinist. Bernard's is a statement of exactly what happens in this tale. Con- stance's fortitude and piety move God to miraculous intervention to save his servant from the disasters threatened in her horoscope. The stars work their evil effects up to a point, but "God liste to shewe his wonderful myracle / In hire" (477–78). The God who had saved Jonah, the Hebrews crossing the Red Sea, and Mary the Egyptian "kepte hire fro drenchyng in the see" and saved "fro the tempest ay this womman," providing her with food on her long journey from Syria to Northum- berland (488–511). Again when Constance is on trial for her life she will surely perish unless "Crist open myracle kithe," (636), and that he does. Another miracle occurs when God strengthened her to the point of being able to throw her would-be ravisher into the sea (912–13). The story does not indicate any scepticism about astrology on Chaucer's part. What it does show, because it is a saint's legend, is that God is lord of the heavens and can miraculously intervene to prevent the direst effects of astral influences.

Constance was a Christian. Arcite, Troilus, and Hypermnestra were not. The "paynems olde rites" provided no escape from the sidereal pattern, but "hooly chirches feith in oure bileve" did. Chaucer's prevailing determinism is modified in the Man of Law's Tale, not logically, to be sure, but practically in the way any medieval Christian would have to have it.

NOTES

1. See Marie P. Hamilton, "The Dramatic Suitability of 'The Man of Law's Tale,'" *Studies in Language and Literature in Honour of Margaret Schlauch* (Warsaw: PWN—Polish Scientific Publishers, 1966), pp. 154–55; Walter Scheps, "Chaucer's Man of Law and the Tale of Constance," *PMLA* 89 (1974), 288–92; Robert E. Lewis, "Chaucer's Artistic Use of Pope Innocent III's *De Miseria Humane Conditionis* in the Man of Law's Prologue and Tale," *PMLA* 81 (1966), 485–92.
2. *Speculum* 23 (1948), 70–75.
3. Hamilton, op. cit.
4. Scheps, op. cit.
5. See Chauncey Wood's treatment of the tale in *Chaucer and the Country of the Stars* (Princeton: University Press, 1970), pp. 192–244.
6. *Teseida* VII: 67; IX: 3.
7. See my essay, "Saturn in the Knight's Tale," in *Chaucer und seiner Zeit: Symposium für Walter F. Schirmer,* ed. Arno Esch (Tübingen: M. Niemeyer, 1968), pp. 149–62.
8. This is the conclusion of J. J. O'Connor, and it seems a reasonable one. See "The Astrological Dating of Chaucer's *Troilus and Criseyde,*" *JEGP,* 55 (1956), 556–62.
9. See Walter C. Curry, *Chaucer and the Medieval Sciences* (New York: Oxford U. Press, 1926), pp. 164–71.
10. Caroline Spurgeon, *Five Hundred Years of Chaucer Criticism and Allusion: 1357–1900* (Cambridge: University Press, 1925), I: 127–99.
11. Derek J. Price, "Chaucer's Astronomy," a paper read at Cambridge on November 28, 1952, at the Weekly Evening Meeting.
12. *The Equatorie of the Planets,* ed. Derek J. Price (Cambridge: University Press, 1955).
13. See James Westfall Thompson, *The Medieval Library* (Chicago: University Press, 1939), pp. 395–96; and F. M. Powicke, *The Medieval Books of Merton College,* (Oxford: Clarendon Press, 1931). The school of astronomy at Merton is treated by R. T. Gunther in *Early Science in Oxford* (Oxford, 1923), II: 42–69.
14. Review of Price's *Equatorie of the Planets, JEGP,* 57 (1958), 536.

15. Nicholas of Lynn, at John of Gaunt's request, had compiled a calendar on the meridian of Oxford, and this Chaucer may have used in the *Astrolabe*. Observations on the weather, purely astrological, were kept for the Oxford district by Wm. Merlee between 1337 and 1344: A. C. Crombie, *Medieval and Early Modern Science* (New York: Doubleday, 1959), I: 99.

16. Price, pp. 129–30, and frontispiece.

17. *De consolatione philosophiae* Bk. IV, pr. 6.

18. See *De caelo,* esp. Bk. II, ch. 3, and Crombie, *Medieval Science* I: 56–58.

19. See A. C. Crombie, *Robert Grosseteste and the Origins of Experimental Science, 1100–1170* (Oxford: Clarendon Press, 1953), Introduction and p. 291.

20. See W. Grundel, *Sternglaube und Sterndeutung: die Geschichte und das Wesen der Astrologie,* 3rd ed. (Leipzig, 1926).

21. *Die philosophischen Werke des Grosseteste, Bischofs von Lincoln,* ed. Ludwig Bauer (Münster: Aschendorf, 1912) in Beiträge zur Geschichte der Philosophie des Mittelalters: Texte und Untersuchungen, 9. For Grosseteste's ideas in the Proemium to his *Hexaemeron* (not yet published) see Richard C. Dales and Servus Gieben, *Speculum,* 43 (1968), 460–61; and Richard C. Dales, "Robert Grosseteste's Views on Astrology," *Mediaeval Studies,* 29 (1967), 357–63.

22. The *Dragmaticon* or *Dialogus de Substantiis Physicis* is a rewriting of Guillaume's *De philosophia mundi* (*PL* 172: 39–102) cast as a dialogue between Guillaume and Geoffrey Plantagenet. It was published in Strassburg in 1597. Guillaume has an interesting comment in his *Glosae super Platonem.* He says that when Plato said the Demiurge distributed the souls to stars he meant "causally, not locally," a metaphor for the influence of the stars on human life; cited by Winthrop Wetherbee, *Platonism and Poetry in the Twelfth Century* (Princeton: University Press, 1972), p. 42.

23. Wood, p. 23, doubts that the fourteenth century was as interested in this question as has been supposed. But certainly as determinism became more prevalent the matter must have been debated a great deal. As the idea of man as microcosm grew, man became fixed to the heavenly bodies that he reflected. Jean Seznec in *The Survival of the Pagan Gods* (New York: Pantheon, 1953), reproduces on p. 66 a miniature from a Copenhagen manuscript showing a figure of man as microcosm depicted as a prisoner of astral forces, and illustrations of this type, he says, appear first in the fourteenth century. See also Harry Bober, "The Zodiacal Miniature of the *Très Riches Heures* . . . Its Sources and Meaning," *Journal of the Warburg and Courtauld Institutes,* 11 (1948), 1–34.

24. Hamilton M. Smyser in "A View of Chaucer's Astronomy," *Speculum,* 45 (1970), 359–73, states with convincing argument his conviction that Chaucer's belief in astrology was genuine and that the Man of Law's Tale is a good test of it.

25. The quotation is from F. N. Robinson, ed., *The Works of Geoffrey Chaucer,* 2nd ed. (Boston: Houghton Mifflin, 1957); Man of Law's Tale II: 190–203, p. 64.

26. Bernardus Sylvestris, *De mundi universitate,* ed. C. S. Barach and J. Wrobel (Innsbruck: Wagner'sche Universitaets-Buchhandlung, 1876), p. 16. This is a very poor text, and a new edition is eagerly awaited.

27. Curry, ch. VII; J. M. Manly, *Chaucer's Canterbury Tales* (New York: Holt, 1928), p. 567.

28. *Timaeus* 36, C: τὴν μὲν οὖν ἔξω φορὰν ἐπεφήμισεν εἶναι τῆς ταὐτοῦ φύσεως, τὴν δ᾽ ἐντὸς τῆς θατέρου [and the outer motion he ordained to be the motion of the same, and the inner motion the motion of the other].

29. I quote Stahl's translation of Macrobius, *Macrobius: Commentary on the Dream of Scipio,* (New York: Columbia U. Press, 1952), p. 157.

30. Lynn Thorndike, *The Sphere of Sacrobosco and Its Commentators* (Chicago: University Press, 1948), pp. 119–20.

31. That Chaucer knew the *Convivio* when he wrote the Man of Law's Tale is proved by his use of it in *Mars* 164–66 and perhaps in *Gentilesse.*

32. He used it in the Knight's Tale, 2045.

33. The *Experimentarius* has been edited by Mirella Brini Savorelli in *Rivista critica di storia della filosofia,* 14 (1959), 283–342. This passage reads: "Credimus etiam eosdem planetas eandem potestatem in rebus nunc habere, et fata unicuique in sua dispositione donare, nisi cum Dominus, aut prece placatus mala in bonis, aut facinore offensus bona in malis mutare voluerit" (p. 313), [and we believe that the same planets have now the same power in affairs, and according to their own order give their destinies to each one, except when the Lord, either pleased by prayer wills to turn evil into good, or, offended by crime, good to evil]. Though the manuscripts assign *Experimentarius,* a work on geomancy, to Bernard, it is not certain that he wrote it. One argument against his authorship is that the prose of the introduction is simple and direct, in sharp contrast to the involved prose of *De mundi.* But then *Experimentarius* is a (pseudo-)scientific manual and *De mundi* is a poem, even in its prose parts.

15

DEREK BREWER

The Arming of the Warrior
in European Literature and Chaucer

It is notable that both Chaucer and the *Gawain*-poet have a formal arming-passage amongst their works—but with how different a hero in either case! To compare Sir Thopas with Gawain is to get a glimpse into the abyss which separates their great contemporaneous authors. A little further acquaintance with European literature soon discovers a very considerable number of other formal arming-passages, strongly resembling each other in structure, though curiously enough no scholar or critic, even amongst those who have commented on the possible allegorical significance of Gawain's armor (which it is not my purpose to discuss here), appears to have remarked upon this phenomenon. The first purpose of this essay is to establish the existence and suggest the varying uses of this formal device, though there is no attempt to list every occurrence. The second purpose is briefly to examine Chaucer's use of it in comparison with that of the *Gawain*-poet and the ancient tradition. Chaucer by his use effectively destroys this tradition in English, as he does others. From this point of view he may be regarded as one of the last traditional poets and the first modern poet in English; or, as I have tried to express it elsewhere, as being both "Gothic," (i.e., traditional) and "Neoclassical" (i.e., modern, naturalistic). I use the term "Neoclassical" to include much of Romanticism.[1]

Chaucer and, to some extent, the *Gawain*-poet, are our principal destination, but the long journey will be clearer if we start as far back as we can. There are three references to arming in Babylonian epic, where heroes are armed by gods for battles with monsters.[2] The details are a strange mixture of realism and cosmic hyperbole without (as far as I can judge) the formulaic structure of later armings, but they suggest the potent emotional and psychological forces, with cosmic mythological resonances, that the physical preparations for battle involved. The primitive quality of Babylonian epic is only approached by the Irish example referred to below.

Our first clear view of the formalized description of the arming of the warrior occurs in the *Iliad*. It is a literary ritual corresponding, I presume, to a solemn and impressive ritual in real life, and the arming marks out both the hero and a combat of some particular importance. A. B. Lord comments briefly upon the arming, and connects it with similar formalized passages in early twentieth-century Yugoslav folk-epic. Thus our topic spans a period from the earliest records to almost the present day in European terms, though in England it faded out in the early fifteenth century.

A question of nomenclature arises here. Lord, followed by Homeric scholars, calls such formal passages "themes." Celtic folklorists, to be referred to later, call them "runs." They may equally well be referred to by the term used by Curtius—*topoi;* or by the Elizabethan term, "commonplaces." Each name emphasizes a certain aspect of the phenomenon and implies a critical point of view, none of which I wish to exclude, but I shall in general use the term *topos.*[3]

II

There are four extended passages of arming in the *Iliad;*[4] when Paris arms for single combat against Menelaus (III: 328–38); Agamemnon arms to lead the Greeks (XI: 15–46); Patroclus arms himself in Achilles' armor (XVI: 130–44); and Achilles arms himself in new armor (XIX: 367–91). Each of the passages begins with the same three lines, which themselves being highly formulaic, clearly signal the recognized theme or topos. Homer had a basic theme for arming, which is given in its normal form in the arming of Paris and Patroclus. The theme is adjusted in the case of the other two heroes to fit the particular circumstances.[5]

The arming of Paris is translated thus by Richard Lattimore.

> First he placed along his legs the fair greaves linked with
> silver fastenings to hold the greaves at the ankles.
> Afterwards he girt on about his chest the corselet
> of Lykaon his brother since this fitted him also.
> Across his shoulders he slung the sword with the nails of silver,
> a bronze sword, and above it the great shield, huge and heavy.
> Over his powerful head he set the well-fashioned helmet
> with the horse-hair crest, and the plumes nodded terribly above it.
> He took up a strong-shafted spear that fitted his hand's grip.
> In the same way warlike Menelaos put on his armour.[6]

The general significance of the arming is as a ritual, "probably one of dedication to the task of saving the hero's people, even of sacrifice.

Each of these men is about to set out upon a mission of deep significance, and the 'ornamental' theme is a signal and mark, both 'ritualistic' and artistic, of the role of the hero."[7] Each description follows the same order, often marking the pieces of armor with identical adjectives; greaves, corslet, sword, shield, helmet with crest, spear. This order is practical. It is probable that once the corslet was put on, a man could not bend over sufficiently far to tie on his greaves (and it may be noted that the heroes arm themselves). At the same time, one should not overemphasize the practicality and potential naturalism at any stage. First, Greek armor of the heroic age appears to have included, besides the items mentioned, footguard, ankleguard, thigh-piece, belt, forearmguard, and upperarmguard.[8] None of these is mentioned. A literal, realistic, naturalistic or mimetic presentation of "how things actually are" is not the primary aim of traditional literature. Second, though the "framework" of the arming topos in the *Iliad* is invariable, and to some extent expressed in unchanging verbal formulae, variations may be introduced in a manner familiar in traditional (including folklore) literature. In the *Iliad* the variations are mostly additions, of an elaborate kind, which are slotted into appropriate parts of the framework, on their minute scale quite comparably with the way Chaucer "slots in" additions to the framework provided by *Il Filostrato* when he composes the *Troilus*. Such additions both enrich and subtly change the received standard. It may be that the great poet reveals himself by the way he accepts with all its advantages of accumulated feelings the traditional topos, and yet adapts it to the purposes of his own poem, or to the limited context of one small section of his own poem. Such adaptations require a response in the reader or hearer different from that evoked by passages which claim to be both original and naturalistically mimetic, as in such "Neoclassical" writing as the novel.

III

Before the advent of gunpowder the basic armor of the warrior was the same at any period, as Stubbings remarks,[9] so that local inconsistencies and anachronisms, in a traditional style of writing or speaking which does not primarily cherish naturalistic accuracy, are easily accepted even when not understood. The basic similarity is illustrated from a source perhaps even older than the *Iliad,* and much better known in the Middle Ages, where the topos had apparently not developed so far:

> And Saul clad David with his apparel, and he put an helmet of brass upon his head, and he clad him with a coat of mail. And David girded his sword upon his apparel, and he assayed to go, for he had not proved it. And David said to Saul, I cannot go with these; for I have not proved them. And David put them off him.
>
> (1 Samuel 17:38–39, Revised Version)

Even here there is clearly a ritual as well as practical element in the deed, if not in the literary treatment, and that the armor is borrowed is a curious coincidence with the armor which is borrowed in the first three instances of the topos in the *Iliad* (and in the fourth it is new).

Armoring has an intrinsic significance, and so in Isaiah it is said of the Lord that:

> he put on righteousness as a breastplate, and an helmet of salvation upon his head; and he put on garments of vengeance for clothing, and was clad with zeal as a cloak.
>
> (Isaiah 59:17)

This is taken up by St. Paul—thus we see a topos growing—in the famous passage in Ephesians:

> Wherefore take up the whole armour of God, that ye may be able to withstand in the evil day, and, having done all, to stand. Stand therefore, having girded your loins with truth, and having put on the breastplate of righteousness, and having shod your feet with the preparation of the gospel of peace; withal taking up the shield of faith, wherewith ye shall be able to quench all the fiery darts of the evil one. And take the helmet of salvation, and the sword of the Spirit, which is the word of God.
>
> (6:13–17)

Commentators refer us to the Isaiah passage and Wisdom 5:17–20, as part of Jewish apocalyptic, but surely St. Paul is also here revealing the influence of both the primitive and the secular Greek topos.

IV

Virgil in the *Aeneid* (Book XII) has one relatively full example of the arming of the hero, though he curiously enough applies it to Turnus rather than Aeneas. He uses it as a marker of heroic magnitude, but possibly with some sense of its primitive quality, since it is not applied to Aeneas. The reference to horses precedes the arming of the hero, and the whole description has a more literary flavor. The greaves are omitted; but the corslet is followed by sword and shield and helmet with crest and spear, as in Homer, though Turnus then addresses a speech to his spear:

> Ipse dehinc auro squalentem alboque orichalco
> circumdat loricam umeris, simul aptat habendo
> ensemque clipeumque et rubrae cornua cristae,
> ensem quem Dauno ignipotens deus ipse parenti
> fecerat et Stygia candentem tinxerat unda.
> exin quae mediis ingenti adnixa columnae
> aedibus astabat, validam vi corripit hastam,
> Actoris Aurunci spolium, quassatque trementem
> vociferans. . . .[10]

[Then he placed on his shoulders his corslet stiff with gold and pale orichalc. At the same time he ably adjusts his sword and shield, and his red-plumed helmet. The sword (was that) which the god of fire had made for his father Daunus and had dipped white-hot in the river Styx. Then he vigorously seized a strong lance which stood propped against a huge column in the middle of the palace—it was spoil from Auruncan Actor. He shook the quivering shaft.]

It is to be remarked that the passage seems to have given a slight unease even to Servius, who comments on line 88, "non armatur hac loco, sed explorat, utrum arma apte et congrue ejus membris inhoereant." [In this passage he is not armed, but seeks to discover whether the arms fit his limbs suitably and conveniently.] Servius shows no knowledge of the topos and consequently attempts to rationalize the oddity of Turnus apparently putting on his armor a day too early. J. W. Mackail felt the same difficulty fifteen hundred years later.[11] Traditional and especially oral poetry, necessarily formulaic, often gives rise to such inconsistencies.

Virgil was of course constantly and deeply studied throughout the Middle Ages, and no doubt this passage had its influence and effect, but it seems hardly likely that it itself was the source of such frequent use as will be shown to occur. No doubt there are other instances of the topos in classical Latin, but we may also posit a general oral tradition.

V

This general oral tradition may perhaps be seen to exist in the early period of Irish literature; *The Táin Bó Cúalnge* is very early, though its history and the manuscript tradition are exceedingly complex.[12] It may go back as far as the second century B.C. though perhaps first written down in the seventh century A.D., and then subsequently rehandled after the normal manner of traditional literature. The most recent edition is of the twelfth-century Leinster MS, representing the second recension, said to be more literary than the first, though still extraordinarily grotesque. In the passage concerned, regrettably too long to quote,[13] the charioteer first arms himself, then (as in *Iliad* XI, XVI and XIX) harnesses the horses to the chariot—perhaps once part of the topos. Then Cú Chulainn arms himself. The mixture of militaristic fantasy and hyperbole is characteristic of Old Irish and extraordinarily different from other examples in this paper, which makes the fundamental similarity all the more striking.

The topos is followed by another set piece, even more grotesque, Cú Chulainn's "first distortion." These passages each have the effect of marking out the significant hero and by hyperbole emphasizing his importance.

The latest example of arming the hero in Irish that I happen to have come across is in the probably seventeenth-century tale of decidedly literary flavor entitled in English *The Pursuit of Gruaidh Ghriansholus,*[14] which relates exploits attributed to Cú Chulainn. The author may have known classical Greek tales, according to the editor, as well as traditional Irish tales, and we see here that characteristic intermingling of written and oral elements that marks "traditional" literature (and perhaps, did we but realize it, even some "Neoclassical" and "modern" literature).

Between these two points in Irish literature, however, comes an extensive literature, and for information here, since I do not read Irish, I follow the learned work of Alan Bruford,[15] who has placed in his debt students of literature beyond his specific subject. Bruford's special interest lies in the relationship between oral tales presumed to be of great antiquity in Ireland (but which can be known only in quite recently collected versions), and the medieval Irish romances of a literary kind which date from around the late fifteenth to the late seventeenth century. The relationship is complex and does not concern us here, though we note again the interplay, and two-way influence, between oral and written work. Since Bruford approaches the subject from the folktale he refers to the topos of the arming of the hero as "the arming run," which establishes its highly formulaic nature.

According to Bruford "the arming run is the most celebrated run of all in Ireland. . . . Folk versions may expand the framework of literary arming runs in two ways: by adding extra articles of clothing or weapons (boots, breeches, knife), and by adding clauses—rather than adjectives—describing the history and properties of the article and how it was put on."[16] The literary Romantic tales of the fifteenth century retain the "basic equipment of warriors in Old Irish tales—a pair of javelins, sword and shield, and sometimes a helmet."[17] There may or may not be a tunic or breastplate mentioned, or other weapons. In late literary or in oral versions there may be exchange of formulae between "runs," and even the inclusion of actual nonsense. "Any verbiage will do to fill out a run."[18] Even in the literary tales, however, Bruford detects something of the same tendency. In his valuable chapter on runs, where he distinguishes between folk runs and literary runs, he concludes that at least they have in common that they were intended for oral delivery. "The big set pieces are rhetorical purple passages, designed to sweep away the hearer in a sonorous wash of verbiage whose actual meaning was of little importance. They could well have been the high points of the story if read by a good performer, though the silent reader is likely to skip them."[19] (Here is one of the origins of the differences between traditional, whether oral or written, and "Neoclassical" literature; that is, the ultimately oral origin of traditional literature, to be contrasted with the more fixed nature of "Neoclassical" literature, as determined both by its own theory and the dominance of its origin in print, and which leads to an attempted close correspondence between "word" and "thing.") It is important to recognize Bruford's thesis that in many cases his "oral" examples derive from earlier "literary" ones, though both are traditional. There are complex processes at work of both decay of meaning and rationalization.

VI

As might be expected, the topos appears in both *Beowulf* and the *Chanson de Roland,* the two major "epics" (if rightly so called) of medieval European vernacular literature. Since *Beowulf* was not known in Middle English literature we can regrettably do no more than notice the passage (1441–64), substantial as it is.[20] It is admirably assimilated to the style and structure of the poem. First we have the corslet (*here-byrne*) characteristically described, then the *hwita helm,* again adorned, and then the *hæft-mece, Hrunting nama.* The poet selects the essentials and weaves around them potent words that evoke the notes of ancient power and splendor. The passage occurs just before Beowulf's fight with Grendel's mother and thus shows that for the poet this is the key battle of the poem, undertaken voluntarily and solemnly by the hero, no mere response to an attack, as was his encounter, however heroic, with Grendel when Grendel came to the hall. But it has been pointed out to me that Beowulf's taking off his armor in the hall, when he goes to bed on the evening of Grendel's attack, is as it were an inversion of the topos. Beowulf takes off corslet and helm, neither qualified by so much as an adjective, and his *hyrsted sweord, irena cyst,* and gives them to a servant (671–74). This inversion of the topos is of great originality and power, of a kind hard to describe. Perhaps it is designed to show Beowulf's fundamental lack of aggressiveness, in that he is attacked as a defenseless sleeping man before moving to the offensive himself—though he knows very well how to be heroic when need be, and is then heroically armed. Such would fit in well with the poet's Christian yet heroic temper.

Le Chanson de Roland makes a surprisingly less specific use of the topos. It occurs, probably, in the *laisses* 55, 79, 136, 217, 231 (ed. F. Whitehead, Oxford, 1942) but it is used indiscriminately for pagan and Christian and certainly does not mark the hero. The passages are very brief with only minimal formulaic usages.

The topos is much more obvious in such poems as *Le Couronnement Louis* (405–13). It has been pointed out that it occurs with the same vocabulary and in the same order of corslet, helmet, sword, mounting a horse, taking a shield, then another sword, and a standard, as in many other *chansons de geste*.[21]

Even more striking than the topos in the *chansons de geste* is the use made of it by Chrétien in *Erec et Enide*. The first occasion is early in the poem when Erec is to defend the hawk on behalf of Enid, and is betrothed to her. Already armor has been mentioned by his host, Enid's father, in the conversation of the previous night. At dawn Erec, who has slept little, arises and hears mass. He is impatient for the battle, calls for his armor; Enid herself arms him.

> Les armes quiert et l'an li baille;
> la pucele meïsmes l'arme;
> n'i ot fet charaie ne charme,
> lace li les chauces de fer
> et queust a corroie de cer;
> hauberc li vest de boene maille
> et se li lace la vantaille;
> le hiaume brun li met el chief,
> molt l'arme bien de chief an chief.

Au costé l'espee li ceint.
Puis comande qu'an li amaint
son cheval, et l'an li amainne;
sus est sailliz de terre plainne.
La pucele aporte l'escu
et la lance qui roide fu;
l'escu li baille, et il le prant,
par la guige a son col le pant;
la lance li ra el poing mise,
cil l'a devers l'arestuel prise.[22]

[Erec was eager for the battle, so he asks for arms and they
are given to him. The maiden herself puts on his arms
(though she casts no spell or charm), laces on his iron
greaves, and makes them fast with thongs of deer-hide. She
puts on his corslet with its strong meshes, and laces on his
ventail. The gleaming helmet she sets upon his head, and
thus arms him well from tip to toe. At his side she fastens
his sword, and then orders his horse to be brought, which is
done. Up he jumped clear of the ground. The damsel then
brings the shield and the strong lance; she hands him the
shield and he takes it and hangs it about his neck by the
strop. She has placed the lance in his hand and he has
grasped it by the butt.][23]

Here we have the order: greaves, corslet, helmet, sword, horse,
shield, spear, slightly different from that in the *Iliad,* which also is
clearly required by practical necessity. Chrétien uses the topos, but has
brought it back into line with the facts of the case. Chrétien is both
realistic and traditional. Erec is successful in his battle and marries
Enid to their mutual joy. That his beloved should arm the hero is an
important contextual addition, giving the topos an emotional power
and direction very characteristic of Chrétien's genius.

The second arming is even more elaborate and is also a significant
marker. It occurs soon after Erec has overheard Enid bewailing the
reproaches he has incurred for his uxoriousness. He orders her to dress
in her finest robes, and she does so, lamenting. Then Erec summons a
squire, not Enid, to arm him, and the elaborations underscore the
ominous yet splendid style of the occasion, as music might sound a rich
foreboding bass figure (2620–60). It is somewhat too long to quote,
though its variations, to properly constituted minds, ensure that it is
not to be skipped. The arms are brought and laid upon a Limoges
carpet, where Erec also sits upon the image of a leopard which is
portrayed on the carpet. Then greaves are laced, corslet (not at all

rusty), helmet, sword (which he girds on himself); and then he calls for his horse. The order of arming is the same, notwithstanding the rich elaborations.

The formality of the topos, as opposed to its realism, is here notice-able in that neither shield nor lance is mentioned and must be taken for granted, because Erec certainly has them when he is soon attacked by three robber knights. Yet realism is perhaps not quite abandoned, if we reflect that after this arming Erec has elaborate conversations in the courtyard with his father and other persons, during which scene to have had him holding his shield and certainly a spear would have been otiose. That he has been formally armed guarantees that we feel, when the occasion soon after arises, that he has the necessary weapons.

Chrétien does not seem to make use of the arming topos in his other poems. If *Erec et Enide* is a relatively early work, as is usually supposed, he may have felt he had used the topos enough, or that it was too crude; but he used it well in this poem.

If a conjecture that I have made elsewhere has any substance, Chaucer may have known Chrétien's work, which was certainly avail-able in England in the fourteenth and presumably thirteenth cen-turies.[24] The French and Anglo-Norman works referred to were cer-tainly known in England, though it is interesting that the thirteenth-century English *King Horn,* for example, does not take over the arming topos. There was however another literary channel which leads directly into English, to which we now turn.

VII

It would be wrong to distinguish this channel clearly from that of the works discussed in the previous section, for this other channel is the Arthurian series emanating from the *Historia Regum Britanniae* of Geof-frey of Monmouth, which was certainly known to Chrétien, and which could easily have at least encouraged his own use of the arming topos.

In Book IX Arthur succeeds to the kingdom and is attacked by the Saxons, who after a setback return with renewed strength. The Arch-bishop addresses the army who then, cheered by this, all rush to arm themselves. There is a detailed description of the arming of Arthur, of a kind now familiar to the reader:

Ipse vero Arthurus, lorica tanto rege condigna, indutus, auream galeam simulacro draconis insculptam capiti adaptavit. Umeris quoque suis

clipeum, vocabulo Prydwen, imposuit, in quo imago sanctae Mariae, Dei
genitricis, inerat picta, quae ipsum in memoriam ipsius saepissime re-
vocabat. Accinctus etiam Caliburno, gladio optimo, in insula Aval(l)onis
fabricato, lancea dexteram suam decorat, quae Ron nomine vocabatur: haec
erat ardua lataque lancea, cladibus apta.[25]

[Arthur himself, however, having put on a corslet worthy of such a king,
drew upon his head a golden helmet carved into the likeness of a dragon.
Also he placed on his shoulders the shield, Prydwen by name, inside which
the image of holy Mary, mother of God, was painted, which very often
recalled the memory of her to him. He was also girt with Caliburn, best of
swords, made in the vale of Avalon; and the lance which was called Ron
adorned his right hand. It was a tall, thick lance, well suited to slaughter.]

The greaves have got lost again; corslet, helm, shield (called Prydwen), sword (Caliburn), and spear (Ron) are the usual significant items,
with the French order of accepting shield and sword. Hammer notes
Geoffrey's debt to Virgil's account of the arming of Turnus (part of a
very extensive verbal borrowing by Geoffrey from Virgil and other
classical Latin authors), but the names of the weapons may suggest that
Geoffrey knew other armings, in Welsh. The names may be a clue to
the vexed question of Geoffrey's sources, to what extent they were
Welsh, to what extent oral, which cannot be followed here. The topos
once again marks the hero, and marks a very significant stage of his
career. It seems not to be used by Geoffrey elsewhere. He seems to have
given it a literary flavor, whatever his oral sources. He is interested in
adorning his narrative, but not much interested in armor.

Geoffrey seems also to have invented the detail of the picture of the
Virgin inside the shield, which is in the characteristic manner of local
adornment of the given basic structure of a topos. Unlike most of the
description it may be a rare example of Geoffrey borrowing from contemporary practice. If he did so he perhaps changed a secular and coarse
chivalric joke to a pious and serious use. Joan M. Ferrante notes that
the so-called first troubadour, Count William IX of Aquitaine (1071–
1127), is reported by William of Malmesbury as having the picture of
someone else's wife (whom he had seduced after rejecting his own wife)
painted on his shield so that he could carry her in battle as she carried
him in bed. Ferrante also notes that in the twelfth-century *Roman de
Thèbes* Ethiocles, one of the heroes, rides a horse given him by one of his
mistresses, whose legs he has painted on his shield as a joke (6273).[26]

We look forward now to those texts which were based on Geoffrey.
The literal translation from the Welsh text in Jesus College Oxford

MS LXI printed by Griscom[27] shows the topos taken back into Welsh
in a fairly close version. Since the names given in the Welsh text are
fuller, it may be that the translator knew some general Welsh tradition
that Geoffrey might himself have drawn upon.

Wace seems to have translated the *Historia* with an interesting independence, though lack of space forbids quotation. We may note immediately that he reveals acquaintance with the topos from sources
other than Geoffrey's *Historia,* and since he finished *Le Roman de Brut*
in 1155 these must be earlier than Chrétien. Wace's influence on
Chrétien is held to be doubtful by his editor,[28] so that it is likely that
both draw on a common tradition. Wace's order of arming is slightly
different. The greaves come back and are put on first, then corslet,
sword, helmet, horse, shield, lance. The inversion of sequence between
sword and helmet recalls the *Iliad.* There seems no special reason for it.
Otherwise, Wace's adornments are of the usual kind. He takes twenty-
five lines, so he does not spread out unduly. His rapid narrative has had
no time for the good Archbishop's allocution reported by Geoffrey, so
that the arming stands out a little more vividly as a marker.

It is even more vivid when we at last come to English with the
translation in its turn of Wace by Laȝamon. Here is a different world,
wilder and stranger; and the topos looks different.[29]

> Þa he hafde al iset and al hit isemed,
> þa dude he on his burne ibroide of stele,
> þe makede on aluisc smið mid aðelen his crafte;
> he wes ihaten Wygar, þe Witeȝe wurhte.
> His sconken he helede mid hosen of stele.
> Calibeorne his sweord he sweinde bi his side;
> hit wes iworht in Aualun mid wiȝelefulle craften.
> Halm he set on hafde, hæh of stele;
> þeron wes moni ȝim-ston, al mid golde bigon;
> he was Vðeres þas aðelen kinges;
> he wes ihaten Goswhit, ælchen oðere vnilic.
> He heng an his sweore ænne sceld deore;
> his nome wes on Bruttisc Pridwen ihaten;
> þer wes innen igrauen mid rede golde stauen
> an onlicnes deore of Drihtenes moder.
> His spere he nom an honde, þa Ron wes ihaten.
> Þa he hafden al his iweden, þa leop he on his steden.
>
> (2828–44)

[When he had arranged all, and everything was satisfactory, then he put on his corslet of woven steel, which a

smith with magical powers made by his noble skill; it was
called Wygar, which Widia made. He covered his legs with
steel stockings. Caliborn his sword he hung by his side; it
was made in Avalon with magic skills. His tall helmet of
steel he set on his head: there were many jewels on it, and it
was encircled with gold. It was the noble king Uther's; it
was called Goosewhite, and was unlike any other helmet.
He hung a precious shield around his neck: in British it was
called Pridwen. On the inside was engraved with red-gold
markings a precious likeness of God's Mother. He took his
spear, which was called Ron, in hand. When he had all his
equipment then he leaped on to his horse.]

The order has been changed: corslet, greaves (*hosen of stele*), sword,
helmet, shield, spear, horse. What strikes one immediately is that
Laȝamon cares little or nothing for armor, and pays little attention to
the topos. This seems a strange omission, since Laȝamon normally
expands Wace by choosing topics from Old English poetry, namely
journeys, arrivals, and feasts.[30] Why should he not use the arming
topos? The reason may partly be that it is of the essence of the medieval
topos that it should normally be used only once, in a single work, in
order to emphasize the role of the dominant hero and his first significant battle. Laȝamon liked to use topoi several times. But the omission
remains effectively unexplained.

We may briefly note that the topos appears in medieval German at
least once, and other instances may well be known to the learned.
Gottfried von Strassburg has a most elaborate account of the arming of
Tristan before the battle with Morold. The basic order is greaves,
corslet, sword, helmet, shield, horse, though the passage is remarkable
for the elaboration with which they are described, the addition of spurs
and tabard, presumably correctly after the greaves and corslet, and for
the tone of the whole.[31]

VIII

The lines established by Geoffrey and the French texts generally are
continued in English in the fourteenth century in the two main streams
of alliterative poetry and rhymed romance (especially tail-rhyme romance). The alliterative tradition may be taken first, as somewhat more
closely associated with the Arthurian series initiated by Geoffrey, and
less near to Chaucer. Without attempting to list occurrences we may

select the striking example found in the alliterative *Morte Arthure*, probably to be dated roughly in the second half of the fourteenth century. As is usual (but not inevitable) the arming topos occurs early on to mark and establish the hero.[32] (The topos does not occur in the corresponding passage in Geoffrey or Wace because they have already had the arming in an earlier episode). Arthur has dreamed his first dream and now proceeds to Mont St. Michel to accomplish the heroic deed which establishes him in the poem, the killing of the giant. He orders Sir Cayos and Sir Bedbere to be armed after evensong, then proceeds to arm himself.

The editor considers this arming to be an example of descriptions of dress, which may have influenced it, but the framework and placing show that it is specifically the arming topos. The elaborations, it can now be easily recognized, are of a kind very familiar from the *Iliad* onwards. The order is corslet (elaborated by mention of the preliminary jacket and tunic and the subsequent surcoat of Jerodyne), helmet (with crest and additions), gloves, shield, sword, horse—in other words, the usual, or, as we may even say, the correct order. The gloves and other garments are unusual additions, but not out of the way. The greaves as so often have been lost. There is nothing in this passage that is strange to either courtly or "heroic" poetry, and it can hardly be used, in the way that the editor suggests, to determine the level of audience or the turn of the author's mind, except to establish both in the broad category of "traditional."

The other notable passage in alliterative verse is the arming of Sir Gawain in *Sir Gawain and the Green Knight,* which is so well known and easily available that I shall not quote it here.[33]

The passage is placed, as we should expect, to mark the hero and his beginning on the great adventure. But it is better integrated into the narrative than is usual, for before Gawain comes to his horse he hears mass and takes leave of the king and his courtly companions. The order is elaborated. Gawain is dressed in the necessary preliminary clothing (as is Arthur in the *Morte Arthure*) but then proceeds to the steel shoes and greaves (elaborated with realistic detail of knee pieces and cuisses), corslet (with more detail), gloves, surcoat, spurs, and sword. Then, as remarked, he must hear mass and take leave before he is presented with his horse, which is almost as elaborately attired as himself. The poet has of course not forgotten helmet and shield, or omitted them as Chrétien omitted shield and spear in the second arming of Erec. The helmet, very practically, is not put on until he has finished leave-taking. The shield, now so famous in academic discourse, is offered to him quite realistically after he has mounted, and the separation of the shield from the rest of the armor allows the poet to elaborate the shield's description—an extreme case of the normal license to adorn exercised from Homer onward. No other arming that I know has so elaborate a description of the shield. The *Gawain*-poet has presumably developed it from Geoffrey's detail of the picture of the Virgin on the inside of Arthur's shield, which the *Gawain*-poet also takes over. Finally, Gawain takes his lance (667) and gallops vigorously away, as he and the court believe, to his doom. Without losing the formality of the topos the poet has wonderfully well integrated it with his narrative, to the gain of both realism and splendor. Yet it remains the local "marker" topos it has been since the *Iliad*. The shield is only briefly mentioned later in a purely practical way. The pentangle and the picture of the Virgin are never mentioned again. They are the local adornments of the given basic structure of the topos, emblematic of Gawain's goodness, as the poet makes clear, but are in no way incorporated into the general narrative with an organic, thematic, or allegorical function. The absence of a second formal arming is in no way significant. It would distort and overload the poem without adding anything useful. The shield, incidentally, was going out of practical use in the second half of the fourteenth century.[34] The *Gawain*-poet is deeply traditional.

Nothing better illustrates the difference of attitudes between those two contemporaries of supreme genius, the *Gawain*-poet and Chaucer, than their respective treatments of the arming topos. One might say of the *Gawain*-poet that he finally naturalizes the literary topos, while Chaucer, naturalistic, or realistic in a quite opposite way, effectively kills it. The *Gawain*-poet was as old-fashioned in his day as Shakespeare was in his; in contrast to both, Chaucer holds "with the newe world the space."[35]

As already noted, *King Horn,* amongst the earliest of the vernacular English rhyming romances, does not take over the arming topos from his Anglo-Norman source. The vernacular romances of the fourteenth century, deriving from the Midlands and South-East England, including the tail-rhyme romances, at least reach out to the topos. They may be represented by the romances in the Auchinleck Manuscript, usually dated about 1340, which it has been argued that Chaucer knew.[36] Whether or not he knew this particular manuscript may not be quite certain, but what is beyond doubt is that he knew very well similar versions of such romances as it contains, and initially derived from them not the least effective part of his style. His parody of them is in part the witness of his deep and early engagement, but there is other evidence also.[37]

The Auchinleck MS offers a formal arming in the romance of *Sir Beues of Hamtoun,* 969–88, which is adapted from the French.[38] Here it follows the dubbing of hero as knight, and therefore presumably emphasizes his prowess, but it also immediately precedes the battle, which is the right place. Possibly the dubbing affects the order, which is shield, sword called Morgelay, then gonfanoun (brought by his lady Josian). Beues then puts on his "actoun," followed by corslet and horse named Arundel. No helmet is mentioned. It is on the whole a feeble performance. The Manchester MS, which Kölbing prints beneath Auchinleck, is more "correct," having habergeoun, corslet, helmet, sword, horse, in that order (739–52), but is not much more impressive. The translators have hardly got hold of the formal topos, and Chaucer would not have learned much about it from *Beues.*

The Auchinleck *Guy of Warwick* does rather better, and may be quoted.[39]

> He oxed his armes hastiliche,
> And men es hi*m* brou3t sikerliche.
> Hosen of iren he haþ on drawe,
> Non better nar bi þo dawe.
> In a strong hauberk he gan hi*m* schrede,
> Who so it wered, þe ded no þurt hi*m* drede.
> An helme he haþ on him don:
> Better no wered neuer kni3t non;
> The sercle of gold þer-on was wrou3t,
> For half a cite no worþ it bou3t:
> So mani stones þer-in were,
> Þat were of vertu swiþe dere.
> Seþþe he gert him wiþ a brond
> Þat was y-made i*n* eluene lond.
> His scheld about his nek he tok,
> On hors he lepe wiþ-out*en* stirop,
> On hond he nam a spere kerueinde,
> Out of þe cite he was rideinde.
>
> (3849–66)

This is much better. The presence of the greaves as usual for some reason suggests that the writer has a better grasp on both the realistic and formalistic elements. Here we have greaves, corslet, helmet, sword, shield, horse, spear, with admirable vigor and a small amount of adornment, and in the right place, just before a major battle with the Saracens. The other parallels between *Sir Thopas* and *Sir Guy* that Loomis presents in *Sources and Analogues* are not of actual armings, and the diction is so commonplace that it must be risky to suppose borrowing of any specific kind on Chaucer's part. Loomis also quotes an arming topos from *Libeaus Desconus* from British Library MS Cotton Caligula A. II.[40] Three others are quoted by Irving Linn from the fifteenth-century version of the fourteenth-century English rhyming romance, *Otuel and Roland*.[41] They all follow the usual general pattern, with individual (but still highly typical) adornments: aketoun, habergeon (Clarel only), corslet, shield, sword, helmet, saddle (Roland only), spear, horse, spurs. Different characters bring various parts of the armor to the various heroes, and it is clear that this is as usual a commonplace device for enriching but also individualizing the use of the topos to make some point about the hero's relationships.

Another instance where the topos is well handled (doubtless thanks chiefly to a French original) is *Octavian*, where Clement arms his foster-son (who like Sir Thopas is to encounter a giant) so sorrowfully with rusty old armor: "hacton," corslet, shield, spear, sword. Perhaps the disorder, with sword last, expresses the unfamiliarity of armor to Clement but it is more likely to be due merely to the exigencies of the rhyme-scheme.[42]

These are all poetic uses of a poetic topos, but it will be well to remind ourselves just before turning at last to Chaucer that an actual everyday reality was not far beneath the topos. We have a genuine practical fifteenth-century set of instructions how to arm a man.[43] This work concerns complete plate-armor, which was only beginning to be used late in the fourteenth century, and there are two swords. The order is usual, except for the second sword, and there are practical additions that few poets (except in part the *Gawain*-poet) concerned themselves with, such as vambras and serebras; but even so the list is not complete, for there are, for example, no spurs. There is also no shield.

It will not do, then, when we come to Chaucer, to argue that the omission of spurs is part of the absurdity of the description.[44] Even at the risk of anticlimax that description need not be quoted here, since every friend of Father Beichner and any other likely reader of this essay no doubt has a copy of Chaucer at his "beddes heed" and in every room.

The arming of Sir Thopas contains a very usual selection of usual elements, with the quite reasonable and realistic addition of breeches and shirt beneath. Even the coat-armor and bridle can be found elsewhere. The greaves are present, but they indeed are in a wrong and silly place. What is ridiculous is the presentation of the details with certain modifications, exaggerations, and oddities such as, possibly, the white surcoat; certainly the shield of *gold,* so soft and heavy; the leathern, not steel, greaves; the sword-sheath of ivory yet no sword mentioned; the helmet of the cheap soft metal, latten; the shining bridle; the mild horse; etc. The placing and pomposity of the arming, the prelude of the wine (of which I have noticed no precedent), Sir Thopas's swearing on ale and bread, are all splendidly absurd, and even more so when read against the long tradition of solemn splendor. Though the English verse romances are certainly mocked in the arming of Sir Thopas, it seems hardly likely that the topos would have made such an impression on Chaucer if he had not known it elsewhere in European literature, for it is not so exceptionally frequent in the English romances themselves. Chaucer was mocking, no doubt, the Flemish bourgeoisie, and aligning himself with courtly sneers at lower classes. But he was also mocking, it would seem, the whole ancient formal aggrandizement of fighting, Arthurian bravery and bravado, "and al that longeth to that art." In the Knight's Tale Chaucer does not mock chivalry, and it is notable that he had in it some fine opportunities for the arming topos: one, especially good, when Palamon and Arcite arm each other before their fight in the grove (CT I: 1649–52). But there is nowhere the least hint of the traditional formulae. When Chaucer describes Troilus in his armor as a knight, he shows him *returning* from battle, with much damage to his armor (II: 624–44). There is no arming topos attached to Troilus. Yet, as we see from *Sir Thopas,* Chaucer knows the topos perfectly well. Both his treatment of it and his refusal to use it elsewhere are significant. What Chaucer finds moving is suffering, not aggression. Even the Knight in *The Canterbury Tales,* hardbitten fighting-man that he is, and is praised for so being, is shown in his habergeoun, without armor, seeking forgiveness for sin.

IX

The topos soon disappeared in English literature. Chaucer and the *Gawain*-poet have been contrasted. Chaucer as usual is the more modern. Use of the topos gives us some insight into the character of an author. Recognition that a description of arming is a topos guides us to a correct understanding of its literary function and meaning. As already noted above, the topos continues in folk literature in Ireland and Yugoslavia until the twentieth century. In England, no major author

uses it seriously, to my knowledge, after Chaucer—nor any minor
author either, apart from scribes and translators. Here it is interesting
to note Malory. The critical cliché about Malory is that he is "nostal-
gic." Such a view should have been long dispelled by Vinaver's demonstration of Malory's forward-looking rationalization of the excessive
complexities of the French cyclic romances. Malory rationalizes the
arming topos almost to the point of extinction. When he is turning
into prose the alliterative *Morte Arthure* and comes to the arming topos
he practically demolishes it, simply referring to three items that Arthur
took for his fight with the giant—gesseraunt (or corslet), bacinet (helmet) and shield. No sword is mentioned, no formality of diction is
used. Even this residuum is reduced by Caxton, who tells us simply
that Arthur "armed hym at alle poyntes and took his hors and his
sheld."[45] Shakespeare does not appear to use the topos, though there is
probably an echo of it when Cleopatra attempts to arm Antony. This
will be Antony's first battle in the play and thus the arming comes in
the "right" place. Although Antony is at first successful in the battle
he ultimately fails, and it is significant that in helping him to arm,
Cleopatra is conspicuously inept. There is a light-hearted burlesque of
arming in *The Rape of the Lock* I: 121–48 ("Now awful beauty puts on
all its arms"), and an even more light-hearted inversion of the topos by
W. S. Gilbert with Arac's song in *Princess Ida,* Act III, where the
greaves as so often give difficulty: "These things I treat the same / (I
quite forget their name) / They turn one's legs / To cribbage pegs /
Their aid I thus disclaim."[46]

Yet one final piquant use remains to be noted. In Ariosto's *Orlando
Furioso,* that immensely long, half-mocking, half-self-indulgent romance, coming towards the very end of the whole tradition of romance,
there are surely hundreds of armed encounters between outstanding
heroes. In not one case is there a formal arming, until the very end,
almost the last page (quite the "wrong" place), when Ruggiero, whom
of all the heroes Ariosto most wants to exalt (despite the name of the
poem), comes to his greatest and final battle. Then his famous armor is
brought that was won from the realms of Tartarus; Orlando puts on
Ruggiero's spurs; Charlemagne girds on his sword; Bradamante (his
newly-wedded wife) and his sister Marfisa bring the corslet, with the
rest of the harness; and that famous English duke with the well-known
English name of Astolfo brings the horse. Ogier the Dane holds the
spear for him.[47] The order is different, but the passage seems as serious
as anything in the poem can be. It is strange to find so archaic a topos
in so sophisticated a poem; its presence illustrates that deep ambiva-

lence of Ariosto towards the subject-matter and manner of romance, ostensibly mocking it in order to indulge it, which was no doubt the reason for the enormous popularity of the *Orlando Furioso* in Europe in the sixteenth century. Ariosto pretends to be more modern than he is—surely an infallible recipe for a best-seller. For once, Chaucer seems less ambivalent, sharper, less sentimental.

NOTES

1. Derek Brewer, "Gothic Chaucer" in *Geoffrey Chaucer,* ed. Derek Brewer, Writers and Their Background (London: Bell, 1974), 1–32; "Towards a Chaucerian Poetic," Sir Israel Gollancz Memorial Lecture, *Proceedings of the British Academy,* 60 (1974), 219–52; "Some Observations on the Development of Literalism," *Poetica,* 2 (1974).

2. I am much indebted to Professor Canon J. R. Porter of the University of Exeter for references to arming in Babylonian epic: first, the *Eruma elish,* telling how the god Marduk was armed by other deities for his fight with the female chaos-monster Tiamat (tr. E. A. Speiser, in the edition by J. B. Pritchard, *Ancient Near Eastern Texts Relating to the Old Testament,* 2nd ed. [Princeton: University Press, 1955], p. 66); second, two passages from the Epic of Gilgamesh, telling how the two heroes Gilgamesh and Enkidu are armed for combat with a monster, (tr. A. Heidel, *The Gilgamesh Epic and Old Testament Parallels,* 2nd ed. [Chicago: University Press, 1944], pp. 36–39).

3. Albert B. Lord, *The Singer of Tales,* Harvard Studies in Comparative Literature, 24 (Cambridge, Mass.: Harvard U. Press, 1960), esp. pp. 68–98. I am generally much indebted to this remarkable book, of such importance for the study of medieval and folk literature. When, however, Lord associates the formalized description of dressing in the medieval Greek epic *Digenis Akritas* with the arming (p. 89) I believe he is confusing two different types of formalized topic. For use of the term *topos,* see E. R. Curtius, *European Literature and the Latin Middle Ages,* tr. W. R. Trask (London: Routledge and Kegan Paul, 1953).

4. Lord, pp. 89–92; A. J. B. Wace and F. H. Stubbings, *A Companion to Homer* (London: Macmillan, 1962), pp. 30, 190–91, 504–14. I am also indebted to my colleague Dr. Stubbings of Emmanuel College for personal advice on this topic. See also Harald Patzer, *Dichterische Kunst und poetisches Handwerk im homerischen Epos, Sitzungsberichte der Wissenschaftlichen Gesellschaft an der Johann Wolfgang Goethe-Universität,* 1971, vol. 10, no. 1 (Wiesbaden: Steiner, 1972). I am indebted for this reference to Mr. A. M. Bowie, Lecturer in Classics in the University of Liverpool.

5. A. B. Lord, "Homer and Other Epic Poetry," in Wace and Stubbings, p. 191.

6. *The Iliad* (Chicago: University Press, 1951), III: 330–39.

7. Lord, *Singer of Tales,* p. 91.

8. See the museum at Olympia in Greece where there are actual pieces of armor used and pictorial reconstructions, which I follow. There is also a portrayal of a warrior arming on a vase in the Greek National Museum in Athens, item 363. He appears to be putting on his greaves, i.e., going through the initial significatory stage.

9. F. H. Stubbings, "Arms and Armour," in Wace and Stubbings, pp. 504–505.

In one of the tombs, the "Giglioli," of the Great Etruscan Necropolis at Tarquinia in Italy, dated about the third century B.C., the painted decoration on the walls consists of the armor of warriors, painted as if hanging by nails from the wall. The only items represented are helmet, corslet, greaves, sword, spear, shield. These, it would seem, constitute the intrinsic "idea" of armor, to which the smaller practical necessities, real pieces to cover feet, joints, thighs, such as are preserved in the museum at Olympia in Greece, are quite irrelevant.

Pictures of ladies saying goodbye to armed knights, especially if handing them a helmet or a weapon, probably reflect the topos, with some extra meaning associated with love, as occurs in Chrétien.[48] A clear example occurs in the Luttrell Psalter (British Library MS. Add. 42130, f.202, reproduced in Derek Brewer, *Chaucer in his Time* [London: Longmans, 1973]); Cf. also the Bermondsey Dish of c. 1325, in the Victoria and Albert Museum, reproduced in Derek Brewer, *Chaucer and His World* (London: Eyre Methuen, 1978); and Bibliothèque Nationale MS. Fr. 2186, f.8^v, reproduced in R. W. Barber, *The Knight and Chivalry* (Ipswich: Boydell Press, 1974).

10. *Aeneid,* ed. J. W. Mackail (Oxford: Clarendon Press, 1930), XII: 87–96.

11. Ibid., p. 468.

12. *Táin Bó Cúalnge from the Book of Leinster,* ed. and tr. Cecile O'Rahilly (Dublin: Institute for Advanced Studies, 1967). See also *The Táin,* tr. Thomas Kinsella (London and New York: Oxford U. Press, 1970).

13. *Táin Bó Cúalnge,* ed. and tr. Cecile O'Rahilly, pp. 200–201.

14. *Tóruigheacht Gruaidhe Griansholus,* ed. and tr. Cecile O'Rahilly, Irish Texts Society, 24 (London: Simpkin, Marshall, Hamilton, Kent, 1924 for 1922), pp. 44–47.

15. Alan Bruford "Gaelic Folktales and Medieval Romances," *Bealoideas: The Journal of the Folklore of Ireland Society,* IML, 34, 1966 (Dublin: 1969). I am indebted for this reference to Mr. Patrick Sims-Williams.

16. Bruford, p. 184; see also p. 36. The author, unfortunately for our purposes, gives no list or specific example of arming runs.

17. Bruford, p. 27.

18. Bruford, p. 199.

19. Bruford, p. 37. In concluding the Irish references it may be noted that the arming of the hero probably lies behind the popular hymn attributed to St. Patrick and known as "St. Patrick's Breastplate" (e.g., *Hymns Ancient and Modern,* no. 162).

20. I am grateful to the Notre Dame Press's reader and to the editors of this volume for calling this passage in *Beowulf* to my attention.

21. J. E. Martin (now J. E. Weiss), "Studies in Some Early Middle English

Romances," Diss. University of Cambridge, 1967. See pp. 80–82. As examples she refers to the Anglo-Norman *Hom* 1408–41; *Raoul de Cambrai,* 4934 ff.; *Roland,* 3140–56; *Guillaume de l'Angleterre,* 132–40.

22. Chrétien de Troyes, *Erec et Enide,* ed. Mario Roques, Classiques français du Moyen Age, 80 (Paris, 1952), pp. 708–26.

23. Translated by W. W. Comfort, *Arthurian Romances* (London: Dent, 1914), p. 10.

24. D. S. Brewer "Chaucer and Chrétien and Arthurian Romance," *Chaucer and Middle English Studies in Honour of Rossell Hope Robbins* (London: Allen and Unwin; Kent, Ohio: Kent State U. Press, 1974), pp. 255–59.

25. I quote from Geoffrey of Monmouth, *Historia Regum Britanniae, A Variant Version,* ed. Jacob Hammer (Cambridge, Mass.: Mediaeval Academy of America, 1951), Liber IX: 2; pp. 154–55 (lines 104–11), corresponding to *Historia Regum Britanniae,* ed. A. Griscom (New York: Longmans Green, 1929), Liber IX: iv; pp. 438–89, which has verbal differences insignificant for the present purpose.

26. *In Pursuit of Perfection,* ed. Joan M. Ferrante and George D. Economou (Port Washington, N.Y.: Kennikat Press, 1975), pp. 138, 174.

27. See note 25.

28. *Le Roman de Brut de Wace,* ed. I. Arnold, 2 vols., Société des anciens textes français, 56 (Paris, 1938–40), pp. lxxviii (on the date); xlv (on Chrétien); the arming is on pp. 489–90 (lines 9275–9300).

29. *Selections from Laȝamon's Brut,* ed. G. L. Brook (London: Oxford U. Press, 1963).

30. Håkan Ringbom, *Studies in the Narrative Technique of Beowulf and Lawman's Brut,* Acta Academiae Aboensis, Ser. A, 36, no. 2 (Åbo: Åbo Akademi, 1968), p. 154.

31. Gottfried von Strassburg, *Tristan,* tr. A. T. Hatto (Harmondsworth: Penguin Books, 1960), IX: 129–30.

32. *Morte Arthure,* ed. John Finlayson, York Medieval Texts (London: Edward Arnold, 1967), pp. 43–44 (lines 900–16).

33. Lines 566–89, ed. R. A. Waldron, York Medieval Texts (London: Edward Arnold, 1970); and E. V. Gordon and J. R. R. Tolkien, 2nd ed. revised N. Davis (London: Oxford U. Press, 1967).

34. May McKisack, *The Fourteenth Century, 1307–1399* (Oxford: Clarendon Press, 1959), p. 238.

35. Another example of the topos in alliterative poetry occurs in *Sir Ferumbras* ed. Sidney J. Herrtage, EETS E.S. 34 (London, 1879), p. 8 (lines 235–40). The hero Oliver is armed early in the poem just before the first major enterprise (as usual, a battle). The topos is not elaborated. The order is greaves (hosen of mayle); hauberk of steel; helm (with aventail, as usual in the fourteenth century); sword (Hautecer); horse (Garyn).

36. Laura Hibbard Loomis, "Chaucer and the Auchinleck MS." *Essays and Studies in Honor of Carleton Brown* (New York: University Press, 1940), pp. 111–28. See also her admirable chapter on Sir Thopas in *Sources and Analogues of Chaucer's Canterbury Tales,* ed. W. F. Bryan and G. Dempster (Chicago: University Press, 1941), pp. 486–559.

37. I have argued this fully and I believe conclusively in "The Relationship of Chaucer to the English and European Traditions," *Chaucer and Chaucerians,* ed. D. S. Brewer (London: Nelson, 1966), pp. 1–38.

38. Ed. E. Kölbing, EETS E.S. 46, 48, 65 (London 1885, 1886, 1894), pp. 45–46. The other MSS have corresponding passages. It derives from the French version; see *Der anglonormannische Boeve de Haumtone,* ed. Albert Stimming, Bibliotheca Normannica, 7 (Halle: Niemeyer, 1899), pp. 532–45.

39. *Guy of Warwick,* ed. J. Zupitza, EETS E.S. 42, 49, 59 (London, 1883, 1887, 1891), lines 3849–66.

40. Ed. Joseph Ritson, *Ancient English Metrical Romances,* II (London: Bulmer, 1802), pp. 10 ff., 217–40.

41. Irving Linn, "The Arming of Sir Thopas," *Modern Language Notes,* 51 (1936), 300–11; *Otuel and Roland,* ed. M. I. O'Sullivan, EETS O.S. 198 (London, 1937), 282–320, 357–86, 1217–46.

42. *Octavian,* lines 877–88, ed. Maldwyn Mills, *Six Middle English Romances* (London: Dent, 1973), p. 99.

43. Harold Arthur, Viscount Dillon, "On a MS. Collection of Ordinances of Chivalry of the Fifteenth Century, Belonging to Lord Hastings," *Achaeologia,* 57 (1900), 29–70; the extract occurs on pp. 43–44, and I quote the slightly modernized version by Edith Rickert, *Chaucer's World,* ed. Clair C. Olson and Martin M. Crow (New York: Columbia U. Press, 1948), p. 156. The MS is now New York, Morgan Library, MS. 775.

44. S. J. Herben, "Arms and Armor in Chaucer," *Speculum,* 12 (1937), 475–87, shows that the actual underclothing and armor of Sir Thopas is quite normal and accurate.

45. *The Works of Sir Thomas Malory,* ed. Eugène Vinaver, 2nd ed. (Oxford: Clarendon Press, 1964), I: 200.

46. *The Savoy Doeras* (New York: St. Martin's Press, 1967), p. 260.

47. *Orlando Furioso,* Canto XLVI: 109–10.

16

ROSSELL HOPE ROBBINS

The Structure of Longer
Middle English Court Poems

The court verse of the fifteenth century in England comprises many miscellaneous short formal lyrics and the so-called Chaucerian Apocrypha, those longer courtly poems erroneously associated with Chaucer in the black letter editions of Pynson in 1526, Thynne in 1532, Stow in 1561, and Speght in 1598.[1] Probably the best known of the longer *dits amoureux* (to use the name given their French counterparts) include the Middle English translation of Chartier's *La Belle dame sans merci, The Court of Love, The Flower and the Leaf,* and *The Assembly of Ladies.* In addition, because of their generic similarity, should be included James I's *Kingis Quair,* and those secular poems attributed to Lydgate like *The Complaint of the Black Knight, The Flower of Courtesy,* and *The Temple of Glass.*

During the past fifty years, Middle English *dits amoureux* have begun to receive a little attention: a major but solivagant book,[2] a few dissertations (all unpublished),[3] an occasional article,[4] and good editions of three typical poems.[5] Critical opinion, such as it is, still rests on the largely textual work of Skeat, Hammond, and Berdan.[6] There are several reasons for this neglect:

One is embarrassingly obvious: these are not major poems. Not every one deserves Skeat's criticism of *The Craft of Lovers,* "too bad even for Lydgate."[7] Keats praised *The Flower and the Leaf* for its "honied lines... What mighty power has this gentle story!"[8] A few of the short items merit Hammond's comment on *The Lover's Mass:* "Chaucer need not have been ashamed to sign [it]."[9] As a group, however, these court love poems are often dull, often uninspired.

A second reason is their relative inaccessibility. Skeat's additional volume (VII) to the *Oxford Chaucer* can still be obtained; and Volume I of Chalmer's *English Poets* of 1810 has been reprinted. But many of the rest are shy: *The Isle of Ladies* available only in a Berlin doctoral dissertation of 1903;[10] *The Letter of Dido to Aeneas* only in the Pynson print of 1526.[11]

A third is the lack of an appropriate criticism. Recent studies in rhetoric, exegesis, and iconography have provided some underpinning to develop a critical approach for these poems, which then might justify considering *How a Lover Praiseth His Lady,* for example, with its appeal to "mayster Chauser sours and fundement," as an exercise "with wordys of Rethorique."[12]

Nothing can be done to remedy the first reason for neglect: a bad poem remains a bad poem no matter how brilliantly a critic explicates it. As for the second, my forthcoming anthologies will soon make all the texts easily available. About the third, I would like to present some suggestions on the design and construction of the longer court love poems which may perhaps aid in understanding and appreciating them.

As a basis for a critical rationale for the court verse of the fifteenth century, I propose the following theses:

1. The short love lyrics and the longer love poems were composed under the same social conditions, for intellectual and social diversion and amorous dalliance among a minuscule elite group. There is no essential difference between the two groups in manuscript preservation, in core subject matter (*fin amor* or "fine loving"), in skillful use of rhetoric, and in structure.

2. Most of the two or three hundred short love lyrics fall into two main genres: the lover's salutation (the *salut d'amour*) describing and praising his lady, and (more numerous) the lover's plea or *complaint d'amour*, complaining to or about his lady.

3. The longer love poems (the Chaucer Apocrypha *par excellence*) are simply literary and social exercises extending the salutation and complaint.

4. The elaboration in the long love poems of these two short, simple lyric genres is achieved by surrounding them or embedding them in formal set pieces, minor genres, themes, topics or figures (often occurring independently in the shorter lyrics). The contemporary readers of Chaucer and of the fourteenth- and fifteenth-century French *dits amoureux* and their Middle English counterparts were quite familiar with such rhetorical devices as the seasonal-astrological gambit, the garden locus, dialogues, the catalogue of lovers, the temple locus, epistles, ballades, allegorical attendant figures, and the court of love. The salutation and the complaint determined the whole ornamental superstructure of rhetoric, without which the longer poems could not exist. Only rarely in Middle English, unlike French, are the *salut* and *complaint* resolved by a *confort* (e.g., as in the very late *Comfort of Lovers* and the *Castell of Pleasure*).

Both the lyric salutations and complaints and the longer court love ditties bear little relation to reality. The Hundred Years War or the

Wars of the Roses, or even the everyday concerns of the aristocracy, as recorded in contemporary letters and chronicles, are never discussed.

Even the few complaints of women are literary: their lover image is absent. Never do court ladies complain they are pregnant. Gentlewomen, however, did get pregnant, and not every lady was as fortunate to have her pre-marital progeny legitimized, as was Katherine Swynford, erstwhile mistress to John of Gaunt, Duke of Lancaster; or Eleanor Cobham, erstwhile mistress to the Duke of Gloucester. Most trees of medieval gentry show a few grafts outside the family orchard. But the court poets certainly did not record the complaints of those duchesses—or "queens."

Real life situations are found only in the non-court verse, the popular-by-destination and probably clerically-composed songs and carols, like:

> he seide his sawus he wolde fulfille,
> þerfore y lat him haue al his wille;
> now y sykke and morne stille,
>   For he is far.[13]

This lass has trouble on her hands, and well may she "unburden" herself:

> Were it vndo þat is y-do
> I wolde be-war.

Another betrayed leman laments Sir John's "crook":

> I go with childe, wel I wot;
> I schrew the fadur þat hit gate,
> with-outen he fynde hit mylke and pap
> a long while-ey.[14]

Yet another scorns her jolly Jankin:

> Benedicamus domino, cryst fro schame me schylde.
> Deo gracias þerto—alas, I go with schylde![15]

And yet another, a certain Jack (an appropriate name, if we know our John S. Farmer):

> sone my wombe began to swelle
> as greth as a belle;
> durst y nat my dame telle
>   Wat me betydde þis holyday.[16]

Court ladies are never solicited by courtly lovers, as were peasant wenches, in the direct words of a popular lyric scrap, "Ly þow me ner, lemmon, in þy narms."[17] Nor does a gentleman invoke the Western Wind and Christ that "my loue wer in my armys, / And I yn my bed Agayne"[18]—at least, never before the beginning of the sixteenth century, when a court song reminisces, "I was wont her to behold, / And take in armys twayne."[19]

The lyric *saluts d'amour* are much fewer than the pleas or plaints. It is convenient to describe this group by the French term, although it is actually more specialized in French. The basic form consists of a brief celebration of the lady, for her beauty (the *effictio*) and personality (the *notatio*), sometimes little more than a series of anaphora or a catalogue of delights. Many *saluts* are couched as epistles; the metrical pattern is variable, but most are seven- or eight-line stanzas. While they may even mention her lack of mercy, or end in a plea for favors, their essence is praise, and for any lover's sickness the lady is always herself the doctor and the medicine.

An early-fifteenth-century manuscript, Lambeth 306, has a pleasant little poem which neatly epitomizes the type:

> My hertes ioie, all my hole plesaunce,
>   whiche that y sarue, and schall do faithfully
> with treue Entente and humble obseruaunce
>   you for to please in that y cane treuely,
> Besechynge youe, this litil bille and y
>   may hertely, with som pleasaunce and drede,
> be Recomaundide moste specially
>   vnto you, the floure of goodely-hede.[20]

If she is not the "floure of goodely-hede," the lady will be the "frische flour of womanly nature,"[21] or "the floure of formosyte,"[22] who "is so trew and kynde,"[23] with her "crystal eyen stablyd in countenaunce."[24] The whole thrust may conveniently be distilled in a little five-line chanson of the early sixteenth century:

> O what a treasure ys love certeyne
> When hertes be sped and cannot refrayne;
>   my ladye loveth me well,
>   my ioy no tong can tell,
> in her ys petye and no disdayne.[25]

The second lyric genre, the complaint of a lover to his lady, is closer to "the statement of injustice suffered" by a feudal vassal justifying himself to his lord, than to a lamentation, grieving, or grumbling, though these attitudes ultimately enter; it corresponds to the French *complaint d'amour*.

The amorous complaint, if it is to remain a complaint, works within certain boundaries. The boundary was clearly defined in *Troilus and Criseyde*:

> He spak, and called evere in his compleynte
> Hire name, for to tellen hire his wo . . .
> Al was for nought: she herde nat his pleynte.
> (I: 541–44)

In the same way that today anybody who is anybody has a psychiatrist, the fifteenth-century man-about-court had a mistress. In neither case was any cure expected—"al was for nought"; but it's fun, conspicuously expensive, satisfies the ego, and allows for one-upmanship: my psychiatrist is better than your psychiatrist; my mistress is better than your mistress. And to show you, I'll write a *salut d'amour* or maybe a *complaint d'amour,* because she says she doesn't love me. But even if by granting favors my mistress thereby removed the cause of complaining, I would never celebrate her surrender. So whether she shows pity or not, I'll go on writing my complaints. It's all part of a ritual game.

Generally, the cause of the complaint is that the mistress—most lyrics are male oriented—does not accept his devotion; she is simply merciless: only infrequently is she upbraided for loving a rival. Or else she may be far removed, or the poet himself may be distant from his lady. One poem shows unhappy lovers assembled at the *Parliament of Cupid* presenting the various impediments to requited love:

> And vpon this, they present vp their byllys
> Vpon her knes, wyth facys pale of hewe,
> Compleynyng sore for many dyuerse skyllys:
>   Sum sayed playnly, that fortune was vntrew,
>   And sum bygan a long proces to sewe
>   Of seuen yere enduryng in seruyse
>   Wyth-out coumfort in any maner wyse.
>
> Sum sayd that they were hyndryd causeles,
>   And how thay couthe not fynd no remedy;
> Sum sayd absence had causyd their dystres,
>   Thus were they hurt, god wot, full pittuouslye;

> And wyth o woys they sayd all openlye,
>   Bothe one and othir, wyth a rewful mon,
>   "Of Daunger we compleyn vs euerychon."[26]
>   (50–63)

In Lydgate's love aunter, *The Temple of Glass,* in addition to the ever-menacing Daunger, other possible reasons for complaint are catalogued more fully, and include, surprisingly, some real-life situations as well as purely literary misfortunes: the young forced to marry pre-selected mates, young women forced to become religious before "þei hade yeris of discresioun," or coupled to old mates, or sold as spouses. Usually complaints are made up of rhetorical reasons, and seldom (as here in *The Temple of Glass*) is a really valid reason for despair mentioned, such as the parental pressure exerted on Elizabeth Paston[27] for a commercial marriage—pressure that included beatings, "sometimes twice in one day." But Lydgate's most detailed reasons for making a complaint are largely literary and derive from the *Roman de la Rose:* hindrances due to Envy, Jealousy, Exile due to Wicked Tongue and False Suspicion, Danger and Disdain, Lack of Response, Poverty, Bashfulness (fearing scorn), Falseness, or Newfangleness. And these are impediments to Romance, not impediments to Marriage, and indeed in court verse a marriage complaint is rare.

Most of the stock reasons for complaining or presenting the injustice of the lover's lot appear as themes of the anonymous short love lyrics. One of the simplest is an unspecified general-purpose complaint:

> My self Alon I mak grete mone
> And sygh full sore both ny3t and day
> For comfort now hath ever me foregone. . . .[28]

Another poet likewise gives no clue to his misery: he is "past all despeyre and owte of all gladenesse," and nothing can comfort him "tyl deith come forthe and make of me an ende."[29] Love unrequited is basic to most situations: one poet merely requests his lady to consider "what payne I suffer be gret exstremytte";[30] another is "In bytter bale . . . y-brent" because his heart "wyth dart of loue . . . ys slayn."[31] Another, "your seruant In grete distresse," asks for "sum sygne of loue."[32]

Lyrics which lament the sorrows of separation are especially common. One short lyric shows the lovers prohibited from seeing each other:

> Is it not suer a dedly Payne
> to you I say, that Lovers be,
> when faithfule hartes must nedes refrayne
> th'oon th'other for to see?
> I you assure, you may trust me,
> of all the Paynes that euer I knewe,
> It is a payne that most I rewe.[33]

And here is another example of the absence motif, from a poem attributed to Lydgate:

> And yit ageyne for hevynesse I gane me to compleyne,
> þat she was so fer away, myn hertes soueraine,
> Which to spek of wommanhed haþe in þis world no peer.[34]

Some lyrics are set to music, like:

> Alas, departyng ys ground of woo!
> Oþer songe can y not synge.[35]

Another chanson begins, "I ne haue ioy, plesauns, nor comfortt / In your absenss, my verrey hertes queene."[36] Another: "Ther may no barn my balyes on-bynd, / Tyll y onys may sse my leffe."[37]

A complaint must never become an attack on a lady for withholding her "solace"; to do so would not only be bad form socially, but would direct attention away from the poet himself. Within the court tradition, the moment a lover begins an attack, the poem turns into a hostile antifeminist tirade where the "temple of Venus" becomes "the water gate."

How is the lover-poet to proceed if he wishes to vary his salutation or his complaint or, in other words, how is he to structure a longer love poem? If he is stylistically inclined, he can use more intricate stanzaic patterns, like a triple ballade,[38] or the rare virelay,[39] introduce French lines and make a macaronic,[40] contrive an acrostic,[41] or incorporate stanzas from other better-known poems.[42] Even a dull rhetorician can list catalogues of famous lovelies of antiquity, from Penelope to Bersabee, a topos found throughout Middle English court verse, sometimes occurring as an independent poem, like the *Nine Ladies Worthy.*[43] And of course a modesty topos will take up a stanza or so, useful because it can double either for *salut* or *complaint.*

To go beyond such Phase One developments, the poet must first have a basic *salut d'amour* or *complaint d'amour,* and then develop a chain of topoi or themes to introduce it, and another chain with which to conclude it. It helps if one topos leads organically into another, and such an embroidery as birds' songs in praise of love is better structured if preceded in a house-that-jack-built crescendo by a garden topos with a catalogue of trees. And if the poet copies from a source naming Mediterranean trees or birds he had best blur identification with a dream-vision opening. And his eyelids should become heavy because he is sleepy from too much reading some book (like Macrobius' *Somnium Scipionis,* which can be abstracted) or from overexcitement at the arrival of spring (which may also be described).

To illustrate the agglutinated stretching of a core *salut d'amour* into a love ditty I have selected three poems: *How a Lover Praiseth His Lady, The Lover's Book,* and *The Parlement of Love.*

In *How a Lover Praiseth His Lady,*[44] a very simple exercise (though it has 467 lines) in binary form, the formal *effictio* is introduced at line 191, when the poet sees a lady, "an angel and woman ifere." But it is not until fifty lines later (244) that the *effictio* proper begins. The poet's rhetorical approach is emphasized by his marginal rubrics, *descripcio capitis* (248–57) and *descripcio crinium* (258–69). The "gylt tresses," "Inogh to wrap al hir fair body in," are enumerated along with a comparison with famous beauties, an astrological description of the sun, and a simile to a mine of gold. The face takes ten couplets (employing the whale bone metaphor of the Harley lyrics, at least two centuries earlier), the eyes (13 couplets), then, methodically continuing at length, the brows, forehead, nose, mouth, tongue, teeth, neck (19 couplets), breasts (11 couplets), arms, sides (2 couplets only), and a twenty-one-inch waist dismissed in one couplet. Five couplets are devoted to "the paleys of Venus the quene," which the poet explains is "the golden cloyster of maydenhode." This description is possibly unique in Middle English. With puritanical primness the poet warns that

> Hyt was none ostry nor loggyng place
> But for wedloke the sacrement of grace.

The lady has no legs or feet.

Those 250 lines comprise, I believe, the longest *effictio* in Middle English. It is introduced by a garden topos almost as long, prefaced by a highly aureated midsummer gambit. The garden is leisurely analyzed, with detailed catalogues of trees, herbs, spices, birds, and animals. In the garden the poet ultimately sees a woman dancing, and thereupon writes his extended *effictio.* The poem concludes with a summary of "parfyte womanhede"; three white, three red, three long, three round, and three little.

The second example of the agglutinated salutation is *The Lover's Book*,[45] a late-fifteenth-century poem of thirty-two stanzas, which further clarifies the process of rhetorical accretion. It is built round four stanzas of an almost classic illustration of *effictio*, unfortunately of scant poetic merit, starting with the yellow hair, fair forehead, lusty eyebrows, and continuing through crystal eyes, unspecified nose, mouth, teeth, chin, and on to "rosy lyppes tweyne." En passant, this poet invoked Geoffrey of Vinsauf's doctrine of decorum, that for "the parts just below, more fittingly does the imagination speak of these than the tongue."[46] But at least Geoffrey's idealized beauties came equipped with a leg of graceful length and a wonderfully tiny foot. Like the preceding English paragon and many others, this lady is footloose; perhaps future research will establish, as well as the *anglicus caudatus*, an *anglica depeditata*.

And how does an uninspired poet like the author of *The Lover's Book* expand this core? He even profits by his dullness, and after an opening statement about his writing a bill or epistle, launches into a modesty topos (stanzas 3–5), truly a genuine apology. Then come four stanzas of a typical *salut* and the core *effictio* (stanzas 11–15), with a bridge passage introducing the clouds (not personages) of Danger and Absence which conceal from him the sight of his lady. Then a dialogue in seven stanzas where the Lover upbraids Nature for making his lady subject to death. Alas, that such beauty should disappear. The six concluding stanzas parallel several of the devices in the opening six stanzas: the epistle, the modesty topos again (stanza 29), False Tongue, a request for sympathy from other lovers hearing the poem, and a final brief salutation, culminating in a whirl of alliteration to that "woman wyse wythoute werking wylde."

A third and final example of the expanded *salut* shows the core shrunk to eight lines out of a total of 174. *The Parlement of Love*[47] draws on a variety of set topics (instead of limiting itself to an extended garden topos, as in *How a Lover Praiseth His Lady*). The theme is described in the opening couplet: "What so euyr I syng or sey, / My wylle is good too preyse here welle." The poet then

1. Describes how the God of Love summoned a parliament,
2. At which gentlewomen sing a ballade (included here) praising Cupid,
3. And where the poet sees the *ne plus ultra*, "the feyrest creature that euer was formyd by nature."

4. Gives his brief *effictio,* followed by a longer *notatio.*

5. Then withdraws into a corner to pen a general bill of devotion (three stanzas rime royal), concluding with a modesty topos.

The raison d'etre for this composition, which demands the setting of a parliament of Love, and which is made up of at least two independent lyric themes, is the eight-line catalogue of charms:

> Too speke of schape and semelynesse,
> Off stature and of goodlynesse;
> Here sydes longe with myddyll smale,
> Here face well coulord and not pale,
> With white and rode ryth well mesuryd;
> And ther-too schee was well emyred,
> And stode in euery mannes grace,
> This goodly yong and fresche of face.
>   (52–59)

Just as the poet writing an extended *salut d'amour* amplified the basic lyric with literary devices and decorations, so the same poet made the grain of a complaint the nucleus of a pearly extended *complaint d'amour.*

Most *dits amoureux* or long love ditties are structured about a complaint. Three typical poems, *The Supplicacio Amantis, The Temple of Glass,* and *The Assembly of Ladies,* illustrate how poets could ring the changes.

The Supplicacio Amantis,[48] a "compleynt" following in some manuscripts *The Temple of Glass,* relates the poet-lover's departure from his mistress Margaret on March 30. The deviousness with which he extends his lament into 628 lines is clever: he plays on variation after variation, always returning to simple direct complaints when he feels he has been circumlocutious. For example, in lines 137–73 he asks his lady to accept him as a servant to delight her; then he recalls their last parting, unable to speak, struck by a sword of love, angry with the sun for shining; he describes his lady in a catalogue, invoking March for contrariness, a fitting background for an unstable mistress, though she is the flower of womanhood with all the moral virtues; then, some 200 lines further on (at 351) he notes her lack of mercy and pity, the standard grounds for complaint. He starts another cycle: he pleads to Fortune (variable, like March) to turn her wheel and change his lady's attitude; he hopes the healing powers of the daisy will relieve him, he describes the daisy in a rare Middle English pastourelle, he pleads again to Fortune, then once more after 100 lines he comes back to the complaint: may his lady have mercy on her faithful lover. Then off

again: he will do any bidden service, he praises her in a "Myn"
anaphora, he is all "masid," and like the variable elements his heart
burns, he is wounded, he is getting worse, then after some 150 more
lines he comes to the final complaint: he prays forgiveness and writes
this bill!

The list of ingredients is not entirely haphazard; there is some formal
progression. His lament in line 99 that she never bade him serve her is
picked up again in line 461; his description of her beauty in line 71 is
paralleled in line 318. The sword-of-love theme appears first at line
210, and is repeated in line 556. The scaffolding is clear: three main
complaints along with short complaints repeated throughout at reasonable intervals. For example, at lines 11–12:

> That wel I fele by myn smert
> That I from deth may not astert.

at lines 35–37:

> For verry wo and dystresse
> Ne myghte I not a word expresse
> Of al myn wo.

at line 51:

> I fele smert, and can not pleyne.

And so on, at lines 100, 115, 166, 210, 220, 280, 295, 381, 442,
460, 520, 538, 582, and 625. The near isolable quatrain at line 381
can summarize them all:

> Thus may I seyn, allas, allas!
> That causeless, for no trespas,
> Hast mad myn lady most soueryn
> Myn symple seruyse to dysdeyn.

Because it never strays beyond the strict boundaries of a complaint,
The Supplicacio Amantis is therefore different from *The Temple of Glass*,
the second example of extended complaints. *The Temple of Glass*[49]
introduces quasi-narrative themes and digressions, to turn what promises to be a simple extended dramatic complaint into a *dit amoureux* of
promised fulfillment.

The Temple of Glass is ascribed to Lydgate, and Lydgate was a monk
as well as the unofficial poet laureate at the court of Henry VI. As a

monk he may well have excused this theme on ironic and exegetical grounds; but at face value *The Temple of Glass* is a blatant promotion of adultery, all cleared by Venus and the whole pagan heaven of gods as "clene" and virtuous. A married woman hates her husband and yearns for another man. Previously unaware of the woman's love for him, when he sees her, the man reciprocally falls in love. They pledge troth and agree to be faithful. Where does this lead? The woman has already pledged to be faithful to her husband. Is she supposed to wait until her husband has died before she and her lover bed together? Or should they plan to murder him? This dilemma in situational ethics is not common in Middle English court verse, and may be the result of Lydgate's attempt to give relevance to the lady's initial complaint. The actual phraseology would have been the same, however, had the woman not been married.

The Temple of Glass is a choice illustration of a poet's centering a whole love aunter on the complaint theme, and with *deus ex computante machina* dexterity simultaneously matching two would-be lovers. It also illustrates the formalized way of composing court verse, as if the poet had stocked in his mind a pile of rhetorical and topical building blocks descriptively labelled Spring Topos, The Garden, Lover's Request to his Mistress, Commandments of Love (the medieval sensuous man's guide to sex: twenty-one times a night), Lover's Appeal to Venus, Lover's Reproach to Fortune, Birds' Songs, and so forth, almost like some electronic bard programming his oral formulae. Almost every block is found as a separate short lyric, so that all a poet writing a longer poem had to do was to assemble a chain of little lyrics and provide some continuity.[50]

Some of these blocks, as has been shown, were used by the poet of *The Supplicacio Amantis*—the complaint to Fortune, the Request to his Mistress, a modified spring topos (serving as pastourelle), and some others. The poet selects what blocks he will need and then arranges them in a certain order. He is not required to be original: his audience is happy and satisfied with the familiar, may in fact be waiting for the conventional formulas, sometimes joyfully anticipating a deviation from the norm.

More than other *dits amoureux, The Temple of Glass* lends itself to a building-block breakdown: it is a series of set pieces, including catalogues, *saluts d'amour*, ballades and envoys, clustered round three sets of complaints and responcios: the first the lady's complaint (321–69) to Venus and Venus' reply; the second the man's complaint (701–847) to Venus with her reply; and the third the man's complaint

(970–1102) to the lady, the lady's responcio, and then Venus' responcio to both lovers, individually and together. Each complaint might be
extrapolated from the poem and serve as a short lyric complete in itself.

In *The Temple of Glass,* and in all the other love aunters, both
extended salutations and complaints, there is actually very little plot or
action in the conventional sense; there is, however, what Charles Muscatine called a "lyric commentary" and the action is implied. Thus if a
lover makes a complaint, the reader might assume a prior meeting
where the lady rejected the lover's suit. Such an assumption is taken for
granted in a sonnet sequence by, say, Shakespeare, Elizabeth Browning, or Meredith.

In a number of these Middle English *dits amoureux,* both *saluts* and
complaints, however, the implied narrative itself breaks down, because
the poet is not interested in it. He is interested in something else:
decoration and embellishment have become ends in themselves.
Rhetoric takes the place of experience. For example, *The Flower of
Courtesy*[51] is a valentine greeting in 270 lines and is plotless: praise of
his lady who lacks pity becomes the sublimation for any actual love
experience. *The Complaint of the Black Knight*[52] has no narrative line:
the knight goes every year, in May, to a country lodge just to express
his "wofull compleynt," which is the literary equivalent of a game of
solitaire:

> And to a lodge went there be-syde,
> Where al the May his custom was to abide,
> Sole to compleyn of his peynes kene,
> For yer to yer under the bowes grene.
> (585–88)

The Black Knight is not even trying to change his woe to bliss: his is a
masochistic ritual. The poem's expressed aim is to do pleasance to you
lovers that be true. Whether us lovers' awareness of the faces of love is
increased is doubtful. The interest lies in the technical skill of explicat-
ing the complaint. Unlike the complaints in *Troilus and Criseyde,*
which may be dramatic and heighten the narrative, in most of these
Chaucerian Apocrypha the complaint is not even a method of examining a love experience. The unimportance of what happens is clearly seen
where the style and diction are the same for the poet who has lost his
mistress as for the lover who never had a lady.

The third and final example of an expanded complaint, although the
core comprises only eighteen stanzas out of a total of 108, nevertheless
presents the complaints of no less than nine women to form the techni-

cal or structural culmination and climax. In *The Assembly of Ladies*[53] the 83 preceding stanzas and the seven concluding are simply devices in yet another effort to give a new format to an old form. The poet posits four ladies lamenting somewhat vaguely on traditional grounds: 1. Broken promises; 2. Insufficiently rewarded desert; 3. Lack of stability in lover; 4. Difficulty of seeing lover. Their four attendant gentlewomen present other grounds: 5. No thanks for merit; 6. Fidelity scorned; 7. Unfaithfulness; and 8. Lack of "good continuance." the *poetria* herself adds a ninth bill of complaint, but it is not clear just what her problem is:

> Nothyng so lief as death to come to me
> For fynal end of my sorwes and peyne;
> What shuld I more desire . . .
>
>   (694–96)

Beyond adding that she has in patience suffered very much for a long time, she tells the reader nothing more about her sorrow; and this indefiniteness may perhaps explain why the recent editor, Derek Pearsall, wrote that all these complaints "mark a low-ebb in fifteenth-century verse."[54]

But the nine complaints themselves are typical enough, parallel to the shorter lyrics in similar generalized terms, like:

> Constraynyd am I
> With wepynge eyes
> To morne and pleyne.[55]

It might be observed that six of the nine complaints in *The Assembly of Ladies* are duplicated in short poems in my *Secular Lyrics,*[56] and numerous other parallels to these six and the remaining three can also be found.[57]

The poet's device of dividing among nine women the reasons for unhappiness in love may explain the lack of specificity; whereas had all nine troubles befallen one woman, as in Lydgate's "balade sayde by a gentil womman whiche loued a man of gret estate," they would have given more substantiality to the narrative.[58] On the other hand, the series of nine bills serves as the mechanics to introduce a series of allegorical figures out of the *Roman de la Rose,* keepers of the castle of Lady Loyalty, who themselves lead to the climax of the poem, built up with considerable suspense, which is the court of Love. One can here follow the fusing of various ingredients of shorter love lyrics, which by being arranged in a certain order end up as a love aunter. Venus, or (as

here) her human equivalent, judging love problems, is a common
enough theme; the fifteenth-century *Parliament of Cupid* presents an
abbreviated version (in sixteen stanzas) of *The Assembly of Ladies,* where
"In hir presence we kneled doune echeon / Presenting up oure billis."
So *The Parliament of Cupid* tells:

> And vpon this, thay present vp thair byllys
> Vpon her knes, wyth facys pale of hewe,
> Conpleynyng sore for many dyuerse skyllys . . .[59]
>
> (50–52)

And the "dyuerse skyllys" are familar (though given from a man's
viewpoint): "seuen yere endurying in seruyse Wyth-out coumfort. . . . /
Absence had causyd their dystres." As in *The Assembly of Ladies,*
The Parliament of Cupid has a spokesman who begs Cupid "to voyd
daunger out of [t]her coumpany," and both poems conclude with
the promise of another parliament (the same word in both poems).

In *The Assembly of Ladies,* the emphasis on a mortal, Lady Loyalty,
raises the suspicion that the whole poem might be as much a salutation
to some great lady (for example, Queen Margaret or the Duchess of
Gloucester) as it is a complaint, for Lady Loyalty's resolution of the
complaints is merely to set a later date for "open remedy." The complaints could be straw men because Lady Loyalty does not hold a *cour
d'amour,* nor is she arbitrating a *cas d'amour.* Had the poet wanted or
needed a parliament, then he would have moved the complaints from
their present position so near the end to the beginning—as happened
in *The Book of the Duchess*—or else he could have continued the whole
poem for as long as necessary. Without the complaints, however, there
would be no reason to introduce Lady Loyalty and hence no poem.

So highly did some writers of the *dits amoureux* regard the inserted
complaints that occasionally they changed the stanzaic form to emphasize the position and importance of the complaint, and in poems
like *The Lay of Sorrow*[60] introduced a sixteen-line complaint after the
French fashion. So Chaucer in *The Book of the Duchess* varied the stanza
form of the Knight's complaint to a different and unusual meter.

There is a complementary and obverse side to this presentation of the
longer court verse as agglutinated *saluts d'amour* or as agglutinated
complaints d'amour, comprising basic, simple lyric forms barnacled with
many smaller lyric forms, patterns, and themes. This process can be
seen in reverse, with a long poem being partly broken down into its
lyric components.

Longer court poems were pillaged for extrapolable stanzas for shorter lyrics or else for isolable lyrics complete in themselves. For example, one of the poems in Trinity College Cambridge MS 599, which Stowe did not take for his 1561 edition, is an epistle to his mistress rubricated "Chaucer."[61] It is typical of the late court-coterie verse, with classical and Biblical allusions, protestations of literary incompetence, and the formal diction of the psychology of love. But four of its stanzas are taken from *The Craft of Lovers;* in that longer poem the borrowed stanzas were originally satirical, but divorced from their context they here adapt to the courtly tradition of the new pastiche. Another piece from Trinity MS 599, which Stowe also omitted, *O Merciful and O Merciable,*[62] borrows its first four stanzas from *The Court of Sapience;* originally religious, the stanzas are here wittily twisted to a secular amorous purpose. Another stanza is borrowed from *The Craft of Lovers.*

Nor is this all. From *The Temple of Glass,* various phrases and lines were culled for a five-stanza composite, signed incidentally by the Secretary to the Duke of Bedford, with the original "her" changed to "youre" to make the poem seem a direct petition of a lover to his lady, instead of a lover's remarks to Venus.[63] Another three stanzas of this extract appear in the Bannatyne MS as a *salut d'amour.*[64]

The early-sixteenth-century Devonshire MS, compiled in the household of Anne Boleyn, has nearly two hundred short lyrics, about a third attributed to Wyatt.[65] But copied there without any identification are several fragments from the older court verse, like Hoccleve's *Letter of Cupid,* where one stanza has been selected to make a lyric in praise of women. We also find an attractive little *salut d'amour.*

> Alas! what shuld yt be to yow preiudyce
> Yff that a man do loue you faythfully
> To yowr worshyp eschewyng euery vyce?
> So am I yowrs and wylbe veryly.
> I chalenge nowght of ryght, and reason why
> For I am hole submyt vnto yowr servyce:
> Ryght as ye lyst yt be, ryght so wyll I,
> To bynd myself where I [w]as at lyberty.[66]

If a reader did not know the translation of Chartier's *La Belle dame sans merci,* how could he decide this extract was not an original court lyric? Here is another complaint, borrowed from an original composition:

> For thowgh I had yow tomorow agayne,
> I myght as well hold Apryl from rayne

> As holde yow to maken stedfast.
> Allmyghty god, off treuthe the souerayne,
> Wher ys the truthe off man? Who hath yt slayne?
> She that them loueth shall them fynde as fast
> As in a tempest ys a rotten maste.
> [A]s that a tame beest that ys aye fayne
> To renne away when he ys le[s]te agaste.[67]

These lines come from Chaucer's *Anelida and Arcite* (308–16). And in the Devonshire MS there is more of Chaucer: six stanzas are extracted from *Troilus and Criseyde* to form six independent lyrics;[68] and there is a composite from Book IV, the complaint of Troilus on the departure of Criseyde for the Greeks.[69] The adapter has boldly omitted the name of Criseyde, jumped a couple of stanzas, added a couplet heading, and come up with a brand new complaint, in fact, a well-unified lyric. Incidentally, a leading authority on the sixteenth century ascribed this poem to Sir Thomas Howard.[70] And there are quite a number of other extrapolations,[71] including the celebrated *Cantus Troili,* which appears separately in three manuscripts, with a Scottish version in the Bannatyne MS.[72]

If we try to judge these English court poems, both the short lyrics and the longer *dits amoureux,* by standards of high seriousness, they will be found wanting. On the other hand, if we regard them as ephemeral, occasional pieces, designed to please for the moment, to provide an escapist interlude from a harsh society, "to make your hertes gaye and lyght,"[73] then we may appreciate them as eminently fitting to their function in palace and court circles.

Examining the court poems will not, I am afraid, rediscover by-passed masterpieces; but an awareness of the techniques of composition will, in the words of that poet whose earliest poem was entitled "A Tale of Chaucer lately found in an old Manuscript," help

> A perfect judge [to] read each work of wit
> With the same spirit that its author writ.

And that is something.

NOTES

1. Described in my "Chaucerian Apocrypha," in *A Manual of the Writings in Middle English, 1050–1500,* ed. Albert E. Hartung (New Haven: Connecticut Academy of Arts and Sciences, 1973), IV: 1061–1101, 1286–1306.

2. Ethel Seaton, *Sir Richard Roos, Lancastrian Poet* (London: Heart–Davis, 1961).

3. E.g., Ruth Fisher [Smith], "The Flower and the Leaf and the Assembly of Ladies: A Study of Two Love-Vision Poems of the Fifteenth Century," Diss. Columbia 1955, *Dissertation Abstracts*, 15: 1233; F. J. Chiarenza, "Chaucer and the Medieval Amorous Complaint," Diss. Yale 1956, *Dissertation Abstracts*, 16 (Index): 143; Prajapati Prasad, "The Order of Complaint: A Study in Medieval Tradition," Diss. Wisconsin 1965, *Dissertation Abstracts*, 26: 3930A; Stephen Robert Knafel, "A Variorum Edition of the Kingis Quair," Diss. Brown 1967, *Dissertation Abstracts*, 26: 3147A.

4. E.g., F. W. Bonner, "The Genesis of the Chaucer Apocrypha," *Studies in Philology*, 48 (1951), 461–81; Derek Pearsall, "The English Chaucerians," in *Chaucer and Chaucerians*, ed. D. S. Brewer (London: Nelson, 1966), pp. 201–39; John Stephens, "The Questioning of Love in the *Assembly of Ladies*," *Review of English Studies*, N.S. 24 (1973), 129–40; and part of the chapter, "The Chaucerian Tradition," in A. C. Spearing, *Medieval Dream Poetry* (Cambridge: University Press, 1976), pp. 171–87.

5. D. A. Pearsall, ed., *The Floure and the Leafe and the Assembly of Ladies* (London: Nelson, 1962); V. J. Scattergood, ed., *The Works of Sir John Clanvowe* (Cambridge: D. S. Brewer Ltd., 1975).

6. Walter W. Skeat, *Chaucerian and Other Pieces* (Oxford: Clarendon Press, 1897); Eleanor Prescott Hammond, *English Verse between Chaucer and Surrey* (Durham, N.C.: Duke U. Press, 1927; repr. New York: Octagon, 1965); John M. Berdan, *Early Tudor Poetry 1485–1547* (New York: Macmillan, 1920).

7. Walter W. Skeat, *The Chaucer Canon* (Oxford: Clarendon Press, 1900; repr. New York: Haskell House, 1965), p. 120.

8. Sonnet written at the end of "The Floure and the Lefe," in *The Poetical Works of John Keats*, ed. H. Buxton Forman (London: Oxford U. Press, 1926), p. 292.

9. Hammond, *English Verse*, p. 210.

10. Jane B. Sherzer, "The Ile of Ladies," Diss. Berlin 1903 (Weimar: Mayer & Müller, 1903).

11. *The Boke of Fame*, R. Pynson, 1526 (STC, no. 5088), ff. iii[b]–vii[b].

12. Carleton Brown and Rossel Hope Robbins, *The Index of Middle English Verse* (New York: Columbia U. Press, 1943); and Rossell Hope Robbins and John L. Cutler, *Supplement to the Index of Middle English Verse* (Lexington: U. of Kentucky Press, 1965), no. 4043. Eleanor Prescott Hammond, "How a Lover Praiseth His Mistress," *Modern Philology*, 21 (1923–24), 379–95.

13. *Index* and *Supplement*, no. 1330. Rossell Hope Robbins, *Secular Lyrics of the XIVth and XVth Centuries*, 2nd ed. (Oxford: Clarendon Press, 1955), p. 18. For a fabliau in *Les Cent nouvelles nouvelles* about a gentlewoman who had a child by her coachman and was ostracized by polite society as "the most reproached and most dishonored woman in the world," see my translation, *The Hundred Tales* (New York: Crown Publishers, 1960), pp. 225–27.

14. *Index* and *Supplement*, no. 3409. *Secular Lyrics*, p. 20.

15. *Index* and *Supplement*, no. 377. *Secular Lyrics*, p. 22.

16. *Index* and *Supplement*, no. 225. *Secular Lyrics*, p. 25. See also John S. Farmer, *Vocabula Amatoria* (1896; repr. New Hyde Park, N.Y.: University Books, 1966), p. 162.

17. *Supplement*, no. 1871.5.

18. *Supplement*, no. 3899.3. *Secular Lyrics*, p. xxxviii.

19. *Supplement*, no. 14.5. John E. Stevens, *Music and Poetry in the Early Tudor Court* (London: Methuen, 1961), p. 395.

20. *Index* and *Supplement*, no. 2247. Frederick J. Furnivall, ed., *Political, Religious, and Love Poems*, EETS, O.S. 15 (London, 1866), p. 40; (rvsd. ed. London, 1903), p. 68.

21. *Index* and *Supplement*, no. 868. Furnivall (1866), p. 41; (1903), p. 69.

22. *Supplement*, no. 2384.8. Kenneth G. Wilson, "Five Unpublished Secular Love Poems from MS. Trinity College Cambridge 599," *Anglia*, 72 (1953), 402–404.

23. *Supplement*, no. 3880.6. Edward Bliss Reed, "The Sixteenth Century Lyrics in Add. MS. 18,752," *Anglia*, 33 (1910), 360.

24. *Supplement*, no. 2478.5. Wilson, *Anglia*, 72: 407–15.

25. *Supplement*, no. 2579.3. Bernard M. Wagner, "New Songs of the Reign of Henry VIII," *Modern Language Notes*, 50 (1935), 455.

26. *Index* and *Supplement*, no. 2595. Henry Noble MacCracken, "An English Friend of Charles d'Orléans," *PMLA*, 26 (1911), 171–74.

27. H. S. Bennett. *The Pastons and Their England* (Cambridge: University Press, 1932), p. 30.

28. *Index* and *Supplement*, no. 2268. Previously unpublished. The last line, very faded, reads " . . . I morn . . . ys well Awaye."

29. *Index* and *Supplement*, no. 3163. *Secular Lyrics*, p. 156.

30. *Index* and *Supplement*, no. 2318. *Secular Lyrics*, p. 152.

31. *Index* and *Supplement*, no. 152. *Secular Lyrics*, pp. 152–53.

32. *Index* and *Supplement*, no. 2475. *Secular Lyrics*, p. 149.

33. *Supplement*, no. 1620.5. John Saltmarsh, "Two Medieval Love-Songs Set to Music," *The Antiquarian Journal*, 15 (1935), 18 (punctuation mine).

34. *Index*, no. 1496; *Supplement*, no. 837.5. Henry Noble MacCracken, ed., *The Minor Poems of John Lydgate*, II, EETS, O.S. 192 (London, 1934), p. 425.

35. *Index* and *Supplement*, no. 146. *Secular Lyrics*, p. 150. Cf. *Index* and *Supplement*, no. 767 (Advocates MS).

36. *Index* and *Supplement*, no. 1334. *Secular Lyrics*, p. 151.

37. *Index* and *Supplement*, no. 2245. *Secular Lyrics*, p. 151.

38. *Index* and *Supplement*, no. 828. Henry Noble MacCracken, "Lydgatiana II: Two Chaucerian Ballades," *Archiv*, 127 (1911), 326.

39. Seemingly amorous, in fact grisly political: *Index* and *Supplement*, no. 1288; *Supplement*, no. 3193.5. Exclusively a love lament, *Index* and *Supplement*, no. 267. *Secular Lyrics*, p. 173.

40. *Index* and *Supplement*, nos. 16 and 19. See under *macaronic* in *Supplement*, p. 540 (twenty-five items listed).

41. See under *acrostics* in *Supplement*, p. 526 (seventeen items listed).

42. See note 60.
43. *Index* and *Supplement,* no. 2767. In Stowe's *Chaucer* and early editions; last ed., Alexander Chalmers, *The Works of the English Poets from Chaucer to Cowper* (London: J. Johnson, 1810; repr. New York: Johnson Reprints, 1969), I: 561–62.
44. See note 12.
45. *Supplement,* no. 2478.5. Wilson, *Anglia,* 72: 407–15.
46. "The New Poetics," tr. Jane Baltzell Koop, in *Three Medieval Rhetorical Arts,* ed. James J. Murphy (Berkeley: U. of California Press, 1971), p. 54.
47. *Index* and *Supplement,* no. 2383. Furnivall (1866), pp. 48–51; (1903), pp. 76–79. Arthur K. Moore, "Chaucer's Use of Lyric as an Ornament of Style," *Comparative Literature,* 3 (1951), 46, regards the lyric insertions as interpolations; similarly in Lydgate's *Temple of Glass.*
48. *Index* and *Supplement,* no. 147. J. Schick, ed., *Lydgate's Temple of Glass,* EETS, E.S. 60 (London, 1891), pp. 59–67. Seaton, *Sir Richard Roos,* p. 370, interprets the poem as a daisy (Margaret) tribute.
49. *Index* and *Supplement,* no. 851. Schick, pp. 1–57.
50. This is the essence of the *dit amoureux* or love aunter. These poems are designedly static; there is no story line as in a conventional romance. Rather, the poem is built on set pieces, comparable to the frames of a cartoon film strip. Passing from one frame to the next, the reader himself creates a kaleidoscopic effect which gives the illusion of action (i.e., narrative). The same techniques had, of course, appeared in French at least fifty years earlier. See James Wimsatt, *Chaucer and the French Love Poets* (Chapel Hill: U. of North Carolina Press, 1968; repr. New York: Johnson Reprints, 1972).
51. *Index,* no. 1487. MacCracken, EETS, 192: 410–17.
52. *Index* and *Supplement,* no. 1507. MacCracken, EETS, 192: 382–410.
53. *Index* and *Supplement,* no. 1528. See note 5.
54. Pearsall, p. 167.
55. *Supplement,* no. 1295.8. Rossell Hope Robbins, "Middle English Texts: Handlist of New Lyrics," *Anglia,* 83 (1965), 46.
56. *Secular Lyrics,* nos. 132, 135, 137, 138, 139, 150.
57. See my two forthcoming anthologies of Middle English court verse. E.g., *Supplement,* nos. 190.5, 763.5, 2261.6, 3785.5.
58. *Index,* no. 154. MacCracken, EETS, 192: 418–20.
59. MacCracken, *PMLA,* 26: 172.
60. *Index* and *Supplement,* no. 482. Kenneth G. Wilson, "*The Lay of Sorrow* and *The Lufaris Complaynt:* An Edition," *Speculum,* 29 (1954), 708–26. In French, examples of many lyric forms inserted in a single *dit amoureux* include Machaut's *Remede de Fortune* and *Voir Dit,* and Froissart's *Espinette amoureuse* and *Paradys d'amours.* The *ne plus ultra* is Froissart's romance, *Méliador,* in which are inserted many lyrics by Froissart's patrons.
61. *Index* and *Supplement,* no. 1838. Rossell Hope Robbins, "A Love Epistle by Chaucer," *Modern Language Review,* 49 (1954), 290–92.
62. *Index* and *Supplement,* no. 2510. Chalmers, *English Poets,* I: 562–63.

63. *Index* and *Supplement*, no. 2161. *Secular Lyrics*, pp. 141–42.

64. *Supplement*, no. 1598.3. W. Tod Ritchie, ed., *The Bannatyne Manuscript*, III, Scottish Text Society, N.S. 23 (Edinburgh and London, 1928), p. 270.

65. See Raymond Southall, "The Devonshire Manuscript Collection of Early Tudor Poetry 1532–1541," *Review of English Studies*, N.S. 15 (1964), 142–50.

66. *Supplement*, no. 1086, MS 7. Kenneth Muir, "Unpublished Poems in the Devonshire Manuscript," *Proceedings of the Leeds Philosophical and Literary Society*, Lit. and Hist. Section, 6, pt. 4 (1947), 279.

67. *Supplement*, no. 3670, MS 9. Muir, p. 279.

68. *Supplement*, no. 848.5. Southall, p. 144. Also *Supplement*, no. 1418.5 (Muir, pp. 279–80), followed by four other single stanzas from Chaucer's *Troilus and Criseyde*, II: 344–50, 778–84, 785–91, 855–61; all printed by Muir, pp. 279–80.

69. *Supplement*, no. 2577.5. Muir, pp. 265–66.

70. Muir, p. 281.

71. *Supplement*, no. 1926.5. Frederick Morgan Padelford, "The Songs in Manuscript Rawlinson C. 813," *Anglia*, 31 (1908), 362–63. Corrections by Wilhelm Bolle, "Zur Lyrik der Rawlinson–MS C. 813," *Anglia*, 34 (1911), 273–307.

72. *Index* and *Supplement*, no. 3327 (Extracts B, F, J); and *Supplement*, no. 1422.1. See Ernest H. Wilkins, "Cantus Troili," *ELH*, 16 (1949), 167–73.

73. Chaucer, Rom, 32.

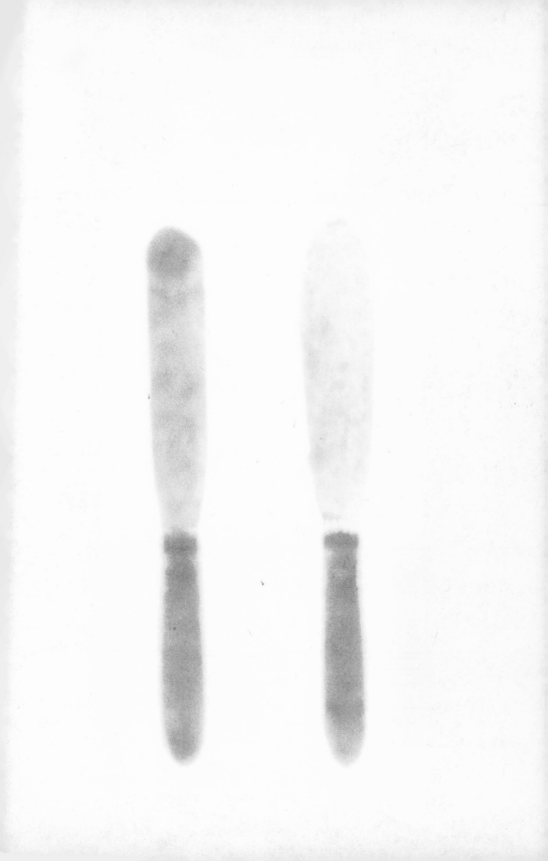

PR
1924
.C47

Chaucerian problems and
perspectives